A Theological Jurisprudence of Speculative Cinema

T0386705

Visit the **Edinburgh Critical Studies in Law, Literature and the Humanities** website at http://www.euppublishing.com/series-edinburgh-critical-studies-in-law-literature-and-the-humanities.html

A Theological Jurisprudence of Speculative Cinema

Superheroes, Science Fictions and Fantasies of Modern Law

Timothy D. Peters

EDINBURGH
University Press

Edinburgh University Press is one of the leading university presses in the UK. We publish academic books and journals in our selected subject areas across the humanities and social sciences, combining cutting-edge scholarship with high editorial and production values to produce academic works of lasting importance. For more information visit our website: edinburghuniversitypress.com

Edinburgh University Press Ltd
The Tun – Holyrood Road
12(2f) Jackson's Entry
Edinburgh EH8 8PJ

First published in hardback by Edinburgh University Press 2022

Typeset in 11/13 Adobe Garamond by
IDSUK (DataConnection) Ltd, and
printed and bound by CPI Group (UK) Ltd, Croydon, CR0 4YY

A CIP record for this book is available from the British Library

ISBN 978 1 4744 2400 4 (hardback)
ISBN 978 1 3995 2242 7 (paperback)
ISBN 978 1 4744 2401 1 (webready PDF)
ISBN 978 1 4744 2402 8 (epub)

Contents

Acknowledgments

This book is a work of particular times and places. It arose out of my PhD thesis, which was completed at the Griffith Law School (GLS), Griffith University, from 2007 to 2014 with Professor William (Bill) MacNeil as supervisor, joined ably and indefatigably by Professor Kieran Tranter. The most significant work was completed in the period from 2011 to 2014, when I joined the GLS as a full-time academic at what was the height of the GLS's cultural legal turn (extending from its critical and socio-legal eras). Bill was Dean at the time and the myriad of new hires, including Dr Karen Crawley, Dr Ed Mussawir, Dr Edwin Bikundo, Associate Professor Olivera Simic, Professor Jay Sanderson and myself, fitted with the broad programme of Cultural Legal Studies and Law and Humanities scholarship. We joined an already impressive line-up of critical and cultural legal scholars, including Bill and Kieran, Professor Afshin Akhtar-Khavari, Dr Chris Butler, Merran Lawler and Dr Roshan de Silva Wijeyeratne, as well as prior and present PhD candidates Dr Daniel Hourigan, Dr Robbie Sykes, Dr Ben Wardle and Dr Alex Deagon. As often happens, due to a variety of institutional, family and other 'life' circumstances, this presence of cultural legal scholars has since spread further afield: with Jay, Ben and myself moving to the University of the Sunshine Coast (where Jay is now Head of School), Bill to Southern Cross University (where he is Professor of Jurisprudence and Dean of Law), Daniel to University of Southern Queensland and Kieran, Afshin and Alex to Queensland University of Technology. All of these individuals—and Bill and Kieran in particular—have contributed to my growth as a scholar and my gratitude here is but a small part of the return that I present to them.

The completion of this book occurred at my new institutional home at the University of the Sunshine Coast. This has proved an innovative and exciting context for both legal and interdisciplinary conversations. I have greatly appreciated and acknowledge the lively intellectual camaraderie of all my colleagues in the School of Law and Society, *née* School of Law and Criminology (SLACers rule!), *née* the USC Law School. In particular, I would like to think my past and present Heads of School, Professor Pam O'Connor and Professor Jay Sanderson, for the many opportunities provided and the incredible support of my scholarship. I would also like to provide 'call outs' to Dr Drossos Stamboulakis (now at Monash) for many winding and lively conversations, to Dr Dominique Moritz, Dr Lara Christensen and Dr Nadine McKillop for always being up for a 'chat', and to Kay Meredith and Kylie Fletcher for the incredible (and now further dispersed) administrative support. It has also been a great delight to have been joined at USC by my fellow cultural legal aficionados Dr Ashley Pearson and Mr Dale Mitchell. More broadly within USC, I have been blessed by numerous interdisciplinary engagements and I would like to thank, in particular, Dr Clare Archer-Lean, Dr Theresa Ashford, Dr Ginna Brock, Professor Lisa Chandler, Professor Gary Crewe, Dr Peter English, Dr Thomas Hamlyn-Harris, Professor Sandy O'Sullivan (now at Macquarie) and Dr Ross Watkins.

For the practice of the generosity of scholarship I owe much to the Law, Literature and the Humanities Association of Australasia (formerly the Law and Literature Association of Australia) and the numerous organisers of its conferences since 2006. Each of these chapters has been presented in some form at one of those conferences; the opportunity to present and the generosity of engagement and feedback that I have received have always challenged and stretched my thinking and have impacted on the quality of the work in this book. Many thanks to the organisers of and participants in these conferences (Melbourne—2006; Griffith—2009; Wollongong—2011; ANU—2013; UTS—2015; Hong Kong—2016). Special thanks, for questions, conversations and support, go to Professor Maria Aristedemou (Birkbeck), Dr Olivia Barr (Melbourne), Associate Professor Penny Crofts (UTS), Professor Ian Duncanson, Dr Maria Elander (La Trobe), Dr Thomas Giddens (Dundee), Professor Judy Grbich, Dr Daniel Hourigan (USQ), Professor Marett Leiboff (Wollongong), Professor Desmond Manderson (ANU), Professor Shaun McVeigh (Melbourne), Dr Joshua Neoh (ANU), Dr James Parker (Melbourne), Dr Connal Parsley (Kent), Dr Honni van Rijswik (UTS), Associate Professor Juliet Rogers (Melbourne), Professor Peter Rush (Melbourne), Associate Professor Cassandra Sharp (Wollongong), Associate Professor Marco Wan (Hong Kong) and Professor Alison Young (Melbourne). That, in the context of the neoliberalisation of the university and the constant pressures on academia, this association and its scholars have continued to thrive is a testament to the importance of our approaches to thinking and re-envisioning law and the cultural legal.

Presentations of various components of this book have also been made at conferences of the Law and Society Association of Australia and New Zealand (Wollongong—2006) and the Association for the Study of Law, Culture and the Humanities (Texas Wesleyan, Fort Worth—2012, Birkbeck, London—2013), as well as at the following symposia and seminars: 'Law as Site and Sound', Emerging Scholars Network Colloquium, Griffith

Law School (2010); 'Representational Legality: Reading Culture, Thinking Law', Griffith Law School and Socio-Legal Research Centre (2012); 'Cultural Legal Studies Methodology: Wherefore Art Thou?', Legal Intersections Research Centre, University of Wollongong (2012); 'Law/Trauma', School of Arts & Communication, University of Southern Queensland (2016); and the Arts Research in the Creative Humanities Research Showcases, University of the Sunshine Coast (2017). Thanks to the organisers of and participants in those events.

I owe great thanks for the 'gift' of teaching much of this material in both Bill's elective, *Legal Fictions*, and my own elective, *Cultural Legal Studies*, at the GLS. The opportunity to present this work and have students critically interrogate it is one of the highlights of my teaching career to date. It is further gratifying to see a number of those students go on to complete cultural legal or related honours projects and PhD scholarship—including Dr Ashley Pearson, Dale Mitchell, Emily Muir, Rudolf Ondrich, Tara Mulroy and Liz Englezos. Thank you also to those students and research assistants who contributed to the preparation of this manuscript: to Samantha Nean for her incredible early assistance with referencing, to Joanna Dohler for the formatting of early drafts, to Michaella Duggan, who took oversight of both (as well as chasing down random sources, and mastering Endnote) in the final completion of the project, and to Eloise Turnbull for her work compiling the index.

A number of the chapters of this book have earlier incarnations in various forms: a version of the Prologue was published as 'Reading the Law Made Strange: Cultural Legal Studies, Theology and Speculative Fiction', in *Cultural Legal Studies: Law's Popular Cultures and the Metamorphosis of Law*, edited by C. Sharp and M. Leiboff, Routledge, 2016; parts of Chapter 1 were published in early form as 'Comic Book Mythology: Shyamalan's *Unbreakable* and the Grounding of Good in Evil' (2012), 16 *Law Text Culture* 242; aspects of Chapter 2 appeared as '"The Force" as Law: Mythology, Ideology and Order in George Lucas's Star Wars' (2012), 36 *Australian Feminist Law Journal* 125; Chapter 3 was published as 'Beyond the Limits of the Law: A Christological Reading of Christopher Nolan's *The Dark Knight*' (2015), 24(3) *Griffith Law Review* 318; and an early version of Chapter 5 was published as 'Allusions to Theology: I, Robot, Universalism and the Limits of the Law' (2008), 13 *Media & Arts Law Review* 77. Small components of Chapters 3 and 4 are also drawn from '"Seeing" Justice Done: Envisioning Legality in Christopher Nolan's *The Dark Knight Trilogy*', in *Envisioning Legality: Law, Culture and Representation*, edited by T. Peters and K. Crawley, Routledge, 2018. To the managing editors and special issue editors of those journals and collections (Professor Marett Leiboff, Associate Professor

Cassandra Sharp, Professor Andrew Kenyon, Associate Professor Peter Rush, Dr Judith Grbich, Dr Ed Mussawir, Dr Karen Crawley, Professor Luke McNamara, Associate Professor Julia Quilter, Dr Luis Gomez Romero and Ian Dahlman), as well as the many anonymous reviewers, I say thank you for the invaluable input and feedback and for publishing this work. Thanks must also go to Edinburgh University Press, and in particular to Laura Williamson and Sarah Foyle for their support of this project and their patience in seeing it materialise—and to the anonymous reviewer for their supportive comments.

Whilst many are already mentioned above, particular thanks are owed to Professor William MacNeil, Professor Kieran Tranter, Dr Karen Crawley, Dr Edwin Bikundo, Dr Ed Mussawir (who also gets credit for suggesting the subtitle), Dr Ashley Pearson, Dale Mitchell, Eddie Ngaluafe, Rev Dr Andrew Peters, Rev Jock Dunbar and Chantelle Peters for reviewing and commenting on drafts of various chapters, and for discussions that have helped move it forward in multiple ways—along with Professor Adam Gearey and Professor Jason Bainbridge, who examined my PhD thesis and provided incredibly supportive feedback. The work here does not represent fully or sufficiently their intellectual impact on me, but its quality would have been significantly less without it. Thanks must also go to Professor Shaun McVeigh, Professor Marett Leiboff, Associate Professor Cassandra Sharp, Professor Jay Sanderson and Dr Thomas Giddens for their support in a variety of ways of my scholarship and my career to date.

Academia is a calling in which serendipitous and unexpected connections make significant differences—two I wish to highlight and acknowledge here. First is to Associate Professor Dean Knight (Victoria University of Wellington), who I met by chance at the 2006 conference dinner of the Law and Society Association of Australia and New Zealand in Wollongong. It is in part due to the off-hand comment Dean made at the later 2009 conference of that association in Brisbane—'why haven't you become an academic yet?'—that I made the decision to leave a career in banking for the calling of the scholar. For his intellectual camaraderie, and for seeing something in myself that I had not yet seen, I give him thanks. Second is to Bill MacNeil himself. From the moment I offered to type up his overhead transparencies for the first-year course *Introduction to Legal Theory*, Bill has been unceasing in his generosity, encouragement and support—as a lecturer, supervisor, colleague, dean, conference confrère, editor and friend. Thank you for 'sharing the luv' of both legal theory and cultural legal studies. This book would not have taken shape without you.

The life of the scholar does not cease with the academy. Whilst there is much made to date of the importance of 'engagement and impact' *of* scholarship, what is not always as significantly recognised is the impact *of* engagement *on* scholarship. In this context, I would like to thank in particular the members of St Jude the Apostle Anglican Church, Everton Park, for the opportunity not only to be part of your community but to explore the highs and lows of 'being the Church' together. I greatly appreciate your love and support over the many years of the writing of this book. To my parents, Rev Dr Andrew Peters and Lynette Peters, and sisters, Samantha Peters and Maxine Burnett, thank you for your love, encouragement and support in the numerous ways that make up family life.

This work would not have been possible, and would never have seen its way to completion, without the unceasing belief of my best friend and wife, Chantelle Peters (who also had the 'joy' of reading the entire manuscript in various stages of its completion). My sincere thanks and heartfelt appreciation do not capture enough her willingness both to engage with this work, and to provide the time for me to complete it and support as I did so. To Elsie, Lucia and Annabelle: you are each a joy and it has been wonderful to begin to share the delights of the cinematic with you. I love you all very much.

I conclude this book with a consideration of gift and generosity. In many respects, these 'acknowledgments' highlight the way in which generosity and gift exchange is fundamental to academic life and to the type of scholarship that Cultural Legal Studies produces. The theological jurisprudence that I argue for in this book is not one that can occur only in the mind but must also be lived and breathed, and which is a return of the gifts given to us. It is also to acknowledge that, as the epigraph to the concluding chapter notes, every good gift is from above.[1]

---

[1] James 1: 17.

Prologue
Reading the Law 'Made Strange'

I. Introduction

A top one of the LexCorp skyscrapers in the 2016 *Batman v Superman: Dawn of Justice*, Lex Luthor (played with semi-psychotic brilliance by Jesse Eisenberg, in a film distinctly lacking brilliance) challenges Superman's virtuous status as follows: 'If God is all powerful, he cannot be all good. And if he is all good, he cannot be all powerful. And neither can you be.'[1] Luthor's diabolical plan is to show the world the 'holes in the holy', to encourage 'the almighty' to come 'clean about how dirty he is when it counts', by requiring Superman (Henry Cavill) to kill the Batman (Ben Affleck) in order to save his mother. This discussion of Superman in theological terms brings to a head the prominent Christological themes in his filmic presentations: Superman (Kal-El) as sent by his 'heavenly' father (Jor-El), embodying both *divinity* (super-strength, X-ray vision, the ability to fly) and *humanity* (human appearances, emotional struggles, the desire to fit in), along with a mission to save the world.[2] Whilst the 2013 *Man of Steel* presents Kal-El in these Christological terms (beginning his mission at thirty-three years of age, making the momentous decision to reveal himself to the world in a country church with stained-glass windows of Christ forming the background, and raising explicit questions of faith and trust),[3] *Batman v Superman* interrogates the implications of these connections: Superman is proclaimed a false idol; Batman, after defeating him in the fight that gives the film its name, notes that he was 'never a god' and 'never even a man'; and numerous news interviews and talking heads engage in religious debate

---

[1] *Batman v Superman: Dawn of Justice*, film, directed by Snyder.
[2] The Christological aspects of the filmic representations of Superman have been central since Richard Donner's *Superman: The Movie* and were developed by Bryan Singer's *Superman Returns*. *Superman: The Movie*, film, directed by Donner; *Superman Returns*, film, directed by Singer. See Schenck, 'Popular Culture Messiah'; Barkman, 'Superman'.
[3] *Man of Steel*, film, directed by Snyder.

over whether Superman is a 'Jesus figure', a devil or 'just a guy who is trying to do the right thing'. In this context, Luthor's Nietzschean desire for, and fulfilment of, the 'death of god' (Superman is killed at the end of the film) emphasises these Christological themes in a secular context—promoting the importance of humanity throwing off reliance on such a religious saviour figure.

That Luthor's challenge to Superman is presented in the form of a discussion of theodicy—the attempt to justify the existence of an all-powerful and all-virtuous God with the existence of evil in the world—is significant, not just because of the fact that theodicy is a *modern* phenomenon,[4] but also because of the way in which it raises questions about meaning and authority that are also foundational to modern law.[5] For modern law and its embodiment in the rule of law face a similar conundrum—that of the existence of violence and evil in the context of a supposedly 'civilised' and ordered society. At one level, it is the religious that is often presented as the source of 'contaminations' to secular liberal modernity—the causes of violent uprising, terrorist attacks by fundamentalists or religiously driven racial politics. Yet, at the same time, modern law itself is caught within the frame of this violence and evil—a point that is implicit in *Batman v Superman*. For the counterpoised question to Superman's virtuousness in the film is: how does the modern condition of the rule of law deal with a superhero who is not only *acting* beyond the law but is fundamentally beyond the law's power to constrain?[6]

Senator June Finch (Holly Hunter) heads a range of Senate hearings and inquiries into deaths associated with Superman's interventions—in particular, the devastation and destruction caused by the fight between Superman and General Zod in *Man of Steel*. Whilst the world praises Superman for his acts of salvation, the political concerns are about the impossibility of restraining him and bringing him *within* the system of law and legality which governs both domestic and international actions. Finch challenges Superman as to whether he acts by his own will—unilaterally—or with 'the consent of the governed': that is, the modern foundation of law in the *demos*, in the 'consent' of the people, gives the legitimacy to the law. This challenge invokes the modern system of legality, state sovereignty and law which encompasses a monopoly on the *legitimate* use of violence—of justified violence.[7] The concern is that Superman is not simply a figure of good, aimed at helping people,

---

[4] Surin, *Theology and the Problem of Evil*; Milbank, *Being Reconciled*, pp. 1–25.

[5] Cover, 'Nomos and Narrative', p. 35.

[6] Manderson, 'Trust Us Justice', p. 33.

[7] Weber, 'Politics as Vocation'; see also Fitzpatrick, *Modernism*, p. 77.

but that his unilateral actions beyond and outside the law *also* cause considerable death, destruction and suffering. To put it back in terms of theodicy, if Superman's saving actions *also* cause evil and suffering in the world, then he cannot be a figure that is all-good and all-powerful. He must therefore be brought within the bounds of the law, which, if it does not necessarily prevent suffering, at least provides a mechanism for the deployment of justified violence.[8] Senator Finch emphatically asserts this jurisdictional claim over Superman: 'Let the record stand that this committee holds him responsible.' But this assertion of the authority of law is immediately undercut by the emotional response from one of the witnesses: 'He'll never answer to you. He answers to no-one. Not even, I think, to God.' Superman is therefore a challenge both to the rule of law, to which *everyone* is subordinate, and to modern law's self-grounding that rejects a transcendent beyond.

We live in a world of law and legality, not just in the sense of the globalisation of the rule of law and the infiltration of legalistic thinking into all realms of life,[9] but in the sense of what Robert Cover in 1983 called a *nomos*—a normative universe where we 'constantly create and maintain a world of right and wrong, of lawful and unlawful, of valid and void'.[10] The formal institutions of law and justice form only a small part of this normative universe and it is only when they are situated within the 'narratives that locate [them] and give [them] meaning'[11] that we can understand their role. In an era in which law 'lives in the image',[12] the multiplicity of texts of popular culture have become integral narratives informing our *nomos*. Though in its multiplicity popular culture offers many differing narratives, certain recurrent themes can be drawn out: themes of law and legality, of good and evil, of the questioning of unilateral or vigilante justice versus the importance or significance of lawful violence. These texts provide a questioning or critique of the nature of law and a 'barometer', as Richard Sherwin has noted, of social and cultural disenchantment with the legal system.[13] Whilst pop culture may also provide a source of re-enchantment and affirmative myth-making with regard to law, such affirmation requires a working through of the very *challenge* of fictional representations and images to law's ability to derive and provide meaning in modernity: if law lives in the image, what does it mean if we lose faith in the

---

[8] Cover, 'Violence and the Word'; Benjamin, 'Critique of Violence'.
[9] Comaroff, 'Reflections on Legal Theology', pp. 193–6.
[10] Cover, 'Nomos and Narrative', p. 4.
[11] Ibid.
[12] Sarat, 'Imagining the Law of the Father', pp. 9, 39; Sherwin, *When Law Goes Pop*.
[13] Sherwin, *When Law Goes Pop*.

image itself?[14] What does it mean if the very affective function of our popular narratives and images are deceptive—if, for example, the witness's challenge in *Batman v Superman* was staged by Luthor, so as to produce a justification for legal intervention? It is in this context that this book argues that the stories told within popular culture—in particular those of speculative fiction (science fiction, fantasy, superheroes) so favoured by Hollywood in recent years—inform our concepts of law and justice but also challenge, question and 'make strange' our received understandings and justifications of legality, reorientating our quest for legal meaning today.

The brief analysis above of *Batman v Superman*'s interwoven narratives of a secularised theodicy aiming at the 'death of god', along with demands for responsibility and the authorisation of violent interventions under the rule of law, highlights the way in which our texts of popular culture and the speculative fiction so dominant on our screens give rise to questions of what could be called modern theo-legality.[15] It is towards an interrogation of the way these filmic narratives explore not just questions of law but their interrelation with the theologico-political in our post-secular times that this book aims. This is not simply to note the way in which a figure like Superman might be considered an 'Americanised Christ', or how science fiction is a secularised myth of modernity, or the ways in which fantasy texts draw on historical religious beliefs in the divine and supernatural, but rather to identify the way in which our popular culture represents and attempts to work through a range of the *tensions* of modern law, still bound to, and interwoven with, its theological roots. In doing so, it questions the presumed secularity, objectivity and universality of modern law, revealing that, despite its attempts to relegate religion either to a historical antecedent long forgotten, or simply to an aspect of the private domain to be regulated and protected, that law itself remains caught in the theological. The theological aspects of modern law are often opaque, not visible to our modern secular eyes so bound to an underlying faith in legality. My argument throughout this work is that speculative fiction's genres of estrangement provide a way for us to see, engage and render visible these theological concepts of modern law in our era of late capitalism, global empire and the crises of neoliberalism. It is for this reason that I turn to a cultural legal analysis of speculative fiction as a way of discussing and reflecting on the intersections of theology and law—and, in particular, unpacking an examination of the *meaning* of law, which runs aground if we ignore the theological position that it takes up in secularised form.

---

[14] Sherwin, *Visualising Law*.
[15] Comaroff, 'Reflections on Legal Theology'.

II. The Theo-legality of Modern Law: Towards a Theological Jurisprudence Today

If our understanding of law and legal meaning is embedded in the narratives we tell about it, then our modern concept of law is captured within what Mark Lilla has described as the fairy-tales of modernity.[16] To describe modernity in relation to fairy-tales would appear paradoxical, given modernity's distaste for myth, superstition and fantasy. However, the movements of modernity themselves—including those of modern law—are caught within a narrative mythos. As the late Peter Fitzpatrick described it, modernity is mythic—it is the myth of being without myth.[17] In *The Stillborn God*, Lilla describes the stories of modernity (secularisation, democratisation, disenchantment) as the 'fairy-tales of our time', arguing that they have been presented as simple, straightforward and inevitable on a supposed march from political theology to secular liberalism.[18] Instead, he suggests that secularism and liberalism are not inevitable but experimental and fragile, and that they have an urgent need to be nurtured and maintained against the returned spectre of political theologies. As Ronald Beiner and Charles Taylor have pointed out, Lilla's description of modernity is premised on a particular story that is seen as essential to modernity and modern law: the 'great separation' of theology from secular politics, religion from secular law, the church from the state.[19] Lilla argues for a re-establishing of such a 'great separation', wanting, therefore, to return to narratives of secular modernity which would see a focus on the 'immanence' of modern law as opposed to its 'transcendence'—a reaffirming of its objectivity, secularity, rationality and neutrality.

Whilst acknowledging the role of religion and theology in its historical development, the dominant narratives of modern secular law affirm this 'great separation' and, in particular, the severing of law from religion.[20] From this perspective, the intersections of law and religion either are of historical interest only or concern the protection and regulation of religious freedoms which are relegated to the private domain, minimising or limiting the role of religion in the 'public sphere'.[21] Such an approach is one that

---

[16] Lilla, *Stillborn God*, p. 6.

[17] Fitzpatrick, *Mythology*, p. ix.

[18] Lilla, *Stillborn God*.

[19] Beiner, 'Has the Great Separation Failed?'; Taylor, 'Two Books, Oddly Yoked Together'.

[20] See discussions in Hunter, 'Law, Religion, Common Good'; Calo, 'Post-Secular Legal Theory'.

[21] See discussion in Babie, 'Breaking the Silence', pp. 296–314.

presumes the gaze of secular legality itself—a neutrality that is able to tran-scend the particularities of individual theological or religious positions and personal beliefs—and encompasses the Enlightenment idea of a purely secu-lar basis for law as self-grounding, autonomous and universal.[22] This aligns legal modernity with the 'secularisation thesis', which presupposed the co-development of modernity and secularity, positing that modernisation would undermine the need for, and authority of, religion and theology[23]—an automatic extension of what Max Weber described as the rationalisation and dis-enchantment of modernity.[24] The secularisation thesis has, however, been called into question in recent decades from empirical, sociological and philosophical perspectives. The 'return of religion' (a term which assumes that religion had been away somewhere—exiled or on holiday) has chal-lenged the idea that religion was something diminishing in modernity, and instead we are considered to inhabit a 'post-secular world', which involves 'the empirically undeniable persistence of religion in the late modern world, the recognition of the limits of secular epistemology and reason' and 'an intensifying and unstable pluralism'.[25]

Whilst this turn to the post-secular would appear to be a debunking of the Enlightenment trajectory, at the level of philosophy, as Slavoj Žižek has noted, the post-secular can be understood as a *result* of the Enlightenment. The attempt, following Immanuel Kant, to separate religion from reason results not in the elimination of religion but rather in a space for religion to return in the form of the irrational. The repression of religion by the Enlight-enment—its attempt to segment it off—does not eliminate religion or God, but results in its return in a space *outside* of reason where reason's own limita-tion is that it cannot know everything.[26] This very aspect of *finitude* seems to allow a space of the transcendent beyond, but which can now be conceived only in terms of negative theology—an absolute Other that cannot be known but to which we can remain 'open'.[27] Modernity's focus on finitude, and therefore also on contingency, has its own theological genealogy—one which can be traced back to theologians such as Duns Scotus and philosophers

---

[22] Calo, 'Post-Secular Legal Theory', pp. 507–8; see also Fitzpatrick, *Modernism*.

[23] See Habermas, 'Notes on Post-Secular Society', pp. 17–18.

[24] Weber, *Economy and Society*; Weber, *Protestant Ethic*.

[25] Hunter, 'Law, Religion, Common Good', p. 1067; see also Calo, 'Faithful Presence'.

[26] Žižek, 'Two Questions', pp. 215–16; Kant et al., *Religion*; Milbank, *Being Recon-ciled*, pp. 1–25.

[27] See Žižek, 'Two Questions', referring to the work of theologians like John Caputo; see, for example, Caputo and Vattimo, *After the Death of God*.

like Descartes who point to the absolute contingency of creation founded in God's untrammelled will: that God could have decided that things were other than what they are, not just in terms of the modes of creation but in terms of the very laws of existence.[28] Questions of the post-secular would seem to emphasise, therefore, not just a 'return of religion' but also the way in which the rise of religious fundamentalisms (whether Christian, Muslim or other) is essentially a response or reaction to modernity itself—it involves an attempt at determining the realm of specific knowability with claims to absolute knowledge within a particular domain.

The issue of the post-secular in relation to law is that it encompasses a *challenge* to the fundamental tenets of legal modernity: both its secularity and its universality. It therefore calls into question the sharp distinction between law and theology—its grounding in the 'great separation'. But the idea that there ever was such a great separation in law has *also* been called into question by recent scholarship.[29] As Winnifred Sullivan, Robert Yelle and Mateo Taussig-Rubbo have pointed out, the assertion of both the secularity and the universality of modern law itself embodies a theological move: the positing of separation between sacred and profane is inherently religious, and a number of religious traditions, most notably Christianity, arrogate to themselves the power to 'succeed and contain' religious traditions that came before, in the same way that 'secularism asserts its authority to displace and locate religion'.[30] In a more general sense, much of the work on law and religion has asserted the *similarities* in the function of law and religion: they each seek to frame human behaviour and govern both private and communal life; they embed a commitment to certain foundational obligations, institutions and ideologies; they each focus on the hermeneutical interpretation of founding texts; and they both engage in a production of foundational meaning-making and the construction of a normative reality.[31] Thus, even though attempting to distinguish itself from religious particularity, modern secular law fulfils a similar function to religion, but also takes within itself concerns with the sacred and theological, even if it attempts to do without recourse to transcendence.[32] From a more

---

[28] Žižek, 'Two Questions', p. 221; see also Milbank, *Theology and Social Theory*.

[29] Barzilai, 'Introduction', p. xi.

[30] Sullivan et al., 'Introduction', p. 2; see also Yelle, 'Moses' Veil'; Fitzpatrick, *Mythology*; Goodrich, *Oedipus Lex*.

[31] Sullivan et al., 'Introduction', p. 3; Barzilai, 'Introduction'; Neoh, 'Text, Doctrine, Tradition'; Calo, 'Faithful Presence'. See also, for example, Harris-Abbot, 'On Law and Theology'; Marty, 'The Religious Foundations of Law'; Sharp, 'Religion and Justice'.

[32] Umphrey et al., 'The Sacred in Law: An Introduction', pp. 10–15.

historical perspective, we can also turn to the theological origins and roots of the Western legal tradition (and, by association, all those legal systems that have come under its influence). Such has been explicitly established by the detailed work of Harold Berman, who outlines the way in which the modern Western legal system has direct theological roots which involve 'a secular residue of religious attitudes and assumptions which historically found expression first in the liturgy and rituals and doctrines of the church and thereafter in the institutions and concepts and values of the law'.[33] The significance of this theological history is that 'Western legal science is a secular theology, which often makes no sense because its theological presuppositions are no longer accepted.'[34] As such, our 'modern' conceptions of law, justice and judgment are drawn from theological underpinnings.[35] Whilst these two points (law's analogous role to religion and its theological roots) are generally not considered controversial, they are often still viewed from the perspective that modern law has been successfully secularised, promoting a neutral and objective 'rule of law' not bound to particular theological dogmatisms.

The undermining of the presumed separation of secular law from theology by the post-secular is further emphasised by the renewed scholarship and interest in the field of political theology over the past twenty years. At one level, this interest has also arisen out of the 'return of religion', focused on the increasing theocratic claims for the involvement in politics of what Jose Casanova has described as 'public religions'.[36] This view of political theology retains the inherent modern sense of separation between fundamental theocracy on one side and secular democracy on the other, and emphasises the challenges and debates between the two. At a more conceptual and foundational level, however, are approaches to political theology that follow (in some form or another) Carl Schmitt's proclamation that 'all significant concepts of the modern theory of the state are secularised theological concepts'.[37] On this view, political theology is not so much a separate enterprise to modern secular politics and law, but rather the only way to understand modern

---

[33] Berman, *Law and Revolution*, p. 166. See also Mohr, 'Christian Origins of Secularism', p. 34.

[34] Berman, *Law and Revolution*, p. 165.

[35] Ibid., pp. 171–85.

[36] Casanova, *Public Religions*; Comaroff, 'Reflections on Legal Theology'. For a variety of approaches to the interactions of law and religion in terms of political theology see Vries and Sullivan, *Political Theologies*; Kirsch and Turner, *Permutations of Order*.

[37] Schmitt, *Political Theology*, p. 35. See also Kantorowicz, *King's Two Bodies*.

politics itself.[38] Following and extending Schmitt's thesis, Giorgio Agamben has argued that secularisation is not a de-theologising or dis-enchanting of the world (as is posited by Weber), but rather a process in which theological concepts and frameworks are transitioned into a secular domain but which still have effect.[39] Agamben therefore argues that

> secularization is a form of repression. It leaves intact the forces it deals with by simply moving them from one place to another. Thus the political secularization of theological concepts (the transcendence of God as a paradigm of power) does nothing but displace the heavenly monarchy onto an earthly monarchy, leaving its power intact.[40]

From this perspective, the establishment of a supposedly secularised law in fact leaves intact the theological structure of that which is secularised. Theology is therefore a means for understanding the political—a point which has been taken up by a range of other critical theorists who, following in particular Jacob Taubes's *The Political Theology of Paul*, have (re)turned to the writings of Saint Paul as fundamental texts of the Western tradition that need to be reclaimed, resituated and 'fought for', even in their process of being overcome.[41] Of note here, of course, is that even though this would seem to be the privileging of a particular religious tradition, at the same time it involves a reclaiming of Paul's *universalism*—a point highlighted by Alain Badiou and Žižek.[42]

As such, despite the presumed separation of theology and the secular, and, more specifically, religion and law, theology has returned as the discourse *du jour* for developing an increased understanding of the immanent working of

---

[38] See, for example, Kahn, *Political Theology*; Crockett, *Religion and Violence in a Secular World*; Vries and Sullivan, *Political Theologies*.

[39] Weber, *Protestant Ethic*; Weber, 'Science as Vocation'.

[40] Agamben, *Profanations*, p. 77. He thus contrasts secularisation with profanation, which 'neutralizes what it profanes. Once profaned, that which was unavailable and separate loses its aura and is returned to use. Both are political operations: the first [secularisation] guarantees the exercise of power by carrying it back to a sacred model; the second deactivates the apparatuses of power and returns to common use the spaces that power had seized.' See also Agamben's discussion of secularisation as a 'signature': Agamben, *Kingdom and the Glory*, pp. 3–4.

[41] See Taubes, *Political Theology of Paul*; Badiou, *Saint Paul*; Žižek, *The Fragile Absolute*; Žižek, *On Belief*; Agamben, *Time That Remains*; Caputo and Alcoff, *St. Paul Among the Philosophers*; Milbank et al., *Paul's New Moment*. On the turn to St Paul, in particular, see Chapter 5 below.

[42] Badiou, *Saint Paul*; Žižek, *The Fragile Absolute*.

the state, politics and law. This shift has not gone unnoticed by theologians, who also have, not unsurprisingly, engaged substantially with the traditions and ideas of political theology as well as the theological origins and precursors of modernity. The theological movement operating under the moniker 'Radical Orthodoxy' has consistently demonstrated the way in which modernity itself encompasses a particular response to theology that is not simply its repression but also its deployment in heterodox form.[43] In particular, this involves a tracing of the 'invention' of the secular back to shifts in medieval theology with the rise of the voluntarism and nominalism of Duns Scotus and William of Ockham.[44] John Milbank, for instance, argues that the construction of modernity and secular social theory is always defined *against* or in terms of theology and can thus be understood only *as* a form of theology.[45] In engaging the depths of the Christian theological tradition along with modern critical theory and philosophy, Radical Orthodoxy seeks to overcome the deadlocks of modern theology, which either limit theology to its determination by the secular (such as in liberal theology) or close off the space of revelation and religion from an autonomous secular sphere (such as occurs in both neo-orthodoxy and fundamentalist theology).[46] Radical Orthodoxy challenges these 'modern' theologies by identifying their problems as being those of modernity itself, which seeks to promote an autonomous space of secular reason devoid or detached from theology and revelation—in this sense, a parallel challenge to the 'great separation' of theology and politics, law and religion discussed above.

Much of the work that goes to uncovering, revealing and rendering visible modern secular law's theological traces—and the 'machine' of political

[43] Milbank et al., *Radical Orthodoxy*; Milbank, *Theology and Social Theory*; Milbank, *Beyond Secular Order*. See also Ward, *Cities of God*; Smith, *Introducing Radical Orthodoxy*; Oliver, 'From Participation to Late Modernity'. For a critical jurisprudential use of John Milbank's work in particular, see Deagon, *From Violence to Peace*.

[44] Milbank et al., *Radical Orthodoxy*; Milbank, *Theology and Social Theory*; Milbank, *Beyond Secular Order*.

[45] Milbank, *Theology and Social Theory*; Milbank, *Beyond Secular Order*. Even a cursory reading of Hobbes's *Leviathan*, which Lilla takes to be a founding text of modernity and the inauguration of the 'great separation' between secular and religious in politics, identifies that Hobbes is engaging and responding to theology, as well as constructing his own. See Lilla, *Stillborn God*; Milbank, *Theology and Social Theory*, pp. 19–27.

[46] See discussion by Milbank et al., *Paul's New Moment*, pp. 7, 11–13; Davis, 'Holy Saturday or Resurrection Sunday?', pp. 5–13.

theology that undergirds it—is often presented with the aim of escaping from or exiting its logic, further de-theologising or dis-enchanting the world and leaving bare the very immanent and human operations of power.[47] This, for Lilla, would involve a reaffirming and reinstituting of the 'great separation' between theology and law—political theology and secular politics. At times, this comprises a desire to ensure that law maintains its secular neutrality, seen as a necessary foundation for the globalisation of the rule of law, *increasingly* needed in the context of post-secularity and religious pluralism. Alternatively, further de-theologisation can involve attempts to think the operations of law, power and governance outside of the bind between transcendence and immanence that law's inherent theological roots account for and the machinery it encompasses.

My approach in this book, however, is not to engage in a reaffirmed process of de-theologisation or dis-enchantment but rather to explore and seek to re-examine the 'theatrics' of theo-legality that we already inhabit.[48] In this sense I take up Zachary R. Calo's call for a 'theological jurisprudence' which seeks not only to 'escape the captivity of modern logic' so that we can interrogate the 'deeper assumptions informing legal scholarship', but also to engage in a constructive and transformative approach that moves *beyond* Lilla's 'Great Separation'.[49] Calo argues that the post-secular further challenges the foundational secularity of modern law, and argues for a drawing on theological traditions not as a complete rejection of modernity but as a way of engaging in a constructive approach to legal meaning today.[50] In the context of the post-secular's destabilisation of legal modernity's claims to universality, '[t]he issue is no longer whether there should be more or less secularism, but rather how to give law meaning within a cultural environment where there is no possibility of deep moral consensus.'[51] Following Calo, my argument is not to subordinate law to a particularistic theological position, but rather to engage with theological traditions so as to redefine our way of seeing law—seeing law not as an autonomous, self-grounding and universalising enterprise but rather as 'grounded necessarily in a basic act of trust in the meaningfulness of creation and the possibility of justice'.[52] It is with this approach to theological jurisprudence in mind that this book is written. It seeks to engage in the

---

[47] On the machine of political theology, see Esposito, *Two*.
[48] Goodrich, 'Theatre of Emblems', p. 67.
[49] Calo, 'Post-Secular Legal Theory', p. 517.
[50] Ibid.; Calo, 'Faithful Presence'.
[51] Calo, 'Faithful Presence', p. 1086.
[52] Ibid., p. 1088.

development of a critical theological jurisprudence which both critiques and renders visible the fractures in modern law's secularity, but also draws on the theological tradition as a way of re-envisioning law today. In doing so, I not only draw on the developments of Radical Orthodoxy's approach to theology and critical theory, but also take up the aspects of its sensibility which sees theology found as much, if not more so, in art, symbols, images and narratives as much as in reason.[53] Taking up this approach, I argue that a theological account and critique of law needs to look to its cultural texts as much as its legal ones for its elaboration—and thus I situate my work clearly within the developing jurisprudence of 'cultural legal studies'.

III. Cultural Legal Studies as 'Making Strange'

The question of law's meaning today cannot be understood purely within the bounds of positivist accounts of law and its focus on the relationship between the individual and the state—or even in the frame of reference of the formal institutions and practices of justice. We need a greater understanding of the cultural contextual frames of legal meaning—and this is precisely what the emerging field of Cultural Legal Studies focuses on. Cultural Legal Studies does not just involve critical readings of cases, legal treatises, legislation and other legal instruments, but also it turns to find legal meaning and law in *cultural* texts as much as, if not more than, explicitly legal ones. Marett Leiboff and Cassandra Sharp have described it as concerned 'with animating law's popular cultures—the multivalenced forms and practices ranging from the humanities to videogames and beyond—as a means through which to transform or animate questions of law and justice'.[54] Whilst it sits within the broad range of disciplines operating under the banner of 'law and the humanities',[55] and draws on the earlier approaches to law and literature involving the use of literature to 'humanise' the law and legal profession, the analysis of law and legal text's *literary* characteristics and

[53] See Milbank, 'Fictioning Things'; Milbank, *Chesterton and Tolkien*; Blond, 'Perception'; Pickstock, 'Liturgy, Art and Politics'.

[54] Leiboff and Sharp, 'Cultural Legal Studies', p. 5; see also Peters and Crawley, *Envisioning Legality*; Giddens, *On Comics*. Whilst Cultural Legal Studies often engages in texts of what are considered 'popular culture', this is not in the sense of reaffirming or producing a dichotomy between high and popular culture, but rather recognising the way in which such dichotomies are inherently unstable. Any reference to 'popular' culture is not a limitation upon the types of cultural texts that are considered or the way they constitute law. See Manderson, 'Memory and Echo'.

[55] Sarat et al., *Law and the Humanities*.

critical analysis of law and lawyers in literary, filmic and televisual settings, Cultural Legal Studies goes *beyond* these earlier approaches in a number of ways.[56] First, Cultural Legal Studies is focused not so much on the representation *of* the law, but on a clearer understanding of both how those representations 'work'[57] and the way in which they form part of the *constituting* of law and legality itself. As I have noted elsewhere with Karen Crawley, '[t]he force of law and the possibilities of justice are bound up in the stories or narratives we tell ourselves. Art's images and literature's narratives are central to these stories: they are vital to law's origin, meaning, and legitimacy.'[58] In this sense, Cultural Legal Studies engages in an explicit focus on 'the imagination (and its appropriation)' as central 'to the operation and effectiveness of law and legality'.[59] This means that we need to look not just to *what* cultural texts represent, but the very ways in which they do this—through the forms of story-telling and affect deployed, and the uses of style and genre, as well as the formal characteristics of the particular mediums.[60] Law cannot be separated from culture. Not only is law reflected in and constitutive of culture, but culture infuses, reflects and determines law.[61]

Second ,and following on from the above approach to culture and cultural texts as *constituting* law, Cultural Legal Studies focuses on cultural texts not so much as representations of law but as what Desmond Manderson has referred to as *sites* of law.[62] This includes both the way in which cultural texts *introduce* us into law and legality, as well as provide resistant accounts *to* the formal institutions of law.[63] At one level, cultural texts enthral us with narratives of good and evil, right and wrong, legitimate and illegitimate, and the relations

---

[56] On the humanist tradition, see most significantly White, *The Legal Imagination*; Nussbaum, *Poetic Justice*; Gaakeer, 'Law and Literature'. For a critical engagement of this approach to law and literature, see Manderson, 'Critique of Law and Literature'. On the traditional classifications of law and literature scholarship as 'law *in* literature' and 'law *as* literature' see Weisberg, 'Law-Literature Enterprise'. These have become standard in relation not only to 'law and literature' but also to 'law and film' and 'law and television'. See Gaakeer, 'Law and Literature'; Silbey, 'What We Do'; Silbey, 'Politics of Law and Film'; Robson and Silbey, *Law and Justice on the Small Screen*.

[57] Crawley, 'Critical Force of Irony'; Crawley and Peters, 'Representational Legality'.

[58] Crawley and Peters, 'Representational Legality', p. 2.

[59] Ibid., p. 3.

[60] Young, *Scene of Violence*. See discussion in Crawley, 'Critical Force of Irony'. See also Manderson, 'Critique of Law and Literature'; Crawley, 'Reproducing Whiteness'.

[61] Manderson, 'Memory and Echo', p. 12.

[62] Manderson, 'From Hunger to Love', pp. 91, 93; Manderson, 'Trust Us Justice'.

[63] Manderson, 'Trust Us Justice', pp. 25–7; see also Manderson, 'Memory and Echo'.

of power, justice and authority. It is not just, as Jessica Silbey notes in relation to films, that cultural texts go to 'constitute a legal culture beyond law' but that they are involved in 'particular ways of world-making' which 'shape our expectations of law and justice in our world'.[64] The forms of story-telling embodied in film imagine the law, and construct and institute us into law and legality itself. As Orit Kamir has noted, both film and law construct a world and a *nomos*.[65] The significance of this approach to cultural texts is that it goes beyond the traditional idea of a 'legal' text, or canonical debates about what is or is not a 'law film'.[66] For rather, it understands the very narrative, constructed and affective forms of cultural texts themselves as being imbued with legality but also introducing us and engaging us in the *nomos* of legality itself. At the same time, Manderson argues that cultural texts are also 'a *source* of law', one which does not involve just depictions of formal law but, even despite their technologised and commercialised mediations today, are sites of 'resistance to it, as the effort to preserve or to resuscitate an alternative *nomos*'.[67] In this sense, cultural texts also encompass a *critique* of the formal law and a challenge to it by offering alternative normative frameworks— alternative *nomoi*.

The fact that popular culture can operate as both a source of law and a site of resistance to it goes, then, also to the third significant aspect of Cultural Legal Studies, which is the way in which it *reads* cultural texts themselves as providing critical encounters and engagements with law, legal theory and jurisprudence. Whilst early work on law and film referred to 'cinematic jurisprudence', it is potentially William MacNeil's method of 'reading jurisprudentially' that offers the most sophisticated form of this approach—and which has since been adopted, adapted and deployed in a multitude of contexts and by a range of authors.[68] At one level, 'reading jurisprudentially' takes up the idea that pop culture 'has something to say about law', but what is more important is the way in which it involves a process of critique that, in a sense, 'defamiliarises' our approach to the traditional questions of law, legality and jurisprudence—to borrow a term from Žižek (one of MacNeil's influences), 'reading jurisprudentially' involves a process of reading the law 'awry' through the texts of popular culture.[69] MacNeil's mediation of law and

---

[64] Silbey, 'Politics of Law and Film', p. 757. Buchanan and Johnson, 'Strange Encounters'.

[65] Kamir, 'Why "Law-and-Film"', p. 257.

[66] See Bergman and Asimow, *Reel Justice*; Machura and Robson, 'Law and Film'; Greenfield et al., *Film and the Law*.

[67] Manderson, 'Trust Us Justice', p. 25; Manderson, 'Memory and Echo'.

[68] MacNeil, *Lex Populi*; MacNeil, *Novel Judgements*.

[69] Žižek, *Looking Awry*.

jurisprudence through fiction privileges the process of reading as much as the texts under consideration, as a way of seeing the cultural texts as well as the law and legality anew. It 'produces not just mutually illuminating readings, but an alternative intertext'—a text between texts—which 'synthesizes, sublates . . . and enables us . . . to look at "the legal" and "the literary" *otherwise*—as a site of discursive difference rather than binary stasis, of theoretical inquiry rather than socio-legal representation'.[70] Through a critical reading of cultural texts, Cultural Legal Studies uncovers not just their legal narratives but a critical theorisation of law, legality and justice. As Leiboff and Sharp have put it, Cultural Legal Studies 'generat[es], produc[es] and creat[es] complex encounters between different manifestations of the popular cultural and law as jurisprudence, as a means through which to think about how to *do* law well'.[71]

As noted above, Cultural Legal Studies therefore extends the earlier bounds of law and literature, and law and humanities, in a number of respects. There are two additional extensions that are particularly relevant here. First, it recognises that texts that do not specifically engage in representations of law, the legal system or even traditional representations of crime and justice as their central focus are still significant both as constitutive of our *nomos* and as sources of jurisprudential analysis. Texts from the speculative genres such as fantasy, science fiction and the gothic, for example, have as much to say about law and legal theory as many of the texts traditionally explored by law and popular culture scholarship. Following MacNeil in particular, a range of scholars have engaged in jurisprudential analyses of everything from science fiction to superheroes, and music to video games.[72] Second, as MacNeil's work makes clear, the approach to cultural texts embodied in Cultural Legal Studies does not simply provide an insight into what people think about

---

[70] MacNeil, 'One Recht', p. 280; MacNeil, *Lex Populi*, pp. 155–6.

[71] Leiboff and Sharp, 'Cultural Legal Studies', p. 6.

[72] On science fiction and fantasy see, for example, Tranter, *Living in Technical Legality*; Hourigan, 'Breach!'; Hourigan, *Law and Enjoyment*; Peters, '"The Force" as Law'; Rogers, 'Free Flesh'. On superheroes, see Bainbridge, 'This is the Authority'; Bainbridge, 'Spider-Man, The Question and the Meta-Zone'; Giddens, 'Navigating the Looking Glass'; Giddens, *On Comics*; Mitchell, 'Legal Reading of She-Hulk'; Peters, 'Globalisation, Persona and Mask'. On role-playing games and video games, see Beattie, 'Voicing the Shadow'; Pearson and Tranter, 'Code'; Pearson, 'Legal Persona of the Video Game'; Mitchell, 'Masterful Trainers'; Barnett and Sharp, 'Moral Choice of inFAMOUS'; Sykes, '"Those Chosen by the Planet"'. On music see Sykes and Tranter, '"You Gotta Roll/Rule With It"'; Sykes and Tranter, 'A Just (Electric Lady) Land'.

law but, through the text's modes of story-telling, its tropes, stylistic turns, plot devices and affective features, provides the possibility for rethinking the law and for 'doing' jurisprudence. The construction of an intertextual juris-prudence elevates the status of the cultural text to theoretical work that can re-sign, re-signify and re-imagine traditional understandings of law and juris-prudence in ways not possible via either cultural studies or jurisprudence themselves as independent disciplines. In this sense, Cultural Legal Studies breaks down certain disciplinary boundaries, as well as 'modern' divisions in respect of what can be considered the canonical or 'authoritative texts' of law and jurisprudence.[73] It not only understands law as being 'opened up' to its literary and cultural 'other', but recognises that the boundaries imposed between them are themselves illusory (though not insignificant) constructs of modernity and modern law themselves.[74]

My aim in the present work is to take up these approaches of Cultural Legal Studies, which emphasise the critical analysis of cultural texts as sites and sources of law and forms of critical jurisprudence. But I do this through deploying the leitmotif of 'defamiliarisation' or 'estrangement' as a way not only of enabling us to see the world differently or as constructed but of return-ing us to the world itself. At times, the very narratives of law and legality that we live and breathe—and which Cultural Legal Studies seeks to analyse—are ones that we take for granted. As such, we need to find a way to return to and see differently the narratives of law today—still dominated by legal moder-nity and its presumed secularity. It is for this reason that I turn to the genres of speculative fiction, which take a mode of estrangement or 'making strange' as foundational to their presenting of both alternative worlds and alterna-tive visions of our world as a means for turning to the construction of legal meaning in the context of our post-secular times. In doing so, I am arguing that Cultural Legal Studies *also* encompasses a process of defamiliarisation— a process of approaching questions of law and legality *otherwise* through the texts of popular culture. At the same time, I also contend that speculative fiction provides a way of returning the world to us and affirming its mean-ing, and therefore engages in a particular form of theologising—a point I will elaborate on in the next section.

IV. The Law 'Made Strange': Taking Speculative Fiction Seriously

Whilst 'speculative fiction' has traditionally been understood as a commercial, rather than literary, classification which therefore struggles with definitional

---

[73] MacNeil, *Lex Populi*. For a discussion of this, see Giddens, *On Comics*, pp. 2–14.
[74] Giddens, *On Comics*, p. 5.

boundaries, R. B. Gill provides a useful working definition: 'works presenting modes of being that contrast with their audiences' understanding of ordinary reality'.[75] This means that the focus is not only on the alternative worlds or 'modes of being' presented in speculative fictions, but, more importantly, on the alternative *to* the ordinary perceived reality of the reader or viewer. What would be deemed speculative fiction for a nineteenth-century reader is inherently different from that for a twenty-first-century reader or viewer. At the same time, as Carl Malmgren has pointed out, these genres tend to focus on the question of the *world*, rather than the story[76]—they situate themselves in worlds '*other* than the basic narrative world' that is the empirical world of the author.[77] In contrast to 'realistic' or 'naturalistic' fiction, which, whilst positing fictional narratives and characters, generally does so in a world that conforms to that of the author and reader, the genres of speculative fiction imagine a world that is fundamentally different from what the author or reader understands as ordinary reality.[78] The differences of such an imagined world may be naturalised via a scientific explanation as logically possible (as in science fiction) or relegated to the imaginable but impossible or unreal (as in fantasy) or explained with references to various modes of the supernatural (as in much gothic literature).

What all of these genres have in common is the deployment of the concept of estrangement or 'making strange'. Darko Suvin famously defined science fiction as a form of 'cognitive estrangement', situating it as one of a number of 'estranged genres' (including fairy-tale, fantasy and myth), which he opposed to naturalistic ones.[79] This concept of estrangement has a particular artistic and intellectual heritage—one which Suvin draws on explicitly by reference to the work of Victor Shklovsky and Bertolt Brecht. Shklovsky, one of the Russian Formalists, developed the concept of *ostranenie* (estrangement, defamiliarisation or 'making strange') as a theory of art, whose purpose is to 'impart the sensation of things as they are perceived and not as they are known'[80]—to 'de-autonomise' us from our habitualised and desensitised experience of the world and enable us really to *see* what we often take for

---

[75] Gill, 'Uses of Genre', pp. 72–3.

[76] Malmgren, 'Definition of Science Fantasy', p. 259.

[77] Ibid., p. 260. Darko Suvin describes this as the 'zero-world' of the author: Suvin, *Metamorphoses of Science Fiction*, p. 11.

[78] Malmgren, 'Definition of Science Fantasy', p. 276 n. 2; see also Suvin, *Metamorphoses of Science Fiction*, p. viii.

[79] Suvin, *Metamorphoses of Science Fiction*, pp. 3–4, 7–10; see also Spiegel, 'Things Made Strange', p. 371.

[80] Shklovsky, 'Art as Technique', pp. 3, 12.

granted. Art 'removes objects from the automatism of perception'[81]—it 'exists that one may recover the sensation of life; it exists to make one feel things, to make the stone *stony*'.[82] Rather than involving a transparent or direct access to the world of the thing represented, art should make objects 'unfamiliar' and '[i]ncrease the difficulty and length of perception'—the focus is not on the object itself but rather on *experiencing the artfulness of an object*.[83] Whilst Shklovsky draws on a range of examples from both literature and painting, he argues that estrangement applies to *all* forms of art: 'defamiliarization is found almost everywhere form is found'.[84] When it comes to painting and images, the aim is not to provide a *clear* perception of the image but rather to impede or slow perception so as to allow a focus on the *presentation* of the representation rather than on *what* is being represented.

Brecht's *Verfremdung* or *V-Effekt* in theatre drew on a similar understanding of estrangement: '[a] representation which estranges is one which allows us to recognise its subject, but at the same time makes it seem unfamiliar'.[85] Whilst similar to Shklovsky's definition, Brecht's focus is political and didactic.[86] The practice of the *V-Effekt* in theatre is aimed at blocking empathy and *interrupting* the audience's perception.[87] Instead of engaging with or 'delving' into the play, in Brecht's Epic Theatre, the spectator 'is obstructed from regarding it as "natural"',[88] and the activity occurring on the stage should be rendered visible in itself (not simply in terms of the world it represents).[89] The artifice of the performance (and, by comparison, politics and the social order) should become clear, rendering visible its constructedness. In seeking to develop a 'theater of the scientific age', Brecht sought to replicate the naïve, objective gaze of the scientists that would see things as estranged in terms of looking at them as if for the first time.[90] As Spiegel notes, the result of the estrangement techniques for Brecht should be 'the realization that things do

---

[81] Ibid., p. 13.

[82] Ibid., pp. 11–12.

[83] Ibid., p. 12. Emphasis in original.

[84] Ibid., p. 18.

[85] Brecht, 'Short Organum for Theatre'; quoted in Suvin, *Metamorphoses of Science Fiction*, p. 6, where he changes the translation of 'alienation' to 'estrangement'.

[86] There is speculation as to whether Brecht was directly influenced by Shklvosky or not. See discussion in Tihanov, 'Politics of Estrangement', pp. 687–8, n. 42.

[87] Brecht, 'Short Organum for Theatre', pp. 190–2.

[88] Spiegel, 'Things Made Strange', p. 370.

[89] For a use of Brecht's *V-Effekt* in the context of legal analysis, see Leiboff, 'Of the Monstrous Regiment'; Leiboff, 'Cultural Legal Studies as Law's Extraversion'.

[90] Spiegel, 'Things Made Strange', p. 370.

not have to be the way they are, that any current state of things is not a natural given but a product of historical processes, which can change and will be changed'.[91]

Whilst Suvin alludes to Brecht's aim of replicating the objective gaze of the scientist in his discussion of science fiction as a 'factual reporting of fictions', his deployment of the idea of *estrangement* functions not simply as a technique (which may or may not be deployed in works of speculative or science fiction) but in terms of the '*formal framework* of the genre'.[92] For Suvin, 'the approach to the imaginary locality, or localized daydream, practiced by the genre of S[cience] F[iction] is a supposedly factual one'.[93] It encompasses a 'look of estrangement' which is 'both cognitive and creative'.[94] At times, Suvin's use of the term estrangement at the level of genre has been criticised as misinterpreting Shklovsky and Brecht's focus on technique (particularly because what appears estranged to the reader is naturalised at the level of the story).[95] However, Suvin's discussion of the genres of estrangement also operates in a critical and satirical context. Works of speculative fiction *do* engage in a form of making the familiar unfamiliar, which is Shklovsky's definition of art. The factual reporting of fictions—the naturalised presentation of the unnatural at the level of the story—also returns us to a reflection on the world itself and a way of seeing it anew. Despite these genres' engagement with and creation of different worlds, novums and characters, they involve a 'reflecting *of*' reality but also a critical reflecting '*on* reality'.[96] In this sense, the deployment of estrangement at the level of world or genre *does* display a difference from Shklovsky's and Brecht's approach because it aims at defamiliarising our perception of our own world at the same time as returning us to it. The aim is to engage not simply in a viewing of art itself but in a viewing of art that, in its artfulness, returns us to a consideration of the world and its meaning.

The argument that both the techniques and the genres of estrangement involve a returning of us to our world is of particular significance in the context of the theological jurisprudence that I explore and develop in this book. This is in part because of the way in which Cultural Legal Studies reads and understands law itself as captured in the narratives that we tell ourselves, but

[91] Ibid.; Brecht, 'Short Organum for Theatre'.
[92] Suvin, *Metamorphoses of Science Fiction*, p. 7.
[93] Ibid., pp. 5–6.
[94] Ibid., p. 6.
[95] See Spiegel, 'Things Made Strange', p. 375. For a more favourable rendering of Suvin's analysis of estrangement in science fiction, see Mather, 'Figures of Estrangement', p. 187.
[96] Suvin, *Metamorphoses of Science Fiction*, p. 10.

also because of the significance of the imagining of an alternative world as a commitment to a particular metaphysics, a particular *belief* in the world itself. Alison Milbank, writing on the works of G. K. Chesterton and J. R. R. Tolkien as prominent authors in the 'MacDonald tradition', points to the way in which they both drew on concepts and techniques of defamiliarisation and 'making strange' in their speculative fiction and as essential to their view of the role of art in 'revealing the createdness of the world'.[97] She situates Chesterton and Tolkien not just as fiction writers but as theologians who saw art itself as mediatory—a 'theological tool for opening human eyes to see the reality of God and the reality, albeit contingent, of the world itself'.[98] As engaged in this mediatory process, the artist's creative vocation is neither to describe the world nor to escape from it, but rather to remake it. In Chesterton and Tolkien, Milbank distils a 'theology of the art of invention of stories, fantastic or otherwise':

> To tell a story, whether one's own or a traditional tale, is to mediate the world in its intentionality and narrative character . . . to tell a story is to affirm that there is meaning to life, and that experience is shaped and has an entelechy.[99]

The focus on the telling of stories, and, in particular marvellous or creative stories, is therefore not simply to provide entertainment (though this is certainly an important part of its experience) but to affirm the independence of the world from our perception and appropriation of it. Chesterton and Tolkien saw fairy-tales as a way of looking at the world as storied and gifted. They enable us to see that 'the world of objects is not the product of our own mental perceptions but has its own reality'.[100] Referencing Tolkien's essay on fairy-stories, Milbank notes that 'Faerie', for Tolkien, 'is the site where we encounter other beings and the world itself not just as "enchanted" but as "other"'.[101] This form of enchantment reveals not so much the complete separateness of things from each other but their interrelatedness and relationality—a participation in the created world itself.[102] This is not to say that all forms of speculative fiction and estrangement function in the same way. Following Tolkien himself, Milbank identifies two forms of fantasy in

---

[97] Milbank, *Chesterton and Tolkien*, p. xiv; see also Milbank, 'Fictioning Things'.
[98] Milbank, *Chesterton and Tolkien*, p. xiv.
[99] Ibid., p. 11; see also Ward, 'Belief and Imagination'.
[100] Milbank, *Chesterton and Tolkien*, p. 12.
[101] Ibid., referring to Tolkien, 'On Fairy-Stories'.
[102] Milbank, *Chesterton and Tolkien*, p. 12.

Chesterton and Tolkien's fiction. Chesterton's work is associated in particular with a form of 'making strange' or 'defamiliarisation' which, rather than privileging the viewer over the object (as Shklovsky's approach does), focuses on empowering the object itself and its givenness as part of the world.[103] He uses 'making strange' to 'sunder our lazy ownership of perception, so that we lose our apprehension of the phenomenal world in order to find it again: as something coming to us which is a mystery in its quiddity, its individuality and its difference from ourselves'.[104] That is, it is a process of returning us to the world to see it anew and see its enchantment and wonder in the world's very ordinariness. Tolkien's approach also involves a similar recovery of vision but aligned with a sense of 'escape'—not in terms of escapism but in terms of how, in fairy-stories, normal daily objects and materials, such as stone, wood and iron, 'are made all the more luminous by their setting'.[105] Tolkien's approach therefore seeks to highlight the independence of the imaginary (the 'sub-created', to use Tolkien's term) fictional universe, which both reflects and sets free elements of the world of the artist. Whereas Chesterton's aim is to show the marvellous or transcendent *realism* of objects—making us actually *see* them—Tolkien's aim is to show their independence. Fantasy, for Tolkien, is about liberating things to be themselves: '[b]y being freed into new life, however, they also become *more* than themselves'.[106]

Whilst it is not necessarily unsurprising to find that both Chesterton and Tolkien, the devout intellectual Catholics, saw their artist and literary works as engaging in a particular form of theologising, is it appropriate, therefore, to extend this argument more broadly to works of speculative fiction in general? This question comes back to the nature of our narrative cultural texts and the 'worlds' that they construct.[107] Milbank's argument is that the very process of creating an alternative fictional world itself requires a commitment to meaning and to metaphysics:

> In order to create an alternative fictional world, it is not enough to write beautifully and persuasively: the world described has to have coherence and teleology. It has to make sense as a way of viewing the whole of reality in order for the narrative to work.[108]

---

[103] Ibid., pp. 36–7.
[104] Ibid., p. 37.
[105] Tolkien, 'On Fairy-Stories', p. 59.
[106] Milbank, *Chesterton and Tolkien*, p. 51.
[107] Yacavone, *Film Worlds*, pp. 9–13.
[108] Milbank, 'Literary Apologetics', p. 97; Milbank, *Chesterton and Tolkien*, p. 11.

This does not mean that there cannot therefore be literary *contest* or conflict between different ideas and accounting for the world:

> Fantasy writing may seek to present a wholly material universe or, like Neil Gaiman's *American Gods*, a world in which gods wane and grow with the strength of human belief in their existence. Necessarily, however, such work must leave postmodern equivocation behind and commit to metaphysics, thus allowing a space for theological contestation but equally an opening into mystery.[109]

Milbank herself constructs a theological dialogue between Philip Pullman's 'new atheist' fantasy trilogy, *His Dark Materials*, and J. K. Rowling's *Harry Potter* stories—both of which engage in processes of enchantment and dis-enchantment and a reflection on our world. But in doing so, they also engage in a certain commitment to the world and the way in which it is storied. As Milbank points out, these fictional fantasies have also taken on the status of myth for many of their readers and fans—they have become 'a story within which its readers live and through which they think and interpret experience—their episteme'.[110]

Speculative fiction therefore has the capacity to become the way in which we read and engage with the world—it involves a certain affirmation of the world, even in the process of constructing a 'film world' itself.[111] It is by taking up this approach to the possibilities of speculative fiction that I therefore seek to engage in the development of a theological jurisprudence. Whilst, as noted in Section II above, legal modernity involved a dis-enchantment of the world, a removing of law from its traditional and religious foundations, this dis-enchantment was not complete—law is still intertwined with the religious, sacred and theological. Certain responses to this realisation would desire, therefore, a greater process of secularisation—ensuring law's neutrality so that the vision of a global legal order may be brought into reality and an attempt to escape or leave behind the traces of the machinations of political theology. However, even such a vision itself is caught within the process of speculative world-making, and therefore, I argue, also encompasses its own theology—not just at the level of content (debates over whether human rights are a return to religious natural law or the formation of a new secular morality) but at the level of legal form. For law itself comprises a form of envisioning of the world, a sense of what Cover called law's 'world creation'

---

[109] Milbank, 'Literary Apologetics', p. 114.
[110] Ibid., p. 97.
[111] Yacavone, *Film Worlds*.

via which the practices of law engage in 'the projection of an imagined future upon reality'.[112] The institutions of law and the practices of legal interpretation are always caught not only in their own mythos, their own process of envisioning the world, but also in a process of violently making or bringing this world into existence. Law plays a very specific role in this process because law's implementation and actualisation always involve a violent bringing into force of a particular imagined future: the law operates in the tension between reality and 'an imagined alternative—that is, as connective between the two states of affairs, both of which can be represented in their normative significance only through the devices of narrative'.[113]

If the characteristics of narrative world-making that I have described above always involve a particular metaphysical affirmation of the world as storied and meaningful, then the very process via which law brings into existence an alternative imagined world is *itself* also theological—it involves questions of the transcendence of the law, the sacrality or inviolability of the sanction, and the metaphysical justification of the imposition of violence. It is these forms of justification of violence that are encompassed in the narratives of law itself—a form of legal theodicy, as I alluded to in the opening analysis of *Batman v Superman*. It is these aspects of law that can be 'made strange' through readings of the modern myths told by our popular cultures—readings which provide a way to unpack and explore the theological structures of law. The estranged texts of speculative fiction provide a way of de-autonomising us, as Shklovsky would say, from our habitualised way of viewing the law and its world-making capacities. In considering the structures of law as they are 'made strange' by speculative fiction, not only do we see them anew (and thus are able to conceive them otherwise), but also we can bring to light, and make available for critique, the latent theologies of modern law. The normative aspects of legal analysis and legal interpretation are always about the enforcing of a particular vision of the world on the factual situation in which it engages. The legal imaginary that informs such a process of enforcement therefore has parallels with the artist's process of creation or subcreation in the remaking of the world through art. The mythologies and stories of law involve a speculative recreating of the world. However, the risk of viewing the law in this way is that we see the world as being able to be simply constructed and created through law—modernity's deployment of law as a process of mapping and regulating the world. My turn to speculative fiction from a

---

[112] Cover, 'Violence and the Word', p. 1604. On law as 'world-creation' see Cover, 'Nomos and Narrative', pp. 12–19.

[113] Cover, 'Nomos and Narrative', p. 9.

theological perspective therefore involves a returning of the world to us as gifted and not simply constructed, created as well as contingent. As a result, it is important to understand our fictional narratives not simply as a means of artifice, of pure imagination with no bearing or relationship to the world— for such then comprises a naïve utopianism that would see us being able to imagine and then create a new future. Rather, in taking us out of our present world, this approach to speculative fiction and to estrangement is about a returning us *to* the world anew. That is, to make us return to and reflect on the given, not as arbitrary matter that can be deployed for instrumentalised purposes, but as gifted and created. Speculative fiction not only provides the ability to uncover the *theological* aspects of law in the process of estranging our ordinary conceptions of it. It also provides a theological revelation of the world as created and contingent, and with which we should engage.

V. Overview of Work

Whilst the aim of this book is to render visible various aspects of modern law's theological underpinnings, this work is not just descriptive or analytical. Rather it is performative—it seeks to engage in a depth of analysis of the otherwise superficial, to take seriously our speculative narratives and our fictional films as a means of our being-in-the-world. It sees in these genres not just a way of imagining the world differently but a process of returning the world to us through our imaginative works. In the reflections on law and theology that arise at their intersections and overlaps in popular film, I engage in a particular process of 'doing' law and theology through Cultural Legal Studies. My aim is both to 'make strange' our approach to law and to estrange our considerations of the theologies of legal modernity and elaborate a theological jurisprudence in response. This is not a focus on the periphery or the margins (though noting the *importance* of such marginalia[114]), but aims to identify the way in which the imaginative narratives that dominate our screens in the twenty-first century provide a way of critically engaging with the most central narratives and ideologies of law today. That in doing so I also engage in a process of theologising is significant, not only because of the tradition of religious and theological groundings of law and justice, but also because of the need for us, today more than ever, both to understand our theological contexts and to return to seeing the world storied in a way that requires a turn to the theological itself. This does not mean a return to a presumed synthesised and uniform way of being of an earlier time—this would,

---

[114] See the 2017 special issue of *Law and Humanities* on 'Legal Marginalia': Matthews and Wan, 'Legal Marginalia', pp. 3–6.

in itself, only be trading one dominant theological legality for another. That we live in a world of multiple *nomoi*, of pluralised accounts of law, of conflicting and competing claims to authority is not here contested. At the same time, the narratives of law that dominate are ones that still remain by and large caught within the jurispathic dominance of the state and its own theological heritage.[115] By engaging in the process of seeing the world as storied, and deploying and 'using' our popular narratives to do just this, we enable a pluralising and diversifying approach—even, at the same time, making clear the way in which the telling of stories itself involves a sharing of such stories and an entering into a joint story-telling.

In performing this form of cultural legal studies, the book progresses through a range of interrelated readings of speculative fiction films: from M. Night Shayamalan's *Unbreakable* and Zack Snyder's *Man of Steel* to Peter Jackson's *The Hobbit*, from Christopher Nolan's *The Dark Knight Trilogy* to George Nolfi's *The Adjustment Bureau*, and from Alex Proyas's *I, Robot* to the *Star Wars* of Lucas (et al.). Each of these 'readings' explores a particular theme of law (justice, the exception, law's violence, revolution, law's universality, sovereignty, property as theft) and theology (Manichaeism, mysticism, atonement, sacrifice, visions of the divine, compassionate acts, charity as gift). Aside from the concluding chapter, the book is split into three sets of pairs. Chapters 1 and 2 take up the already presented theme of legal theodicy by examining the relationship (or non-relationship) between law and evil by working through the presentations of the battle between Good and Evil so replete in speculative fiction. Chapter 1 takes the obvious starting point of the superhero genre, but engages in a reading of two critical texts, one *prior* to the dominance of the superhero on film (Shyamalan's *Unbreakable*) and the other towards its epitome (Snyder's *Man of Steel*). These texts both engage in a *realistic* take on the superhero in the Superman mythos, but in two different forms. Central to each is a question about the nature or justification of violence, the role of the law in its consideration and the *co-dependency* of Good and Evil. At the same time, they both present theological questions about the *meaning* of violence: in *Unbreakable* this comes in the form of the need to explain or provide meaning to suffering; in *Man of Steel* it comes in the question about the legitimacy of power and justice beyond the law. Chapter 2 then turns to one of the most well-known depictions of the battle between Good and Evil in recent times: Lucas's and Disney's *Star Wars* saga. There, the mystical Force not only presents Good and Evil as a fundamental unity, but also represents the self-grounding nature of modern legality and its

---

[115] Cover, 'Nomos and Narrative', pp. 40–2.

mythic oscillation and reconciliation between law understood as will and law understood as order. These two chapters therefore set up the themes that are progressed throughout the book: first, law as opposed to, and holding at bay, a fundamental chaos; and second the rule of law and its exception.

Chapters 3 and 4 continue the consideration of the superhero genre by focusing on Nolan's *The Dark Knight Trilogy*, in particular the latter two films, and examine the narrative of sacrifice and atonement that they encompass whilst matching them against a critical account of the law and its exception (in *The Dark Knight*) and the rule of law and revolution (in *The Dark Knight Rises*). In these films Nolan 'makes strange' the superhero genre by taking it out of the tradition of the 'hero myth' and into the realms of theology by presenting Batman as a non-heroic Christ figure who challenges the co-dependency of Good and Evil (explored in Chapters 1 and 2), as well as the inherent violence and arbitrariness of modern secular legality with an alternative compassionate act. It is here that a particular *Christian* theological challenge to both modern accounts of evil *and* the ability of law to shore up protection against it is evoked, and the beginnings of a theological jurisprudence founded on trust is elaborated.

Chapters 5 and 6 then turn to particular theological accounts of the secular and secular law via considering the filmic reworking of two significant twentieth-century science fiction writers: Isaac Asimov and Philip K. Dick. Chapter 5 provides a jurisprudential reading of Proyas's *I, Robot* in the context of the critical return to St Paul. It argues that the film presents a Pauline theological jurisprudence that calls for a deactivating and fulfilling of the law through a love that challenges the abstract universality of modern law as legality without exception. Chapter 6 extends the consideration of a love beyond the law, by presenting a theological jurisprudence that challenges the modern form of secular sovereignty. Through a reading of Nolfi's *The Adjustment Bureau*, the modern theology of will which undergirds both sovereignty and the liberal legal subject is contrasted with a participatory theological understanding of free will not as an autonomous willing of Good or Evil, but as gift. Here these sci-fi narratives, whilst at one level encompassing myths of modernity, deal with specific theological concerns that render visible a particularly modern account of the law: as a system without exception, an unlimited sovereign authority, a form of secularised providence.

The concluding chapter returns us to fantasy and to Tolkien, though in terms of Peter Jackson's re-envisioning of *The Hobbit*. It presents a culmination of the book's argument by elaborating the basis of a theological jurisprudence founded on trust and friendship—rejecting the autonomous self-interested legal subject for a vision of legality based on reciprocity. As such, the overall narrative of the work marks a course from antagonism to reconciliation, from autonomy to reciprocity and from law to love. Through-out the work, the book draws on resources within the Christian theological tradition's critical engagement with law, as a means for rethinking and re-imaging our post-secular legal modernity—enabling both a deactivating and a fulfilling of the law. In exploring speculative film's estranged accounts of the mythos of modernity and modern law, it articulates an alternative theological jurisprudence based on a love that takes us beyond the law.

1

From Shyamalan's *Unbreakable* to Snyder's *Man of Steel*: Comic-book Mythology on Screen and the Co-implication of Good and Evil

'Do not be overcome by evil, but overcome evil with good.'

Romans 12: 21

I. Introduction

'It's a classic depiction of Good versus Evil,' Elijah Price tells a potential buyer at his art gallery, Limited Edition, in the world of M. Night Shyamalan's 2000 film *Unbreakable*—now referred to as the first of Shyamalan's 'Eastrail 177 Trilogy'.[1] The 'piece of art' in question is neither a medieval image of Christ versus Satan, nor an early modern representation of John Milton's *Paradise Lost*, but rather an early sketch of a battle between two characters from a superhero comic. Whilst popular culture is replete with such dualities of Good and Evil—the *good* hero inevitably battling the *evil* villain—it is in the superhero genre that this duality has a foundational structure. This structure was part of the reason for the superhero genre's rise to dominance in Hollywood in the context of post-September 11 anxieties around terrorism and the need for 'extraordinary measures' to contain, overcome or respond to terrorist actions—a mythologising of the global war on terror. My argument in this chapter, however, is that the superhero is reflective *not* of a capturing of a pre-modern desire for hope or a saviour, but rather of our secular modernity itself. For in addition to the alignment of the superhero genre with the political use and abuse of the language of Good and Evil, the genre also demonstrates the co-implication of both the Superhero and Supervillain *and*

---

[1] *Unbreakable*, film, directed by Shyamalan. *Unbreakable* was initially released as a stand-alone film in 2000, with the second and third instalments coming only recently (2017 and 2019): *Split*, film, directed by Shyamalan, and *Glass*, film, directed by Shyamalan.

Good and Evil within this framework. This chapter therefore explores the structural aspects of the superhero genre in relation to this duality of Good and Evil, but also recognises that the deeper questions of the dealing with suffering and the 'problem of evil' can be understood, as Susan Neiman has argued, as the 'guiding force of modern thought'.[2] As such, I seek to situate the rise of the superhero genre in relation to the resurgence of scholarship on Evil that began at the end of the last century and then increased in intensity with the use and abuse of the language of Good and Evil in political and religious rhetoric following the terrorist attacks on September 11, 2001.[3]

This more 'serious' approach to the question of Evil would seem to be significant in the context of the turn of the genre, at least on film, towards a 'gritty realism' that wants to put aside the superhero's association with the camp and kitsch of its earlier incarnations. This chapter therefore proceeds via a reading of two 'telling instances' (to use Peter Fitzpatrick's term) of such a turn: Shyamalan's *Unbreakable*—released *prior* to September 11 but at the beginning of the rise to dominance of the superhero genre on film to dominance—and the 2013 reboot of the Superman franchise by Zack Snyder's *Man of Steel*.[4] Whilst both of these films comprise a *realist* approach to the genre (taking seriously the traditional tropes of the Superman mythos in particular), Shyamalan's film sees the genre as essentially mythic and highlights the link between myth and reality. Snyder, by contrast, seeks to present a Superman narrative *as real*, at the same time emphasising Superman as a Christ figure. This mythic reading of the superhero genre has a long history— going back to Richard Reynold's claim in 1992 that it is a 'modern mythology', and before that to Umberto Eco's 'The Myth of Superman'.[5] More recent iterations of this approach have analysed the interconnections between superheroes, religion and theology with titles such as *The Gospel According to Superheroes*, *Our Gods Wear Spandex* and *Do the Gods Wear Capes?*[6] At the same time, there has been a significant development of work analysing the superhero's murky relationship with law from both cultural criminological

---

[2] Neiman, 'Undeniable Evil', p. 6; Neiman, *Evil in Modern Thought*.

[3] See, for example, Copjec, *Radical Evil*; Bernstein, *Radical Evil*; Bernstein, *Abuse of Evil*; Singer, *President of Good and Evil*; Jeffery, *Evil and International Relations*; Hirvonen and Porttikivi, *Law and Evil*.

[4] *Man of Steel*, film, directed by Snyder. On 'telling instances' as methodology, see Fitzpatrick, *Modernism*, pp. 4–6.

[5] Reynolds, *Super Heroes*. See also, the classic essay: Eco, 'Myth of Superman'.

[6] See Oropeza, *Gospel According to Superheroes*; Knowles, *Our Gods Wear Spandex*; Garrett, *Holy Superheroes!*; Saunders, *Do the Gods Wear Capes?*

and cultural legal perspectives.[7] However, there has been limited analysis of the interactions between these two sets of literature—the mythological–religious reading of the superhero genre and the legal one. Bringing these two approaches to the superhero together is important for it makes clear the way in which popular culture both represent and reproduce our modern mythologies of law. That is, in this chapter I wish to analyse the superhero genre not simply as a modern mythology, nor as a resource for the working through of debates amongst readers or viewers of 'how law and justice can work together in the real world',[8] but rather the way in which the genre constitutes a form of secular legal theology.

Section II begins by situating this analysis in *Unbreakable*'s call to take the superhero genre seriously as a form of mythology and the way in which the genre itself encompasses both mythic and legal readings. Section III goes on to explore the two different forms of visual realism that *Unbreakable* and *Man of Steel* engage in, and the way in which this affects the mythic nature of the genre and the viewer's engagement or participation in it. Sections IV and V then take up explicitly the mythic and legal readings of the genre: first, by analysing the thematic and visual links between the superhero genre and dualist mythologies of Good and Evil such as Manichaeism; second, by looking at the way in which the superhero genre constructs Evil as a means for justifying the response to it—including, therefore, providing a justification of the law and its judgment. These sections demonstrate the way that *Unbreakable* and *Man of Steel* present mythic dualities of the superhero and supervillain, but also explicitly situate the superhero alongside the role of the law, each engaging in a judgment of what Nickie D. Phillips and Staci Strobl refer to as the 'death-worthiness' of the villain.[9] The mythic and legal readings of the genre *align* in presenting a particularly *modern* mythology. My argument here is that, rather than simply being a throwback to a pre-modern desire for justice in contrast to modern legality,[10] the superhero genre is actually a reflection of modern accounts of both law and Evil.

---

[7] See, in particular, Bainbridge, 'This is the Authority'; Bainbridge, 'What is so "Super"'; Giddens, 'Navigating the Looking Glass'; Giddens, 'Natural Law and Vengeance'; Giddens, 'Anderson v Dredd'; Mitchell, 'Legal Reading of She-Hulk'; Phillips and Strobl, 'Cultural Criminology and Kryptonite'; Phillips and Strobl, *Comic Book Crime*; Sharp, 'Riddle Me This'; Sharp, '"Fear" and "Hope"'; Taslitz, 'Daredevil and the Death Penalty'; Vollum and Adkinson, 'Portrayal of Crime and Justice'.

[8] Bainbridge, 'What is so "Super"', p. 386.

[9] Phillips and Strobl, *Comic Book Crime*.

[10] See, for example, Bainbridge, 'This is the Authority'.

However, if the genre itself reflects these modern accounts of law and Evil, then it also presents the aporias of such approaches. For, as Section VI will show, whilst the law itself incorporates a modern addressing of Evil—attempting to restore a sense of order to otherwise senselessly violent acts, by determining the responsibility of the perpetrator or criminal—it cannot explain the *suffering* of the victim. At the same time, as Section VII will demonstrate, if we take seriously the law's claim to a rational accounting of crime, the law's response to Evil remains fundamentally ambiguous. For the law encompasses a particular modern 'positive' account of evil, focused on a legal subject held responsible only for a 'willed' and 'rational act'. This positive account of Evil, which is the paradigm for both modern philosophical and legal accounts, is constantly at risk, however, of *failing* to hold the subject responsible. By contrast, the traditional and theological 'negative' understanding of Evil as privation actually provides a greater accountability for Evil committed (despite the 'modern' criticisms of this understanding of Evil). *Unbreakable* reveals these problematics and leaves the viewer with the need to think through their own understanding of what occurred in the film, but also our relation to evil and suffering today. By contrast, *Man of Steel* covers over such an approach and leaves the viewer with a sense of the justification for Superman's actions and the ongoing necessity of the superhero.

II. Superheroes and Justice: Comic-books as Visual Legal Mythology

Superman in particular, and the superhero genre in general, have been read as 'modern mythology' that not only takes up earlier hero myths and deploys mythical structures and motifs,[11] but has taken the place of mythology in terms of defining our position in an uncertain world. Leo Partible, for example, has argued that the superhero genre is 'an artistic vehicle that conveys the collective hopes and dreams of humankind', answers important questions about life and explores 'the human condition, oftentimes better than stories grounded in reality'.[12] Comics artist Grant Morrison argues that, despite being 'about as far from social realism as you can get', superheroes give us images of hope in times when we are deprived of such images and 'deal directly with mythic elements of human experience that we can relate to'.[13] Ben Saunders reads superhero comics as crossing the bounds of philosophy, literature and theology and finds

---

[11] Reynolds, *Super Heroes*; Eco, 'Myth of Superman'; Lawrence and Jewett, *Myth of American Superhero*; Garrett, *Holy Superheroes!*; Knowles, *Our Gods Wear Spandex*; Alsford, *Heroes and Villains*.

[12] Partible, 'Superheroes in Film', p. 247.

[13] Morrison, *Supergods*, p. xvii.

that their 'fantastic, speculative, and distinctly modern' expressions 'attest to the strength of our demand that the world should make sense (and the depth of our fear that it may not)'.[14]

Drawing on the work of Joseph Campbell in particular (to which I will return in the next chapter), these approaches to the superhero genre see it as having 'taken the place' of earlier traditions, with Superman, as noted in the Prologue, as an 'American Christ'.[15] These stories often centre around a saviour figure, 'a pure Christ-like deliverer', and the turn to 'these motifs give[s] us something to trust and a way to interpret our world'.[16] John Shelton Lawrence and Robert Jewett, in their classic *The Myth of the American Superhero*, argued that these stories involve a retelling and replacing of the Judeo-Christian redemption narrative, combining 'elements of the selfless hero who gives his life for others and the zealous crusaders who destroy evil'.[17] The mythic structures of these narratives, however, encompass a very particular sense of society—a harmonious paradisal community, which is under siege from some evil, monster or other external threat that extends beyond what 'normal' institutions have the capacity to deal with. This society under threat requires 'a selfless superhero' to emerge, 'renounce temptations and carry out the redemptive task', thereby restoring the community to its condition of paradise.[18] These stories thus tell a tale about the nature of the saving of society, in the context of a particularly *American* 'mono-myth'.

It is this aspect of the mythic structure that intersects with the role of the law, for the very need for the superhero is premised on the failure of traditional social institutions, and the legal system in particular, to be able to deal adequately with the threat to the social order. Whilst this is often because of the excessive nature of the threat to society, it also points to the limits or deficiencies of the legal system and its ability to achieve justice. As Cassandra Sharp notes, '[t]he very existence of the superhero . . . presupposes that justice has not and cannot be achieved by the legal system.'[19] The superhero genre does not just operate on the basis of potential heroic ideals, but connects these to a sense of vigilantism and a seeking of justice instead of or beyond what the law can achieve. It is this aspect of the genre that has seen increasing interest from

[14] Saunders, *Do the Gods Wear Capes?*, pp. 3, 6.
[15] See Schenck, 'Popular Culture Messiah'; Barkman, 'Superman'.
[16] Partible, 'Superheroes in Film', p. 248.
[17] Lawrence and Jewett, *Myth of American Superhero*, pp. 6–7. See also Garrett, *Holy Superheroes!*
[18] Lawrence and Jewett, *Myth of American Superhero*, p. 6; Nichols, 'Reading of the Batman/Joker Comic'.
[19] Sharp, 'Riddle Me This', p. 359.

cultural criminologists and cultural legal scholars, who argue that superheroes give us a powerful way to think about our understanding of law, the deficiencies or inconsistencies of the legal system, and the inexorable gap between law and justice.[20] At the same time, superheroes essentially encompass a *critique* of the law.[21] As Jason Bainbridge has noted, 'superheroes . . . personify the tension between a modern adherence to the rule of law' and pre- or post-modern explorations of justice.[22] Modern legality has a focus on the rule of law, on a *system* of justice and on due process. The superhero, by contrast, presents a fundamental critique of the ability of the modern system of law to achieve 'true justice'. Desmond Manderson argues that '[t]he superhero's preparedness to act against and despite due process and law is surely an implicit—indeed, increasingly explicit—critique of the established order's ability to achieve justice at all.'[23]

That the mythological and legal approaches to the superhero genre intertwine is not surprising, given the intersections between law and mythology itself, both providing a sense of 'how social relations are and should be constituted'.[24] As Penny Crofts has noted, drawing upon the work of Robert Cover, the law is involved in 'projecting and routinely authorising an image of the ways in which individuals relate or ought to relate to each other in society'.[25] The cultural legal analysis of the superhero genre itself often examines these mythological characteristics, arguing that these narratives comprise a way of dealing with the larger questions of life and society in the context of uncertainty. For example, Nickie D. Phillips and Staci Strobl, in their *Comic-book Crime*, argue that 'comic-books offer expressions of contemporary life that tap into our hopes, fears, personal insecurities, and uncertainties about the future'.[26] The negotiation of meaning about crime and justice in comic-books therefore forms 'part of a broader cultural context in which readers

---

[20] See, in particular, Bainbridge, 'This is the Authority', p. 476. See also Vollum and Adkinson, 'Portrayal of Crime and Justice'; Reyns and Henson, 'Superhero Justice'; Phillips and Strobl, 'Cultural Criminology and Kryptonite'; Phillips and Strobl, *Comic Book Crime*.

[21] Sharp, 'Riddle Me This'; Manderson, 'Trust Us Justice'.

[22] Bainbridge, 'This is the Authority', p. 457.

[23] Manderson, 'Trust Us Justice', p. 33.

[24] Crofts, *Wickedness and Crime*, p. 16.

[25] Ibid.; Cover, 'Nomos and Narrative'. I will turn to a more general consideration of Peter Fitzpatrick's claim that modern law is mythic in Chapter 2. Fitzpatrick, *Mythology*.

[26] Phillips and Strobl, *Comic Book Crime*, p. 10.

absorb, reproduce, and resist notions of justice'.[27] Similarly, for Bainbridge, the superhero genre 'continues to interrogate the law and push the boundaries of what law can be',[28] as well as performing 'intellectual work' which 'suggests one way of moving the law closer to justice'.[29] Superhero comics and films therefore encompass a particular form of meaning-making, providing a way for readers and viewers to 'work through their own understandings of the world'.[30] Bainbridge thus argues that the superhero genre

> prompts debate amongst viewers . . . around how law and justice can work together in the real world because it presents viewers with a character (the superhero) with the ability to appropriate and enact their own vision of justice (by virtue of their being super)[31]

—a point echoed by scholars considering the superhero genre in religious and theological contexts.

M. Night Shyamalan's *Unbreakable*, whilst pre-empting the climactic rise of the superhero film, brings together and renders visible these two approaches to the superhero genre. For the central premise of the film is that superhero comics are a form of mythology and meaning-making, exaggerations of narratives about real-life heroes and villains. Such an argument is central to Shyamalan's film-making more broadly, which often involves 'stories about stories', looking to narratives as ways for creating meaning in an unstable and uncertain world, and working through trauma and suffering.[32] As a result, in considering the superhero genre, his focus was *not* on the spectacular and fantastic nature of these tales but rather on the underlying *form* of the stories told. Shyamalan presented a 'realistic' superhero story well before the 'gritty realism' that has dominated superhero films since Nolan's *The Dark Knight Trilogy* and is evidenced in Snyder's *Man of Steel* and *Batman v Superman: Dawn of Justice*.[33] In focusing on the 'everyday' rather than the extraordinary, and drawing on the genre of melodrama as much as superhero adventure, Shyamalan placed as central to his narrative the interconnected formation of

---

[27] Ibid.

[28] Bainbridge, 'What is so "Super"', p. 386.

[29] Ibid. Bainbridge, 'This is the Authority', p. 476; Bainbridge, 'Call to Do Justice'; Bainbridge, 'Spider-Man, the Question and the Meta-Zone'.

[30] Phillips and Strobl, *Comic Book Crime*, p. 228.

[31] Bainbridge, 'What is so "Super"', p. 386.

[32] Weinstock, 'Telling Stories about Stories', p. xi.

[33] *Batman Begins*, film, directed by Nolan; *The Dark Knight*, film, directed by Nolan; *The Dark Knight Rises*, film, directed by Nolan; *Man of Steel*, film, directed by Snyder; *Batman v Superman: Dawn of Justice*, film, directed by Snyder.

both a hero and a villain as representations of Good and Evil.[34] This approach involves a particular treatment of superhero comic-books themselves, proposing that they are a form of mythology through which we tell stories about ourselves and to which we can look for guidance, direction and meaning.[35]

This argument is presented by Elijah Price (Samuel L. Jackson), the proprietor of the comic-book art gallery *Limited Edition*. Price, having been born with the disease osteogenesis imperfecta (which makes his bones extremely fragile and susceptible to breaking), has spent much of his life reading and studying the form of comic-books and believes that they are 'our last link to ancient ways of passing on knowledge'. Price explains to David Dunn (Bruce Willis) and Dunn's son, Joseph (Spencer Treat Clark), that he believes that 'comics are a form of history that someone, somewhere, felt or experienced'. He goes on to elaborate that if there is someone like him, who is 'at one end of the spectrum' and extremely fragile, then potentially there is someone at the other end, who does not get sick or hurt. That is, he presents the idea that a superhero, 'a person put here to protect the rest of us', might actually exist.[36]

Shyamalan thus engages in the debates about the place and importance of popular culture, and Price in particular represents a view that comic-books are texts of social significance and worthy of cultural and philosophical study.[37] Furthermore, Price's arguments that comics are a form of art—he refuses in outrage to sell a piece from his gallery to a prospective purchaser who discloses that it would be a gift for his four-year-old son—implicitly draw on the first wave of comics scholarship and the work of artists and scholars such as Will Eisner, Scott McCloud, Arthur Asa Berger and David Carrier, who sought to legitimise the study of comics as an art form.[38] Price's broader theory that comic-books are a 'last link' to forms of pictorial history (emphasised by the hieroglyphics and other icons that are in the background

---

[34] See Palmer, 'Melodrama and Male Crisis'; Yockey, 'Unbreak My Heart'.

[35] Regalado, 'Limits of Transgression'.

[36] As Regalado has noted, *Unbreakable* therefore 'argues that superhero comic books . . . are cultural productions that do more than merely entertain audiences or reflect cultural realities. Instead, they are dynamic forms of cultural expression that individuals actively employ to shape and give meaning to individual as well as social existence.' Ibid., p. 133.

[37] Ibid.

[38] Eisner, *Comics and Sequential Art*; Eisner, *Graphic Storytelling*; McCloud, *Understanding Comics*; Berger, *A Study in American Satire*; Berger, *The Comic-Stripped America*; Berger, *Narratives in Popular Culture*, pp. 99–110; Berger, *Manufacturing Desire*, pp. 93–131; Carrier, *The Aesthetics of Comics*. For a critical response to the 'legitimacy' approach of early comics scholarship, see Pizzino, 'On Violation'.

of the frame when he is speaking) explicitly parallels McCloud's tracing of the lineage of the comic back to include the French Bayeux Tapestry, reaching as far back as Egyptian paintings.[39] This link is important, given the seminal nature of McCloud's work for the development of comics studies as its own discipline (despite the later critiques of his approaches, including both his definition and his history of the comic).[40] It is also significant in the context of *Unbreakable* because Shyamalan's cinematography itself attempts to draw on a number of aspects of the comics form.

III. Visual Realism and Viewerly Engagement: The Superhero Film *as* a Comic

Whilst comics have become a dominant source of material for Hollywood, film-makers face a range of challenges in the process of adaptation because of the differences of 'visual ontology' between comics and film.[41] Drawing styles themselves are more readily understood to include a certain level of abstraction and therefore a more intentional *interpretation* of reality.[42] Photographic images or film, by contrast, tend to imply a 'more realistic' depiction.[43] In addition to the 'reality' of the film-image creating a question about the nature of a genre that is traditionally fantastic and speculative in its content, the superhero film's attempt to re-present drawn stories also raises a range of other stylistic questions for adaptation: how to deal with the unique characteristics of page layout versus film screen; the dilemmas of translating drawings to photography; and the importance of sound in film compared to the 'silence' of comics, to name only a few.[44] Some film-makers have deployed a form of direct 'stylistic remediation', such as Ang Lee's use of multi-frame or split screen imagery in *Hulk*, or the use of comic panels as part of the narrative or screen credits, such as in Edgar Wright's *Scott Pilgrim vs. the World* and

[39] McCloud, however, specifically excludes Egyptian hieroglyphics, like the ones seen behind Price when he outlines his comic-book theory, from his genealogy of comics as they are not directly pictorial. As hieroglyphs represent sounds, they are an antecedent of the written word and not comic: McCloud, *Understanding Comics*, pp. 12, 17.
[40] See Hatfield, *Alternative Comics*. For a recent collection of critical essays on the field, see Giddens, *Critical Directions in Comics Studies*.
[41] Lefevre, 'Problematic Adaptation of Drawn Images', p. 9.
[42] On the intersubjective nature of comics creation, see Grennan, *Theory of Narrative Drawing*.
[43] McCloud, *Understanding Comics*, pp. 28–9.
[44] Lefevre, 'Problematic Adaptation of Drawn Images', pp. 3–4.

Dean Parisot's *RED 2*.[45] Yet one of the challenges of such approaches is that they are unable to reproduce the comics experience itself.[46]

Shyamalan's cinematography, by contrast, takes more seriously the process of stylistic remediation of the comics form, whilst also paying particular attention to the *form* of the film. For example, instead of using multi-frame or split-screen imagery to reproduce a comics panel, Shyamalan deploys physical props in his shots to recreate a panel-like perspective. When the audience first meets Dunn as a passenger on the train at the beginning of the film, the shots of both Dunn and the lady who sits next to him are individually framed by the seats in front of him. A few scenes later, curtains at the hospital frame Dunn in a similar way, reproducing the sense of separate close-up panels. The use of such framing techniques throughout the film recreates the visual effect of the comic-book—a remediation of the comics form.[47] Shyamalan also recreates what has been referred to as the 'mono-sensory' aspect of comics: the way that comics use their visuality to engage and communicate multiple sensory experiences—hearing, smell, touch and taste.[48] *Unbreakable* has an exceptionally minimalist soundtrack and uses singular forms of dialogue where voices and sounds rarely, if ever, overlap (only one voice or sound is heard at a time). This restrictive use of sound recreates a sense of the 'silence'

---

[45] On 'stylistic remediation' see Morton, *Panel to the Screen*. *Hulk*, film, directed by Lee; *Scott Pilgrim vs. the World*, film, directed by Wright; *RED 2*, film, directed by Parisot. For a discussion of Ang Lee's *Hulk* in particular, see both Lefevre, 'Problematic Adaptation of Drawn Images', p. 6; and Morton, *Panel to the Screen*, pp. 76–86.

[46] On the multi-sensory experience of reading comics, see Hague, *Comics and the Senses*.

[47] In addition to the consistent use of physical objects to frame shots (whether it is curtains, window panes, doorframes, fence railings or shelving), some distinct camera angles are employed that also distance the viewer from what is being seen and reproduce the sense of a panel. An innocuous version of this is when David reaches into the top of his cupboard, the camera angle is from above, showing the shelf, clothing and David's head. A more signficant example comes later in the film, when Price falls down the stairs and his glass cane shatters—again, the camera angles here reproduce the sense that you are viewing specific comic-book panels.

[48] It is important to note, however, that despite comics operating in a visual medium, they do *engage* with these other senses through the process of synesthesia. McCloud, *Understanding Comics*, pp. 89–92. McCloud argues that this *does* involve an engagement of the other senses as well. For a critical discussion of McCloud on this point, see Hague, *Comics and the Senses*. See also Peters, 'Theological "Seeing" of Law'.

of comics—dialogue, sound and mood are communicated more by the visual form than by the use of sound.

The effect of Shyamalan's cinematography reproduces not only the stylistic features of the comic-book, but also the readerly or viewerly engagement with it, which goes to a specific point about the nature of the comics form as engaging in a process of meaning-making. For McCloud, what is significant in comics is not just what goes on *in* the separate images or panels, but what occurs *between* them in the 'gutter'.[49] The reader of comics is therefore central to the process of meaning-making, not simply as an observer but as an active participant.[50] As McCloud argues, what holds the narrative or meaning of the comic together is the process of 'closure'—the way in which we, as the reader, 'fill in the gaps' between images generating rather than simply perceiving the narrative and aesthetic meaning.[51] Whilst film constantly guides the viewer and we are incessantly in the 'present' of what is being shown to us, comics allow a more subjective recognition of the movement between panels and the functioning of time. Ian Hague, although critical of McCloud's approach, has described a similar aspect of comics in terms of understanding them as a performance rather than simply a static text—but a performance in which the reader is involved.[52]

Shyamalan's stylistic remediation of the comics form reproduces aspects of this viewerly engagement by making the viewer *more* aware of their participation in the construction of meaning, along with the constructed nature of the film itself. This approach is not dissimilar to Bertolt Brecht's *V-Effekt* in theatre, which aimed at making the audience aware of the constructed nature of the performance.[53] Shyamalan uses long-timed shots, very deliberate shifts in camera angle and a minimalist soundtrack. The result is that, rather than getting lost in the film and superhero narrative, the viewer's experience is slowed, providing a sense of estrangement from

---

[49] McCloud, *Understanding Comics*.

[50] Ibid., pp. 49, 104; see the discussion of this in Crawley and van Rijswijk, 'Justice in the Gutter', p. 101.

[51] McCloud, *Understanding Comics*, pp. 62–73. Crawley and van Rijswijk emphasise that the formal properties of comics also provide a way of working through the 'unrepresentability' of trauma and its *resistance* to closure. The comics form can therefore 'resist law's demands for interpretative and normative finality by drawing our attention to the structural or endemic traumas which constitute legal subjectivity, and the representational practices through which meaning—and justice—become possible'. Crawley and van Rijswijk, 'Justice in the Gutter', p. 95.

[52] Hague, *Comics and the Senses*, pp. 34–8.

[53] Brecht, 'Short Organum for Theatre'.

the narrative.[54] This involves a dynamic contrast with the plot itself, which presents the idea that superhero narratives themselves might be 'real', and that the viewer might be watching one (though the conclusion of the film dramatically challenges this approach). Shyamalan's presentation of a 'realistic' superhero narrative is thus undercut by the cinematography, which makes the viewer reflect on the constructedness of the filmic narrative, as well as their participation in such a narrative construction.

This cinematography is in stark contrast with the fast-paced, gritty and jolting action of the contemporary superhero film, which allows little time for the viewer to catch their breath. Whereas Shyamalan allows the viewer to come to an awareness of the *construction* of the film and its narrative, the visual realism of the modern superhero film encourages us to get lost within the film world because it appears to be so similar to our own. As Jela Krečič Žižek has pointed out, the problem with this approach is that it presumes a progression from the 'naïve' and simplistic iterations of the earlier genre, to a more serious and socially relevant realist approach.[55] The comical interventions and asides by the characters in earlier incarnations involved a form of self-reflexivity that meant the reader was aware of the type of story that it was engaging in (whilst still allowing for some modes of social critique).[56] By contrast, presenting audiences with gritty, realistic and challenging narratives with more humanised superheroes asks the viewer to forget that they are watching fantastic and unrealistic tales. These films seem to want to return us to the real world directly, rather than incorporating the sense of escape and re-enchantment that the speculative encompasses.[57]

Zack Snyder's *Man of Steel* is one of the most significant examples of this 'realist' approach. As critic Lev Grossman noted just after its release, '[w]hile the story is familiar, *Man of Steel* looks different from other superhero

---

[54] Shyamalan's famous use of the 'click' moment in each of his films *also* reproduces a form of estrangement, more in the tradition of Shklovsky's *ostranenie* or G. K. Chesterton's 'making strange', discussed in the Prologue. This moment towards the end of each film involves a complete reworking of the narrative up until that point—this is most famous (and also most successful) in *The Sixth Sense*, where, at the end, the audience all of a sudden realises that Malcolm Crowe (Bruce Willis) is dead, and that this is why the boy Cole Sear (Haley Joel Osment), who can see dead people, can see him. On Shyamalan's 'click', see Weinstock, 'Telling Stories about Stories', pp. ix–xii.

[55] Žižek, 'Superheroes'.

[56] Ibid., pp. 865–7.

[57] Cf the approach to speculative fiction discussed in the Prologue and in Milbank, *Chesterton and Tolkien*.

movies. It has some of the gritty physical authenticity one associates with documentaries.'[58] This was an intentional aspect of Snyder's cinematography. The movie was shot on actual film (as opposed to using digital cameras) and made use of hand-held cameras, so that 'the point of view shifts and staggers when things explode or superhumans fly by'.[59] The characters themselves appear 'mercilessly unfogged' without the usual Hollywood sheen and a number of shots look like user-generated content uploaded to YouTube.[60] Snyder describes his approach to the film as ironic because 'the most realistic movie I've ever made is a movie about Superman'.[61]

Snyder's realism does not just go to the aesthetic qualities of his cinematography, but is also central to the presentation of Superman as well—an approach which, in many respects, aligns with Shyamalan's. For both films ask the question: what if superheroes were real? However, whereas Shyamalan engages this question through Price's idea that superhero comics might encompass exaggerated and mythicised representations of the actual differences between people, Snyder attempts to present 'what it would be like if Superman actually existed among us'.[62] Snyder's answer, as Kwasu David Tembo points out, can be summarised in a single word: 'destructive'.[63] Whereas Price argues that superpowers (invisibility, X-ray vision) might be a mythic exaggeration of something as simple as instinct, Snyder presents them as real, with the initial ability to control them being completely overwhelming for the superpowered subject. But if a person as strong as Superman existed and entered into battle with another being equally as strong, the result is not a ham-fisted fight presented tongue in cheek with plenty of side jokes, but the utter destruction of multiple buildings and infrastructure, killing, injuring and endangering countless lives. To see Superman operate 'in reality' is to see the potential for mass destruction—and that is exactly what Snyder presented. *Man of Steel*'s realism, therefore, does not render visible the mythic nature of these narratives about superpowered beings with the aim that the viewer reflect on their own process of participating in them. Instead, it presents fiction as 'real life'.[64]

A criticism of the superhero genre, and *Man of Steel* in particular, is that it produces a passiveness in the viewer, who is taught to look for a *deus ex*

[58] Grossman, 'Superman, Grounded', 17 June 2013.
[59] Ibid.
[60] Ibid.
[61] Ibid.
[62] Tembo, 'Pax in Terra', p. 49.
[63] Ibid. Emphasis in original.
[64] Ibid., p. 47.

machina who will come in and save the day, rather than learn to rely upon themselves.[65] Tembo argues, however, that the watching of superheroes' exploits 'invites the reader/viewer to not only imagine feats of spectacular individual power but to desire such power as well'.[66] This is underpinned by the way in which Superman, despite being a powerful alien, is presented in *human form*. There is therefore an 'uncanny resemblance' between Superman (and other superheroes) and the human, allowing for a process of identification in the viewer.[67] This resemblance means that there is not simply a deferral of responsibility to a figure of greater strength or authority, but it allows for the viewer to desire the power of the superhero and to consider the completing of heroic actions.[68] Tembo therefore rejects the mythic reading of the superhero, arguing that *Man of Steel* presents instead a critique of the problem of messianism today: its results are catastrophic and destructive. However, the presentation of superheroes as 'real fictions', humanising and showing their fallibilities and foibles, as well as the collateral damage resulting from their actions, *does not* undermine their mythic status but rather strengthens it.[69] But it does so in a way that covers over such mythic aspects, for in presenting these 'epic battles' as 'real' the film 'presupposes an audience so stupid and ignorant that it will treat the movie as a serious attempt to tell a meaningful story relevant to its time'.[70] Whereas the traditional aspects of the genre acknowledged that it was telling a fantastic fantasy tale full of capes, spandex and the performance of impossible feats, the modern superhero asks the audience to believe a lie which 'resides precisely in the attempt to throw off the disguise and show a realist story'.[71]

---

[65] See discussion in ibid., pp. 37–41.

[66] Ibid., p. 40.

[67] Ibid.

[68] On the significance of Superman as a figure of virtue, see Saunders, *Do the Gods Wear Capes?*, pp. 16–35.

[69] As Krečič Žižek notes, it does this by emphasising the *gap* between the superhero and themselves—engaging in a sense of showing how this person is not really a superhero, but rather has his or her own struggles and turmoil, just like us. However, '[t]he attempts to get us closer to reality or to show things "as they really are", blind us for [sic] the fact that they are no less a fiction than other more humorous approaches—what makes them worse is the way they mask their fiction as an objective realistic document.' Žižek, 'Superheroes', pp. 868–70; Žižek, *Living in the End Times*, pp. 59–60.

[70] Žižek, 'Superheroes', pp. 869–70.

[71] Ibid., p. 869.

As such, whilst Shyamalan and Snyder both engage in forms of cinematic realism, they have a very different effect: Snyder's *Man of Steel*, by asking us to believe in the Superman narrative as a 'real fiction', asks us to *forget* that we are watching a fiction and, as a result, to recognise our own participation in such a narrative; Shyamalan's *Unbreakable* presents a realistic superhero story, which, however, at the level of form, undercuts our belief in the superhero and emphasises our own participation in the construction of the superhero narrative.

IV. Pop Culture Manichaeism: Visualising the Battle Between Good and Evil

What does this realism mean for the mythic narratives of Good and Evil with which the films continue to engage? In addition to the genre's continuous dialectic between the Superhero and the Supervillain, the realistic aesthetic and forms of humanisation that they employ tend to demonstrate and make visible the co-implication of Good and Evil. That this realism arose in the context of the post-9/11 war on terror and its use and abuse of the rhetoric of Good and Evil indicates a particular dialectic between fiction and reality—where reality became more like comic-books with apocalyptic discourses and the attempt to wipe out terror.[72] This rhetoric is often referred back to forms of religious fundamentalism, and Phillips and Strobl explicitly situate their discussion of the superhero genre's 'dichotomous notions of good and evil' within the context of the Western (Christian) tradition's distinction between them.[73] However, the problem with articulating both modern Christian fundamentalism and the Christian tradition within an oppositional structure of Good and Evil is that it misunderstands those distinctions and the way in which they are actually reflected in *modern* rather than traditional theological accountings of evil.[74] The traditional orthodox and classical accounts of Evil did not see it as a positive force, but as an absence of force and quality, a dearth or privation of being itself.[75] A dualistic understanding of the world that pitches a battle between Good and Evil as equally opposed forces is, rather than Christian theological orthodoxy, instead linked to certain Gnostic myths, in particular Zoroastrianism and

---

[72] Bernstein, *Abuse of Evil*; Phillips and Strobl, 'Cultural Criminology and Kryptonite'.
[73] Phillips and Strobl, *Comic Book Crime*, p. 116; Phillips and Strobl, 'Cultural Criminology and Kryptonite'.
[74] Bernstein, *Abuse of Evil*, pp. 116–19; Milbank, *Being Reconciled*, pp. 1–25.
[75] Milbank, *Being Reconciled*, p. 1; Matthewes, *Evil and Augustinian Tradition*.

Manichaeism.[76] If this is the case, then the question is *why*, in the context of secular modernity, are we so interested in these stories that depict a Manichaean dualist mythos?

At one level there is a historical connection between the visuality of superhero comics and films with Manichaeism itself—a connection which could place Manichaean texts within McCloud's 'long history' of comics, and which would seem to undergird Price's sense of the mythology of comic-books in *Unbreakable*. Manichaeism encompassed a dualistic understanding of the world as divided between two forces in being—the Good King of Light and the Evil Archon of Darkness—who are in an ongoing cosmic battle within the universe.[77] What was unique about Manichaeism, however, was that it held as part of its official canon Mani's *Picture-Book* (or *The Image*), a solely pictorial volume attributed to the founder of their religion.[78] Manichaeism made significant use of didactic art as part of their mission.[79] Mani's *Picture-Book* would be reinterpreted (as were the images used in their mythology and teaching in general), based on the particular cultural setting in which it was being communicated.[80] This gives additional genealogical legitimacy to the modern consideration of the superhero genre as forms of religion and mythology, for we can easily point out the comparison with the ongoing battle between forces of Good and Evil (consistent with a dualist mythology), their visual depictions of these forces and the reinterpretation of such a battle into many different forms and versions with the corresponding plethora in both comic-books and films. This *also* undergirds the superhero genre's traditional deploying of visual stereotypes as a shorthand indicating who is 'good' and who is 'evil', reflecting this particular *visual* depiction of mythology.[81]

Price focuses on this visuality of Good and Evil in his analysis of comic-book art. In the first introduction to Price, he is describing a piece of art in

---

[76] The most significant account of this distinction comes from the work of St Augustine who, in a synthesis of Neoplatonism and Christian Theology, argued that Evil is not a 'real substance' but rather a lack of, or turning away from, the Good. Evans, *Augustine On Evil*; Milbank, *Being Reconciled*, pp. 1–25; Matthewes, *Evil and Augustinian Tradition*. For a discussion of Augustine in the context of community, see Hirvonen, 'Civitas Peregrina'.

[77] Renick, 'Manichaeism'.

[78] Gulácsi, 'Searching for Mani's Picture Book'.

[79] Ibid.

[80] Gnoli, 'Manichaeism'.

[81] See the discussion of this in Eisner, *Graphic Storytelling*, p. 12; Kaveney, *Superheroes!*, p. 10; Berger, *Manufacturing Desire*, p. 98. For a more detailed analysis of the aesthetics of the supervillain and their connection to representations of criminality see Fennell, 'Aesthetics of Supervillainy'.

terms of the common visual cues of the characters (the square jaw of heroes versus a slightly disproportionate size of head to body in villains). At the same time, Price also appears to pre-empt the position of the modern superhero film by emphasising realism over exaggeration. He notes that what makes the piece in question 'very special' is the 'realistic depiction of its figures': 'When the characters reach the magazine, they were exaggerated, as always happens. But this is vintage.'[82] Price thus is asserting a certain authenticity to this realistic approach—in contrast to the traditional *loss* of realism of comics as they are 'chewed up in the commercial machine . . . jazzed up, made titillating cartoon for the sales rack'. Yet, despite this criticism of the overtly simplistic and spectacular narratives of Good and Evil in the traditional superhero genre, Price's entire theory is based upon an assumption of a dualistic and Manichaean mythos—something that the modern superhero genre continues, despite its realism. My argument is that this is not so much an incoherence, but rather that the alignment of realism with a dualistic understanding of Good and Evil points to a *positivisation* of Evil which reflects not an earlier theological position but the modern secular theorisation and accounting of Evil. If this is the case, then the issue with the realist approach to the superhero genre is that, instead of returning us to reality, it rather covers over and hides the very construction of Evil in which it is engaging[83]—a construction that continues a certain modern and post-Kantian tradition that starts from the 'self-evidence' of Evil.[84]

The continuation of the Manichaean mythos is most clearly seen, even in the realist approach, in terms of the intimate connection between the

[82] At the end of the film, Price's mother also relays his interpretation of another piece to Dunn: 'This is one of Johann Davis's earliest drawings. See the villain's eyes, they're larger than the other characters. They insinuate a slightly skewed perspective on how they see the world—just off normal.' Both these scenes are revealing within the context of the film: the first because it is the viewer's first introduction to Price (as an adult) and it highlights the attempt to focus on the *realism* of superheroes, which Price goes on to elaborate; the second because the 'skewed perspective on how they see the world' is representative of Price himself, as is revealed in the subsequent and final scene.

[83] This position reflects Brecht's own criticism of realism in art and opera—which is that it produces a sense of passivism in the spectators, who become lost within the narrative of the story being told. His 'epic theatre' and techniques of defamiliarisation themselves were about trying to shock the audience and asking them to engage in their own complicity with oppressive social structures. Brecht, 'Short Organum for Theatre'.

[84] See Badiou, *Ethics*.

superhero and the supervillain[85]—something that both *Unbreakable* and *Man of Steel* place front and centre. At the end of *Unbreakable*, Price makes this explicit by explaining to Dunn that the arch-villain is 'the exact opposite of the hero. And most times they're friends, like you and me.' Even before revealing himself to be the arch-villain, Price continuously referred to the idea that he and Dunn were on opposing ends of the same spectrum—'we're on the same curve, just at opposite ends'. For Price, the idea of these interrelated figures of Good and Evil is the basis for his search for a superhero. He believed that if there was a figure who was stronger than average (Dunn is shown to be able, without training, to lift an incredible amount of weight) and who had an innate desire to protect others (Price points out that Dunn became a security guard, a profession he describes as aimed at helping and protecting others), then that would also explain his own physical weakness (and reflect, as the film reveals at the conclusion, his committing of terrorist actions). This link between the superhero and the supervillain, for Price, becomes the defining trait necessary for proving their existence. The film argues for the existence of these 'superior' individuals that go beyond the ordinary, which, whilst they might be hard to believe in, may give hope in 'mediocre times'.[86] However, Price's 'finding' of the Good superhero is rather about evidencing a dualistic understanding of the world in order to explain and justify his own position—a search which has resulted in Evil actions.

In *Man of Steel* the duality of the superhero and supervillain is presented in a connectedness that comes not from them being friends, but from them being the same alien species on planet Earth. Superman and General Zod are thus not two counterpoints but rather co-equal in every way and literally engaged in an 'epic battle'.[87] More than other representations of Superman's arch-villain as Lex Luthor (including in *Batman v Superman*), which engage in more and more elaborate ways of trying to make entertaining a battle

---

[85] This connection between superhero and supervillain has been identified as a key aspect of the genre: Reynolds, *Super Heroes*, pp. 16–17; Coogan, *Superhero*, p. 76; Bainbridge, 'What is so "Super"'.

[86] This theme is further taken up in the two recent contributions to this narrative, *Split* and *Glass*.

[87] In one sense, these two films therefore represent the two types of supervillain that Price's mother refers to in *Unbreakable*: 'the soldier villain, who fights the hero with his hands' (represented in *Man of Steel*'s General Zod) and 'the real threat, the brilliant and evil arch-enemy, who fights the hero with his mind' (which is clearly alluding to Price in *Unbreakable*). One could also note that in *Batman v Superman*, the sequel to *Man of Steel*, Lex Luthor *also* takes the role of the 'evil arch-enemy'.

between a superhuman superhero and an all too human villain, the extended battle between Superman and Zod focuses on their equality. The character aesthetics impose a certain visual moral judgment: Superman, as the figure of Good, is presented in a muted version of the traditional blue costume with the stylised 'S' (which, on Krypton, means 'hope') versus Zod, the figure of Evil, who is presented in black and is attempting world-wide genocide so that he can rebuild Krypton on Earth. Tembo has argued that the alien characteristics of Superman involve a disruption of what it means for us to be human and thus take us beyond a traditional moral dialectic of Good and Evil.[88] However, despite the realistic approach of the film, it presents a literal Manichaean battle between two co-equal forces, leaving behind extended collateral damage and destruction. Implicit in this is a direct presentation of a particular account of Good and Evil—one that is modern as much as mythic.

In *Man of Steel* this clash is between two theological reference points. At one level Superman is presented as a Christological figure who would fit within Lawrence and Jewett's notion of the American mono-myth—the superhero who, in a Christ-like way, gives himself up to save the community/city/country/world. At a second level, however, this version of American Christianity represents a form of apocalyptic and retributive justice that undergirds American exceptionalism. At the culmination of the battle between Superman and Zod, instead of the Christ figure dying, giving himself up to save others, he rather engages in the ultimate act of judgment and kills Zod. This scene, which attracted significant criticism for contradicting seventy-five years of comic-book history, was an intentional attempt by Snyder to present a more realistic and grounded version of Superman for the twenty-first century.[89] In doing so, what gets reproduced is *not* the Christological vision at all, but a much more nihilistic and secular one—the only solution to a figure of radical Evil attempting global genocide (an attempt which had already been thwarted) is to break his neck. For all Superman's strength, power and virtue, the means he deployed in the end is one of brute death-dealing violence.

In presenting a realistic superhero narrative, whilst explicitly drawing on theological themes, the result is a return not to earlier forms of mythology but explicitly to a secular theology—an attempt at presenting Superman as encompassing a certain sense of responsibility and virtue but which, in the end, is tainted by the reality of circumstances that require exceptional

---

[88] Tembo, 'Pax in Terra', pp. 53–5.

[89] For one of the most significant criticisms of this scene, see Waid, 'Man of Steel, Since You Asked', 14 June 2013. For a discussion of the controversies more broadly, see Holmes, 'Man of Steel Ending Explained', 2015.

death-dealing as its solution. The justification of Superman's actions, as I will show in the next section, are founded in the Evil committed (and threatened) by Zod—an Evil that is presented as a present threat that *must* be dealt with through violence. However, the issue is that the very construction of such a threat, despite its realistic portrayal, remains caught within a particular Manichean narrative. The realist superhero genre as a modern *secular* myth itself reflects a modern account of Evil. In doing so, it does not provide a clearer or more grounded understanding of Evil but rather turns the superhero into the villain themselves.

V. Responding to 'Radical Evil': The Superhero Critique of Law

My argument here is that the superhero genre is both an engagement with the rise, from the end of last century, in philosophical, critical and theoretical considerations of Evil[90] *and* the fact that, rather than being a recourse to an earlier theological or religious tradition, it is in fact a reflection of modern accounts of Evil. Whilst at one level the superhero genre presents a Manichaean dualism, as a modern *secular* myth, it in fact reflects not just the abuse of Evil in political rhetoric of recent years,[91] but also aspects of the attempts of modern and post-modern theories of Evil which seek to understand it as 'really existing' and situate its origin within a subjective will. The fascination with the gritty and realist turn of the genre does not just give the viewer greater insight into the superheroes, diminishing their infallibility and purity, and showing their inner turmoil or struggles and the risks of turning at times to Evil means for achieving Good ends. It also presents the supervillain in a more 'realistic' light—at one level as more complex and sympathetic, or as suffering from certain psychological problems (situating their 'evil' actions within a rational world-view by explaining them away), and at another, attempting to work through and explain the causes or possibility of Evil in the world.

In this sense, the character of General Zod becomes a meditation on the nature of Evil—not so much as the figure of supervillain-as-terrorist, which has dominated much of the recent superhero genre, but reflecting and becoming a stand-in or representation of the ultimate instances of 'radical Evil' of the twentieth century. His plans for and attempt at both world domination *and* genocide, his complete disdain for regular humans as so much beneath the superior beings of Krypton, and his source and origin in a biopolitical

---

[90] Copjec, *Radical Evil*; Neiman, *Evil in Modern Thought*; Bernstein, *Radical Evil*; Singer, *President of Good and Evil*; Hirvonen and Porttikivi, *Law and Evil*.
[91] Bernstein, *Abuse of Evil*; Singer, *President of Good and Evil*.

society focused on genetic engineering present parallels to Nazi Germany and Nazi thanatopolitics. Rather than needing to deploy a massive bureaucratic machine in order to complete this, he has the technological capabilities in terms of an alien World-Engine, which explicitly enables such actions—it is technology itself that enables the possibility of the radical or diabolical Evil of genocide.[92] However, the significance of presenting this 'event' of radical Evil in the context of a particular individual attempting to carry it out feeds into a particular view of the nature of Evil itself: seeing it as that which can be grounded specifically in an intentional act and will.

Such an approach is in contrast to the traditional account of Evil, traceable to the Augustinian tradition, which sees Evil *not* as something positive but rather as something negative—a turning away from the Good. Of significance here is that much of St Augustine's writings on Evil were situated in an explicit historical critique of Manichaeism. Rather than seeing Good and Evil as co-equal entities battling it out, Augustine argued that Evil is not a substantive thing or reality at all but rather a deficiency—a privation of Being, a taking away, a tendency to nothingness and an absence of the Good.[93] As such, it is not seen 'as a real force or quality but as the absence of force and quality, and as the privation of being itself'.[94] Evil is not opposed to the Good in an ontological sense (as in Manichaeism) but is the very lack of the Good. It can be defined only in regard or relation to the Good as its absence. That is, the Good is seen as primordial and the appropriate starting point. It is this traditional account of Evil as privation that Hannah Arendt draws upon with her infamous phrase the 'banality of evil', which she used to describe Adolf Eichmann in her accounting of his trial.[95]

[92] Whilst the Holocaust is often referred to as a new form of Evil (including by Hannah Arendt), what is significant is not the will to wipe out or exclude others, nor is it the attempt at world domination; rather, it is the technological capacity to industrialise the manufacture of death on a large scale that is new. This technology is, as Hirvonen makes clear, fundamentally intertwined with the law, and the Holocaust 'was a legal, bureaucratico-governmental economic–technological event' occurring *through* the law: Hirvonen, 'Total Evil', p. 119.

[93] Evans, *Augustine on Evil*.

[94] Milbank, *Being Reconciled*, p. 1. This does not mean that there is no Evil in the world or that Evil does not have an effect. Rather, it is that Evil, as an end or position in itself, is not possible—Evil can exist only as a corruption or deficiency of the Good. It is that which turns away from, detracts and corrupts that which actually exists.

[95] Arendt, *Eichmann in Jerusalem*.

Modern and post-modern accounts of Evil critique this traditional view of Evil as privation (including Arendt's appropriation of it), arguing that it does not provide a satisfactory way to account for 'really existing' Evil in the world.[96] They dismiss the privation account, arguing that it provided either a *defence* of evil actions (that is, for Augustine, positing them as a result of original sin), or simply an artificial consolation in the face of Evil (in the end this Evil contributes towards a greater Good that we cannot, because of our finite nature, now see). Furthermore, these accounts share an implicit concern that understanding Evil as a 'nothing', rather than a 'something', leaves us open to the very outbursting of the positivity and actuality of Evil that was seen in the twentieth and twenty-first centuries.[97] Jacob Rogozinski, for example, argues that the accounting of the 'radical evil' of the Holocaust is not to be found so much in the agent of evil (criticising, therefore, Arendt's focus on Eichmann), but rather in the Evil decision of Hitler that sits behind it.[98] For Rogozinski, whereas it might be the case that the instrument is a bumbling fool who speaks only in clichés and has no depth, the decision itself to engage in and conduct the Final Solution, whilst clearly mad, is, at the same time, a will to Evil that counters the tradition's sense of Evil as simply a privation of the Good. It is a will to destruction, which must be accounted for because it has been seen and experienced.[99]

This concern with Evil brings into view another alignment between the superhero genre and the law, for the superhero genre is premised on the existence of an Evil that the law is unable to deal with, thus requiring the superhero. This encompasses what I term the 'superhero critique of the law', to which I will also return in Chapter 3. As Phillips and Strobl note, the *need* for the superhero is presented in two fashions: first, in terms of 'the problem of a corrupt and incompetent criminal justice system' that requires the superhero to supplement the law's goal of justice;[100] second, in terms of the 'apocalyptic' level of crime and violence of the supervillains, who 'threaten public safety' and 'are rarely handled adequately by law enforcement and government in general, necessitating heroes and superheroes acting either as adjuncts to the

---

[96] Copjec, *Radical Evil*; Nancy, *Experience of Freedom*; Žižek, *For They Know Not What They Do*; Rogozinski, 'Hell on Earth'; for a discussion of these approaches, see Milbank, *Being Reconciled*, pp. 1–25.

[97] Nancy, *Experience of Freedom*; see the critique by Milbank, *Being Reconciled*.

[98] Rogozinski, 'Hell on Earth'.

[99] Ibid. See also Nancy, *Experience of Freedom*.

[100] Phillips and Strobl, *Comic Book Crime*, p. 116. For other articulations of the same point, see Bainbridge, 'This is the Authority', p. 460; Reyns and Henson, 'Superhero Justice', p. 51; Sharp, 'Riddle Me This'.

authorities or outside the law altogether as vigilantes'.[101] What is presented is the *failure* of the law to deal adequately with or account for Evil. The implication of this is that Evil should be *seen* and *dealt with*, and this is what ties the genre to post-9/11 anxieties around the war on terror and the return to the rhetoric of Good and Evil.

In this way the genre focuses on how Evil is explicitly *seen*, invoking a sense of the *reality* of Evil. The genre presents in visual form the modern *critique* of the privation theory—that is, how, with such a plethora of what would appear to be Evil in our world, can it be that Evil does not exist? To argue that Evil is simply an absence of the Good or a turning away from it would seem to ignore the reality of Evil that people commit and suffer—and would thus leave us without a way of addressing or responding to it. As problematic as it is, the superhero genre thus presents us with a sense of the need to act in response to Evil—the superhero is not so much the *deus ex machina*, upon whom we wait to come in and save the day, but rather the figure who challenges *us* to challenge and resist Evil. It positions a *response* to Evil that asks us to recognise the way in which the evils of everyday life, as well as what would appear to be the 'grander' evils of the twentieth and twenty-first centuries (totalitarianism, genocide, terrorism), indicate that Evil is a 'something' rather than a 'nothing'—and, furthermore, that that 'something' is tied not to an external mythic figure, but rather to very human actions which are culpable and deserving of punishment.

The modern account of Evil, which dismisses the privation approach, is often discussed with regard to the theoretical concept of 'radical Evil'—a term traced to Immanuel Kant's *Religion Within the Limits of Reason Alone*, although often implying something more like what Kant referred to as diabolical Evil.[102] The recourse to Kant is, at one level, as Ari Hirvonen notes, because of its de-theologising of the concept of Evil—removing it from an Augustinian/Christian theological context, as well as from a more fundamental Manichaean dichotomy.[103] Joan Copjec argues that what is new in Kant's

---

[101] Phillips and Strobl, *Comic Book Crime*, p. 120.

[102] Kant, *Religion*. For Kant the 'radicalness' of radical Evil was a point about its universality rather than its extremity. By contrast, the concept of a pure will to Evil itself is what Kant describes as diabolical—something which he did not think was possible for humans. Ibid., pp. 32–3. Having said that, psychoanalytical philosophers have argued that the very structure of Kant's notion of the categorical imperative and the Good is one that, because it is devoid of content, can apply equivalently to the idea of ultimate Evil. See, in particular, Zupančič, *Ethics of the Real*.

[103] Hirvonen, 'Problem of Evil Revisited'.

thought is that he 'sees evil as uniquely the product of a free humanity'.[104] For Kant, human beings, as finite rational agents, are free and thus solely and completely responsible for their moral choices.[105] As such, it is the will and not natural inclination or reason which is the only possible source of Evil. He notes that we call a man evil not because he performs actions that are evil, 'but because the actions are of such a nature that we may infer from them the presence in him of evil maxims'.[106] Evil, for Kant, is the failure to adopt good maxims, failing to give priority to the moral law. Radical Evil, then, is the fact that there is a universal propensity in the human animal to evil, which is both innate and inborn. It is the propensity *not* to do what duty requires, or to do your duty but for a reason that is not solely the moral law. As a starting point, Kant's position is seen as a more palatable understanding of Evil than the privation theory.

The structure of the modern gritty superhero genre presents a form of this articulation of the notion of Evil because it situates the superhero as a figure constructed in response to Evil: both the everyday and the grand. As noted above, the need for the superhero arises *first* as the result of the deficiency of the law to deal with the plethora of crime and everyday evil; and *second* in response to the villain or arch-enemy engaged in the 'grander' evils that stand in, as General Zod does in *Man of Steel*, for the horrors of the twentieth and twenty-first centuries, by attempting mass terrorism or genocide. Whilst the blockbuster special effects of Hollywood's superhero films seem to align themselves with these 'grander' evils, Shyamalan's films, by contrast, tend to focus on the pervasiveness of the everyday evils.[107] In *Unbreakable*, when Dunn starts to explore his 'superhero intuition', Price tells him that he will not need to go far. In fact, standing in the midst of a train station, within a matter of minutes he touches multiple people who have committed crimes (theft, racist violence, rape). These crimes are

---

[104] Copjec, *Radical Evil*, p. 139.

[105] Bernstein, *Radical Evil*, p. 33.

[106] Kant, *Religion*, p. 16.

[107] Think of *The Village* (2004), in which every member has experienced a tragic loss as a result of some violence, thus believing they need to leave society and start their own village. *The Sixth Sense* (1999) presents the need for the dead to tell their story—for us to *see* the evil done to them. *The Happening* (2008) shows us nature's response to the evils we have enacted against it (that is, nature seeking its revenge). In *Devil* (2010), written by Shyamalan but directed by John Dowdle, everybody trapped in a lift has committed Evil: *The Village*, film, directed by Shyamalan; *The Sixth Sense*, film, directed by Shyamalan; *The Happening*, film, directed by Shyamalan; *Devil*, film, directed by Dowdle.

visually presented to the viewer as having occurred (though within the film they are psychic visions in Dunn's mind). In one sense, this scene seems to literalise Kant's concept of radical Evil, which he describes as follows: '[t]hat such a corrupt propensity must indeed be rooted in man need not be formally proved in view of the multitude of crying examples which experience of the actions of men puts before our eyes.'[108] The reference to these experiences being put 'before our eyes' points both to *experience* itself as being the basis for our understanding of the existence of evil, and to visual framing of this evidence: a visuality that Shyamalan's filmic presentation of this evil explicitly provides. Dunn's intuition or psychic vision is visually depicted for the viewer, convincing us that these actions have actually occurred within the filmic universe and positioning us to judge them as crimes or Evil.

It is in this way that *Unbreakable* points to the particular moral vision of the superhero genre and the way in which it constructs this as an aesthetic and visual narrative. Because of the superhero's alignment with the law, this *also* highlights the way in which modern discourses of legality, human rights and ethics are situated as an ability to judge *a priori* what is Evil. As Alain Badiou notes, the modern paradigm of ethics is conceived 'both as an a priori ability to discern Evil . . . and as the ultimate principle of judgment', in which 'good is what intervenes visibly against an Evil that is identifiable a priori'.[109] As such, the law is presented as 'first of all "against" Evil'.[110] The essence of the superhero can thus be understood not so much as about capes and powers, identities and costumes, but most essentially about providing a response to a self-evident Evil.[111] Shyamalan's *Unbreakable* makes this explicit by tying Dunn's psychic capabilities to visual depictions that demand judgment—a visual *seeing* of evils that then justifies the actions of the superhero in responding to them. In doing so, the visual depiction itself encompasses a mode of judging by the viewer which parallels the mode of judgment imbued by the law in response to Evil.[112] In contrast to the traditional privation account which starts from the idea of the Good, the modern account of Evil begins its analysis—and therefore also its justifications for actions in response—from the idea and prevalence of the experience of Evil itself. In so doing, Evil becomes *not* an explanation of that which exists in the world, but rather a

---

[108] Kant, *Religion*, p. 28.

[109] Badiou, *Ethics*, p. 8.

[110] Ibid. See also Hirvonen, 'Problem of Evil Revisited'; Hirvonen and Porttikivi, *Law and Evil*, p. 6.

[111] For the standard definitions of the superhero see Coogan, *Superhero*; Reynolds, *Super Heroes*.

[112] See Clover, 'Law and Order of Popular Culture'.

justification of a particular response to Evil.[113] It is this that the connection between the superhero and supervillain most clearly presents in the superhero genre—that the superhero's actions become defined in terms of a *response* to Evil and to the villain.

This point is made clear in both *Unbreakable* and *Man of Steel*, which have their culmination points in the process of both Dunn and Clark/Kal-El 'becoming' the superhero, specific heroic acts which are not just preventative, but engage in retribution, judgment and death. In *Man of Steel* the conclusion of the fight between Zod and Kal-El/Superman comes when Zod threatens to kill a number of innocent people caught in the battle as an attempt to spite Kal-El by making him watch them die. As noted above, in contradiction of seventy-five years of comic-book history, Kal-El breaks Zod's neck and kills him. Whilst this would appear to be a wielding of death-dealing justice beyond the law, it is tied explicitly to a legal question of judgment. For the action by Kal-El is presented to the audience at one level as a 'hard decision'—one that challenges him to the core, as his scream of anguish after having killed Zod evidences. The film presents this supposed 'necessary act' of preventative violence—necessary because of Zod's threat to the innocent victims; supposed because, as with all 'necessary acts', there were other options (such as flying away with Zod in his arms or taking the fight out of the city)—as an act of judgment and execution combined. The scene comes *after* Superman's foiling of Zod's plans for gaining control of Earth and building a new Krypton to destroy the original. Superman's killing of Zod is therefore not just about the saving of a few innocent people in immediate danger, but a rendering of judgment for attempted crimes against humanity—Zod is presented as deserving of death.[114]

Whilst *Unbreakable*'s version of superhero realism does not engage with the same extreme battles across the city-scape, or a threat of genocide, it *does* engage in the same logic of death-dealing justice. This is clearest when Dunn goes to engage in his first 'heroic act'. Dunn, at Price's prompting, goes searching not for someone who has committed crimes, but for someone who is *going* to commit one. He finds a man who has broken into a family's home, killed the father, raped the mother, tied up the two children and is now living in the home, with the mother and children as prisoners. Dunn, in following the man back to the house, breaking in and freeing the children, is found and then thrown out the window into the pool. Almost drowning (as water

---

[113] Badiou, *Ethics*, p. 9.

[114] On the way in which superheroes at times are engaged in the judging of 'death-worthiness', see Phillips and Strobl, *Comic Book Crime*, pp. 135–42. And on *Man of Steel* in particular: Phillips and Strobl, 'Should Superman Kill?', 1 July 2013.

is Dunn's 'kryptonite'), he is rescued by the two children. Dunn then goes back into the house, attacks and, in what must be one of the longest strangle scenes on film, kills the man. The following day, Dunn has been written up in the newspaper as a superhero—appearing to fulfil Price's vision, presenting his act as a noble rescue and a killing of a criminal deserving of death.[115]

What is important to recognise in these two examples is the way in which the justification of the death-worthiness of these characters is demonstrated visually in cinematic form. In both cases, they function in relation to a particular vision. In *Unbreakable*, the viewer is explicitly shown Dunn's psychic vision, seeing the man force his way into the house, killing the husband and raping the wife. This vision is then affirmed when Dunn breaks into the house and provides a justification for his attacking of the perpetrator—a murderer, kidnapper and rapist who 'deserves to die'. In *Man of Steel*, both Kal-El and the viewer are presented with an understanding of Zod's plans through a vision that Kal-El has of the skulls of the millions (or billions) that would be slaughtered by Zod in carrying out his plan. Like Dunn's intuitive visions of the Evil committed by individuals, Kal-El's psychological vision of the outcomes of Zod's actions becomes the basis for judging Zod's death-worthiness.[116] It is the very affect of these 'scenes of violence'[117] that is deployed to invoke a response of horror in the viewer and is thus a justification of the actions taken by the superhero. Their 'good' response is justified by the very evilness of what has been seen, of what has been literally put 'before our eyes'.

The significance of this visual depiction of evil is that it orientates itself towards a modern positive theory of evil, presenting these characters as manifestly Evil. In articulating their death-worthiness, their deservingness of punishment, it presumes a subjective responsibility for their actions and positions the viewer to judge such responsibility—with the superhero becoming a stand-in for the law in enacting judgment.[118] The problem with this depiction, however, is twofold: first, the rendering of judgment is still unable to provide a satisfactory explanation of Evil and the suffering that it results in; second, the attempt to hold these characters responsible for their evil actions, by grounding their actions within a subjective will, also fails—with the result

---

[115] In this 'becoming' of the hero, Dunn also regains his manhood, saves his marriage and gains the respect of his son. See Palmer, 'Melodrama and Male Crisis'; Abele, 'Home-Front Hero'.

[116] Phillips and Strobl, 'Should Superman Kill?', 1 July 2013; Phillips and Strobl, *Comic Book Crime*, pp. 135–42.

[117] Young, *Scene of Violence*.

[118] Clover, 'Movie Juries'; Clover, 'Law and Order of Popular Culture'.

that the punishment would seem to be perverse rather than justified. The next two sections work through these two failures.

VI. Justice-dramas, Law's Mythic Restoring of Order and Evil as 'Meaningless Suffering'

The superhero genre can be understood as a genre of legality not simply because of its depiction of crime and the failures of law to do justice, but because of its mythic structure as a justice narrative.[119] This mythic structure aligns with the mythic nature of law and its social function.[120] As Benjamin Berger has noted, one of the roles of the law (focusing in particular on the criminal law) is mythic—it is an attempt to provide order and meaning to actions that would otherwise seem disordered and disruptive.[121] Crofts's critical recuperation of the idea of malice in the criminal law also points to the way in which the law encompasses a sense of restoring meaning and order.[122] She highlights the historic role of the criminal law, which was understood not simply in individualist terms, but also as involving ritual extirpation, a cleansing of society by dealing with and responding to harmful acts that have disrupted the *concordia* of the community.[123] This approach sees the criminal law's role in providing meaning by defining the injustice of certain actions and the significance of punishment as being about restoring community. When a superhero acts to deal with a crime—or, even more violently as noted above, to render judgment and punishment upon criminals—this comprises for the viewer a certain mythic resolution and restoration of a disrupted community.[124] The superhero's role, whilst often extra-legal and antagonistic towards the law, fulfils this mythic sense of justice *for* or on behalf of the law. At the same time, the realist mode of the superhero narrative I have been examining parallels shifts in modern legality to a more rationalised account of the law alongside a greater rationalistic accounting of Evil and responsibility. What these modern secular myths demonstrate are the challenges and *failings* of the modern 'positive' account to explain Evil in terms of the idea of human responsibility and freedom.

This accounting for or dealing with evil and suffering is part of the broader aspect of Shyamalan's film-making which focuses on depicting those who are trying to make sense of physical or emotional suffering. As such, his films fit

---

[119] Phillips and Strobl, *Comic Book Crime*, pp. 15–16.
[120] Fitzpatrick, *Mythology*.
[121] Berger, 'On the Book of Job'.
[122] Crofts, *Wickedness and Crime*.
[123] Ibid., p. 26.
[124] Lawrence and Jewett, *Myth of American Superhero*.

broadly within the tradition of theodicy discussed in the Prologue—attempts to justify or explain evil and suffering in the context of the world (and in conjunction with the idea of a good God). However, Shyamalan's films also highlight the connection between Evil and the *meaninglessness* of such suffering—the inability to reconcile the suffering experienced with any sense of meaning to the world.[125] *Unbreakable* thus can be understood as a challenge to the 'meaning' of the superhero genre and whether the actions of the superhero themselves can provide meaning—a challenge that is also put to the law. Whether it is the superhero or the law, the desire to do justice and to restore a sense of order, meaning and reason to an otherwise senseless, disordered or unjust act by determining and punishing it as evil, fails actually to explain suffering.[126] Whilst the law can determine a measure of culpability, denouncing certain actions as blameworthy and aberrant to society and punishing those carrying out such actions, this operation does not resolve the senselessness to which it is attempting to respond.[127] The perpetrator can be designated as Evil and processed in relation to justice, but the *victim* cannot. As Berger notes, '[p]unishment does not speak to *why* the act happened in the first place, so the senselessness of victimhood remains untouched.'[128] The victim's questions of 'why me?' or 'why do I suffer?' endure. The committing of violence (by the superhero or by the law) does not counter-balance the violence already suffered by the victim—despite the attempt of law and human rights to address the vision of the human as victim.[129]

What both *Unbreakable* and *Man of Steel* reveal is the way the question of meaning—and of attempting to impose meaning upon 'meaningless suffering'—is used to justify greater acts of Evil. Both films focus on the finding of one's 'place in the world' as part of the construction of the superhero and supervillain. In *Unbreakable*, this is the reason for Price's theory of the 'real'

---

[125] Jeffery, *Evil and International Relations*, pp. 28–30. See also, in a Levinasian context, Minkkinen, 'The Expressionless'.

[126] As Minkkinen notes, whilst in 'the trial, law imposes narrative meaning to suffering and consequently gives it a utilitarian value in the task of assigning responsibility', at the same time 'it falls necessarily short of any profound way of coming to terms with the agony of the injured individual'. Minkkinen, 'The Expressionless', pp. 65–6.

[127] Berger, 'On the Book of Job', p. 107. For a critical working through of the way in which victims are constituted in their representation by the law, see Elander, *Figuring Victims*.

[128] Berger, 'On the Book of Job', p. 108.

[129] Badiou, *Ethics*, pp. 10–12. See also Elander, *Figuring Victims*; Minkkinen, 'The Expressionless'.

mythology of comics. In the dénouement at the end of the film, Price rhetorically asks David: 'Do you know what the scariest thing is? To not know your place in this world. To not know why you're here. That's, that's just an awful feeling.' As it is revealed that Price had been committing terrorist acts to see if there is an individual who would survive unharmed when all else did not, Price is then able to claim: 'Now that we know who you are, I know who I am. I'm not a mistake.' This defining of one's place in the world is also part of David's own narrative. After Price first gets in touch with him, David notes: 'This morning was the first morning that I can remember that I didn't open my eyes and feel sadness.' His actions as a 'hero' were, therefore, about providing his own sense of purpose and enabling him to reconnect with his family, as much as taking up this particular role. However, whereas David seems to gain a sense of his own purpose whilst taking up the mythic role of restoring a sense of order, Price imposes meaning upon his own meaningless suffering by defining himself as a villain and committing terrorist acts.

What this reveals is the reverse side of the modern positive theory of Evil and its critique of the privation theory. The concern with seeing Evil as a privation of Being is that, in doing so, we let the perpetrator off the hook, arguing that it was their limited capacity to seek the Good (the limitation of finitude) that resulted in Evil actions. In doing so, it feels as if we can no longer hold them responsible and that the suffering that they inflicted loses all reason—it is the offshoot of the seeking of lesser goods or a failure to care. However, if we can identify that Evil is a positive substantial 'thing', an intentional act of a particular individual, then we impose meaning on suffering in terms of that intentionality. Price's actions are an attempt to impose meaning upon the world and are a justification of the disease and suffering that he has experienced.[130] In this sense, Price is taking seriously the problematic stereotypical tropes of many comic-books (and other forms of pop culture), which

---

[130] Early in the film there is a flashback to when Price was a boy and his mother was encouraging him to go outside. He was refusing because he did not want to get hurt again. His mother replies with: 'You can't do anything about that. You might fall between this chair and that television, if that's what God has planned for you, that's what's gonna happen. You can't hide from that sitting in a room.' This presents a particular account of the predetermined nature of our actions being caught up with God's plans. It also shows a nascent aspect of Price's theory of comics because Price's mother encourages him to go outside by giving him a comic-book each time he does. As such, the readings of comics themselves become attached to Price's overcoming of his fear of getting hurt.

link disability and the disabled body explicitly to Evil and villainy.[131] He is seeking a reason for his suffering and finds that *reason* in terms of *who he is*. In trying to enact this stereotype, Price then commits terrorist actions—the very enacting of Evil becomes an attempt to restore meaning to the world and provide an explanation for his suffering.

This sense of the determining of meaning for suffering as the inverse of the positive theory of Evil as an intentional subjective act is made even more clear in *Man of Steel*. There, much of the narrative around Clark/Kal-El's growing up is about him finding his place in the world, which culminates with his pensive consideration of whether he should reveal himself to Earth. But here also there is an essentialism depicted—the 'naturalness' of his own conception (his being the 'first natural birth on Krypton in centuries') versus the genetic programme that had dominated reproduction on his home planet. Zod is the representative of Krypton as an 'ultra-modern society', whose genetic engineering does not simply eliminate the weak but designs *every* person to fulfil a particular societal need. Jor-El's claim that Krypton had lost the 'element of choice' embodies an (admittedly Hollywoodified) privileging of choice, freedom and free will that reflects the modern account of Evil. But the implicit counter-point is that Zod's very 'evil-ness' comes not as a result of a freely chosen action, but rather from a *lack* of choice—in effect, a fulfilment of his pre-determined role.

What is exemplified, therefore, is the aporia of the positive account of Evil which subordinates Evil to an intentionally willed act in order to hold the human subject responsible for it. At one level, situating Evil in a subjective will and an autonomous choice is *not* a solution to the accounting for Evil because such autonomy cannot distinguish between Good and Evil—what is there to determine that when the will wills, such willing is either Good or Evil?[132] At the same time, when it comes to the enacting of Evil by Zod, this

---

[131] Norden, '"Uncanny" Relationship of Disability and Evil'; see also Fennell, 'Aesthetics of Supervillainy'; Alaniz, *Death, Disability and the Superhero*.

[132] Both Milbank and Bernstein, while approaching the issues from different directions, point to a similar critique of Kant: that his articulation of the nature of the will and its predispositions leaves one *unable* to distinguish between a will that wills the Good and one that wills Evil. As such, placing Kant as a founder of the modern account of Evil results in a *lack* of explanation of Evil actions. Milbank, *Being Reconciled*, pp. 12–15; Bernstein, *Radical Evil*, pp. 11–45. Milbank goes on to argue that the privation theory, by contrast, enables both an accounting of Good and Evil, as well as still holding us responsible for Evil actions. See also Matthewes's critique of Arendt's accounting of action and spontaneity as also pointing to a similar Kantian problem. Matthewes, *Evil and Augustinian Tradition*, pp. 157–8, 174–8.

is also *not* attributable to his subjective will or autonomy. Rather, he expresses his 'pre-determined nature' explicitly in a fulfilment of duty: 'I have a duty to my people and I will not let anyone prevent me from carrying it out.' At the beginning of the final battle with Kal, this duty itself becomes a justification for Zod's violent and cruel acts: 'I exist only to protect Krypton. That is the sole purpose for which I was born. And every action I take, no matter how violent or how cruel, is for the greater good of my people.' This recourse to duty thus takes aim at a particular aspect of the Kantian paradigm of Evil. For Kant, the fulfilment of duty is the greatest exercise of freedom and autonomy (fulfilling one's duty for the sake of duty), whilst it is the failure of doing duty for its own sake that goes to the heart of the human propensity for Evil.[133] That Zod presents his actions in terms of a sense of duty and the 'greater good', however, reveals the problematic aspect of both the Kantian paradigm *and* the modern positive account of Evil: that the fulfilling of duty can, in fact, be the committing of diabolical Evil.[134]

We can see here a parallel to Arendt's critique of the Eichmann trial. Arendt noted that Eichmann had a self-admitted, Kantian habit of mind—he asserted explicitly that 'he had lived his whole life according to Kant's moral precepts, and especially according to a Kantian definition of duty'.[135] He was also able to provide a reasonable summation of the categorical imperative— though he acknowledged that, once tasked with carrying out the Final Solution, he was no longer 'master of his own deeds'. Arendt argues that, from that point on, it was not that Eichmann had 'dismissed the Kantian formula' but rather had distorted it: 'Act as if the principle of your actions were the same as that of the legislator or of the law of the land.'[136] This popularised Kantianism demands 'that a man do more than obey the law, that he go beyond the mere call of obedience and identify his own will with the principle behind the law—the source from which the law sprang'.[137] Whereas, for Kant, the source of this is the judgments of practical reason, the sovereign law of free will, for Eichmann it was simply the sovereign 'will of the Führer'.[138] Arendt thus

---

[133] Kant, *Religion*, pp. 32–4.

[134] See Lacan and Swenson, 'Kant with Sade'; Zupančič, *Ethics of the Real*.

[135] Arendt, *Eichmann in Jerusalem*, pp. 135–6.

[136] Arendt also notes the link to Hans Frank's Nazi formulation of the categorical imperative: 'Act in such a way that the Führer, if he knew your action, would approve it.' She goes on to defend Kant, noting that 'to him every man was a legislator the moment he started to act: by using his "practical reason" man found the principles that could and should be the principles of law'. Ibid., p. 136.

[137] Ibid., pp. 136–7.

[138] Ibid., pp. 135–7, 146–50. Milbank, *Being Reconciled*, p. 23.

defends Kant by arguing that Eichmann had confused the command with the categorical imperative. However, as John Milbank points out, there is a question as to whether *in practice* the two are distinct, for Kant's philosophy of law is undergirded by his moral philosophy, which asserts the goodness of following the law above all else. That is, in his moral philosophy he praises autonomy, which is the giving to oneself of the law, but in his jurisprudence this becomes a recognition that the positive law itself is that which is given to society by itself and therefore should also be followed without question.[139] As such, Eichmann was more right than Arendt allowed: following the law itself *becomes* fulfilling the categorical imperative.[140]

What *is* important in Arendt's critique is the way in which the attempt to indict Eichmann either as the bearer of a demonic will *or* as caught within greater social or historical forces actually risks letting Eichmann off the hook.[141] That is, the modern subjective account of criminal culpability and justice *fail* in the face of Eichmann, the 'bumbling bureaucrat' who went to the end to fulfil his duty.[142] The very attempt to explain Evil as a positive entity, to determine the reason *why* such actions were taken and suffering imposed (and, as a result, to demonstrate that Eichmann had acted explicitly out of both intention *and* base motives), in effect fails because Eichmann exhibited *no* capacity for such will or intention beyond aspects of self-preservation and a deficient desire to carry out his duty.[143] Arendt's resuscitation of the privation theory with her reference to the 'banality of Evil' is therefore an attempt to demythologise this desire for a subjective demonic will, rather holding to the very *inexplicability* of Evil.[144] For, in trying to explain Evil one finds that there is nothing there—Evil itself is not meaningful but *meaningless*. This does not mean that those who conduct or engage in Evil, such as Eichmann,

[139] For Kant, Milbank notes, 'sovereign political authority is the point where moral and political rule, categorical and contingent imperative, actually come together. Since the sovereign power embodies the collective general will, and is the absolute source of all legality, to will against the sovereign power in person is to will against political legality. This cannot be universally willed, under the maxim "I will to destroy a corrupt sovereign power", because it removes the very basis of legality ... Hence regicide *does* fall foul of the categorical imperative, and to oppose the political sovereign *is* to oppose the moral sovereign.' Milbank, *Being Reconciled*, p. 24. See also discussion in Maris and Jacobs, *Law, Order and Freedom*, pp. 185–7.
[140] Milbank, *Being Reconciled*, p. 24.
[141] Matthewes, *Evil and Augustinian Tradition*, pp. 188–9.
[142] Arendt, *Eichmann in Jerusalem*, pp. 26–7.
[143] Ibid., p. 25. Cf Matthewes, *Evil and Augustinian Tradition*, pp. 185–6.
[144] Matthewes, *Evil and Augustinian Tradition*, pp. 188–9.

should not be punished. Rather it is that his culpability should not be limited to a determination of a particular subjective account of intention and action, but should also encompass the emotional and social context of the commission of Evil deeds and, in particular, the lack of care for the outcomes.[145] It is this approach, which focuses on Evil not as a positive thing but a lack, a dearth, an absence and, in particular, a lack of care, that Crofts argues for in her recuperation of a jurisprudence of malice as essential for modern criminal law.[146] Modern legality's focus on an individualised, subjective account of Evil risks letting Evil slip through its net by failing to account for it.

It is at this point that we can see the way in which the modern, gritty superhero film reproduces and puts on display this modern vision of legality. Whereas Eichmann, as a figure of the 'banality of evil', shows a complete *lack* of agency, Snyder attempts to produce Zod as embodying a demonic Evil will. Yet, as demonstrated above, this 'realistic' presentation doubles down on the problem because Zod is presented as *without* choice (his actions being determined by his genetic programming), whilst at the same time encompassing a fulfilment of a Kantian-esque duty. This calls into question our ability to hold Zod subjectively culpable and my earlier argument that Superman, in killing Zod, is rendering punishment for his 'crimes against humanity'. Because the film attempts to *explain* why Zod committed such actions it also reveals that this is *not* simply an abominable will to Evil for its own sake. Because it cannot reveal such a will in Zod the film has to go to great lengths to present Zod's death-worthiness—not only the fact that he attempted global genocide and then proclaims a hell-bent determination to make Kal suffer by killing humans one by one, but also the very specific circumstance of an imminent threat to a family who he is about to slaughter. However, this intense focus on presenting Zod's death-worthiness in the end does *not* demonstrate so much a positive account of Evil as it does a *justification* for the action that is taken by Superman. Evil here is not something in and of itself, but a justification for the *response* to Evil that is being taken.

Snyder's cinematic build-up to the killing of Zod demonstrates this point, presenting the viewer with scene after scene of massive destruction in the brawl between Superman and Zod (and no regard from *either* side for the thousands that may be killed in the fallout). Crashing into a subway station, Superman manages to get a stranglehold on Zod, who then threatens to kill innocent bystanders with his laser vision. The music and dialogue at this point, after having been clear and dynamic in the lead-up, become muffled, as if one's ears are blocked—you have to struggle to hear them. The music

---

[145] Ibid., pp. 166–9.
[146] Crofts, *Wickedness and Crime*. See, in particular, Chapter 6.

is muted but has an intensity that builds anticipation. Camera angles shift from Zod's laser vision coming closer to the family in question to focusing on the intensity of the faces of Superman and Zod—presenting the latter's rage and the former's anguish. Superman begs for Zod to stop ('don't do this!') and Zod responds with a defiant 'never!' The intensity of the scene is brought into immediate relief when Superman breaks Zod's neck, with an oppressive silence and a broader shot focusing on Superman himself—who then, in a scream of anguish, falls to the ground. This image of a scream of anguish is significant here, for it points to a question about the nature of suffering in the midst of the rendering of judgment. After Zod is killed, his 'potential victims' are not seen or presented again, but the focus is rather on the impact on Superman of having killed Zod. That is, the cinematic concern is *not* over this 'innocent family' and Superman's ability to save them, but rather their presentation as 'potential victims' who justify the action taken by Superman. As such, the film structurally represents the law's utilitarian deployment of suffering and victims as simply a component within the task of assigning responsibility. The 'victims' are structurally presented and constituted *not* as individuals bearing a suffering to which the law is responding, but as those necessary to affirm Zod's death-worthiness and justify Superman's killing him—the victims are a 'necessary' representational ground for the law.[147] The focus on the anguish of Superman in a way reproduces a particular aspect of his Christological figuring—the anguish, particularly emphasised in certain artistic renderings, of Christ's suffering. However, whereas for Christ the depiction of anguish is about rendering the humanity of the man-God in his suffering upon the cross, in *Man of Steel* this becomes a sense of suffering at having to engage in the act of judgment. This form of cinematic judgment renders visible modern legality's deep discomfort with its own constitutive violence as a rendering of punishment. The positive view of Evil imbues the deservingness of punishment within a subjective intentional will, but in doing so is always concerned about its lack of ability to identify such a will. It therefore has to turn to circumstances in order to try to present a justification for the punishment that it inflicts—and victims and victim suffering become subordinated to that justification. In doing so, suffering is taken within the law, and instead of it being a response to the suffering of victims, it becomes the suffering of the law itself—brought to bear because of the law's own self-anxiety about its capacity to judge Evil and deliver justice, a point to which I now turn.

---

[147] Elander, *Figuring Victims*, pp. 72, 79–87, 104–7.

VII. Rethinking the Law's Response: Demythologising the Subjective Account of Evil

At one level, as Hirvonen has pointed out, law is concerned with and deals with evil—the evil deeds or motivations that result in conduct that transgresses the law.[148] In this sense, law encompasses the ability to determine what is Evil and there is alignment between a modern 'positive' account of Evil and modern law's subjective account of human actions, focusing on will, intent and action.[149] However, if one turns to contemporary law and jurisprudence itself, one will find an *absence* of the language of evil.[150] In the context of the criminal law, one no longer finds 'evil persons' but rather 'wrongdoers, illegal risk takers, deviants, socio- and psychopaths, the socially deprived, the economically marginalised and potential lawbreakers, who should be identified already before any act'.[151] Such a 'withering away of the concept of evil' aligns with the rise of the therapeutic state which reduces Evil to social problems—and would seem therefore to result in a *loss* of the 'idea of freedom and the responsibility of the subject'.[152] Law's ability to determine clearly what is Evil and to assure justice through the punishment of the wrongdoer has thus become subordinated to *other* ends—such as efficiency, order, normativity or security.[153]

If such is the case, the law's role and legitimacy would appear to be called into question.[154] For, as Crofts has demonstrated, the law's claims to be able to determine and punish wickedness and evil are part of its jurisdictional claims—historically shoring itself up against religious or theological domains, today against other domains that would seek to influence it.[155] The legitimacy of legal judgment required ensuring that evil or 'malice' did not escape the law. Interrupting the history of progress towards a modern rational legality, Crofts demonstrates the way in which a broader, more

[148] Hirvonen, 'Problem of Evil Revisited', p. 29; Hirvonen and Porttikivi, *Law and Evil*, p. 6.
[149] As Crofts notes, the dominant subjective account of modern criminal law aligns with the modern 'positive' theory of Evil. Crofts, *Wickedness and Crime*, pp. 9–10; see also Midgley, *Wickedness*.
[150] Hirvonen, 'Problem of Evil Revisited', pp. 29–30. Notable exceptions include Pillsbury, *Judging Evil*; Crofts, *Wickedness and Crime*.
[151] Hirvonen, 'Problem of Evil Revisited', p. 30.
[152] Ibid., p. 31.
[153] Berkowitz, 'Justice to Justification'.
[154] Crofts, *Wickedness and Crime*, p. 4.
[155] Ibid., in particular Chapter 2; Berkowitz, 'Justice to Justification'; see also Berkowitz, *Gift of Science*.

malleable and contextualised approach to malice was needed to assist in ensuring law's claims. The move to a rationalised approach of law is that the 'positive' account of the human subject's responsibility, based on action, intent and consequence, failed to take into account other aspects of the subject, which earlier considerations of malice did (such as emotion, place, social relationships and character before and after the criminal act), as well as the social context in which such judgment must occur. The result is that the rational account of crime risks failing to be able to account for the Evil done by human subjects—and those who do not fit within the mode of this rational subject must be pushed into other categories outside its explanatory power. The rational account of malice in the criminal law does not escape monstrous Evil but rather *produces* 'monsters' in terms of those beyond or outside its account.[156] This essentially returns us to the superhero genre, for the supervillain is not that which is simply beyond the law but that which is a product of the rational mode of legality that is unable to conceive of or explain subjects outside its frame.

At the same time, the trajectory of rationalisation of the criminal law *also* reveals concerns about the law's own relation to malice and Evil. What is it that distinguishes between the violence committed by the law and the violence committed by the outlaw? The nineteenth-century dominance of legal positivism, which undergirded the move to rationalisation, had to come to terms with the law's use of force—explained by Jeremy Bentham and James Fitzpatrick Stephen in terms of utility.[157] 'On this argument, although intentionally violent and thus an evil, the use of force by the law is without malice because unlike the outlaw, the law is acting for the good of the major- ity.'[158] The law's violence is legitimate because of the ends which it serves. However, on a cognitive model of subjectivity, '[b]oth the law and outlaw were intentionally harming another.'[159] The crucial distinction between the two was articulated in terms of the law's *absence* of malice. That is, there are two intertwined grounds for the legitimacy of law: first, that it is capable of consistently and accurately determining and punishing those who do evil; second, that, in doing so, it is free from the malice which forms part of the actions of the outlaw.

The significance of the superhero genre as a subject of cultural legal analy- sis is that it points to these very aporias of the legitimacy of the law. As discussed above, the premise of the superhero is that the law has *failed* in its

[156] Crofts, *Wickedness and Crime*, p. 125ff.
[157] Ibid., p. 152.
[158] Ibid.
[159] Ibid., p. 153.

ability to punish, consistently and accurately, those who do evil. At the same time, the superhero's actions can be called into question if they are not able to distinguish themselves from those of the outlaws that they are fighting. There must be an ability to separate themselves from evil and malice. This goes to the core of Bainbridge's analysis of the superhero genre, arguing that it allows for a working through of these issues, enabling viewers to engage in questions about what is the right or wrong way of dealing with criminal (or terrorist) violence. Whilst I agree that superheroes provide a means for working through issues of law and justice, these issues function at a different level to that which Bainbridge presumes. It draws out not the *difference* or *distance* between law and superhero justice, but rather *their interrelation*. When the superhero stands in the place of the law, it presents to us the deficiencies not of the law itself but of the *vision* of legality that undergirds it. The realist superhero genre, in attempting to present to us a greater explanation of the supervillain, as well as a greater justification for the superhero's actions, in fact reveals the tensions of modern legality itself.

Let us return, for a moment, to Dunn's first action as a superhero in *Unbreakable* as an example of these aporias. At first glance, Dunn seems to have engaged in a heroic act—taking his first step towards a superhero career of fighting crime and Evil. However, what did Dunn actually do? He broke into a private residence and strangled a man to death. On what evidence or authority did he do this? Simply the speculative theorising of an art gallery owner and an intuition regarding what the man had done. This intuition—Dunn's psychic vision—is visually depicted for the audience, thus convincing us that it has actually occurred in the filmic universe. As with the scene above from *Man of Steel*, the cinematic positioning here is important. Shyamalan's slow-paced cinematography and the sense of realism mean that, instead of dramatic build-up and instant relief with the snapping of Zod's neck, Dunn's strangling of the perpetrator is extended, difficult and challenging—it requires Dunn to hold on whilst being beaten against the wall, and the sense of 'relief' of the tension is only marginal and gradual, as one is not entirely sure at what point in time the intruder dies. The follow-on from the actions focuses on Dunn returning to untie the mother of the children he has already saved, only to find that she has died. The victims remain an essential part of the action—but Dunn has also *failed* to save two of them.

The issue with the actions taken by Dunn is not just the fact (as noted above) that killing the intruder and saving the children cannot explain the suffering experienced by them. Rather it is the question that goes to the essence of the law itself: that is, is the superhero (or law) consistently able to determine justice? What if, for example, in his desire to respond to Evil, Dunn had in fact attacked and killed the wrong person? An attempted *response* to Evil would then have been an *enacting* of Evil, inflicting senseless suffering rather than responding to it. This is where the law's awareness of the possibility of its own failure is inherent and instituted in the requirements of rights to a fair trial and due process. William Blackstone's famous maxim that 'it is better that ten guilty persons escape than that one innocent suffer' is often referred to as providing a guiding principle of the criminal legal system—focusing on the necessary link between guilt and punishment, and the cruelty of punishing those who are not guilty.[160] The risk for the law is that it will inflict suffering (that is, wrongful conviction/punishment) where none is due and thus act *as* Evil instead of doing justice and restoring the Good.[161]

Whilst the normal reading of the superhero genre is that it involves a justification of extra-legal actions in responding to a failure of the law, or a crisis or state of emergency (an argument I will return to in Chapters 3 and 4), what this analysis points to is not so much the *distance* between the superhero and the law, but their similarity. Because the superhero steps into and takes the place of the law in the context of these comics and films, what is being presented to us is in fact a vision of modern legality in stylised form. It positions the viewer as engaging in a process of judging the guilt of the criminal or supervillain, based on the manifest visuality of their Evil actions placed before our eyes. Whereas the comic form engages the reader/viewer in a degree of complicity through the very functioning of its *form*, the filmic form situates the viewer as judging that which is occurring before us. The battles of Good and Evil, and the narratives of death-worthiness that are presented, are in fact a reflection of modern legality. The question that is presented is: what is the *justification* for the violent actions of the superhero, which often are transgressive of the law itself? At one level this can be read in a straightforward fashion, arguing that the violence of the law is legitimated through its structures of authority, its formal process of decision making and the *systematic* exercise of violence.[162] What is central to such an account is an argument that the law *must not* engage in Evil or malice in its actions.[163] And yet, at the same time, the very limits of legal judgment must acknowledge that the exercise of violence always involves the risk of it being Evil—of punishing the innocent. When the law's own anxiety is then matched against a subjective account of Evil, the law, as Berger has noted, risks making no

[160] Ibid., pp. 4–5.
[161] Berger, 'On the Book of Job', pp. 11–12.
[162] Cover, 'Nomos and Narrative'.
[163] Crofts, *Wickedness and Crime*.

sense at all.[164] The rationalised account of the subject risks *failing* to explain or account for actions as Evil except in a very precise sense—and, as with the discussion of General Zod, and as Arendt made clear in her analysis of Eichmann, the commission of extreme or exceptional Evil may in itself escape a subjective account of Evil.

It is here that the conclusion of Shyamalan's *Unbreakable* becomes significant because it provides an attempt to break free of the intertwined mythic framing of the law and the superhero, understanding the way in which we are complicit in the narratives of legality and evil in which we participate. The film concludes with the revelation that Price's theory of there being actual superheroes is all about justifying his own being-in-the-world, which has taken the form of a supervillain. This revelation is presented as the culmination of Price's theory—as he says to Dunn, 'now that we know who you are, I know who I am'. This would appear to be the conclusion of an origin story, leaving open the possibilities of many escapades of Price and an epic battle between the supervillain, Mr Glass, and the superhero, Securityman (or, as he is referred to in *Glass*, the 'Overseer'). This revelation that Price is in fact the one who committed the terrorist actions which gave rise to the discovery of Dunn functions aesthetically as a version of what has been termed Shyamalan's 'click' moments.[165] However, the significance of *Unbreakable* is not so much the revelation that Price is in fact the supervillain—which would seem to *affirm* his theory and provide the sense of this all being a demonstration of the way in which superheroes are real. Rather, it is in the postscript that is superimposed at this point in time, which, instead of *affirming* Price's theory (there *are* 'superior' beings amongst us), negates it—the theory is simply a deranged delusion and, as such, Price is placed in an 'institution for the criminally insane'.[166] Whereas *Man of Steel* goes to extreme lengths to justify Superman's role as the superhero, these few words completely undermine the whole of the superhero mythos. When Dunn goes to tackle the 'invader', resulting in his death, he takes upon himself the mantle of the law-cum-superhero—he *does not* go to the police or authorities, but rather steps in and

---

[164] Berger, 'On the Book of Job', p. 116.

[165] Weinstock, 'Telling Stories about Stories', pp. ix–xii.

[166] As Palmer notes, Shyamalan's original cut of the film had an open-ended conclusion, paving the way for a series of films about Dunn as superhero (which, after fifteen years, became the 'Eastrail 177 Trilogy' with the release of the subsequent films in 2017 and 2019). However, in response to pre-release marketing feedback, Shyamalan became convinced that there was a need for at least a token gesture towards a restoration of the social/moral order at the end of the film. As such, the postscript text was added. See discussion in Palmer, 'Melodrama and Male Crisis'.

responds himself because of his apparent acceptance of Price's theory (he is actually a superhero put here to protect others). By contrast, at the conclusion, the postscript notes *not* that there was an epic battle between Dunn and Price, but simply that 'David Dunn led authorities to Limited Edition where evidence of three acts of terrorism was found.' Dunn therefore *rejects* his positioning as a superhero because it reveals explicitly the type of 'Good' which can be conceived only *as a response to* Evil (both requiring and justifying a fight against Evil).

Here the aesthetics are important. In *Man of Steel*, the viewer is asked to forget the mythic and stylistic forms that we are being presented with, instead believing that this is a 'real' presentation demonstrating the actuality of Evil in the world and the type of response that it requires. At the same time, it retains the traditional mythic structure of the superhero genre, which involves the supervillain as protagonist who moves the story along, whilst the superhero is simply a conserver of the status quo, called upon to defeat the rise of a monstrous or external Evil.[167] The result of this mythic form is that, despite its implicit or explicit allusions to the superhero as a Christological saviour figure, it essentially posits a notion of the Good as reactive or responsive to Evil—a direct by-product of the modern positive accounts of Evil. By contrast, as Milbank has noted, as exemplary of the privative account of Evil, the Christian paradigm for a virtuous act is *not* one that assumes a prior Evil to be contained, but rather a spontaneously creative one.[168] It is when one starts from the position of the Good as something spontaneous or creative, or a truth that can be 'eternal' (to use Badiou's terminology), that the concept of Evil can be recognised not as an end in itself but as a negation.[169] By contrast, the attempt to depict or conceive of an Evil in and of itself that justifies extreme and superheroic acts in response (as *Man of Steel* does) is not so much something that 'really exists' in the world, but rather a particular narrative structure.[170] Such structures have benefit *only* if they are recognised as presenting for us in stylised form certain aspects of ourselves that we need to deal with in order to grow, but they *should not* be taken as a literal or realistic depiction of Evil.

Whereas *Man of Steel* in the end affirms both Superman as a superhero, and the validity (hard or discomforting thought though it might be) of his

---

[167] Lawrence and Jewett, *Myth of American Superhero*; Reynolds, *Super Heroes*; Eco, 'Myth of Superman'.

[168] Milbank, *Word Made Strange*, pp. 219–21.

[169] Badiou, *Ethics*, pp. 72–87.

[170] On the narrative function of Evil, see Cole, *Myth of Evil*; discussed by Crofts, *Wickedness and Crime*, p. 125.

'necessary' actions to eliminate or eradicate the threat of Evil, *Unbreakable* calls into question this entire narrative. Shyamalan's 'making strange' of the superhero genre, positioning it within a realist context, challenges the viewer by revealing in the end all these 'narrative elements' as just that, certain aspects of stories that we tell ourselves about the role of superheroes and supervillains in life—and, by association, the role of modern legality. The point of revelation (not just Shyamalan's 'click', but the explicit *explanation* of its meaning) is a process of defamiliarisation that makes the viewer *aware* of the explicit *construction* of a superhero narrative that is occurring, and in which we as viewer are participating. The end-point is to reveal this as a distorted view of the world, not to punish the villain (who, in the end, is presented rather as suffering from mental illness—and, as such, being *excluded* from the law's rational accounting of subjective culpability), but rather as a distortion that we ourselves *also* participate in, because we have been positioned to *want* Dunn actually to become the superhero.[171] That is, despite drawing upon the Manichaean nature of the superhero genre, *Unbreakable* in fact demythologises Evil, by arguing that it is part of our interpretation of the world, rather than an essential aspect of it. Evil is not a positive, really existing reality, but a negating of the Good that is the world with which we should engage.

It is significant that the sequels to the two films I have been discussing both *invert* these positions. Whereas *Man of Steel* seems to affirm the role of Superman and his 'necessary' elimination of Zod, *Batman v Superman* challenges the role of Superman, raising questions about his actions as being unilateral and outside the domain of the state. However, whilst these questions are raised by the Senate hearings and Senator Finch's inquiries into Superman's actions, the end narrative reveals two things: first, that the Senate hearings themselves are based on an emotional manipulation that is set up by Lex Luthor, and which would seem to call into question the validity of the way in which the law challenges Superman; second, that Superman in the end *is* a saviour figure, here giving up his life to save others. The conclusion of the film, following Superman's sacrificial death, focuses both on the state funeral for Superman, and on the personal funeral for Clark Kent. In the background, Bruce Wayne (Ben Affleck) complains to Dianna Prince (a.k.a. Wonder Woman, played by Gal Gadot) about the 'circus' burying an empty box. Dianna notes that they 'don't know how to honour him, except as a soldier'. Bruce then comments that he failed him in death but he won't fail him in life, and that there is a need to find the others like them, because there will be a need to fight (as a precursor to the 'epic battle' that proceeds in the

---

[171] Berger, 'On the Book of Job', p. 116.

following film, *Justice League*).[172] One of the final lines of the film, however, comes from Lex Luthor, now imprisoned (though unfit to stand trial) and proclaiming that 'the god is dead'. While the film at one level raises questions about the nature of a figure of the Good acting unilaterally beyond the law and the state, in the end it affirms, in the eyes of the viewer, the role of such a figure—with the need for others, such as Batman and Wonder Woman, to take up Superman's salvific mantle.

By contrast, *Glass*, the recent sequel to *Unbreakable*, which *does* explain how a figure like Price (Mr Glass), in a 'realist' narrative, is able to escape an institution for the criminally insane (despite having been locked up for twenty years, he is able to hack into the security system and design an escape), provides an affirmation of the superhero mythos instead of retaining its faithfulness to the process of 'defamiliarisation' and demythologising deployed in the earlier film. This occurs in an aesthetic dimension, which in part moves *away* from the comic-book stylisation and the 'silence' of the filmic qualities to include aspects of a more modern aesthetic similar to those deployed by the gritty style (though in a more muted tone). It *also* occurs in a thematic sense. The *starting* premise of the film, and supposedly consistent narrative throughout, seems to be that of the earlier conclusion: that *both* Price and Dunn (as well as 'the Beast', played by James McAvoy, another 'superior' individual whose origin is told in the film *Split*) are in fact simply delusional, suffering from certain forms of mental illness and therefore all the ideas that they might be superheroes or supervillains are fabricated or inexistent. In this sense a psychoanalytic reading is privileged over the legal one. However, the revelation at the end of *this* film is that there is a secret society hiding the 'truth' that there are superior people in the world, in the belief that such knowledge would have disastrous consequences for society. The concluding move is for Price to release imagery of the actions of Dunn and the Beast to the world, distributed via social media so that the world 'will know' the truth—that is, that 'true life' reflects the weirdness of what can otherwise be found on YouTube, FaceBook, Instagram and Twitter. This affirmation of the superhero mythos thus undermines Shyamalan's immanent *critique* of the genre that his earlier film deployed.

---

[172] The funeral ceremony for Clark is *also* a precursor to the return of Superman in *Justice League*, with the quotation from Isaiah 26: 19: 'The dead shall live. My slain shall rise again. Awake and sing ye that dwell in dust, for thy dew is like the dew of the morning, and the earth shall give birth to her dead.' This trope of 'resurrection' affirms again the Christological nature of Superman.

VIII. Conclusion: Superheroes as Figures of Law and Justice

The realist superhero genre, in attempting to present to us a greater explanation of the supervillain, as well as a greater justification for the superhero's actions, in fact reveals the tensions of modern legality. It is *not* presenting a recourse to a pre-modern form of justice focused on crime control versus modern legality focused on due process. In this sense, it is *not* hearkening back to earlier Christological modes of justice. Rather, it is presenting the very ambivalence of modern legality: that in attempting to reduce Evil to subjectively willed human actions, it removes the ability to distinguish between Good and Evil altogether. In doing so, it provides a sense of culpability and responsibility that is unable to respond to the way in which Evil in the world affects society. The solution is *not* therefore to involve a greater recognition of Evil as something which is 'actually existing' in the world—such would be to fall into the trap of the realistic mode of the superhero genre and presume that 'this is' the real world. Rather, the solution is to recognise the way in which Evil itself is always negative, parasitic on the Good arising not so much from intentional cruelty as from a failure to care. This would encompass at one level a richer jurisprudence of malice and wickedness, whilst at the same time decentring Evil from the law's focus, enabling us to embrace a law that is not simply a response to Evil, but a vision of the Good itself. This involves, therefore, a recognition that the delight we see in the superhero genre on screens today is reflective of, as well as feeding, our own sense of modern legality.

Unbreakable's conclusion and critique of the superhero genre also reveal the more significant critique of the law that undergirds it. This is not the naïve concern that law is fallible and failing, needing a superhero to 'fulfil' justice, but rather reflects a greater symptom of modern legality which is, in itself, its detachment from a greater vision of Justice and the Good. In analysing the positioning of the superhero in relation to the villain in *Unbreakable* and *Man of Steel*, law is unable to explain the suffering caused by the villain *or* to account for their actions as an Evil attached to an autonomous human will which we can hold responsible. But, more significantly, the superhero genre's *desire* for a justice beyond the law is actually a desire for the law itself to encompass a greater consideration of justice. In this sense, as a modern secular myth, the superhero genre reflects the way in which modern law, shorn of its traditional and religious foundations, is unable to do anything other than articulate a justice as a means to an end—a response *to* Evil, rather than an envisioning of the Good.[173] Whilst the superhero may appear to be

---

[173] Berkowitz, 'Justice to Justification', p. 627.

able to provide justice where the law fails to do so, what is presented, rather, is the aporias of modern legality which are resolved only by presenting a 'seeing' of Evil that is put before the eyes of the viewer. The modern subject-based legality has, at its roots, a particular modern conception of the subject, which sees freedom and free will as its goal, without a consideration of the ends or purposes for which such a will is given or used. In response, we need to envision an alternative response not grounded in a heroic reaction to Evil, but a conception of the Good as a radical creative and spontaneous act.

In *Man of Steel*, despite presenting Superman as a figure of the Good, an ideal that we can live up to, we are left with him committing Evil and violence only ever as a *response* to Evil. This fails to think of either Zod as a political actor, or Superman as an appropriate bearer of the Christian mythos. What remains, despite all its gritty realism, is an attempt to present a form of Manichaeism, which can understand Good only in its battle with and as a response to Evil. Snyder's 'gritty realism', here, tries to make us believe that this is the nature of the real world itself. That the Evils we confront in this world are unstoppable and need to be destroyed. Such an approach forgets both the mythic nature of the genre and the own fictionality of the filmic medium which is being deployed—we are asked to enter not *another* world, but what is supposedly a representation of our own world. By contrast, *Unbreakable* begins by making a Manichaean dualism more explicit, but in doing so it also makes clear the problems and risks of such an approach, for it demonstrates explicitly the way in which the vision of the Good of the superhero is tied to a response to Evil, determined *a priori* and explicitly attached with a particular form of seeing. If the superhero stands in for modern secular legality, then the issue is the way in which it constructs and articulates a vision of the Good based on an *a priori* vision of Evil. What Shyamalan's filmic exploration of superheroes makes clear in its pre-empting of the climactic rise of the superhero film is the precariousness of a Good (the hero, democracy, the law) that is constructed in and via Evil itself (the villain, terrorism, crime): that is, the presentation of a Good to be constructed in terms of an Evil that must be defeated. Yet such a concept of the Good is inherently unable to explain either the nature of Evil or the suffering it inflicts. This is the significance of Shyamalan's aesthetic presentation, in the deployment of the participatory dimensions of the comics medium, as well as in the dénouement which reveals to us the narrative construction of the superhero and supervillain. In doing so, Shyamalan asks us to be *more* aware of the fictions that we engage with and therefore reflect those that govern and structure our lives.

Having said this, whilst *Unbreakable* presents us with a critical account of the superhero genre—one which asks us to take stock of our own complicity in the narratives we tell of the world—it also leaves us without the greater sense of wonder at the world which a form of Christian 'making strange' makes possible. As such, Shyamalan provides us with only a half-step, for he points to the way in which we are complicit in the particular narratives of the world that we participate in but fails to reveal a possibility of seeing the world otherwise, of returning to us and rendering the world more luminous. In the next chapter I turn to explore one attempt at doing this in terms of one of the most significant Hollywood texts which presented itself explicitly as a modern myth: *Star Wars*.

2

The Force of/as Modern Law: Justice, Order and the Secular Theology of *Star Wars*

'Jurisprudence is the knowledge of things divine and human, the science of the just and the unjust.'

Bracton[1]

I. Introduction: An Eternal Recurrence

Why is it that *Star Wars* seems to be enacting an eternal recurrence of the same?[2] Having had dramatic cultural impact across multiple generations, *Star Wars* was a mainstay and touchstone of science fiction, fantasy and space opera throughout popular culture even *before* Disney's acquisition of the series from Lucasfilm. Now with Disney's sequels, spin-off films, animated and live-action series (*Clone Wars*, *Rebels*, *The Mandalorian*), we seem once again to have the *dominance* of *Star Wars* as a global cultural multitext—one which, if we are to concur with legal scholar Cass Sunstein in his *The World According to Star Wars*, is universal.[3] But what is it that is universal here? Is this simply a case of cultural imperialism, the globalisation of Hollywood and a myth of American exceptionalism, or is there something more fundamental at stake in the *Star Wars* saga? My answer to this question is that the significance of *Star Wars*, specifically *because* of its cultural imperialism, is that it provides a key example of contemporary secular legal theology. This is because what undergirds and 'binds' the *Star Wars* galaxy together is not simply its mythic tropes, its battles between Good and Evil, its visions of spectacular light-sabre battles or spaceship dogfights, but the religion of the Force itself. However, the central argument of this chapter is that we should understand the Force not simply as a religion but rather as a

---

[1] Bracton, *De Legibus et Consuetudinibus Anglia*, p. 25.
[2] A Nietzschean point made, slightly differently, in a brief review of *The Force Awakens* by philosopher Eric Winsberg: Winsberg, 'Is This the Eternal Recurrence', 21 December 2015.
[3] Sunstein, *World According to Star Wars*, p. 2. *Star Wars: The Clone Wars*, film, directed by Filoni; *Star Wars: The Clone Wars*, TV series, directed by Lucas; *Star Wars: Rebels*, TV series, directed by Kinberg et al.; *The Mandalorian*, TV series, directed by Favreau.

representation of the fundamental nature of modern law: its ability mythically to resolve, as Peter Fitzpatrick's work has made clear, the transcendence, certainty and determination of law on the one hand, with its immanence, social construction, contingency and responsiveness on the other.[4] In its 'secularity', modern law is positioned *against* a religion that has supposedly been jurisdictionally separated and subordinated to the private realm. At the same time, modern law becomes 'deified', taking up the very qualities of transcendence that the secular supposedly banishes from religion. The significance of *Star Wars* as a 'modern myth' is that it *does not* present the Force as a transcendent divinity but rather as an immanent presence, a 'force' created by all living things, which binds the universe together. That is, we find a representation of a modernity that has 'let go' of the transcendent, focusing on an immanent normativity and *nomos*.

In one sense, this chapter extends the argument from the previous one, which focused on the way in which law is envisioned as a response to Evil, in particular a modern positivised sense of Evil situated in the human will of the subject. But here the argument is presented in a different key by demonstrating the way in which the traditional alignment with justice and the Good is one that, in the modern development of positive law, has lost its connection to such insight and connection to justice. Modern law becomes caught up with a focus on order, not simply as a link *to* an underlying order of the world, but as a construction or 'making' of such order itself—an imposition of 'order' and 'civilisation'. Law's consistent *failure* to achieve such order, however, retains the need for a belief or faith in the possibility of legality, once again linking the theological with the jurisprudential in secular form. Law thus functions (and has at times been described as) a 'civil religion' which is supposedly able to 'bind us' together, just as the Force does in *Star Wars*. At the same time, if my outrageous argument that the Force stands in the place of modern law and legality holds, then such a 'binding' is presented as fractured and riven, always at risk of its own destruction. In this sense, *Star Wars* also provides a *critique* of modernity which separates the law from faith, belief, ethics and morality— that is, the way in which the law 'let go' of its groundings, internal authority and sense of reason and insight, replacing it with claims of certainty, universality and its ability to produce order and security. As such, the Force presents not a religion but rather a secular theology of modern law and legality.

My rendering visible of this connection of the Force to law focuses mainly on the three *Star Wars* film trilogies (Lucas's 'original' and 'prequel' trilogies, along with the more recent Disney 'sequel' trilogy – now together referred

---

[4] Fitzpatrick, *Mythology*; see also Fitzpatrick, *Modernism*.

to as 'the Skywalker Saga'[5]), as not only a 'telling instance' of popular culture (one that is globalised and universalised) but as a 'making strange' of the mythology of modern law. Section II situates my arguments for reading the Force as a mythology of modern law explicitly *within* the mythic readings of *Star Wars*, drawing on Lucas's personal and intellectual relationship with Joseph Campbell and the intentional construction of a modern mythology. Section III extends this consideration by working through the nature of the religion of the Force, and examining the way in which it relates not to specific other religions (Buddhism, Taoism, Christianity), but to religion in general in a pluralist form. This pluralist approach is significant because it undergirds the way in which Lucas's 'modern myth' is one that presents a *modern* view of religion—both in a sociological sense in which all religions are presumed to serve the *same* function; but also in terms of their relation to law in terms of being subordinated to the private realm and thus governed by public legality.

Sections IV and V turn to a more explicit examination of the central theme of the *Star Wars* saga: that of 'letting go'. This theme functions not simply as a particular 'ethic' undergirding *Star Wars*, but is linked to the ideological functioning of this series in what Michael Hardt and Antonio Negri have termed the 'age of Empire'.[6] Important in this context is the way in which the religion of the Force is not simply pluralist but is explicitly *immanent*, having 'let go' of an external or transcendent divinity, and rendered in terms of being *created* by life itself. Such a focus on immanence is worked through in relation to the law in Section VI, which outlines the way in which the Force is a representation not of a pre-modern natural law, but more explicitly of the immanence of modern law understood particularly in its liberal form: grounded in a 'rule of law' that is based on protecting a separate and independent legal order both from the risk of a transcendent deific, totalitarian sovereign *and* from the external threats to the realm of legality. Section VII turns back to transcendence in terms of the way in which such a 'protection' of legal order must, in the end, remain *subordinate to* a transcendent sovereign, seen not only in

[5] The original trilogy: *Star Wars Episode IV: A New Hope*, film, directed by Lucas; *Star Wars Episode V: The Empire Strikes Back*, film, directed by Kershner; *Star Wars Episode VI: The Return of the Jedi*, film, directed by Richard. The prequel trilogy: *Star Wars Episode I: The Phantom Menace*, film, directed by Lucas; *Star Wars Episode II: Attack of the Clones*, film, directed by Lucas; *Star Wars Episode III: Revenge of the Sith*, film, directed by Lucas. The sequel trilogy: *Star Wars Episode VII: The Force Awakens*, film, directed by Abrams; *Star Wars Episode VIII: The Last Jedi*, film, directed by Johnson; *Star Wars Episode IX: The Rise of Skywalker*, film, directed by Abrams. At times, reference is also made to the two stand-alone 'Star Wars stories' films: *Rogue One: A Star Wars Story*, film, directed by Edwards; *Solo: A Star Wars Story*, film, directed by Howard.

[6] Hardt and Negri, *Empire*.

the 'state of exception' of the 'prequel' trilogy, but in terms of the tension between transcendent 'aristocratic' mediation and the immanent 'democratic' multitude in the 'sequel' trilogy. The chapter concludes with a critique of the constant invocation of this immanent legality in the Jedi farewell and blessing, 'may the Force be with you'. The result is that *Star Wars* is presented as a text that not only demonstrates but critically explicates and 'makes strange' our understanding of law and its relation to society, taking that intersection elsewhere, not just to a mythic juridical galaxy 'far, far away . . .' but immanent in our very understanding of the role of law today.

II. *Star Wars* as Legal Mythology: 'I've got a bad feeling about this'

Where is the law in *Star Wars*? Why, in films so resonant with our current age and touted as a mythology of our time,[7] saturated with technology (droids, ships, blasters), enmeshed in political turmoil (the manoeuvring in the Galactic Senate, the Emperor's and then First Order's totalitarian rule of the Galaxy, the political struggles of the Rebels and the Resistance) and permeated with international—or, rather, intergalactic—commerce (trade federations, commerce guilds, a military–industrial complex and wars over the taxation of trade routes), has the law been jettisoned like space trash from an Imperial Cruiser? Law breakers (Jabba the Hut, Han Solo, Poe Dameron) and even law enforcers (stormtroopers, bounty hunters) abound, but no court scenes are dramatised in *Star Wars* and no lawyers are figured. Despite *some* mention of slow and bureaucratic courts and the need for a treaty to make the Trade Federation's invasion of the planet of Naboo 'legal' in *Episode I: The Phantom Menace*, and the revolutionary claims for droid rights by L3–37 (Phoebe Waller-Bridge) in *Solo: A Star Wars Story*, there is almost no reference to law or legality at all in these films, which, despite their mythological structuring and space opera setting, are otherwise so reflective of their times.[8]

In fact, as the opening words of *Solo: A Star Wars Story* note, it is 'a lawless time', dominated by crime syndicates. Whilst an appropriate exposition of the context which might give rise to a character such as Han Solo (Alden Ehrenreich), such a claim of the *absence* of law would appear strange—not least because we are presented with a galaxy literally being fought over by multiple claims to sovereignty: the Old Republic, the Galactic Empire, the New Senate and the First Order. Such sovereigns are backed by the physical force of traditional armies (whether droid, clone or forcibly conscripted), as

---

[7] Gordon, 'A Myth for Our Time'.

[8] My focus in this chapter is restricted to the *Star Wars* live-action films, leaving aside both the canonical *Clone Wars*, *Rebels* and *The Mandalorian*, and the now non-canonical Extended Universe.

well as, particularly in the case of the Empire and First Order, technologi-cal power (death stars, starkiller bases, planet killer star destroyers). Between these two claims—of 'lawlessness' and the abundance of the 'force' of law—what is on display would seem to be, rather, the *failure* of law: whether this is in terms of the constant struggle for the Galactic Empire and First Order to shore up its rule, or the ineffectiveness of the laws of the Old Republic or the new Senate actually to sustain any sense of 'peace and justice' in the galaxy by, for example, abolishing slavery (which, as is seen in *The Phantom Menace*, is clearly permissible on Tatooine and other planets in the outer rim) or to regulate arms dealers or the excesses of a casino capitalism (presented in terms of the luxurious gambling city of Canto Bight in *The Last Jedi*).

Such an apparent absence of specific presentations of legality might pro-vide an explanation for the dearth of cultural *legal* analyses of *Star Wars*: an absence that is conspicuous amongst the plethora of other critical readings and scholarly engagements with the series, with monographs and collections of essays covering the relation of *Star Wars* to politics and history,[9] philosophy and ethics,[10] technology[11] and religion,[12] not to mention its often questionable representations of race, gender, sexuality and identity.[13] Given that *Star Wars* was central to the corporatised and merchandised, special effects-orientated, big-budget blockbuster associated at the time with 'New Hollywood'—now transmogrified into the franchise-focused trans-modal production model being deployed by Disney and others[14]—it is not surprising that considerations of

[9] Machaj, *Rise and Fall*; Meyer, 'Star Wars, *Star Wars*, and American Political Cul-ture'; Kuiper, 'Star Wars: An Imperial Myth', Brode and Deyneka, *Myth, Media, and Culture in Star Wars*; Brode and Deyneka, *Sex, Politics, and Religion in Star Wars*; Kaminski, *Secret History of Star Wars*.

[10] Decker and Eberl, *Star Wars and Philosophy*; Eberl and Decker, *Ultimate Star Wars and Philosophy*; Robinson, 'Far East of Star Wars'; Cooke, 'Environmental Ethics in Star Wars'.

[11] Silvio and Vinci, *Culture, Identies and Technology*.

[12] The Jedi and the Force have formed the basis for a consideration of both 'new religion' or spirituality, as well as being mined for connections to numerous older religious traditions. Jones, *Finding God in a Galaxy Far, Far Away*; McCormick, 'Sanctification of Star Wars'; Possamai, 'Cultural Logic of Late Capitalism'; Possa-mai, *Religion and Popular Culture*; Possamai and Lee, 'Hyper-Real Religions'; Farley, 'Virtual Knights and Synthetic Worlds'; Bortolin, *Dharma of Star Wars*; Grimes, *Star Wars Jesus*; Porter, *Tao of Star Wars*; McDowell, *Gospel According to Star Wars*.

[13] de Bruin-Molé, 'Space Bitches, Witches, and Kick-Ass Princesses'; Lee, *Galaxy Here and Now*; Frankel, *Rey of Hope*; McDowell, *Identity Politics*.

[14] Kunz, 'Canonicity Management and Character Identity'; Hassler-Forest and Guynes, *Star Wars and the History of Transmedia Storytelling*; Zornado, '*Star Wars* as Disney Fantasy'.

questions of 'ownership' and intellectual property have been raised and discussed.[15] However, other critical analyses of the legality of *Star Wars* remain few and far between. Adam Gopnik made some allegorical remarks about the US Supreme Court and the Jedi Council, as depicted in the prequel trilogy,[16] and Julie Lovell has provided a more sustained jurisprudential consideration of human rights within the original films and *The Phantom Menace*.[17] Even Sunstein's pithy interrogation of the series, when it comes to a consideration of the links to law, focuses more on the questions of authorship, narrative and canonicity—comparing the approach of writers and film-makers with judges, in a Dworkinian consideration of legal interpretation and the constraints of tradition and meaning—rather than the legality of the narrative content or formal cinematic rendering of the saga.[18] What, instead, dominates the readings of *Star Wars* is not its *legality*, but rather its mythology, looking at the way in which Lucas did or did not draw upon particular mythic tropes, and the purpose and function of such myths today.[19]

This consideration of *Star Wars* as mythic can be traced to Andrew Gordon's description of *Episode IV: A New Hope* (simply titled, upon release in 1977, as *Star Wars*) as a 'myth for our time', and has focused on Lucas's alignment with (or distance from) Joseph Campbell's articulation of the 'monomyth' and the adventure of the hero in his famed *The Hero with a Thousand Faces*.[20] Drawing

[15] Lomax, '"Thank the Maker!"'; Proctor and Freeman, 'Transmedia Economy of Star Wars'; Wolf, *Building Imaginary Worlds*; Kunz, 'Canonicity Management and Character Identity'.

[16] Gopnik, 'Lessons for the Supreme Court', 18 February 2016.

[17] Lovell, 'Great Disturbance in the Force'.

[18] Sunstein, *World According to Star Wars*, pp. 149–61; see also Sunstein, 'How Star Wars Illuminates Constitutional Law', 2015; Somin, 'Star Wars, Science Fiction and the Constitution'.

[19] Though there are significant calls to go *beyond* such an analytic focus for *Star Wars* scholarship. See Silvio and Vinci, *Culture, Identies and Technology*.

[20] Campbell, *Hero With a Thousand Faces*. The trajectories of Luke Skywalker in the original trilogy of films have been mapped to this adventure of the hero both for each film individually and for the trilogy as a whole: see Gordon, 'A Myth for Our Time'; Voytilla, *Myth and The Movies*, pp. 273–91; Galipeau, *Journey of Luke Skywalker*. While it has been argued that Lucas drifts further from Campbell's hero quest in the prequels (Lawrence, 'Campbell, Lucas and the Monomyth'), at least *The Phantom Menace* and the prequel trilogy as a whole also conform to this form of the monomyth: Lancashire, '*Phantom Menace*: Repetition, Variation, Integration'. Michael Kaminski has certain misgivings about these connections between Lucas and Campbell. See Kaminski, *Secret History of Star Wars*, pp. 213–19. Note, however, John McDowell's extended critique of Kaminski's argument: McDowell, *Gospel According to Star Wars*, pp. 186–8.

on the work of Carl Jung, Campbell engaged in an archetypal analysis which argues that all the divergent and varying *forms* of myth conform, in essence, to a single monomyth made up of two components: the 'Adventure of the Hero' and the 'Cosmogonic Cycle'. According to Campbell, the goal of myth is to effect a reconciliation of the individual consciousness with the universal will, leaving behind the life of ignorance—a coming to 'realization of the true relationships of the passing phenomena of time to the imperishable life that lives and dies in all'.[21] The 'Adventure of the Hero' encompasses: a *departure* or cosmic call upon the hero, summoning him or her beyond their current mundane situation; an *initiation* into a source of power via a number of tests and trials aimed at purifying the self; and then a final *return*, bringing a life-transmitting boon back into the everyday.[22] This departure, initiation and return purifies the ego, reconciling the hero with their opposite and opening their mind to the 'inscrutable presence which exists', not as 'good' and 'bad', but 'as the law and image of the nature of being'.[23] The adventure of the hero, along with the continuous retelling of the story in its various forms, is what achieves this reconciliation to the universal will and it is where the cycle of the hero forms part of the Cosmogonic Cycle. The focus of *this* Cycle is the harmonisation of opposites and a recognition of the totality of the universe—a looking past the appearances of diversity in relation to a unifying underlying essence.[24] As such, there arrives a balance of opposites—between mercy and justice, good and evil, right and wrong—behind which is an energy that is one and the same.

A number of scholars have thus pointed out the structural parallels between Lucas's (and Disney's) saga and the Adventure of the Hero.[25] Each of Luke (Mark Hamill), Anakin (Hayden Christensen) and Rey (Daisy Ridley) are 'called' to the adventure of the hero from a mundane existence (as a moisture farmer, slave or junk trader), undergo a myriad of tests (from pod races to space battles and light-sabre fights to daring rescues and quests to find missing Jedi or lost planets) in order to find greater awareness of themselves and the universe, only to conclude with the question of how to live with the banality of 'ordinary' reality. Yet, what is significant in *Star Wars* is not only

---

[21] Campbell, *Hero With a Thousand Faces*, p. 238.

[22] Ibid., pp. 58, 101, 195–6, 216.

[23] Ibid., pp. 114–15, 146–7.

[24] Ibid., p. 114.

[25] See, for example, Gordon, 'A Myth for Our Time'; Gordon, 'Monsters from the Id'; Gordon, 'End of the Myth'; Wood, 'Growing Up Among the Stars'; Collins, 'Pastiche of Myth'; Lehrer, 'Lucas Weaves New Mythology'; Lancashire, 'Once More With Feeling'; Lancashire, '*Phantom Menace*: Repetition, Variation, Integration'; Lancashire, 'Politics of *Star Wars*'.

the way in which the trilogies can be mapped against this hero cycle, but the way in which what is undergirding it all is the very idea of an energy or 'force' itself. Whilst Lucas attributes his original conception of the Force to Carlos Castaneda's *Tales of Power* and Arthur Lipsett's short film *21–87*,[26] we can see here directly the influence of Campbell, for it is the Force, in *Star Wars*, that provides the reconciliation of the heroes (Anakin, Luke, Rey) with the larger cycle of the films. The teachings of the Force itself are explicit about the process of balancing of the individual with a 'destiny' that goes beyond oneself, needing to involve a reconciliation with one's opposite (Luke with Darth Vader (played by David Prowse, voiced by James Earl Jones), Rey with Kylo Ren (Adam Driver)). Such a balancing is most explicit in the prequel trilogies with the focus on a prophecy about bringing 'balance' to the Force, combined with the teaching of symbiotic relationships and harmony by Jedi Knight Qui-Gon Jinn (Liam Neeson) and his apprentice, Obi-Wan Kenobi (Ewan McGregor), in *The Phantom Menace*.

What is significant, however, in the context of the connections between *Star Wars* and mythology is the way in which both Campbell and Lucas view the status, function and need for mythology today. Campbell argued that, in our modern, mechanised world, mythology has been dismissed as something primitive and false—something which modern society has moved beyond, relying on other discourses. This displacement of mythology creates a number of social problems.[27] While the cosmological, and to some degree mystical, functions of mythology (those that go to provide an explanatory image of the universe and maintain in the individual an experience of awe and respect in relation to it) are now supposedly provided by science, the sociological and psychological functions of myth (those that bind people into particular social groups and that provide certain guides for living, both for a group and for an individual) have tended to be dismissed.[28] Or at least some of the other domains for which myth functions, the law included, seem to have lost symbolic efficiency. Campbell argued that part of this relates to the

---

[26] See McDowell, *Gospel According to Star Wars*, p. 170. Part-way into Lipsett's film there is the following statement: 'Many people feel that in sort of the contemplation of nature and in communication with other living things, they become aware of *some kind of force*, or *something*, behind this apparent mask, which we see in front of us, and they call it God.' *21–87*, film, directed by Lipsett; Castaneda, *Tales of Power*.

[27] Campbell and Moyers, *Power of Myth*, p. 8.

[28] Ibid., pp. 38–9; Campbell, *Masks of God*, pp. 3–7, 608–24. On the functions of myth as they appear in consumer society, see Hirschman, 'Legends in Our Own Time'.

fact that, while the main motifs of myths are always the same, every mythology has grown up in a certain society and in a *bounded* field—providing the origins of a *particular* people or group.[29] With the advent of 'globalisation' and the so-called 'clash of civilisations', such boundaries and boundedness appeared to be fading away[30]—though the resurgence of nationalism over the past decade involves attempts to redraw such boundaries in order to reassert the distinctness of a certain sociality. For Campbell, what was required was a mythology that could be valid for the planet as a whole—one which we did not as yet have.[31]

Enter *Star Wars*. For Lucas, the creation of the *Star Wars* films was about providing this type of mythology. Such a belief is not necessarily unique to Lucas—popular culture itself has been identified as having the potential to serve some of the Campbell-esque functions of mythology.[32] However, Lucas explicitly refers to the alignment of his work with the social and psychological functions of mythology. As reported in an early biography, he said, 'I wanted to make a kids' film that would strengthen contemporary mythology and introduce a basic morality.'[33] Later, prior to the release of the prequel trilogy, he argued that

> somebody has to tell young people what we think is a good person. I mean, we should be doing it all the time. That's what the Iliad and the Odyssey are about—'This is what a good person is; this is who we aspire to be.' You need that in society. It's the basic job of mythology.[34]

At the same time, Lucas did not see himself as simply providing an American myth, localised to a particular bounded space, but rather a global one:

> I'm telling an old myth in a new way. Each society takes that myth and retells it in a different way, which relates to the particular environment they live in. The motif is the same. It's just that it gets localised. As it turns out, I'm localizing it for the planet. I guess I'm localizing it for the end of the millennium more than I am for any particular place.[35]

[29] Campbell and Moyers, *Power of Myth*, p. 27.

[30] See Huntington, *Clash of Civilizations*.

[31] Campbell and Moyers, *Power of Myth*, p. 28.

[32] See Voytilla, *Myth and the Movies*, p. 1; Ferrell, *Modern Mythology*, p. 19; Hirschman, 'Legends in Our Own Time'.

[33] Pollock, *Life and Films of George Lucas*, p. 144; quoted in McDowell, *Gospel According to Star Wars*.

[34] Rayment, 'Master of the Universe', 16 May 1999, p. 20; quoted in McDowell, *Gospel According to Star Wars*.

[35] Moyers, 'Cinema: Of Myth and Men', 26 April 1999.

Here we see, in a sense, an intention for *Star Wars* to be global in its approach—a point which Sunstein emphasises, arguing that 'its appeal is universal', that 'Star Wars unifies people' and (supposedly) that '[i]n all of human history, there's never been a phenomenon like Star Wars.'[36] Such overstated claims, of course, forget much of Lucas's context and source material—that he was part of the driving force of Hollywood's globalisation of the big-budget blockbuster, which *does* impart particular American values and characteristics around the world.[37] That is, as will be seen in Section V below, Lucas is already *within* a particular global myth—the myth of what Michael Hardt and Antonio Negri refer to as 'Empire'.[38]

The key problem with Campbell's approach to the function of mythology, and with Lucas's taking up and attempting to address it, is that it presumes that modernity itself is bereft of myth—that modernity with its scientific, rationalist, materialist and progressive discourses has moved *beyond* mythology. However, this very framing—that modernity is without myth, it having moved beyond a mythic past—is, as Peter Fitzpatrick has made clear, itself mythic.[39] Lucas's attempt to provide a global mythology for the planet misses the way in which modernity *already* functions as a universal and globalising myth, in which Disney and Hollywood's cultural imperialism participate. It is from this perspective that the need for the cultural *legal* analysis of *Star Wars* that this chapter engages in becomes clearer, for if the mythology of *Star Wars* is participating in the myth of modernity, this is a particularly law-full—that is, full of law—myth.[40] Law is what is supposed to distinguish modernity from pre-modernity, civilisation from savagery, secular modernism from a religious or theological past.[41] Modern law is that which secures civilisation both against the historic primitive whence it supposedly has come, and from the risk of falling *back* into a fundamental savagery that always threatens lawful society. Law is constitutive of civilised society.

My argument in this chapter, therefore, is that *Star Wars* constitutes a legal mythology not because these texts *depict* law and legality, but rather because they themselves are mythic *sources* of law. As Desmond Manderson argues in

[36] Sunstein, *World According to Star Wars*, p. 2.
[37] Mirrlees, *Global Entertainment Media*; Ibbi, 'Hollywood'; Brooks, 'Cultural Imperialism vs. Cultural Protectionism'.
[38] Hardt and Negri, *Empire*.
[39] Fitzpatrick, *Mythology*.
[40] As Fitzpatrick has argued, particularly in the context of understanding law's relation to the sacred, law functions *as* a form of modernity. Fitzpatrick, 'Secular Theology and Modernity of Law'.
[41] Fitzpatrick, *Modernism*; Fitzpatrick, 'Secular Theology and Modernity of Law'.

relation to children's literature, they imbricate us into a system of knowing and ways of being in the world, introducing us to appropriate behaviour and the 'social structures of subjectivity in our society'[42]—to questions of authority, right and wrong, good and evil, authorised and unauthorised, legality and legitimacy, a *nomos*, to use Robert Cover's term.[43] That is, they perform the function of law.[44] However, as *modern*, law must also shore itself up with recourse to that which is beyond it. Modern law must be 'self-grounding', for as modern it can no longer have recourse to the transcendent, divine, theological or religious.[45] Yet, if modernity is premised on a turn from transcendence to immanence, from the sacred to the profane, from the religious to the secular, why does Lucas's 'modern' myth make a 'religion' central to it? The answer, as I argue in the next section, goes in part to the way in which *Star Wars* presents a secular legal theology.

III. 'I find your lack of faith disturbing': The Pluralistic Religion of the Force

Lucas's creation of *Star Wars* encompassed not just a process of mythically teaching moral responsibility but also an encouragement for people to think about 'spiritual' matters. He said that he 'put the Force in the movie to try to awaken a certain kind of spirituality in young people—more a belief in God than a belief in any particular religious system'.[46] At the same time, the Force is positioned, most notably in the original film, *A New Hope*, as a particular religion. There, representatives of the Empire twice describe Darth Vader as the last of the 'ancient religion' of the Force—a point which Han Solo (Harrison Ford) *also* alludes to, watching from the side-lines as Luke Skywalker begins his training with Obi-Wan Kenobi (Alec Guinness), with his cavalier reference to 'hokey religions and ancient weapons'.[47] Here the Force is presented

---

[42] Manderson, 'From Hunger to Love', p. 93.

[43] Cover, 'Nomos and Narrative'; Manderson, 'From Hunger to Love', p. 96.

[44] As Manderson notes, such myths are both 'world-creating' and 'world-legitimating and world-harmonizing', for myths 'in creating their *own* world in time or space . . . legitimate and harmonize *ours*'. These myths *mediate* our legal origins, the aporias of the foundation of law and the constitution of society, while also *constituting* 'legal subjects in accordance with the values' they narrate. They do this not by prescribing behaviour or 'lay[ing] down laws for us' but, in their narratives, 'they inscribe behaviour: they lay down ways of being in us'. Manderson, 'From Hunger to Love', pp. 88–90.

[45] Fitzpatrick, *Modernism*, pp. 5–6; Goodrich, 'Fate as Seduction', p. 116.

[46] Moyers, 'Cinema: Of Myth and Men', 26 April 1999; McDowell, *Gospel According to Star Wars*, p. 21.

[47] Howe and Geisler, *The Religion of the Force*, pp. 13–14.

as something which one must believe or 'have faith' in (Luke questions Han by saying, 'you don't believe in the Force, do you?'), alongside evidence of its existence: Luke's ability to fight the remote droid while wearing a blast shield that covers his eyes; Vader's use of the Force to choke Admiral Motti (Richard LeParmentier), noting that he finds Motti's 'lack of faith disturbing'. All of this would seem to indicate, as John C. McDowell points out, that if the Force is a religion, then *Star Wars* is *not* on the side of secularism.[48] As the older and wiser (though no less dashing) Han Solo of *The Force Awakens* notes, although he used to think it 'was a bunch of mumbo jumbo'—'a magical power holding together good and evil, the dark side and the light'—his position has changed, based on his experience: 'The crazy thing is, it's true. The Force, the Jedi, all of it. It's all true.'

Yet if the Force is a religion, what type of religion is it? This question has raised numerous and conflicting answers, with a number of scholars and commentators pointing out the clear connections with both Taoist and Buddhist traditions, other arguing that it resonates with Christianity and the Judeo-Christian tradition, and Lucas himself noting that 'almost every single religion took Star Wars and used it as an example of their religion'.[49] At the same time, a number of Christian commentators have critiqued the idea that the film encompasses an essentially Christian myth, arguing that it presents a pagan, 'Eastern' or mystical context rather than that of Christian redemption and salvation (despite both Anakin Skywalker's (Jake Lloyd) Christological allusions in *The Phantom Menace* and the clear redemptive narrative that comes to a head with the 'salvation' of Anakin/Vader in *Return of the Jedi*).[50] McDowell acknowledges the range of 'Eastern' reference points (for example, 'the samurai-like Jedi Knights', the 'Zen-like Jedi Master Yoda', the resonance of Qui-Gon Jinn's name with both the Taoist concept of Qi and the Jinn of Arabian mythology) whilst also pointing out the range of Judeo-Christian allusions and themes (Darth Maul's devil-like horns, Darth Vader's and Darth Sidious's Satan-like temptations, the *Millennium Falcon*'s Jonah-like emergence from the belly of the space slug, and the virgin-birth imagery of Anakin).[51] This debate over *which* religion the Force is at one level

[48] McDowell, *Gospel According to Star Wars*, p. 21.
[49] Moyers, 'Cinema: Of Myth and Men', 26 April 1999; McDowell, *Gospel According to Star Wars*, p. 23. For examples of the religious readings of Star Wars, see Lott, 'Tao of the *Star Wars* Trilogy'; Porter, *Tao of Star Wars*; Bortolin, *Dharma of Star Wars*; Jones, *Finding God in a Galaxy Far, Far Away*; Grimes, *Star Wars Jesus*.
[50] See, for example, Howe and Geisler, *The Religion of the Force*; Caputo, *On Religion*, pp. 83–4; Robinson, 'Far East of Star Wars'.
[51] McDowell, *Gospel According to Star Wars*, p. 24.

misses the point, for, as Lucas argues, the aim was to present or advocate for, not a *particular* religion or religious system, but rather a more general spirituality and belief in God. Lucas saw *Star Wars* 'as taking all the issues that religion represents and trying to distil them down into a more modern and easily accessible construct'.[52] As Mary Henderson notes, 'the Force combines the basic principles of several different major religions yet it most embodies what all of them have in common: an unerring faith in a spiritual power'.[53] In this sense, as McDowell rightly argues, the Force 'is not a presentation of a *particular* religion but rather a pluralistic account of religion itself.[54] This is consistent with Lucas's drawing upon Campbell, who saw 'the Absolute' as perceived through many different masks—the differences of religions are simply different depictions of an inexpressible 'something that transcends all thinking'.[55] This pluralist account thus presumes that all 'religions' are, in essence, dealing with the same essential 'thing'—an underlying sense of the divine, the true, the transcendent or the mysterious.[56]

Whilst *Star Wars* at one level does not appear to be on the side of secularism, this presentation of a pluralistic religion *does* align with a particularly *modern* understanding of religion and the divine. Its articulation of the commonness or similarity of all religions occurs from a specific standpoint—namely, that of secular Western liberalism—and, in its process, tends to *impose* a common understanding on what are quite diverse elements (to which the debates over the use of the term 'religion' or 'religions' itself points).[57] For John Caputo, *Star Wars* captures a sense of the impossible, mysterious and beyond, to which, for him, all religion at its best alludes. Although he points out that there are no direct representations of the traditional tropes of religion (churches, temples, priesthood, prayers and rituals) in *Star Wars*, he argues that 'the whole thing is religious', 'inasmuch as "the Force" is a religious or mystical structure and everything in *Star Wars* is keyed to the Force'.[58] Part of

---

[52] Moyers, 'Cinema: Of Myth and Men', 26 April 1999, p. 21; McDowell, *Gospel According to Star Wars*.

[53] Henderson, *Magic of Myth*, p. 44.

[54] McDowell, *Gospel According to Star Wars*, pp. 23–5.

[55] Ibid., p. 23.

[56] On the challenges of defining religion as a field of study, and its links to mystery and the transcendent, see Flood, *Importance of Religion*, pp. 5–6, 14–16. See also Caputo, *On Religion*.

[57] Flood, *Importance of Religion*, pp. 12–16.

[58] Caputo, *On Religion*, p. 85. Caputo was writing here just after the release of *The Phantom Menace*. Later films in the prequel trilogy *do* refer to a Jedi Temple (though this appears to be a place of training rather than worship), and there are some indications of other temples, scriptures and even worshippers of the Force in the Disney sequels and *Rogue One*.

what this depiction of the Force in *Star Wars* (and the popularity of the series) indicates for Caputo is that there is 'a certain religion' which flourishes *beyond* or outside the traditions of the confessional faiths: 'Religious transcendence is beginning to transcend the traditional religions.'[59] Whilst Caputo argues that the *Star Wars* universe has *not* succumbed to an intergalactic secularism, this seems to be in part because of his focus on *The Phantom Menace*. If we turn back to the original trilogy, as noted above, *Star Wars* presents not so much a praising of a post-modern 'religion without religion', but rather a 'modern' positioning of religion itself—it is an 'ancient religion', with only a few adherents hearkening back to an earlier era. The Disney trilogy doubles down on this in both *The Force Awakens* and *The Last Jedi*, where the now old and jaded Luke believes that the Jedi Order should be allowed to die—it being the remnants of a bygone era, one particularly dominated by the Jedi's pride, arrogance and vanity.

Rather than a critique of secularism, *Star Wars* supplies a narrative *of* the secular with its key separation of the state, politics and law from religion, as well as the necessity of maintaining such a distinction for the preservation of the liberal order and the justice that it is supposed to guarantee.[60] Modern legality presumes both the neutrality and the value of the rule of law, understood as autonomous, universal and secular. Such an account is said to ensure 'a regime of religious toleration and pluralism, one that allows a zone of "religious freedom" in which individuals and communities are free to follow the dictates of conscience in matters of religious belief and practice'.[61] In this account, both 'private individual' and 'communally bound modes of religion are juxtaposed to and contained within a universal "secular" law'.[62] Modern law is therefore presented as something *separate from* and jurisdictionally *superior to* religion.[63] At the same time, such an emphasis on the *differences* or separateness between law and religion is not simply neutral. As much law and religion scholarship points out, there are similarities of structure and function between the two: both encompass cosmologies, anthropologies, techniques of textual interpretation, regimes of images and representations and even soteriologies.[64] It is therefore the *closeness* of law and religion that gives rise to a competition between them—the need for 'law' to separate itself from and set itself above 'religion'.[65]

---

[59] Ibid., pp. 89–90.
[60] Sullivan et al., 'Introduction'; Lilla, *Stillborn God*.
[61] Sullivan et al., 'Introduction', p. 2.
[62] Ibid., pp. 2–3.
[63] Fitzpatrick, 'Secular Theology and Modernity of Law'.
[64] Sullivan et al., 'Introduction', p. 3.
[65] Fitzpatrick, 'Secular Theology and Modernity of Law'; Sullivan et al., 'Introduction'.

From this perspective, Lucas's attempt at presenting a *global* mythology, underpinned by a particular pluralistic approach to religion functioning as a supposedly 'catch-all concept that assumes a hypothetical commonality in all religions underneath their less important differences', involves, in itself, a presumed universality which is imbued within modern law.[66] This brings us back to the question of what *type* of religion the Force really represents in its attempt at universality. At one level, modern law functions in competition with religion. At the same time, it cannot take recourse to the transcendent as its foundation in the same way that pre-modern legality did. Rather, the 'defining feature' of modern law is 'the attempt to make law self-founding',[67] to position law as self-grounding, assuming within itself a 'deific transcendence' that substitutes 'for the previous variety which has, variously, absconded, been exhausted or disposed of'.[68] It is with this focus on self-grounding that we can see the intersections of modern law and the Force. This is because, whilst McDowell argues that there is much the Christian and Christian theologian can learn from *Star Wars*, the nature of the *source* of the Force is quite distinct from Christian theological orthodoxy. McDowell argues that the Force represents a form of transcendence and thus, by implication, a transcendent deity similar in nature to the Christian triune God. However, this is in direct contrast not just to the way in which the Force is used (deployed by *both* the 'good' Jedi and the 'evil' Sith) but more directly in terms of the way it is described.

Despite some references from Qui-Gon Jinn in *The Phantom Menace* to the Force having a 'will', the way in which the Force is referred to is not so much as an external, divine being 'out there' but rather as something that is internal to and created by all living things. In *A New Hope*, Obi-Wan describes the Force as 'an energy field created by all living things. It surrounds us, it penetrates us, it binds the galaxy together.' Jedi Master Yoda (voiced by Frank Oz) notes in *The Empire Strikes Back* that 'life creates it, makes it grow, its energy surrounds us, and binds us'. In *The Force Awakens*, Maz Kanata (voiced by Lupita Nyong'o) states that the Force 'moves through and surrounds every living thing'. In *The Last Jedi*, the older Luke describes the Force in a similar fashion to Obi-Wan: 'It's the energy between all things, the tension, the balance that binds the universe together.' As Caputo makes clear, 'the Force is not God, not a transcendent creator of the visible heavens and earth . . . but a pervasive mystic–scientific power that runs through all

[66] McDowell, *Gospel According to Star Wars*, p. 25. Sullivan et al., 'Introduction', p. 3.
[67] Goodrich, 'Fate as Seduction', p. 116.
[68] Fitzpatrick, *Modernism*, p. 6; see also Fitzpatrick, 'Secular Theology and Modernity of Law'.

things.'[69] In this sense, the Force is *not* a religion of transcendence (or even a Christian intermixing of transcendence and immanence), but rather a monistic religion of immanence.

This presentation of the Force as an immanent religion, whilst at one level reflective of certain religious traditions that are also *immanent* or pantheistic in nature (versions of, for example, Buddhism, Taoism or Hinduism), is an effect of the pluralised and 'distilled' account of 'spirituality' that Lucas sought to articulate. The result is not an authentic engagement with religion but rather a post-modern myth of the religious, a 'religion without religion' that, because it presumes both a *commonality* of all religions *and* their subordination to the private realm of belief, reproduces religion, as will be seen in the next two sections, as an ideological supplement of the dominant form of rule today: global capitalism undergirded by the rule of law. What is lost in doing so is the way in which different religious traditions operate not *just* through specific symbolism and theological doctrinal tropes, but also through the envisioning of particular social projects and social formations.[70] Rather than viewing religion as a unique way of being in the world that draws forth the subject and provides an account of the subject's relation to the Good and the other, it presents religion as simply a mechanism of binding community or culture together and enabling a degree of order, so that society can function in a peaceful fashion. When religion itself is pluralised in this fashion, it comes to be understood more explicitly as paralleling and serving the same function as modern law: as a mechanism of binding us together and ensuring social order. This has implications, as will now be argued, for the forms of subjectivity that it presents.

IV. 'Train yourself to let go of everything you fear to lose': The Ethics of *Star Wars* or the Subjectivity of Late Capitalism

Despite the saga's continuous focus on destiny, the fulfilment of prophecy and the hero's call, Sunstein argues that the 'hidden message and real magic of Star Wars' is its emphasis on freedom of choice: 'Through acts of personal agency, people can alter the seemingly inevitable moments of history.'[71] We see such an emphasis in Han Solo's decision to return to save Luke at the end of *A New Hope*, Finn's (John Boyega) refusal to shoot at innocent villagers when he is a stormtrooper at the beginning of *The Force Awakens*, Rey's rejection of Kylo Ren's offer to rule the galaxy in *The Last Jedi*, Luke's decision, against

---

[69] Caputo, *On Religion*, p. 83.
[70] Milbank, 'End of Dialogue', pp. 178–9, 184–5.
[71] Sunstein, *World According to Star Wars*, pp. 6, 183–4.

the wisdom of Yoda and Obi-Wan, to leave his training and go to save his friends in *The Empire Strikes Back*, and, most significantly, Darth Vader's final decision to save Luke and kill the Emperor in *Return of the Jedi* (despite his constant claims that he is too far gone to the dark side).[72] It is these types of choices, made at key points by a large range of characters, that, for Sunstein, demonstrate the way in which individual actions are significant in the context of the rise or fall of Empires and Rebellions.[73] Such an emphasis on freedom of choice, the significance of personal agency and an upholding of autonomy idealises a particular form of subjectivity and aligns *Star Wars* with the American monomyth of rugged individualism.[74]

At the same time, this notion of freedom of choice is matched against an apparently contrasting view of subjectivity with multiple claims to 'destiny' and prophecies, along with the Jedi's teaching that encompasses a sense of mindfulness, concentration and control which involves a 'letting go' of attachments—both physical and emotional. This emphasis on 'letting go' was part of the presentation of one's interaction with the Force from the very beginning in *A New Hope*. Obi-Wan exhorts Luke, in his initial training, to 'let go of your conscious self and act on instinct'. This 'letting go' is then emphasised at the end and climax of the film. There the Rebel Alliance mounts an attack on the Empire's Death Star—the space station the size of a moon with the capabilities of destroying an entire planet—based on the technical data stolen by the Rebels and being nobly carried by the droid R2-D2 (played by Kenny Baker). In the attack, squadron after squadron of fighters criss-cross, bob, weave and zig-zag over the textured, corrugated and crenulated cavities of the Empire's 'technological terror', attempting to fire their proton torpedoes into a small exhaust vent, which, if hit, will just happen to set off a chain reaction that will destroy the Death Star.[75] But failure meets every pilot—except, that is, for our hero, Luke Skywalker. This is because, when flying his X-Wing fighter through the trench of the Death Star, he is encouraged to 'let go' and trust his feelings by the voice of his (presumed dead) mentor Obi-Wan—which he does. Unlike the previous fighter pilots,

---

[72] Sunstein also includes in his examples both Anakin's 'decision' to kill Count Dooku and then his later decision to submit the teachings of Darth Sidious. See ibid., pp. 105–13, esp. 110–12. For a critique of this 'choice' see Peters, 'Unbalancing Justice', pp. 263–5.

[73] Sunstein, *World According to Star Wars*, pp. 112–13.

[74] Lawrence and Jewett, *Myth of American Superhero*; Lawrence, 'Campbell, Lucas and the Monomyth'.

[75] In *Rogue One*, this apparent 'coincidence' is presented as an intentional design flaw built into the Death Star by Galen Erso (Mads Mikkelsen).

who relied solely upon the targeting computer and thereby failed to hit the target, Luke turns off his computer and uses the Force instead. The result: a direct hit, with the Death Star exploding spectacularly into millions of pieces.

This iconic scene captures and dramatises a very particular mode of engaging with technology and the material. Despite the numerous advanced technological wonders presented in *Star Wars*, one should 'let go' and trust one's feelings and instincts, rather than directly deploying the technological apparatus available.[76] Given *A New Hope*'s release at the beginning of the rise of the information or knowledge economy, this can be read as a critique of the technologised life of late capitalism. It would appear, as Slavoj Žižek notes, that the only way to 'psychologically cope with the dazzling rhythm of technological development and the accompanying social change' today is to 'renounce any attempts to retain control over what goes on, rejecting such efforts as expressions of the modern logic of domination'.[77] One should draw upon the logic of mysticism or 'Western Buddhism' and 'let go'—'drift along, while retaining an inner distance and indifference toward the mad dance of the accelerated process[es]' of capital.[78] This approach of inner distancing is based on an insight that would seem to align with the descriptions of the Force discussed above: 'that all of the upheaval is ultimately just a non-substantial proliferation of semblances that do not really concern the innermost kernel of our being'.[79] This insight, whilst appearing to present a religious critique of technology and global capitalism, in fact functions, as Žižek notes, as an ideological supplement to it. Its effect is that it presents us with the idea that what we do, in the end, does not really matter because it does not affect our underlying autonomous being.

The consistent exhortation to 'let go' throughout the *Star Wars* series is crucial, therefore, to understanding whether we are being presented with an ethics that is critical of Western liberalism and late capitalism, as McDowell argues, or a form of subjectivity that sustains and supports it.[80] At the same time, the way in which 'letting go' functions is *different* in each of the trilogies. In the original trilogy, as noted above, 'letting go' is one of the first thing

---

[76] For an articulation of the intermeshing of religion and technology in *Star Wars*, see Caputo, *On Religion*. By contrast, see Donnelly, 'Humanizing Technology'.

[77] Žižek, *On Belief*, pp. 12–13. See also Žižek, 'Western Marxism to Western Buddhism'; Žižek, *Parallax View*, pp. 382–5; Žižek, *First as Tragedy Then as Farce*, pp. 65–7.

[78] Žižek, *On Belief*, p. 13.

[79] Ibid. For Žižek's specific connection of Western Buddhism to *Star Wars* see Žižek, 'Revenge of Global Finance', 21 May 2005. See also Žižek, *Parallax View*, pp. 100–3.

[80] McDowell, *Gospel According to Star Wars*, pp. 26–34.

that Obi-Wan instructs Luke to do in his training with the light-sabre. This involves a shift in perspective from seeing with one's eyes to seeing with the mind or feelings—a sensing of not only the interconnectedness of all living and material things, but the nature of being which underlies all appearances. Yoda's training of Luke in *The Empire Strikes Back* further emphasises this approach, noting that Luke needs to unlearn his received way of being in the world, that 'size matters not', that 'luminous beings are we', not the 'crude matter' or materiality that we perceive. This process of 'letting go' is therefore about gaining greater perception into the nature of reality in order to enable the Jedi to manipulate it and to do the amazing feats of wonder with which they are associated.

In the prequel films, by contrast, the injunction to 'let go' is less focused on a physical letting go so that one can see beyond the false appearances of reality to an underlying interconnectedness or symbiosis. Rather it is a psychological or *emotional* letting go of social and familial bonds. This is most obvious with the overall trajectory of the prequels: the fall of Anakin Skywalker and his transmogrification into Darth Vader. Lucas presents this explicitly as a result of Anakin's *inability* to 'let go'.[81] When Anakin reveals to Master Yoda his respective fears of losing his mother and then later Amidala (his girlfriend then wife, played by Natalie Portman), Yoda's advice is to 'train yourself to let go of everything you fear to lose'. McDowell has argued that this letting go removes one's focus on self and self-interested attempts to secure particular objects or persons, so as to enable a more global compassion.[82] To put it in Campbell's terminology, this involves the process of abolishment or annihilation of the ego, enabling its reconciliation to the universal will or, here, the Force.[83] McDowell sees in this *Star Wars'* religious *critique* of liberal individualism, where the sense of detachment as a self-disinterestedness means that you have 'no *need* of others' love', which places you 'in a better position to be endlessly available for creative acts of charity'.[84] In this light, *Star Wars* is thus not exalting the hero but rather recognising their embeddedness—their dependence on others and the world around them, which is presented as the symbiosis of all creation. The Sith are then those who present an inappropriate use or manipulation of the Force focused on self-interest and the desire for power.

The problem with this reading is that it fails to perceive that this letting go—of your conscious self, of those you fear to lose—is *not* a complete letting

[81] Corliss and Cagle, 'Dark Victory', 29 April 2002.
[82] McDowell, *Gospel According to Star Wars*, pp. 127–31.
[83] Campbell, *Hero With a Thousand Faces*, p. 238.
[84] McDowell, *Gospel According to Star Wars*, p. 130.

go, a giving up of oneself for the other. Rather the letting go *physically* and *emotionally* enables a holding on *psychically*—not so much a holding on to the other but rather a holding on to *self* as an autonomous, self-defining entity that is able to determine its own position in the world separate from others: a sovereign and powerful autonomous legal subject. Whilst the injunction to 'let go' is presented as a guard against the dark side—as Yoda explains, 'the fear of loss is a path to the dark side'[85]—it is also that which provides the Jedi with *greater power*.[86] It is here that the distinction between the Jedi and Sith starts to break down, for, despite being presented as a letting go and loss of ego, the Jedi's exhortation to 'let go' is a *holding* on to the ego and one's own ends and desires. Whilst the Jedi supposedly teach compassion and love for all, acknowledging the symbiotic relationship between all living things, at the same time this does not involve a universal respect for all beings as unique, free and autonomous. Rather, what we see is the presentation of a particular elitism that manipulates, uses and disregards the Other. Obi-Wan, Luke, Rey and, most significantly, Qui-Gon Jinn all make use of the Jedi mind control tricks, noting the Force's ability to 'have a strong influence on the weak-minded'. Such manipulation focuses *not* on a 'becoming one' with the Force, but rather on the developing of one's ability to use it to manipulate both things and others. The process of 'letting go' is a way of gaining *increased control*, though this amplification is presented with a façade of peace, compassion and non-intervention.

[85] Yoda goes on to note that 'attachment leads to jealously: the shadow of greed that is'. Lucas is also quoted as saying that an unhealthy form of attachment 'makes you greedy. And when you're greedy, you are on the path to the dark side, because you fear you're going to lose things, that you're not going to have the power you need.' Corliss and Cagle, 'Dark Victory', 29 April 2002. See McDowell, *Gospel According to Star Wars*, p. 63.

[86] McDowell argues that even the notion of 'becoming one with the Force' is not about a disembodying but rather a recognition of our symbiotic relation with the world. McDowell, *Gospel According to Star Wars*, pp. 132–3. However, in a cut scene which appears in the script of *Revenge of the Sith*, there is an interesting discussion between Yoda and Qui-Gon as a Force ghost (which provides an explanation for how Yoda, and then later Obi-Wan, learn how to become Force ghosts). What is significant in this is that Qui-Gon indicates that there is a way in which Yoda can merge with the Force at will and 'Your physical self will fade away, but you will still retain your consciousness.' Qui-Gon points out that this is the aim of the Sith, who attempt to achieve it through compassion, not greed. The aim is to 'learn to let go of everything. No attachment, no thought of self. No physical self.' The significance of this complete 'letting go', however, is that it is *still* described in terms of power. When Qui-Gon says 'You will become more powerful than any Sith,' Yoda notes that: 'to become one with the Force, and influence still have . . . A power greater than all, it is.'

This is most clearly seen in *The Phantom Menace*, when Qui-Gon frees the young Anakin Skywalker and yet will not free Anakin's mother, Shmi (Pernilla August), because their owner (the junk dealer, Watto, voiced by Andy Secombe) 'would not have it'. At one level this seems very noble and non-interventionist: Qui-Gon will adhere to the forms of law applicable on Tatooine, where slavery is allowed (despite having been outlawed by the Senate), to the formality of the freedom to contract (focusing on the terms of the arrangement) and the ability of Watto to determine what to do with his own 'property'. What it *does not* acknowledge, however, is that when betting on which slave to free, Qui-Gon uses the Force to fix the dice roll so that it will turn up on Anakin. Qui-Gon is actually *very* willing to intervene and manipulate circumstances when it suits his purposes, while using the non-interventionist stance as a reason *not* to intervene when it does not (even if that means taking Anakin from his mother and allowing her enslavement to continue when he could have done something about it).

Thus, the focus on 'letting go' is not a dissolving of the self or ego in a pure love or compassion for others. In fact, it is the very holding on to the ego itself—of the individual's ability to take whatever actions they believe appropriate in order to achieve their own ends in disregard for their actual effect on others. This process is seen with greater amplification in *Attack of the Clones* and *Revenge of the Sith* with Anakin's turn to the dark side. Rather than Anakin's turn to the dark side being a result of his inability to let go,[87] it is in fact Anakin's holding on to himself rather than to others that is the problem. Obi-Wan and Yoda's advice to 'let go of everything that you fear to lose', which Anakin attempts to do, promotes an indifference to the plight of the individual involved, rather subordinating such loss and suffering to the will of the Force.[88] It is significant that Obi-Wan and Yoda give the *same* advice to Luke in *The Empire Strikes Back*, where they suggest that he should be willing to sacrifice his friends in order to finish his training rather than running off to help them—advice which Luke ignores. Luke's impatience and desire to help his friends here is presented as a *failure* by Lucas, and therefore is mapped *also* to Anakin's inability to 'let go' of his loved ones.

[87] Corliss and Cagle, 'Dark Victory', 29 April 2002.
[88] Part of Anakin's problem is in fact the attempt to 'let go' and to live the life of a Jedi, when he has fallen in love with Amidala. Instead of 'letting go of all he fears to lose', he should rather have 'held on', allowing his love for Amidala to recoordinate his life completely —leaving the Jedi order to become a fighter pilot, openly loving and having a family with Amidala. It is the very attempt to 'let go' and to fulfil his calling as a Jedi that results in his inability to deal with what Alain Badiou calls the 'event' of love, which I will discuss further in Chapters 5 and 6.

What such advice focuses on, however, is in fact the self or the ego. The release from attachment, the 'letting go', encourages Anakin to ignore those around him in order to increase his focus on himself and his own power (and the reason for advising Luke not to leave his training early is *also* a concern about him not yet being strong or powerful enough to confront Darth Vader). This, in effect, sets Anakin up to be seduced by Chancellor Palpatine/Darth Sidious (Ian McDiarmid) and his offer of the power to save his wife from death. Anakin's goal is not really to save Amidala for her sake, but for his own. Thus, the internal focus of the Jedi, dismissing the worth of the materiality of others' existence, aligns directly with the seeking of power of the Sith. The result is that this form and focus on 'letting go' creates the conditions whereby the mind becomes all-consuming and all-powerful, seeking to control not just machines but the entirety of organic life around this machinic order—in short, the galaxy itself! The logic of this form of letting go makes the autonomous subject the absolute sovereign of the solar system, controlling and manipulating everything to its own ends.[89] The inescapable conclusion, here, is that the Jedi's letting go is the foundation of the Emperor's rule and the source of his power. The path by which the transmogrification—from good Jedi to bad Sith—takes place involves a process which does not so much control as disregard the Other, so that this paradox comes clearly into view: the ultimate control comes through a process of *not* intervening in, or engaging with, the material.

This theme of 'letting go' then reappears at a different level in Disney's trilogy. There, the 'awakening' in the Force is with the rise of Rey—who, throughout the first film, is seeking to get back to her 'home' on Jakku because she believes her family will return to find her there. In this sense, she appears to be holding on to her desire for family. For the fans, the question of Rey's parentage was one of the most anticipated 'reveals' supposed to come in *The Last Jedi*. However, it is presented in the context of Rey's own holding on to the hope of family. After Kylo/Ben and Rey have killed Supreme Commander Snoke (Andy Serkis) and his Elite Praetorian Guard, there comes a point of momentous decision—whereas Rey wants to save the Resistance, Kylo says: 'It's time to let old things die. Snoke, Skywalker. The Sith, the Jedi, the Rebels. Let it all die.' When Rey hesitates, asking Ben not to do this ('please don't go this way'), his response is immediate and angered: 'No, no you're still holding on. *Let go!*' He perceives that her holding on is here about her parents, but he exhorts her to state the truth: 'they were nobody'. And not, according to Ben, just nobodies but 'filthy junk traders—who sold you off for drink money. The dead in a pauper's grave in a junker's desert.' Rey

---

[89] This theme is explored further in Chapter 6 below.

thus apparently has 'no place in this story'—'You come from nothing, you're nothing. But not to me. Join me . . . please.'

This scene makes clear the way in which the notion of 'letting go' is the foundation of a very particular type of subject: a subject who is autonomous, self-defining and explicitly *not* embedded in any pre-determined social and familial relationships; the self-defined individual who can therefore 'let go' of all prior concerns in order to pave the way into the future. What, therefore, becomes most radical in *The Last Jedi* is that it reveals this sense of subjectivity, whilst at the same time rejecting it: Rey's power in the Force *does not* come from her parentage or lineage (her parents were nothing), but rather is independent of this. At the same time, Rey *rejects* the call to complete autonomy in favour of her friendships with Finn, Poe, Leia and the others (similar to Luke's rejection of Obi-Wan and Yoda's advice in *The Empire Strikes Back*).[90] Of course, as I will discuss in Section VI below, this position is then completely altered by *The Rise of Skywalker*.

V. 'We'll use the Force . . . That's not how the Force works': Ideology in the Age of Empire

This emphasis on 'letting go' also dramatises the shift from the mythological to the ideological in *Star Wars*. The disengagement and distancing of oneself from the materiality of the world—this attitude of non-intervention, of 'letting go'—that the Force epitomises can be seen as characteristic of Capital in its current, globalised phase of development. Whereas 'classic capitalism' (that of nineteenth-century modernity) was about controlling productive forces, owning or seizing the means of production, surplus value and so forth, capitalism in its globalised state appears to be about 'letting go' of the productive forces—with the 'decentralisation and global dispersion of productive processes and cites'—to increase the control over production itself.[91] While capitalism was traditionally about the 'thing' and was an economy of objects, our global capitalist form has moved away from the focus on the 'thing' to regimes of immaterial labour, and an economy of signs and ciphers—that is, of information.[92] This 'knowledge economy', as Roberto Unger has argued,

---

[90] An important distinction between *The Last Jedi* and *The Empire Strikes Back*, however, is the way in which, for Luke, this decision ends up *returning* him to family: it is in going to fight Vader and attempting to save his friends that he then discovers that Vader is his father. In *The Last Jedi*, Rey is left completely *without* such familial connections (though in *Rise of Skywalker* she then takes up the Skywalker name, thus claiming familial connection).

[91] Hardt and Negri, *Empire*, p. 297.

[92] Ibid., pp. 284–9.

comprises a 'practice of production that is closest to the mind, and especially to the part of our mental life that we call the imagination'.[93] That is, there is a shift from the material to the mind, with the psyche 'letting go' of the physical. However, as is seen in *Star Wars*, the letting go of the physical does not mean a loss of control. Instead, control is displaced from the old economy, now apparently failing, of industry to the economy of information, of a symbolic universe of textuality, the semiosis of which is mapped digitally.[94] As the use of the Force demonstrates, the 'letting go' of physicality is in order to use the mind to reconceive and recreate the world.

Is it any wonder, then, that in the films made by Disney—a company which encompasses this turn to the knowledge economy with its focus on the imagination, describing certain of its creative workers as 'imagineers'—this theme is taken to its extreme. In Lucas's films the indicators that someone is 'strong in the Force' are subtle and minor, and have to be discerned: Luke does not know that he is 'strong in the Force' at all until Obi-Wan's encouragement; Qui-Gon recognises Anakin's strength because of his quick reflexes in pod-racing. An extensive regime of training is then required before these figures develop any significant capabilities with the Force. In Disney's version, however, the ability to use the Force with exceptional deftness comes *with no training whatsoever*, but is rather a magical ability for the mind to engage with and re-create the world. In *The Force Awakens*, Rey not only has Force visions but is able to fight with a light-sabre, defeating the supposedly strong and well-trained Kylo Ren. The creative capacities of Force use are taken to their most extreme in *The Rise of Skywalker*, where we discover that the Force is able to engage in *productive* capacities themselves, with Palpatine having created an entire fleet of the most advanced and destructive star destroyers *simply through the Force itself* (3D printers, eat your heart out!).[95]

The Force thus becomes an almost *explicit* representation of the shift to a knowledge economy or 'informational capitalism', with expanding productive powers driven by the mind and imagination. Given that this is the case, we should then read Lucas's 'global myth' (and its extension by Disney) directly alongside Hardt and Negri's infamous work, *Empire*, with its charting of the transformations of globalisation and the emergence of a new global

[93] Unger, *The Knowledge Economy*, p. 4.
[94] Hardt and Negri, *Empire*, pp. 290–2.
[95] One should also recognise the way in which it is implied that Palpatine also 'created' Snoke through processes of cloning, as a reflection of what Hardt and Negri refer to as an affirmative biopolitics of life. The 'Emperor', the figure of sovereignty, is *literally* able to manufacture life through the Force.

'Empire'.[96] Hardt and Negri's critical work, which itself is presented as a trilogy (*Empire, Multitude, Commonwealth*) with its own 'prequels' (Negri's *The Savage Anomaly* and *Insurgencies*, and Hardt and Negri's *Labor of Dionysus*) and 'sequels' (*Declaration, Assembly*), analyses and attempts to theorise not simply the transformations of capital with the knowledge economy and global dispersal of productive capacities, but also, even more explicitly, the reformulation of *sovereignty* that is arising with this new mode of global rule.[97] Running through their analysis is a critical consideration of the tensions between the revolutionary and democratic potentials and possibilities of 'the multitude' and the conservative, reactionary and at times totalitarian forms of global control deployed by Empire. This is supposedly *different* to prior forms of rule with a diminished or altered role for the nation-state, which now functions in a 'mixed constitution of global governance' with supra-national governing bodies, transnational corporations and non-governmental organisations (NGOs).[98] Such a transition is sustained and undergirded by the shift in modes of production, which have become more biopolitical, engaging in 'the production of social life itself, in which the economic, the political, and the cultural increasingly overlap and invest one another'.[99] Today's biopolitical production involves 'not only the production of material goods but also the production of communications, relationships, and forms of life'.[100] For Empire, this has meant a transformation in its 'rule' so that it now 'operates on all registers of the social order extending down to the depths of the social world'.[101] 'Empire' is focused on territory and population but

> also creates the very world it inhabits. It not only regulates human interactions but also seeks directly to rule over human nature. The object of this rule is social life in its entirety, and thus Empire presents the paradigmatic form of biopower.[102]

For Hardt and Negri, the internal tension or antagonism that runs through Empire—between sovereignty and democracy, transcendence and

---

[96] Hardt and Negri, *Empire*.

[97] Ibid.; Hardt and Negri, *Multitude*; Hardt and Negri, *Commonwealth*; Negri, *Power of Spinoza's Metaphysics and Politics*; Hardt and Negri, *Labor of Dionysus*; Negri, *Constituent Power and the Modern State*; Hardt and Negri, *Declaration*; Hardt and Negri, *Assembly*.

[98] Hardt and Negri, *Empire*, pp. 304–24; see also Hardt and Negri, 'Empire, Twenty Years On', p. 69.

[99] Hardt and Negri, *Empire*, p. xiii.

[100] Hardt and Negri, *Multitude*, p. xv; Hardt and Negri, *Empire*, pp. 22–41.

[101] Hardt and Negri, *Empire*, p. xv.

[102] Ibid.

immanence—is a resurfacing and reformulation of the tension that gave rise to modernity (or rather the 'two modernities' of Europe). As they set out, the historic precursor of modernity was not simply the secularising process that 'denied divine and transcendence authority over worldly affairs' but rather 'the affirmation of the powers of *this* world' and the discovery by medieval theologian Duns Scotus of 'the plane of immanence'.[103] This discovery is thus argued to have given birth to a 'revolutionary humanism', which resulted not only in a transformation of philosophy and science but also the unleashing of democratic desires in politics. At the same time, this humanism was then to be suppressed by a counter-revolution that sought to 'establish an overarching power' *against* these new forces of freedom. This is the 'second modernity', which posed 'a transcendent constituted power against an immanent constituent power, order against desire' and gave rise to the religious, social and civil wars that ended the Renaissance.[104] For Hardt and Negri, modernity itself is therefore '*defined by crisis*, a crisis that is born of the uninterrupted conflict between the immanent, constructive, creative forces and the transcendent power aimed at restoring order'.[105] In their compressed history, it is the emergence of modern sovereignty and the nation-state (and therefore, as will be demonstrated in the next section, modern law) that mediates and resolves this tension of transcendent constituted power over immanent constituent power. The nation-state provided a 'transcendent political apparatus' that did not simply have recourse to medieval forms of transcendence but imposed 'order on the multitude and prevent[ed] it from organising itself spontaneously and expressing its creativity autonomously'.[106] What is significant, therefore, in the context of globalisation and global Empire is the way in which these tensions between sovereignty and democracy, transcendence and immanence, have been reformulated, revealing 'the emergence of a new global power structure—and, indeed, a new form of sovereignty'.[107] Recent post-mortems of globalisations and calls for a return of national sovereignty do not involve a diminishment of this global command but rather are the very crises through which the 'emerging world order, like capital itself, functions ... and [that it] even feeds on'.[108] At the same time, the fundamental shifts in the nature of capital towards a biopolitical production of social life

---

[103] Ibid., p. 71. They attribute this discovery to Scotus's '*Omne ens habet alliquod esse proprium*'—every entity has a singular essence. I return to the medieval origins of modernity and Duns Scotus in Chapter 6.

[104] Ibid., p. 74.

[105] Ibid., p. 76.

[106] Ibid., p. 83.

[107] Hardt and Negri, 'Empire, Twenty Years On', p. 72.

[108] Ibid., p. 67.

also give rise to new possibilities of resistance—ones which would use the very weapons created by Empire and global capital against it.

It is here that the dualist presentations in *Star Wars* of the Republic, Rebellion and Resistance on one side and the Empire, First Order and Final Order on the other, seem to reproduce and work through the tensions between democracy and sovereignty, immanence and transcendence, to which Hardt and Negri refer. The productiveness of such a comparison arises in the ways in which the Empire's attempts at intergalactic domination are not so much all-encompassing but rather *fail*, with rebellions and resistances not only continuing to resurface but also being victorious. Part of Hardt and Negri's optimistic outlook in their work is the way in which the very foundations of Empire both provide the means for resistance and *prevent* the success of unilateral or totalising power—the symbiotic nature of sovereignty, which requires not only a 'ruler' but also the ruled, gives way, in our current conditions (or so their argument goes), to the *power* of the ruled, who are those that provide the means and knowledge central to today's biopolitical production. As a result, any attempt at a totalising form of power in the context of Empire will *fail* because of the decentralised and dispersed notion of power today, which is unable to submit to the sovereignty of the One. This is what enables the 'multitude' to challenge and contest those forces that would otherwise oppress and control them. Princess Leia Organa (Carrie Fisher) seems to share such a belief in the *limits* of centralising power in the age of (the Galactic) Empire when she retorts to Grand Moff Tarkin (Peter Cushing) in *A New Hope*: 'The more you tighten your grip, Tarkin, the more star systems will slip through your fingers.' Tarkin's direct response would seem to undermine this claim, by using the tremendous power of the original Death Star to destroy the planet Alderaan. Yet, as we know, the conclusion of the film—particularly now read in the context of the additional backstory provided by *Rogue One: A Star Wars Story*—emphasises the power of resistance: a small band of rebels was able to use the *design* of the technology itself to take down the Death Star. The very 'material' grounds of the Empire's totalising powers provide the tools of resistance.

When the first of the Disney films, *The Force Awakens*, *repeats* the narrative of *A New Hope*, which involves a 'new', even more powerful, death star, 'Star Killer Base', we see a focus not just on a rebellion *separate from* the First Order, but also on actions taken by someone who was *within* the First Order: Finn. After oscillating throughout the film between assisting the Resistance and a self-interested desire to *escape* the First Order, along with a desire to save his new friend, Rey, Finn argues that, because of his 'inside information', he is the one who can pull off the shutting down of the Base's defence mechanisms and enable the Resistance's attack. Whilst Finn's claims are a 'bluff', his role in the First Order apparently being sanitation, and his 'suggestion' to Han Solo about how they can disable the defence shields is simply to 'use the Force', the significance here is the way in which, in contrast to the original trilogy, the resistance of the First Order comes from those *within* it. This theme operates throughout the Disney films: in *Rogue One* we discover that Galen Erso (Mads Mikkelsen) has built a design flaw into the original Death Star to enable its destruction; in *The Rise of Skywalker*, it is revealed that there are numerous others in addition to Finn who have resisted the First Order, including Jannah (Naomi Ackie) and her crew; and in *The Last Jedi*, Finn again trades on his knowledge of a Star Destroyer as being one who 'mopped' it.[109] Such an emphasis in these narratives would seem to undergird the comparison with Hardt and Negri's own global myth in terms of the multitude's ability to organise and resist forms of global Empire by using the imperialism, technologies and aesthetics of traditional forms of transcendent sovereignty (with J. J. Abrams, particularly in *The Force Awakens*, taking the Nazi aesthetics of the First Order even further than Lucas's allusions in the original trilogy).[110] Such would seem to be the argument from these films in the contemporary context of a renewed nationalism, the supposed demise of globalisation and calls for a return of the nation-state.

This approach to resistance aligns with Hardt and Negri's argument that the only way of addressing our contexts of global Empire are *immanent ones*— that we must avoid any desire to 'escape' into forms of transcendence, whether religious or political.[111] And it is here that the most significant connection between *Star Wars* and *Empire* appears. The tension that runs through all the battles between Empire and Rebellion, First Order and Resistance, New Imperialisms and Old Republics is undergirded by the creative capacities of the Force as a religion of *immanence*, which, whilst it can and is deployed by the figures of totalitarian sovereignty, *also* provides the productive means of resistance for the revolutionary democratic forces. The Force as an immanent religion, one which is co-constituted and produced *through* the multitude of all created life, presents a form of the Spinozist monism, which underlies Hardt and Negri's paean of 'the multitude'.[112] Such would almost seem to

---

[109] *Solo* even projects this type of complicity and resistance *back* into the history of Han Solo, where it is discovered that he served time in the imperial army of the Empire, before engaging in actions that assist in part of the original formation of the Rebellion.

[110] Skweres, 'Star Wars as an Aesthetic Melting Pot'; Simon, 'Interpellation by the Force'.

[111] See Hardt and Negri, *Commonwealth*, pp. vii, 3–8.

[112] Spinoza features as a prominent source of inspiration and foundation for Hardt and Negri's work and their articulation of the democratic nature of the multitude. See, for particular examples, Hardt and Negri, *Empire*, pp. 77–8, 185–6, 344; Hardt and Negri, *Multitude*, pp. 194, 311, 328–31; Hardt and Negri, *Commonwealth*, pp. 43, 53–5, 189–99.

be directly alluded to in *Multitude*, where Hardt and Negri even include a subsection on the approaches required by 'the multitude', entitled 'May the Force Be with You'.[113] All of this would seem to present an inverse trajectory to Carl Schmitt's political theology—the Force is a theological imagining of a secularised theory of the state, which at the same time presents an *identical* systematic structure between the two.[114]

This emphasis on the immanent nature of the religion of the Force thus takes up, but goes beyond, Žižek's arguments, noted above, around its parallels with Western Buddhism as the ideological supplement of global capitalism. The wisdom that focuses on detaching, uncoupling and 'inner peace' (the sense of mindfulness that Qui-Gon teaches to Obi-Wan, the calm and passiveness that Yoda demands of Luke, or the recognition of the oneness with nature that Luke reveals to Rey) would seem to provide a 'remedy against the stress of capitalism's dynamics'—the incredible pace of consumerist life, technological development and so on—by presenting life as a mere 'theatre of shadows with no substantial existence'.[115] *Star Wars* takes this further by presenting the Force not just as a pantheism, an underlying reality behind the deceptiveness of appearance, but as an immanence that is co-created and constituted *by* life itself. The Force is not simply ideological in the way that Max Weber describes the 'protestant work ethic' as the ideological supplement of classic capitalism.[116] As Hardt and Negri note, it is 'only the productive power of the multitude' that 'demonstrates the existence of God and the presence of divinity on earth'.[117] The Force is a representation not simply of a detachment allowing global capital to function, but of a constituent power in which we participate. In *Star Wars* the evidence of the Force is *explicitly* in terms of its productivity—its capacity to allow for the manipulation and control of the world around you. The immanence and co-creativeness of the

---

[113] The allusions here go both ways, not only from 'culture to theory' (Hardt and Negri's direct allusion here could also be compared to the indirect one in *Commonwealth*, where they seemed to show restraint in *not* titling the chapter 'Empire Returns' as 'The Empire Strikes Back') but also from 'theory to culture', with a number of reviewers and commentators making explicit or implicit connections: Žižek, 'Revenge of Global Finance', 21 May 2005, p. 169; Rofel, 'Modernity's Masculine Fantasies', pp. 188–90; Turchetto, 'On Hardt and Negri'; Kapferer, 'Foundation and Empire'.

[114] Schmitt, *Political Theology*, p. 36.

[115] Žižek, 'Revenge of Global Finance', 21 May 2005. See also Žižek, *Parallax View*, pp. 383–4.

[116] Weber, *Protestant Ethic*.

[117] Hardt and Negri, *Empire*, pp. 164–5.

Force, then, could be understood in terms of the Spinozism that underlies Hardt and Negri's argument that '[p]ower is not something that lords over us but something that we make'.[118]

At the same time, the claim to a pure immanence that the Force represents would seem problematic, given that it *also* founds the transcendence of the Empire. This means that we cannot read, in *Star Wars*, the Empire as separate from the Republic, the Sith as separate from the Jedi, the light side of the force as separate from the dark. Such would seem to involve an ambivalence of the Force and an intertwining of the apparent differences between its 'two sides'—an ambivalence that *also* runs through Hardt and Negri's consideration of power that underlies both Empire and the multitude. How is such a tension now to be resolved? Hardt and Negri seek recourse in an immanent constituent power positioned *against* traditional forms of sovereignty which are the subject of a constituted power.[119] Yet, at the same time, there is a call for *new forms* of institutions to be thought and created so as to prevent the multitude's rule as being simply anarchy.[120] These forms of institution require a new form of global law, one that, like this transformed sovereignty, 'has no actual and localisable terrain or centre'.[121] The result is that this new law or juridical right that would undergird and support these new institutions of constituent power would appear, like the Force itself, to be 'everywhere' and yet 'nowhere' in particular.[122] Such an articulation, as we will see in the next section, is itself something that modern law *already* encompasses in the way in which it functions in the irresolution between determination and responsiveness, transcendence and immanence. It is here, therefore, that we see the way in which the Force is not simply a religion or even an ideological supplement for global capitalism, but rather a representation of constituent power itself. The functioning of the Force is *not* so much religious or theological but rather theologico-political, pointing to a *particular* theological articulation of (post-)modern sovereignty and law.

---

[118] Ibid., p. 165. For an 'immanent' critical discussion of the Spinozist aspects of *Empire*, see Fitzpatrick, 'Immanence of *Empire*'.

[119] See the call for alternatives to Empire in Hardt and Negri, *Empire*, pp. 47–53; on the call to liberate humanity from 'every transcendent power' see also p. 165, as well as pp. xv, 74, 102–3.

[120] Ibid., pp. 161–5; Hardt and Negri, *Multitude*, pp. 348–55.

[121] Hardt and Negri, *Empire*, p. 384.

[122] As Fitzpatrick notes, 'Law cannot be purely fixed and pre-existent if it is to change and to adapt to society, as it is so often said that it must. Its determinations cannot be entirely specific, clear and conclusive if it has integrally or at the same time to exceed all determination, to assume a quality of "everywhereness".' Fitzpatrick, *Modernism*, p. 71, citing Carty, 'English Constitutional Law', p. 196.

VI. 'It surrounds us, it penetrates us, it binds the galaxy together': The Immanent Legality of *Star Wars*

The analysis so far has been leading to a central claim in relation to *Star Wars*: that the Force is a representation of modern law. To sustain such a claim we need to return and examine a different version of the narrative that Hardt and Negri provide of the crisis of modernity, focusing now in particular on the law. Modern law, as noted in Section III, is based on a supposed *separation* of law from religion. This separation, as Fitzpatrick has pointed out, is not so much because of the *differences* between religion and modern law, but rather because of their *similarities*.[123] Modern law has been seen to 'take over' the place of religion both in terms of asserting jurisdictional superiority and in the sense of law operating as a 'civil religion' that ensures social order.[124] At the same time, with the Enlightenment and modernity's rejection of transcendence, the law itself takes on the deific qualities previously reserved for God.[125] In doing so, however, it can no longer secure itself in relation to that transcendence which has been rejected. It is here that, Fitzpatrick argues, modern law takes on a mythic function, mediating its irresolutions:

> Law is autonomous yet socially contingent. It is identified with stability and order yet it changes and is historically responsive. Law is a sovereign imperative yet the expression of a popular spirit. Its quasi-religious transcendence stands in opposition to its mundane temporality. It incorporates the ideal yet it is a mode of present existence.[126]

Prior to the Enlightenment, 'God was considered the supreme lawgiver' and the nature and structure of law, whether it was divine law, natural law or positive human laws, both operated '*in the same sense*' and were dominated by divine law.[127] Though there were diverse theological accountings, 'God remained the necessary and unavoidable source of law's being'[128]—both the laws of nature 'that preserved the stars from wrong' and the human laws

---

[123] Fitzpatrick, 'Secular Theology and Modernity of Law', pp. 176–8.
[124] Fitzpatrick works through a number of the key points of 'rupture' with the past, most notably the French Revolution, which in itself proclaims a 'new religion' of the law and justice. The more modest version of this is Rousseau's determination of the need for a civil religion. See ibid., pp. 165–7, 178–81.
[125] Ibid., pp. 178–80; Fitzpatrick, *Mythology*, pp. 51–63.
[126] Fitzpatrick, *Mythology*, p. x.
[127] Althusser, *Politics and History*, pp. 31–2, cited by Fitzpatrick, *Mythology*, p. 52.
[128] Fitzpatrick, *Mythology*, p. 51.

encompassing 'the rule of duty'.[129] A central precursor to the modern turn from transcendence to immanence arose in the scholastic debates over the nature of God's creative power and intervention in the world. Whilst it was recognised that God had created the world and set in motion its underlying order, the question arose as to what was to prevent him from deciding to make miraculous changes to the world at any point in time, thus disrupting the pre-ordained order. The solution to this dilemma was presented as God's 'self-binding' of his omnipotence. God is all-powerful at the level of his absolute power (*potentia absoluta*), but he self-binds himself in terms of his ordained power (*potentia ordinata*), thus restraining his interference with the order he has pre-ordained.

In Fitzpatrick's outline of law following modernity's rejection of transcendence, he compresses the implications of these debates into the figures of two 'competing Occidental deities': the first is 'the origin and ruler of the cosmos', who can 'alter it at will' and whose laws are to be understood via revelation; the second is a deity 'captured by "his" own creation', who 'is allowed to act only in accordance with the divine order' and whose primary mode of knowledge is acquired through reason.[130] The latter is of first significance, for with the rejection of transcendence, 'order becomes the first law of nature'.[131] When God is the source of law (divine, natural or posited), law is still understood as a 'commandment' needing a 'will to order and wills to obey'.[132] The turn to 'nature', however, involved not so much a focus on *orders* but simply order itself. This gave rise to the objective natural law tradition, which began a secularising trajectory that, following Hugo Grotius, conceived the existence and operation of nature and nature's law without reference to God.[133] The focus was on a law that is determined with recourse to reason, itself prefigured in both Greek and Roman thought.[134]

As Fitzpatrick notes, *this* 'story of law's domestication of deity' is relatively short—not least because the objective natural law tradition proved problematic for determining the content of practical legalities. Instead, what has dominated Western legal thought, from Thomas Hobbes to John Austin, is

---

[129] Ibid., p. 53, citing Willey, *Eighteenth Century Background*, p. 14.

[130] Fitzpatrick, *Mythology*, p. 54.

[131] Ibid., p. 51.

[132] Ibid., p. 52.

[133] Grotius, *De Jure Belli ac Pacis*. Prolegomena, para 11 referred to in Freeman, *Lloyd's Introduction to Jurisprudence*, p. 105; Fitzpatrick, *Mythology*, p. 53.

[134] For example, Cicero spoke of a 'law of reason' that is 'eternal and unchangeable'. Cicero, *Republic*, p. 22, quoted by Lovell, 'Great Disturbance in the Force', p. 230.

the 'tradition of law as command, a tradition which persisted and was not wholly subordinated to objective order'.[135] As such, 'the predominant story of modern law, one told now in the perspective of the nation-state, attributes precedence to the god of will and revelation'.[136] We can see here a point of intersection with the story told by Hardt and Negri, for it is the development of the modern nation-state that becomes the point of resolution, not simply of the tension of transcendent sovereignty and immanent democracy, but its ability to mediate the two. Law is central to this story. With the rise of the nation-state, '[n]atural and divine law become subordinate to the self-sufficient determination of positive law—the law posited by the will of the sovereign', whether royal or popular.[137] This is a law that no longer has recourse to a transcendent origin in the divine, but rather has become 'self-grounding'.[138] Law is no longer an order but rather derives 'its force and origin purely from its intrinsic being'[139]—it is autonomous, self-sustaining and 'independent of any exterior reality'.[140]

The focus on law as ineffable command and will does not mean that the god of cosmic order is not *also* captured within law. It appears now, rather, in the need for 'a stable, independent legal order' guaranteed by an independent 'rule of law' and in 'the mythic equation of Occidental law with order'.[141] We can see the securing of this 'stable and independent "rule of law"' with those celebrated traces of modern law: legal restraints upon the state and limitations upon constitutional changes; and internal restraints built into law in terms of requirements of *generality* and equality before the law.[142] Law came to be both what constituted the nation-state but also that upon which the state is dependent. This stability and order would appear to be in crisis today in terms of both the challenges that globalisation poses to the pre-eminence of the nation-state and the threats to the rule of law that have proliferated. At the same time, Hardt and Negri argue that these

---

[135] Fitzpatrick, *Mythology*, p. 54.
[136] Ibid.
[137] Ibid.
[138] Ibid.
[139] Ibid., p. 55.
[140] Ibid., p. 56.
[141] Ibid., p. 58. To use Fitzpatrick's example, Hans Kelsen declares that 'the law is an order, and therefore all legal problems must be set and solved as order problems'. Kelsen, *Pure Theory of Law*, p. 192.
[142] Fitzpatrick, *Mythology*, p. 58.

'crises' themselves are part of what reveals the new formation of sovereignty that they refer to as Empire.[143]

With its struggles for freedom and concerns over 'restoring peace and justice to the galaxy', *Star Wars* presents its own versions of the crisis of the rule of law. What is significant, however, is the way in which the *immanence* of the Force is not simply a 'modern' positioning of religion in relation to law, as discussed in Section III, but rather a representation of the deific qualities of modern law that *also* function in an immanent fashion. In *Star Wars* this immanence is presented in terms of harmony and symbiosis, a focus on nomological alignment, a submission to 'peace and order' and a desire for *balance*. As I have noted, the Force does not have so much a transcendent 'will'—it having 'let go' of the external divinity—but rather a focus on the balance or order of the universe. The Force could therefore be compared to the secularising movement within natural law, the divinity caught within its own nature, subordinated to the immanence of the natural order which it sustains (that moment of natural law that relinquishes its dependence on God in its focus on reason and order). Such could be gleaned from the way the Force is presented as a regulator of destiny (Obi-Wan tells Luke he 'cannot escape his destiny', Darth Vader and Palpatine also refer to Luke 'fulfilling' his destiny, 'repeating' the terms which Palpatine uses with Anakin in the prequel trilogy, and Snoke exhorts Kylo Ren to fulfil his destiny), the need for internal harmony or 'balance' *within* the Force (particularly with the prophecy of the 'chosen one', destined to 'bring balance to the Force'), as well as the Jedi's role in securing 'peace and justice' in the galaxy. Such a nomological focus on the alignment of destiny and the need for balance reflects this form of natural law's desire for order.

This focus on order would, therefore, seem to be in contrast to modern law's emphasis on will and command. However, as Fitzpatrick notes, modern law involves an irresolution between certainty, fixity and autonomy on the one hand, and responsiveness, change and dependence on the other.[144]

---

[143] However, as Fitzpatrick and others have pointed out, the forms of global institutions and global law that Hardt and Negri seem to allude to are themselves found in the vision of the nation-state and national law. From this perspective, international law or global law is simply a turning outwards or an 'extraversion' of national law—which both historical and present colonialism and imperialism evidence. See Fitzpatrick, *Modernism*, pp. 146–218; Fitzpatrick and Joyce, 'Normality of the Exception in Democracy's Empire'; and on Hardt and Negri in particular, Buchanan and Pahuja, 'Legal Imperialism'.

[144] A point made throughout his work, but see, for example: Fitzpatrick, *Modernism*, pp. 5–6; Fitzpatrick, *Mythology*, p. x.

Whilst pre-modern legality could have recourse to transcendence as a means of mediating and resolving this irresolution, modern law, we are told, has no such recourse. By contrast, the means of resolution is by a 'negative mediator', a savagery and savage violence, to which modern law and law's order are set in contrast.[145] It is in this specific sense that the Force presents us with a view not of natural law but modern legality. Despite the demand for balance, what is central to the Force is not so much internal harmony, but a particular *end*, which it shares with modern law: order. We can see this at two levels, which are reflected in the Force: first, modern law has a foundational relationship with violence in both founding and defending 'civilisation', society or the social order; second, modern law, and the rule of law in particular, have been separated from any intrinsic connection with or insight into justice, becoming instrumentalised and justified by the *ends* which they serve—law is not order but the means for *establishing* order.

Law and violence: 'an elegant weapon, of a more civilised age'

I will start with modern law's role in both instituting and defending 'civilisation' or the social order. In *Modernism and the Grounds of Law*, Fitzpatrick explicates the irresolutions and tensions of modern law via an examination of Freud's myth of the primal parricide—a modern myth of origin which demonstrates the shift from the 'primal horde', dominated by the rule of the father, to the need and development of society through the introduction of the law.[146] This depiction of the transition from primal horde to society is representative of the movement from a 'savage pre-creation' to a civilised society. However, the very focus of this move is on the shift *from* savagery—that is civilisation is what is *not* savage, what is *not* the 'primitive other' from which society has 'developed'.[147] As a 'modern myth' (and for Freud as our 'modern mythmaker') this is significant. Whilst modern law has taken up the deific qualities of pre-modern law, its need to be self-grounding without reference to any form of transcendent mediation means that it cannot define its contents positively. Rather, modern law becomes defined in *negation*—it is that aspect of 'civilisation' that distinguishes us 'moderns' from a primitive or savage 'other' who is 'without' law, or at least law as we know it. Civilisation is thus that which has progressed *from* a savage alterity.[148]

[145] Fitzpatrick, *Modernism*, pp. 19–20, 28–9; see also Fitzpatrick, *Mythology*, pp. 72–87.
[146] Fitzpatrick, *Modernism*, p. 21. For an analysis of the 'evil Father' in relation to *Star Wars* in particular, see Bainbridge, 'Portrayal of the Evil Father in Popular Culture'.
[147] Fitzpatrick, *Modernism*, pp. 72–86.
[148] Ibid., pp. 21–5.

At the same time, civilisation is constantly under threat—disorder seeking to disrupt order. What Fitzpatrick points to in Freud's myth is that this precariousness of civilisation is not so much the attack of a potential savage other from outside, but rather the internal savagery that persists within civilisation itself—the individual is split between a persistent, recalcitrant savagery and the demands of an imperious civilisation.[149] Civilisation is something which is opposed to, or defined in negation of, a 'savage other', but at the same time is always at risk of falling back into such savagery.[150] The result of this inherent savagery within society creates the very need for law and the justification for the law's use of violence to discipline its subjects and prevent a reversion to the state of savagery. Law is both that which must control savagery, but which also draws upon savagery. 'It is precisely as a societal container of savage violence that law comes to be set against savagery and identified civilisation.'[151] For Freud, the first requisite of civilisation is legality: law must constantly be *'made* applicable, not because of its irresolution but as a defence against savagery's constant challenge to civilisation—a savagery which persists in society and the individual alike'.[152] Whilst 'savagery may provoke a civilizing law into being, it is law which delineates that savagery by separating civilization from it'.[153]

To return to *Star Wars*, from the very beginning the Force itself is associated with civilisation, in the same way that modern law is part of the civilising element, distinguishing the modern from that which is imagined to go before it.[154] The first encounter between Luke and Obi-Wan, in *A New Hope*, is *also* the first reference or encounter with the Force. When giving Luke his father's light-sabre, Obi-Wan says:

> This is the weapon of a Jedi Knight. Not as clumsy or random as a blaster. An elegant weapon, of a more civilised age. For over a thousand generations the Jedi Knights were the guardians of peace and justice of the old Republic. Before the dark times. Before the Empire.

What is of note here is not just the hearkening back to the period of the Old Republic, but the fact that the reference to 'a more civilised age' is made in connection with the handing on of a weapon. Whilst the Jedi are described as 'guardians of peace and justice', the associating of a weapon of violence with an age of civilisation reinforces the connection between a law that institutes

---

[149] Ibid., pp. 21, 26.
[150] Ibid., pp. 16, 61; Fitzpatrick, *Mythology*, pp. 63–86.
[151] Fitzpatrick, *Modernism*, p. 36. referring to; Freud, 'Why War?', p. 351.
[152] Fitzpatrick, *Modernism*, p. 36.
[153] Ibid.
[154] Fitzpatrick, *Mythology*, p. 108.

peace and the need for violence to ensure that peace. The vision of the Old Republic in the original trilogy is associated with civilisation, peace, order and justice (in contrast to the 'present times', dominated by the rule and tyranny of the Empire). Violence and disorder are opposed to the Force in the same way that civilisation is opposed to violence and disorder to the law. In *The Empire Strikes Back,* Yoda presents the role of the Jedi in a similar fashion: '[a] Jedi uses the Force for knowledge and defence, never for attack.'[155] The Jedi are associated with the disengagement, passiveness and 'letting go' discussed in Section IV, but as defenders of 'peace and justice' need to engage in violence to ensure the order of the Force and the Republic. In a similar fashion, the law is that which brings order and controls violence *through* violence. The only justified violence is that which preserves the order of law. What the connection of civilisation to the Jedi's weapon references is the way the law must be violent (that is, legitimised violence that is used to restore order) and yet at the same time 'intrinsically associated with non-violence'.[156]

In the prequel films, however, the Old Republic, that supposed bastion of civilisation, is forever under attack. The 'civilised times' that Obi-Wan refers to are in fact full of trade disputes, political manipulations, assassinations, divisions in the Senate and a war in which Obi-Wan played a central role. The 'civilisation' of the Republic, which Obi-Wan praises, is set precariously *against* 'a savage violence [that] ever seeks to destroy it from without'.[157] Yet, this external threat is really only an extraversion of that savagery which cannot be eliminated from *inside* civilisation. It is this which results in civilisation's precarious state—individuals and society are always at risk of reverting to savagery and the savage state of nature.[158] Such is a central theme of *Star Wars*, with the constant internal struggle between the 'good' and the 'dark side' of the Force. As Yoda instructs Luke, anger, fear and aggression are part of the dark side and should be avoided. In the prequels, Yoda also cautions about the dark side and the fear and jealousy which may lead one there. In the sequel trilogy, Luke's concern in training Rey is that her strength in the Force will risk her turning to the dark side as Ben Solo did in becoming Kylo Ren. The risk of violence and savagery that the law must defend against is not external to either society or the individual but is internal to it—and requires protection by the violence of the law itself.

---

[155] An instruction that is *not* emphasised in the prequel films—a point that can also be seen in the change of style of sword fighting used between the two. See Robinson, 'Far East of Star Wars'.

[156] Fitzpatrick, *Modernism*, p. 77.

[157] Ibid.

[158] Ibid., p. 29.

Law and order: restoring 'balance' to the Force

What this internal tension points to is that the good and dark sides are not separate entities but two sides of the *same* entity: the Force. While stark contrasts are presented (good/evil, light/dark, compassion/anger, peace/aggression), what the Jedi seem to miss is the point that Emperor Palpatine makes to Anakin in *Revenge of the Sith*: 'the Sith and the Jedi are similar in almost every way' because they are part of, and draw their power from, one and the same Force. Here the nature of the Force and its association with balance becomes crucial. When Anakin becomes Darth Vader, Obi-Wan is dismayed because, as the prophesied 'chosen one', he was 'supposed to bring balance to the Force, not leave it in ruins'. Upon this understanding, the rise of the Sith caused a great disturbance or disruption in the Force, and eliminating them is what is needed to restore balance. As such, Vader's saving of Luke and 'killing' of Palpatine, at the conclusion of *Return of the Jedi*, could be viewed as a final fulfilment of the prophecy and a restoring of balance to the Force. This approach to the nature of the Force views the differences between the Jedi and the Sith as two different ways of 'living with' the Force—essentially, a 'right' way that comprises the Jedi's ethical duty and being 'mindful of the Living Force', and a 'wrong' way, which is the Sith's selfish ambition for power.[159] Despite the consistent references to Good and Evil, the Force *does not* present a form of Manichaean dualism, as discussed in Chapter 1—there is not a 'good force' and a 'dark force', but rather the Force is only one.

However, whilst *Star Wars* does not present a Manichaean view of Good and Evil, neither does it represent, as McDowell argues, an Augustinian world-view with Evil or the 'dark side' being only a privation, disruption or distortion of the otherwise 'good' nature of the Force.[160] Rather, the Force is

---

[159] McDowell, *Gospel According to Star Wars*, pp. 26–30. Such an approach rightly contrasts with those who take at one level the 'flat' articulations of 'Good and Evil' in *Star Wars* as meaning it is a Manichaean world: see, for example, Rowlands, *Philosopher at the End of the Universe*, pp. 209–32; see also Brown, '*Star Wars* and the Problem of Evil'; Eberl, 'Theodicy of the Force'.

[160] McDowell argues that the series refer to 'the Force' and then 'the dark side' of the Force, indicating that the 'dark side' is a misuse or abuse of an otherwise 'good' entity. One of his criticisms of *The Force Awakens* is the much broader use of good and evil, dark side and light side, to describe the Force. However, such a language *is* used at times in Lucas's films, most notably in *Return of the Jedi*, when Luke is telling Leia that there is still good in Vader: 'there is good in him. I've felt it. He won't turn me over to the Emperor. I can save him. I can turn him back to the good side. I have to try.' Earlier, Luke also notes to Obi-Wan's Force ghost that 'there is still good in him', to which Obi-Wan responds: 'He is more machine now than man. Twisted and evil.'

presented as encompassing not so much an underlying good, but a monism or monistic *tension* or balance *between* Good and Evil.[161] This can be seen both in the way that those who are 'of the dark side' do not have any inhibitions that a misuse of the Force would presume (they are as powerful as the Jedi) and the way in which there are consistent references to an interdependence between Good and Evil, dark and light, with one invoking and calling forth the other (rather than their complete elimination). The series itself oscillates between these two understandings of the balance of the Force (seeing Evil as a disruption of the Good versus seeing Good and Evil in an intertwined tension). Both views can be seen in Luke's training of Rey in *The Last Jedi*. There he notes that, before Ben Solo became Kylo Ren, there *had* been balance in the Force, with the rising of the First Order and Ben's turn to the dark side disrupting this balance.[162] This view is then contradicted in the first lesson he provides to Rey. When Rey reaches out with her feelings, she 'sees' 'the island. Life, death and decay, that feeds new life. Warmth, cold, peace, violence.' When Luke asks what is *between* it all, Rey responds: 'Balance, energy, a Force'. However, when Rey then senses a 'dark place' beneath the island they are on, Luke explains this as reflective of the balance of the Force which incorporates *both* 'powerful light' *and* 'powerful darkness'.[163]

If we read the prophecy of the 'chosen one' from the understanding of the Force as involving a tension between Good and Evil, of encompassing *both* 'good' and 'evil', then we find that the prophecy itself *is* fulfilled at the end of *Revenge of the Sith*. To 'balance' the Force after a period of one thousand years of 'peace and justice' in the 'civilised' Republic *requires* the transition to the Evil Empire. Anakin fulfils the prophecy not by destroying the Sith, but *by becoming one*. The fact that this transition (of Jedi to Sith, Good Republic to Evil Empire) occurs in part through the deftness of Palpatine's ability to use the Force reveals the Force as *neither* Good or Evil, but rather that it can be *both* Good and Evil at the same time—Good and Evil coincide in the operations of the Force. This point is reflected in the original trilogy when Obi-Wan, in *Return of the Jedi*, tells Luke that 'many of the truths we cling to depend greatly on our own point of view'. While the Jedi seem to have some belief in the power of Good over Evil—and separate them out in the

---

[161] This is not so much a Manichaean dualism but rather a Taoist presentation of the interrelation of opposites, which fits explicitly with Lucas's source in Campbell.

[162] In the opening scenes of *The Force Awakens*, Lor San Tekka (Max von Sydow) also refers to the need for the Jedi in order to return balance to the Force—to respond to the disruption of the First Order.

[163] In *The Last Jedi*, Snoke *also* notes that with the rise of the 'darkness' of Kylo Ren, the light would rise to meet it, which occurred with the 'awakening' of Rey.

good and dark sides of the Force—what we find in *Star Wars* is very much that Good and Evil are really only from a certain point of view. Significantly, this view is *also* presented by the hacker or 'slicer' DJ (Benicio del Toro) in *The Last Jedi*. After stealing (with the assistance of the droid BB-8) an arms dealer's ship from Canto Bight, Finn comments: 'at least you're stealing from the bad guys, and helping the good guys'. DJ's response is: 'Good guys, bad guys, made up words.' Flicking through the archive of the ship he brings up an image of a Tie-Fighter and notes that the previous owner 'made his "bank" selling weapons to the bad guys'. Then, revealing an image of an X-Wing Fighter, he goes on to say: 'oh, and the good . . . Finn, let me learn you something big. It's all a machine, partner. Live free, don't join.'

It is here, with this understanding of the way in which 'one and the same' Force can be used for both Good and Evil, that the Force as representation of modern law becomes clear. Just as the Force does not provide a fundamental insight into the Good, so has modern law forsaken its foundational connection with and insight into justice. Instead, it has become an instrument, tool or technology that in itself can be used for both Good and Evil. Such is the alternative genealogy of legal positivism that Roger Berkowitz outlines in his book *The Gift of Science*. There he notes that, alongside the tradition of thinking law as 'wilful', is the way in which law became viewed as attached not so much to justice, but justification, defined by a scientific approach which sought to ground law not in reason in general, but in terms of *reasons*.[164] With the development of a modern law that is no longer able to seek recourse to transcendence, its attempts at self-grounding always risk a justification by ends outside of or beyond law itself. Berkowitz's genealogy marks a series of attempts to shore up law via a recourse to scientific approaches to jurisprudence: Gottfried Wilhelm Leibniz's attempts to ground law in a rational jurisprudence that was able to determine *ius* scientifically; Friedrich Carl von Savigny's historical science that saw law as having 'no existence in itself' but rather in the *Volksgeist* or legal consciousness of a people; through to Rudolf von Jhering's proclamation of law as being a purely human construct justified only by the social or economic 'ends' that it achieves.[165] Each of these approaches sought to ground law in a science, a *justification* of law by the ends that it was aiming to achieve. As the title to one of Jhering's works proclaims, law is understood explicitly as a means to an end.[166] What this genealogy therefore tracks is the way in which

---

[164] Berkowitz, *Gift of Science*.

[165] Ibid.; see also Berkowitz, 'Justice to Justification'.

[166] Jhering, *Law as a Means to an End*. Briana Tamanaha has appropriated Jhering's title in his work tracking the way in which the emphasis on the instrumentality of law came to dominate twentieth- and now twenty-first-century understandings of law: Tamanaha, *Law as a Means to an End*.

law's intrinsic association with justice became a need for justifications, and its intrinsic nature *as* order turned to a means of *establishing order*.

Star Wars' 'modern' religion of the Force functions *explicitly* in the way that modern law does. As an entity that operates in the *tension* or balance *between* Good and Evil, the Force itself becomes an instrument of *both* Good and Evil. The connection to modern law here shifts from the realm of metaphysics or theodicy to legality itself (or, rather, legality *as* theodicy): modern law, in its attempt to be self-grounding, requires a justification in the ends it is to achieve. At the same time, as Fitzpatrick points out, it is always caught 'in between' a transcendent power and determination, and an immanent responsiveness. In its immanent attempt at self-grounding, the desire to shore up its foundations in a scientific approach able to determine justice, it *too* becomes understood explicitly as a human end and tool. The Force is a representation of modern law in the way in which modern law itself has become both an instrumental tool able to *make* or *reform* society and its order (rather than *being* or aligning *with* an underlying order), *and* which must justify itself in terms of the particular ends it achieves: its focus is not on *justice*, but on reasonable *justification*. As I will demonstrate in the next section, this essentially involves a redefinition of justice *as* the particular ends of order and security.

VII. 'More powerful than you could possibly imagine': Exceptional Legality, Transcendent Sovereignty and the 'Democratic' Multitude

This focus on balance and order, as a component of immanent legality represented by the Force, would thus seem to emphasise the Occidental god of order rather than the god of will. Given that the emphasis of positivist jurisprudence has been on will, how does the intersection between will and order function here? As Berkowitz notes, whilst the positivist definition of law as command backed by sanction is correct, this 'does not escape the grounding claims of a scientific legal system'.[167] Rather, 'the radical reduction of law to will merely shifts the metaphysical grounds of the legal system from the pursuit of justice to the preservation of order'.[168] The result of 'the embrace of sovereign and juridical will as the essence of positive law . . . is not a retreat from the scientific grounding of law in justice so much as it is a redefinition of justice as security'.[169] This metaphysical shift is on display in *Star Wars* with the turn from 'Old Republic' to 'Galactic Empire'. When we watch the original trilogy, there appears to be an understanding that the Old

---

[167] Berkowitz, *Gift of Science*, p. 5.
[168] Ibid., pp. 5–6.
[169] Ibid., p. 5.

Republic was taken over by the Empire—that it was a matter of two rivalling claims to rulership and the Empire overthrew the Republic, claiming control of the galaxy. As such, the Empire would be seen as a separate founding of a new legal order resulting from the lawless violence beyond the law of the Republic—the result of a revolution or a war in which one legal order displaces the other. What we *actually* see in the prequels, however, is the exact opposite. It is not that the Republic was 'taken over' by the Empire, but rather that the Republic *becomes* the Empire in response to the threat of disorder and attacks by the band of 'separatist' states. This functions through what Giorgio Agamben, following Carl Schmitt, refers to as a 'state of exception'—which Agamben describes not only as the prevalent 'paradigm of government' today but also as the limit point of the legal or juridical order.[170]

It is here that we can see an essential overlap between the foundational concept of the 'state of exception' and the way in which modern law involves a redefinition of justice as security and order. Law has become not an autonomous system aligned with justice, but, as Berkowitz points out, has been subordinated to the *other* sciences of human ends: philosophy, economics, politics.[171] Modern law is defined by its capacity not simply to institute but also to sustain and protect order. Having 'let go' of its divine grounds, its possibility of being 'the Good' and any intrinsic link to justice, modern law is inherently caught up with its focus on order. The restriction upon the command of the sovereign is the ability to maintain order.[172] Not only the benchmark for actions that are taken but also the justification of the law's suspension in the state of exception become the sustaining of social/juridical order and preserving peace. *Star Wars* situates this deployment of the state of exception with its key historical allusions both to the Roman Empire and to Nazi Germany: both encompass not so much a taking of power but, as we see in *Star Wars*, the 'handing over' of power to the Chancellor-cum-Emperor.[173] However, these allusions undergird more directly the way in which the series represents our modern *global* Empire, in which law has become defined by its exceptionality and the right of intervention is founded not just on 'a permanent state of emergency, but a permanent state of emergency and exception justified by *the appeal to essential values of justice*'.[174] Juridical authority today has become defined in terms of the right to intervene in the name of justice

---

[170] Agamben, *State of Exception*.
[171] Berkowitz, *Gift of Science*; Berkowitz, 'Justice to Justification'.
[172] Fitzpatrick, *Mythology*, pp. 56–8.
[173] Agamben, *State of Exception*, pp. 2, 13.
[174] Hardt and Negri, *Empire*, p. 18.

which is understood explicitly in relation to the capacity to create and maintain order.[175]

What is important to note, therefore, is the way in which the state of exception is deployed. Despite Schmitt's famous 'sovereign is he who decides on the exception', the *form* of exceptionality that both the Roman and Nazi allusions present are ones in which a 'dictator' figure is handed over or *given* emergency powers.[176] In this form, therefore, the functioning of the state of exception is brought *within*—or, rather, put into relation with—the juridico-legal democratic apparatus. Chancellor Palpatine does not 'take' power but rather is given it by the *democratic* Senate, at the proposal (though subject to manipulation) of the Senator Jar Jar Binks (Ahmed Best). The tension that is thereby rendered visible is the way in which the framework of democracy and the rule of law is insufficient for protection against the Evil acts done in the name of protecting the system of rule itself. Whilst Senator Amidala glibly notes that 'this is how liberty dies . . . to thunderous applause', what the irony of this statement reveals is the *democratic* suspending of democracy. This representation of the transition from the democratic Republic to totalitarian Empire rings true with Agamben's point: that the state of exception is 'a creation of the democratic-revolutionary tradition and not the absolutist one'.[177] This should give pause for consideration in an era of the crisis of the rule of law and concerns about it being subordinated to particular political and governmental ends.[178]

The distinction between revolutionary and absolutist traditions also points to the concerns raised by Eric Santner in terms of the way in which modernity has seen not an elimination of political theology but its shift from a localisation in the body of the royal figure of sovereignty to, following the French Revolution, the 'body' of the people.[179] What is significant in the Disney films is the way in which the figuration of the law as an instrument of both Good and Evil is re-presented explicitly as a political theology of the forms of sovereignty. One of the criticisms of *Star Wars* has always been that the rebels, despite apparently fighting for freedom from tyranny and the restoration of democracy, in fact appear in an aristocratic form: not just in terms of 'Princess' Leia and the other references to monarchical sovereignty, but more specifically in the way in which being 'strong in the Force' centres explicitly on particular 'bloodlines'. With Rian Johnson's much criticised *The*

---

[175] Ibid., pp. 16–17.
[176] Schmitt, *Political Theology*, p. 5.
[177] Agamben, *State of Exception*, p. 5.
[178] Tamanaha, *Law as a Means to an End*.
[179] Santner, *Royal Remains*.

Last Jedi, what we see is an explicitly democratising narrative. Luke's desire to see the Jedi order come to an end is *not* simply because he views it as having been arrogant, foolish and vain, but because he fundamentally believes that the Force is automatically *in* everything, and that the Jedi have essentially restricted access to, or control over, it. His criticisms of his own myth (the myth of 'Luke Skywalker, Jedi Knight'), as that which leads to pride and vanity, in the end turn into the possibility of a *true* myth, with *all* being able to have access to both its inspiration and its power. This is seen in Vice Admiral Holdo's (Laura Dern) claim that, simply in surviving, the Resistance will be 'the spark that will ignite the fire that will restore the Republic' (or, as Poe Dameron (Oscar Isaac) later says, 'burn the First Order down'), but more specifically in the way in which Luke's illusory battle with Kylo Ren is now being told around the galaxy, making way (as is seen in the final scene of the film) for younglings to be inspired and develop an ability to use the Force. To borrow Hardt and Negri's language, access to both resistance and the Force is thus an immanent constituent power available to all.

With J. J. Abram's return to direct *The Rise of Skywalker*, this theme is split: at one level it encompasses a *greater* sense of democratisation, whilst *at the same time* it involves a much greater return to the aristocratic narrative of bloodlines than has been seen throughout all the *Star Wars* films. The aristocratic narrative focuses in particular, now, on the discovery that Rey is the granddaughter of Emperor Palpatine/Darth Sidious. Contrary to the narrative of 'letting go' in *The Last Jedi*, where Rey's past and parental lineage is rendered as nothing, she is situated here explicitly within a heritage that explains her incredible power in the Force. What is more, Emperor Palpatine himself, despite having become Chancellor of the Republic in the prequel trilogies through a democratic process, and Emperor of the Empire through the 'state of exception', now presents himself in a specifically aristocratic lineage. He calls Rey to take up her 'birth right', striking him down in order to become Empress. We thus have a blurring of Palpatine's title as Emperor of the Galactic Empire and his role as Sith Lord. This intertwining functions in terms of a sacralisation of power reminiscent of Ernst Kantorowicz's *The King's Two Bodies*—which focuses not only on the human body of the monarch but on their corporate body, both in terms of continuity over time and in terms of the bringing together of *all* past monarchs (or, here, Sith) within a single body.[180]

---

[180] The connections that Kantorowicz identifies between the image of the phoenix and the monarchy would appear particularly pertinent here as well, with Palpatine's invocation for Rey to kill him in order then to 'rise' and take his place as Empress. Kantorowicz, *King's Two Bodies*, pp. 385–95.

This absolutist or aristocratic narrative is presented, however, alongside the democratic one of the Resistance. Early in the film, Poe Dameron meets up with a past co-scoundrel and love interest, Zorii Bliss (Keri Russell), who encourages him to join her and 'get out'. Whilst Poe says that he 'can't walk out on the war, not till it's over', he then reveals his despair: 'Maybe it is. We sent out a call for help at the Battle of Crait [one of the battles in *The Last Jedi*]. Nobody came. Everyone's so afraid. They've given up.' Zorrii responds: 'Nah, I don't believe you believe that. Hey, they win by making you think you're alone, remember? There's more of us.' This inspiring hope in the greater numbers of the multitude across the galaxy reappears at a crucial point in the final battle between the Resistance and the Final Order. Poe, seeing his squadrons of Resistance fighters overwhelmed, outnumbered and outmarched, begins to announce across the radio that he is ready to give up: 'My friends, I'm sorry. I thought we had a shot. But there's just too many of them.' General Lando Calrissian (Billy Dee Williams) all of a sudden comes across the radio with: 'But there are more of us, Poe, there are more us.' Thousands of ships of all sorts have flown to Exegol and are now joining the battle. The response from General Pryde (Richard E. Grant) of the Final Order is disbelief: 'Where did they get all these fighter craft? They have no navy.' To which his aide replies: 'It's not a navy, sir, it's just . . . people.' Here we find, despite all the different narratives of 'separatists', 'rebels' and 'resistance' throughout all the *Star Wars* films, the first time in which there is anything truly representing an uprising of 'the people' themselves. To return to Hardt and Negri's language, what we see is the multitude determining that *they* have the power themselves. This is undergirded with a more discrete narrative around *other* First Order storm-troopers who had refused to obey orders and turned in a similar fashion to Finn—particularly in terms of the band led by Jannah (who then assists with the final battle). This would appear to be the culmination of the democratising narrative of *The Last Jedi*, taken to its conclusion: that instead of being left with no support, no one coming to help, the multitude itself rises up to attack the Empire and Final Order.

Yet, at the same time, the immediate response to this uprising of the multitude is *not* success in battle but rather the unleashing of the 'ultimate power' of the Force by Palpatine, who is able to send his 'force-lightning' not at an individual, group of individuals or a single ship—but at the entire multitude of ships that have come to join the resistance. The visual depiction of this involves a distribution of such power in a network effect out *through* each member of the multitude—the power of transcendent sovereignty is thus able to deploy along the same lines that the multitude uses to resist it. Palpatine's recourse to the language of transcendent sovereignty—able to take up and encompass all the power of the Sith within a single corporate body, reflecting the *source* of Thomas Hobbes's famous figure of Leviathan in the earlier medieval imagery traced by Kantorowicz—seems to undergird a presentation of the power of transcendence. Against such a figure of absolute power, the multitude, despite the vastness of numbers, is rendered *literally* powerless, the force-lightning having shut down all the power systems in their ships. The narrative of the film requires, instead, this figure of sovereign corporate transcendence to be fought and defeated by *another* figure of sovereign corporate transcendence: Rey, who has taken within herself *all* the Jedi in order to fight *all* the Sith. The message of the film would thus appear to be that the solution is *not* that of 'the multitude' winning out, but the need for a sovereign figure to fight back against the sovereign figure. The solution is not, therefore, a 'hero with a thousand faces', but rather 'a thousand heroes with a single body'.

VIII. Conclusion: 'May the Force be with you' or 'Saving what we love'

In *The Last Jedi*, when Kylo Ren and the First Order are about to break into an old Rebel base in which the Resistance is taking refuge, a band of speeders head out to attempt to destroy the technological battering ram being used to gain access. Poe, having finally learned the lesson that sometimes the cost of destroying the enemy is too great, calls for the speeders to retreat. Finn, however, continues, claiming that he is 'almost there' and that he 'won't let them win'. The scene builds with a musical and cinematic intensity, with the sense that we are about to see a 'noble sacrifice' of one of the main characters, giving up his life to save the Resistance (as had already been done by Vice Admiral Holdo in the previous battle). This intensity is brought into relief when, moments before crashing into the battering ram, Rose (Kelly Marie Tran), in another speeder, smashes into Finn, knocking him out of the way. Finn runs to the wreckage of Rose's speeder and, despite her appearing hurt and semi-conscious, challenges her: 'why would you do that? I was almost there? Why would you stop me?' Her response is: 'I saved you . . . dummy. That's how we're going to win. Not fighting what we hate. Saving what we love.' At which point, as the battering ram explosively hits the base behind them, Rose kisses Finn before passing out. This action by Rose (which caused a significant backlash from fans and incredible vitriol against the actress) is profound, particularly in the context of the next line from Kylo Ren, who declares that 'no prisoners' are to be taken by the First Order in its attack on the Resistance.

This call for a *refusal* to attack the other, a call to 'save' rather than fight, is one that would fly in the face of the narrative framework of *Star Wars*—of the need for Good to rise up and fight Evil, no matter what the cost. As I have shown, the culmination of this narrative framework in the conclusion to 'the

Skywalker saga' takes recourse to a political theology of sovereignty. Hardt and Negri have criticised the focus on the theorisation of such sovereignty for fear that it produces the very type of battle between Good and Evil that *Star Wars* presents to us: 'either we submit to this transcendent sovereignty or we oppose it in its entirety'.[181] Their concern is that the 'focus on transcendent authority and violence eclipses and mystifies the really dominant forms of power that continue to rule over us today—power embodied in property and capital, power embedded in and fully supported by the law'.[182] However, the analysis of the immanent legality of the Force in this chapter itself questions their turn to an immanent constituent power of the multitude, for modern law itself, in its very immanent secularity, takes up and incorporates the deific qualities of transcendent sovereignty, now shorn of its religious groundings. It is here that we see the ideological function of these films reproducing that sense in which modern law, in its attempt to cover over its own lack of grounds, takes recourse to an ultimate desire for order, peace and justice (as balance). The rule of law, despite its claim to civilisation and peace, is grounded on the potential of its exception. The idea of the Force as a constituent power of 'the multitude' is one that is ever at risk of appropriation by a transcendent deployment of such constituent power that extends beyond it. Law here is not an underlying 'good' but rather an instrumentalisation of justice that can be deployed *for* both Good and Evil. The result is to render the multitude *not* in a position of strength and power, but forever at risk of being struck by the lightning of law and rendered in that moment powerless.

What is needed, therefore, is not the taking up of arms to fight transcendence with immanence, but to save that which we love. Such a response, as I will outline in the next two chapters, is one that requires not simply a defeating of the 'evil' of Empire, but an envisioning of a new form of community. In this light, we should be wary of the farewell deployed throughout *Star Wars*: 'may the Force be with you'. This very valediction acknowledges the omnipresence of the Force—the everywhereness of law and our embeddedness within it—yet ignores the fact that the Force and the law are 'with' both what we deem as Good (Luke, Rey, the Republic, the Resistance) and the Bad (Darth Vader, Emperor Palpatine, the Empire, the Final Order). Law, having let go of its 'divine grounds' which 'guarantee' its universality, has rather to be *made* applicable. It is the mechanism for the protection of society from violence with violence—a shoring up of community only in terms of what it is against. We need, rather, to think a transformation of the law—a law not

---

[181] Hardt and Negri, *Commonwealth*, p. 5.
[182] Ibid., pp. 3–4.

locked into the tyrannous rule of order and peace justified by exceptionality (the crisis that sustains the 'normal' functioning of the market or state). It is with this aim that, instead of focusing on the Jedi farewell 'may the Force be with you', with its legitimating and 'making applicable' of the existing order, our response should be rather one that invokes the divine itself, as Vice Admiral Holdo does herself: 'Godspeed rebels'.[183]

---

[183] Significant in Rian Johnson's depiction of the *Star Wars* universe is the way in which, despite specific engagements with the Force, there are also allusions that do not fit. After Holdo and Leia have a stilted 'may the Force be with you' on their parting—a phrase that is, itself, a bastardised form of the Christian liturgical 'may the Lord be with you' (to which there is *also* a liturgical response that would have dealt with Leia and Holdo's mismatch: 'and also with you')—the use of 'Godspeed' by Holdo then invokes a similar meaning whilst *not* making reference to the Force: Godspeed, which means 'may God cause you to succeed' or 'may God cause you to prosper'.

3

The Superhero 'Made Strange': A Christological Reading of Christopher Nolan's *The Dark Knight*

'And because lawlessness is increased, most people's love will grow cold.'

Matthew 24: 12

I. Introduction

What vision of legality is driving, undergirding and being propounded by the dominance of the superhero genre on screen and beyond today? Why is it that in recent years we have become so obsessed with these fantastic and powerful personas dressed in masks and capes and engaging in feats of wonder? This chapter considers this dominance of the superhero through an analysis of a crucial text in the gritty and realistic turn of the genre: Christopher Nolan's *The Dark Knight*. In Chapter 1 I explored two key thematic 'readings' of the superhero genre: the 'legal' reading, which sees the superhero as the figure beyond the law who is able to achieve justice where a fallible and inept legal system fails; and the 'theological' reading, which sees the superhero as a Christological or messianic saviour figure who, with great strength, virtue and valour, is able to 'show the way' to humanity and save the city, country or world from peril. The focus here is the way in which *The Dark Knight*, and Nolan's *The Dark Trilogy* more generally, take up but 'make strange' both of these readings. My argument is that, while Nolan draws on the superhero genre and Batman mythos, his filmic remediation of it transcends and transforms that genre and its traditional tropes—going beyond the traditional form of the saviour myth and the genre's inherent critique of the law, to present a more foundational and theological critique of our *vision* of legality.

If the previous two chapters focused on particular presentations of a secular legal theology, encompassing critical examinations of the dichotomies of Good and Evil in the superhero genre and the *Star Wars* saga, my turn in this chapter and the next is to a more direct theological jurisprudential critique. This draws upon and brings together two particular themes that the previous chapters have already alluded to: first, the vision of law as opposed to a fundamental chaos—civilisation to savagery; second, the figuring of a vision of the rule of law and its transgression—legality and its exception. In Chapter 4, I demonstrate the way in which the concept of sacrifice is central to modern secular accounts of law, via a reading of *The Dark Knight Rises* and the particular theme of sacrifice it propounds. In this chapter, however, my focus is on a particular claim in relation to *The Dark Knight*: that Batman (Christian Bale) is a typology of Christ. This is *not* in the mode of sacrifice that the traditional saviour mode of the superhero encounters, and to which the conclusion of *The Dark Knight Rises* alludes. Rather, it is because of a specific *refusal* of the heroic framework—a refusal that makes strange both the legal and the theological readings of the genre. This finds its epitome in the morally ambiguous actions taken at the end of the film. In the final scenes, Batman and Commissioner Gordon (Gary Oldham) conspire to promulgate a lie about Gotham City District Attorney Harvey Dent (Aaron Eckhart), with Batman taking the blame for a number of murders committed by Dent. It is by highlighting the Christological resonances of these actions that we can read *The Dark Knight* as a response to, as much as an expansion and fulfilment of, the rise of the superhero film and the superhero as a figure of the exception beyond the law.

The chapter begins by situating *The Dark Knight* in relation to the critical and scholarly response to it, as well as the general Christological allusions of the superhero genre. Drawing on the work of Carl Schmitt and Giorgio Agamben, it will outline the connections between *The Dark Knight* and a particular form of exceptionalism in which Batman appropriates the sovereign decision on the exception to the norm of the law. What is determinative, however, is that Nolan's Batman does not fit the traditional superhero mythos (fighting for truth and justice) but rather consistently fights *against* particular visions of justice presented by each of the villains in the film trilogy (Ra's Al Ghul, the League of Shadows, the Joker, Two-Face and Bane). With the Joker and Two-Face in *The Dark Knight*, as Sections III and IV explicate, these are visions of justice as legality. In Section III, 'the Joker' is analysed not as being a figure of radical anarchy but as revealing a conservative vision of the law founded on violence—a conception of law as a civilising force that holds at bay a savagery that is also inherent to it. Section IV then considers the way in which Harvey 'Two-Face' Dent takes up the traditional superhero–vigilante critique of the law, but in compressing the legal decision into an arbitrary toss of the coin, he desires a purified vision of the rule of law without exception. In contrast, the actions of Nolan's Batman are grounded in a form of compassion that does not seek a retributive or vigilante justice but enact a form of preventative violence founded in love. It is in this sense that Section V provides a Christological reading of *The Dark Knight* that opens the possibility of a different grounding of law, justice and trust in the community of the city. The chapter concludes with the film's emphasis not on (super)heroism but rather on a theological jurisprudence of the non-heroic.

II. Myths of the Post-9/11 Superhero: Exceptional Saviours and Legal Justice

Following the release in July 2012 of *The Dark Knight Rises*, the final instalment of Nolan's trilogy,[1] which will be the focus of the next chapter, certain critics identified Batman as a Christ figure making the 'ultimate sacrifice' to save the people of Gotham City.[2] As Slavoj Žižek was quick to point out, however, such a crass and superficial reading is patently inaccurate or, at the very least and to follow the theological reference, heretical.[3] In the final scenes of *The Dark Knight Rises*, Batman/Bruce Wayne (Christian Bale) *does not die* but can be found in Venice with Selina Kyle (the cat burglar, played by Anne Hathaway). Such a reading of Batman as Christ, then, is more a gnostic heresy (where Christ did not actually die on the cross but escaped and lived out his life in India or Tibet[4]) rather than the orthodox Christian tradition. The temptation to such an analogy, however, arises from the prevalence of the theological reading of the genre discussed in Chapter 1 and therefore seeing Nolan as simply reproducing the American monomyth, with Batman as an exceptional saviour figure.[5]

My analysis in this chapter rejects this reading of Nolan's film as a straightforward reproduction of the traditional saviour myth, whilst at the same time maintaining a similar claim that contradicts the normal reading of the Batman mythos: that Batman is a typology of Christ. As seen in the Prologue and Chapter 1, if any superhero was going to be compared to Christ, surely it would be Superman and not Batman. For C. K. Robertson, the character of Batman is directly opposed to Superman's 'Christological' connections and is, rather, the real *humanist* myth—the appropriate heir to Nietzsche's self-made *Übermensch* to which we should aspire. Batman as a 'self-made' superhero, relying on his training and technology instead of any inherent

---

[1] Consisting of *Batman Begins*, film, directed by Nolan; *The Dark Knight*, film, directed by Nolan; *The Dark Knight Rises*, film, directed by Nolan.

[2] See, for example, O'Neil, 'Dark Knight and Occupy Wall Street'.

[3] Žižek, 'People's Republic of Gotham', 23 August 2012; Žižek, 'Dictatorship of the Proletariat', 8 August 2012.

[4] Žižek, 'People's Republic of Gotham', 23 August 2012.

[5] This conforms to Joseph Campbell's notion of the hero myth discussed in Chapter 2: see Campbell, *Hero With a Thousand Faces*. See also Lawrence and Jewett, *Myth of American Superhero*.

divine powers, points to a more humanist myth. This Nietzschean reading of Batman has significant merit, particularly if we read the superhero genre in relation to the tales of the Roman and Greek heroes and gods, which embodied a heroic virtue that responds to and overcomes evil. The structural focus of the super*hero* is to demonstrate their virtuous nature by dealing with the evil that arises. As noted in Chapter 1, from the Christian perspective, the problem with this type of virtue is that it secretly celebrates as its occasion a *prior* evil.[6] The virtuous in the Greek and Roman traditions was focused on a heroic overcoming of violence and evil, which means that there

> can only *be* virtue where there is something to be defeated, and virtue therefore consists for them, not only in the attainment and pursuit of a goal desirable in itself, but also in a 'conquest' of less desirable forces, which is always an exercise of strength *supplementary to*, although supporting, a 'right desire'.[7]

At first glance, *The Dark Knight* would appear to be one of the most extreme examples of this type of virtue based on prior *evil*—presenting a form of purifying retributive justice in response to extreme evil. As Michael Nichols argues, it seems to be a modernised version of the 'combat myth', where a figure of order (the hero or god) defends the ordered world or city against the onslaught of chaos (the monster).[8] This model of the combat myth recounts how the social order is continuously preserved from the onslaught of ever-recurring threats to peace and civility by the heroic actions of a particular individual. It thus provides a broad mythic framework in which the superhero genre can be analysed—whenever a monster or villain arises that cannot be dealt with by the normal mechanisms of law enforcement, a superhero arrives on the scene and, after a heroic effort, restores order (until the next monster arrives or the villain escapes).[9] For Nichols, *The Dark Knight* 'updates the mythic theme by casting the opposing characters as representatives of democratic society and terrorism'[10]—a point which John Ip also highlights, describing it as a parable about 'the dilemmas that face society when confronting terrorism and terrorists'.[11]

---

[6] Milbank, *Word Made Strange*, pp. 219–21.

[7] Milbank, *Theology and Social Theory*, p. 393.

[8] Nichols, 'Reading of the Batman/Joker Comic', p. 236; Cohn, *Chaos and the World to Come*, p. 42. This, of course, has parallels with Lawrence and Jewett's discussion of the American monomyth: Lawrence and Jewett, *Myth of American Superhero*.

[9] Nichols, 'Reading of the Batman/Joker Comic', pp. 236–7. See also Reynolds, *Super Heroes*, pp. 41, 65–6.

[10] Nichols, 'Reading of the Batman/Joker Comic', p. 236.

[11] Ip, 'Dark Knight's War on Terrorism', p. 213.

Whilst the rise of the gritty, realist superhero film has been linked to the 'war on terror' environment,[12] it was Nolan's *The Dark Knight* that evoked the strongest identification of such connections between Hollywood and the Bush Administration era of post-9/11 politics, with one critic even describing it as 'the first true, post 9/11 superhero movie'.[13] Following its release in 2008, a number of critics labelled *The Dark Knight* a conservative film that supported and validated the tactics and strategies used by the Bush Administration in the 'war on terror' (presenting coercive interrogation, extraordinary rendition, surveillance and other 'exceptional measures' in a positive and necessary light).[14] On this reading, *The Dark Knight* seemed to present one of the strongest endorsements of the need for exceptional measures in response to extraordinary circumstances.[15] These reviews were met with a cacophony of critical responses, particularly in the blogosphere, that challenged the conservative reading of the film, arguing that, instead, Nolan was presenting a critique rather than an endorsement of Bush politics and that Batman's considered recourse to exceptional measures was in contrast to those seen in reality.[16]

This situating of *The Dark Knight* within the context of the post-9/11 'war on terror' not only highlights the superhero's relationship to the law, as discussed in Chapter 1, but points to a particular reading of that relationship in terms of the concept of 'the exception' described by German jurist

---

[12] See, for example, Treat, 'Post-9/11 Superhero Zeitgeist'; Ip, 'Dark Knight's War on Terrorism'.

[13] Crouse, 'Reviewer Seeking New Words for Awesome', 10 July 2009.

[14] Ackerman, '"Dark Knight" Reflects Cheney Policy', 21 July 2008; Klavan, 'What Bush and Batman Have In Common', 25 July 2008; Allen, 'Batman's War on Terror', 2 August 2008; Bolt, 'Batman Bush True Dark Knight', 30 July 2008; Editorial, 'Batman and the War on Terror', 21 July 2008. See the discussion of these claims by Ip, 'Dark Knight's War on Terrorism'.

[15] See in particular Klavan, 'What Bush and Batman Have In Common', 25 July 2008; Ackerman, '"Dark Knight" Reflects Cheney Policy', 21 July 2008; Bolt, 'Batman Bush True Dark Knight', 30 July 2008.

[16] Cogitamus, 'Dark Knight and International Politics', July 2008; Orr, 'Batman as Bush Ctd', 17 July 2008; Yglesias, 'Dark Knight Politics', 24 July 2008. Ip specifically analyses the post-9/11 context of *The Dark Knight* and proposes it as a critique of the Bush Administration's tactics: Ip, 'Dark Knight's War on Terrorism'. For further examples of the diverse and rich scholarly considerations of the film, see Treat, 'Post-9/11 Superhero Zeitgeist'; Phillips, 'Constructing Images of Good vs. Evil'; Žižek, *Living in the End Times*, pp. 59–61; Schlegel and Habermann, 'Theatricality and Cybernetics of Good and Evil'; Muller, 'Power, Choice, and September 11'; Gaine, 'Genre and Super-Heroism'.

Carl Schmitt and his modern reader, Giorgio Agamben.[17] Whereas Batman's actions are, on the whole, unauthorised and illegal, from this perspective, the role of the superhero could be seen as responding to a 'state of exception' in which the ordinary operation of the law is suspended to deal with a crisis or emergency. This view would see the role of the superhero not as a permanent supplement to an ever-deficient legal system, but rather as a temporary measure to address a specific crisis. Cultural legal scholar Jason Bainbridge posits that the 'superness' of superheroes means that they are automatically outside the law and thus attempts, drawing on Agamben, to think their status in terms of the notion of 'alegality'.[18] However, to describe superheroes as simply exceptional beings (due to their superpowers) is really only to see them on a continuum with ordinary human beings. *Enforcing* the law against someone as strong as Superman may be problematic, but this by itself does not necessarily mean that Superman has an exceptional relation to the law.[19] Figures like Batman, on the other hand—particularly in the 'realist' mode that Nolan adopts in his films—do not have this same innate 'superpower' and derive their status and ability from training, wealth and determination. At the same time, the concept of 'alegality' is important because it points to a different classification or understanding of the role of this type of superhero—not simply as a vigilante who is effectively a criminal, breaking the law in the desire to achieve justice, but as having a different relationship to the law.

For Schmitt, as Agamben points out, the exception is structurally connected to the figure of the sovereign—thus his oft-quoted phrase '[s]overeign is he who decides on the exception.'[20] *The Dark Knight* specifically references

---

[17] Schmitt, *Political Theology*; Agamben, *Homo Sacer*; Agamben, *State of Exception*. The use of Agamben's work on the 'state of exception' to analyse superheroes in general, and particularly based on the status of their superpowers, is taken up by Miettinin and Bainbridge: see Miettinen, 'Representing the State of Exception'; Bainbridge, 'Spider-Man, the Question and the Meta-Zone'; Bainbridge, 'Call to Do Justice'. The connection of Agamben's broader work on the concept of *homo sacer* is also examined by Nayar, *Reading Culture* (referred to by Bainbridge); Spanakos, 'Exceptional Recognition: The US Global Dilemma in *The Incredible Hulk, Iron Man*, and *Avatar*'. McGowan also draws on Schmitt and Agamben in his 'exceptional' (pun intended) analysis of *The Dark Knight*: McGowan, 'Exceptional Darkness'. See also Curtis, *Sovereignty and Superheroes*; Curtis, 'Superheroes and the Contradiction of Sovereignty'.

[18] Bainbridge, 'Spider-Man, the Question and the Meta-Zone', pp. 218–19, 226–7.

[19] Though see McGowan's reference to Hegel, who describes the hero (who is a law unto himself) as the antithesis to modern law: McGowan, 'Exceptional Darkness', paras [4]–[5].

[20] Schmitt, *Political Theology*, p. 5.

this connection between the exception and sovereignty when, early in the film at a dinner with Harvey Dent, Rachel Dawes (Maggie Gyllenhaal) and the Russian ballet dancer Natascha, Bruce Wayne (playing devil's advocate) pitches the question: 'Who appointed the Batman?' Harvey Dent, the District Attorney, then provides quite a specific justification for Batman:

> We did. All of us who stood by and let scum take control of our city . . . When their enemies were at the gates, the Romans would suspend democracy and appoint one man to protect the city. And it wasn't considered an honour; it was considered a public service.

Instead of subscribing to the idea that Batman is a criminal vigilante on a personal vendetta for justice, Dent legitimises the role that Batman has taken. He argues that there is a need for Batman because the people of Gotham have allowed criminals to take over and control the city. Ip rightly identifies this reference to the Roman paradigm of the dictatorship[21]—a 'specific kind of magistrate whom the consuls had chosen and whose *imperium*, which was extremely broad, was conferred by a *lex curiata* that defined its aims'.[22] In this sense, Dent is arguing that the people appointed Batman as their protector to deal with the situation in Gotham, the basis for his position being appointment by popular sovereignty.[23] Agamben, however, makes a distinction between the notion of dictatorship and the theory of the state of exception (despite Schmitt's first examination of the exception being in his work *Dictatorship*[24]). As noted in Chapter 2, rather than embodying the role of dictatorship, Agamben situates the state of exception within the Roman concept of the *iustitium* (distinguished from the *imperium* provided to the dictator). Whereas the dictatorship involved the empowering of a particular magistrate with a specific mandate, such as waging war or quashing an uproar, the proclamation of the *iustitium*, a 'standstill' or 'suspension of the law', would follow a decree declaring a *tumultus*, 'an emergency situation in Rome resulting from a foreign war, insurrection, or civil war'.[25] The *tumultus* was not so much the external threat to the state itself but the effect of that threat on the city in terms of the 'state of disorder or unrest' that the threat produced.[26] Whilst Agamben acknowledges that it has been interpreted in relation to the concept of dictatorship, the result of the *iustitium* is distinct. The *iustitium* suspends the law and all legal prescriptions are put out of operation—at that point

[21] Ip, 'Dark Knight's War on Terrorism', p. 227.
[22] Agamben, *State of Exception*, p. 47.
[23] See Sharp, 'Riddle Me This', p. 360.
[24] Schmitt, *Dictatorship*.
[25] Agamben, *State of Exception*, p. 40.
[26] Ibid., p. 42.

no Roman citizens, whether a magistrate or a private citizen, have any legal powers or duties.[27] For Agamben, the connection of the *iustitium* and the *tumultus* to the state of necessity means that they 'are not categories of criminal law but of constitutional law, and they designate "the caesura by means of which, from the point of view of public law, exceptional measures may be taken"'.[28]

This distinction between the concept of the state of exception and the dictatorship raises a different question about the role of the superhero and, more specifically, Batman's role in Gotham City. Does Batman operate simply as a stop-gap dictator, who always has the potential for never giving up the power provided to him,[29] or does he operate under a 'state of exception'? If the answer is the latter, to return to Schmitt's key point (the link between the exception and sovereignty), then the real question is not 'who appointed the Batman?' but 'who declared the state of exception?'. The way that Batman positions himself and his role in relation to the city is as an agent of change. As such, the state of exception or emergency in the city that he is responding to *is not* the rise of the terrorist activities of the Joker (though, given the tumult that he causes, they would provide grounds for such a declaration) but rather the corruption and domination of the mob. All of this points to the fact that Nolan's presentation of Batman is not as a figure who restores the social order from the disruption by villains such as Ra's Al Ghul, the Joker or Bane, but rather to disrupt the exceptional basis of the situation itself—the corruption and crime-dominated experience of Gotham City. Reading Batman in this way sees him not as a vigilante criminal operating beyond the law, but rather as a figure of sovereignty operating in the space of the law suspended. Batman is neither executing the law (in terms of upholding it as authorised, covertly or overtly, by the police) nor transgressing it (in terms of being a criminal vigilante) but, to use Agamben's terminology, he inexecutes the law in the state of exception.[30]

---

[27] Nissen, *Das Iustitium*, p. 105, quoted in Agamben, *State of Exception*, p. 45.

[28] Agamben, *State of Exception*, p. 46, quoting Nissen, *Das Iustitium*, p. 76.

[29] A point which Rachel Dawes makes, clarifying Harvey's reference to Rome by noting that 'the last man that they appointed to protect the republic was named Caesar and he never gave up his power'. See also Ip, 'Dark Knight's War on Terrorism', pp. 227–8.

[30] Agamben, *State of Exception*, p. 50. Cf. Bainbridge, 'Call to Do Justice', pp. 12–13. Bainbridge makes a similar claim in relation to the role of a number of superheroes more generally, such as Captain America, and, as noted above, has attempted to think the superhero in general through the concept of the state of exception: Bainbridge, 'Spider-Man, the Question and the Meta-Zone'; Bainbridge, 'Call to Do Justice'. However, whilst superheroes, by their very nature, tend to respond to emergencies and extreme acts beyond the law, this does not mean that they are always (or even regularly) 'appropriating the sovereign decision'—rather, in many cases they are either part of the mechanisms of the state (even if only loosely tied) *or* engaging in criminal activity.

This reading of Batman challenges the traditional mythic framework that Nichols proposes and emphasises the way in which Nolan transforms, inverts or otherwise 'makes strange' the superhero genre.[31] It also goes to the way in which Nolan takes up the Nietzschean elements of the Batman mythos that Robertson puts forward but displaces them on to the villains, with Batman consistently fighting *against* their visions of justice. The Joker's (Heath Ledger) first line in *The Dark Knight*—'I believe, whatever doesn't kill you, only makes you *stranger*'—is itself a reworking of Nietzsche's famous 'whatever doesn't kill you, only makes you stronger.'[32] But the Nietzschean villain is much more clearly depicted in the form of Ra's Al Ghul and the League of Shadows in the first film of Nolan's trilogy, *Batman Begins* (and the references back to him in *The Dark Knight Rises*). There, Ra's attempts to destroy Gotham City and its people not for any personal gain but *because* of its corruption. When Bruce Wayne challenges Ra's, noting that he will be destroying millions of innocent lives, Ra's responds by saying: 'Only a cynical man would call what these people have lives, Wayne. Crime, despair, this is not how man was supposed to live.' Ra's is envisioning a form of humanity or life beyond that of the human, which is regularly corrupt and despairing—he desires a new order of humanity that will supersede the corruption that Gotham exhibits. They present a vision of 'justice as balance' which requires them to enact a 'return to harmony' by destroying Gotham City (just as Sodom was destroyed by the hand of God in the Old Testament).[33] Bruce's response recalls the debate between God and Abraham in the Old Testament, arguing that there are still 'good people' in Gotham and that it is worth saving.[34] Ra's responds by saying that Bruce is defending a city whose people are so corrupt that they have infiltrated every level of its infrastructure. He tells Bruce that, as his greatest student, he should be the one 'standing by my side saving the world.' Bruce's response is that he will be standing where he belongs—between Ra's and the people of Gotham. This mediatory role of Batman—standing between the agent of justice and the sinful city of Gotham—thus has Christological resonances to it, where the only thing that

---

[31] For a consideration of the way that Nolan's films transform or cross genre boundaries see McGowan, *Fictional Christopher Nolan*. See also Johnson, 'Nolan's Batman as Moral Philosopher'.

[32] Nietzsche's original is '*From the Military School of Life*—Whatever does not kill me makes me stronger.' See Nietzsche, *Twilight of the Idols*. See also McGowan, 'Exceptional Darkness'.

[33] See Peters, 'Unbalancing Justice'.

[34] See Gen. 18: 16–33 (English Standard Version, ESV).

stands between sinful humanity and the wrath of divine judgment is Christ as defender and advocate.

III. 'When the chips are down, these "civilised people" will eat each other': The Joker, Hobbes and the State of Nature

The Christological aspects of Nolan's trilogy are most strongly emphasised in *The Dark Knight* with the opposition between Batman and the Joker. In his Girardian reading of *The Dark Knight*, Charles Bellinger argues that the Joker is a figurative version of Satan, whose 'main purpose is to sow chaos, confusion and destruction among human beings'.[35] He argues that the Joker claims that it is the system of law and order, as much as the desire to punish criminals, which is immoral and hypocritical.[36] That is, the Joker reveals 'law abiding society' as a mystification, and his proclamation that the 'only sensible way to live in this world is without rules' is an accusation of the failure and hypocrisy of the laws and prohibitions that society invents to contain violence.[37] Žižek picks up on this type of critique by pointing out that, in a film that is all about the privileging of lying as a social principle, the Joker is a revolutionary figure of truth who desires to uncover the lies of society: 'the attacks will stop only when Batman takes off his mask and reveals his true identity'.[38] In this way Žižek privileges the role of the villain. Todd McGowan's reading of *The Dark Knight* also privileges the role of the Joker as presenting a form of social critique and providing the possibility for the otherwise self-interested and self-serving citizens of Gotham City to engage in a truly ethical act. For McGowan, like Bellinger, the anarchic, critical perspective presented by the Joker is related to the role of the law. Drawing on the moral philosophy of Immanuel Kant, McGowan argues that our commitment or devotion to the law is never 'for its own sake but for some attendant pathological motivation'.[39] We are tainted by an originary 'radical evil that leads us to place our incentives of self-love above the law and that prevents us from adhering to the law for its own sake'[40]—we obey the law, not for the law itself, but because it is in our interests to do so. The result of this originary radical evil is a consequentialist ethics that seeks not the moral worth of the

---

[35] Bellinger, 'Joker is Satan', para [5]; cf Nichols, 'Reading of the Batman/Joker Comic', p. 238.

[36] Bellinger, 'Joker is Satan', paras [5]–[6], [9].

[37] Ibid., para [9].

[38] Žižek, *Living in the End Times*, p. 60.

[39] McGowan, 'Exceptional Darkness', para [23].

[40] Ibid., para [24]; Kant, *Religion Within the Boundaries*, p. 59; Kant, *Metaphysics of Morals*.

action itself (obedience to the moral law), but rather the ultimate benefit of the action to the individual.[41] This is a morality of calculation or, as the Joker claims in relation to Gotham City, of 'plans' and 'scheming'.

McGowan argues that the Joker's critique of 'scheming' seeks to overcome this calculating thinking by allowing the space for a truly *ethical* act—one not caught within a consequentialist or utilitarian pathology. After Dent's disfigurement, the Joker provokes him by arguing that the problem with society is that it is full of 'schemers trying to control their little worlds'. The Joker describes himself not as a schemer but as someone attempting to 'show the schemers how pathetic their attempts to control things really are'. Following this reasoning, McGowan argues that when the Joker sets up abhorrent ethical situations (threatening to blow up a hospital unless someone kills the Wayne Enterprises lawyer who is about to disclose who Batman is; or giving a ferry full of criminals and a ferry full of 'innocent citizens' the detonator to blow each other up and threatening to do it himself if they do not decide in fifteen minutes), he in fact provides a way for the people in those situations to break out of their self-interested calculating and scheming—giving them the opportunity to privilege the act itself rather than any benefit they may gain.[42] These opportunities present a utilitarian calculation—justifying the death of one man to save all those in the hospital, or justifying the deaths of the criminals who have 'had their chance' in order to save the 'innocent civilians'. The result, in McGowan's view, is that

> [t]he Joker's evil provides the basis for any ethical heroism because it highlights and strives to eliminate the evil of calculation that defines the subject's original relation to the law. He thereby constitutes the ground on which the ethical act can emerge.[43]

The problem with this reading of the Joker is that it is based in substance upon the Joker's self-description. McGowan argues that, when the Joker describes himself as 'a dog chasing cars' that 'wouldn't know what to do if [it] caught one', he is presenting a priority of 'the act' over its consequences. That is, that the Joker does not have a plan and is focused on the ethical stance of 'the act' itself. As the Joker says to Harvey Dent, 'I just *do* things.' Yet, to take anything that the Joker says at face value is problematic. In line with his mythical figuring as a Satan or trickster figure, the Joker operates on the premise of deceptions, half-truths and bad jokes. For example, after having recovered the mob's pile of cash, the Joker emphasises that he is a 'man of his

---

[41] McGowan, 'Exceptional Darkness', para [30]. Kant, *Metaphysics of Morals*, p. 89.
[42] McGowan, 'Exceptional Darkness', para [30].
[43] Ibid., para [46].

word'. The mobster finds this hard to believe when the Joker's men start to burn the cash. In response, the Joker claims that he is only burning *his* half. This is, of course, true, though it makes no guarantees as to what will happen to the other half. If the Joker consistently operates through half-truths and deceptions, then can we believe his discussion with Harvey?

In response to Harvey's rage towards the Joker about the killing of Rachel, the Joker explains that he was 'sitting in Gordon's cage' when she was kidnapped. Dent's response is that it was the Joker's men and the Joker's plan. The Joker, dressed as a female nurse (complete with wig), turns and poses the question to him: 'Do I really look like a guy with a plan?' Throughout the rest of the dialogue, when the Joker accuses the mob, the cops, Gordon and even Dent of having plans which he takes pleasure in disrupting, he never actually says that he himself does not have a plan. The truth of the matter, as is unveiled throughout the film, is that the Joker *does* have a plan.[44] The Joker meticulously maps out his escapades, taking into account the expected responses to his actions and incorporating them into his plan. For example, the Joker allows himself to be caught by the police (after a spectacle-filled chase scene which includes the vertical flipping of a semi-trailer) so that he can be put in the holding cell at the Major Crimes Unit, where Lau, the mob's accountant, is also being held. His subsequent *escape* is enabled by the use of a 'human bomb' in the holding cell, which the Joker triggers via a phone call after goading the supervising officer into attacking him. Thus, despite all the rhetoric presented by the Joker about being a disrupter of plans, he, in the end is the greatest planner and schemer of them all. The question, then, is: what is the Joker's plan? Is it simply that, as is so often quoted, he just wants to 'watch the world burn'?[45]

It is here that the Joker's alignment with Satan that Bellinger points out becomes particularly relevant. In the Old Testament Book of Job, the role of Satan or 'the Accuser' is to challenge God's valorisation of Job.[46] Whereas God boasts to Satan that there is none like Job on earth, that he is a 'blameless and upright man, who fears God and turns away from evil',

[44] The question raised by Dent is accusatory, indicating that it was the Joker's plan that resulted in the death of Rachel (which, of course, is true). The Joker magnificently deflects this accusation by posing the question above and asking Dent to make a judgment about whether the accusation makes sense. He never answers the question himself.

[45] See, for example, Phillips, 'Constructing Images of Good vs. Evil', pp. 33–5; McGowan, 'Exceptional Darkness', note 15; Nichols, 'Reading of the Batman/Joker Comic', p. 241, who descibes this as a neat summary of 'the Joker's sole motive'.

[46] For a more detailed working through of the Joker and Dent in relation to Job, see Peters, '"Seeing" Justice Done'.

Satan challenges the reason for Job's goodness.[47] He argues that it is only because God has blessed Job (he is rich, well thought of and prosperous) that he is good, and that if he lost it all, he would turn and curse God.[48] God therefore allows Satan to test Job, initially destroying his children and possessions, and then finally afflicting his health.[49] Job, of course, passes the test, refuting Satan's challenge that goodness and integrity are purely dependent upon good circumstances. It is this accusatory nature of Satan that is referenced by the Joker's operation and behaviours in Gotham. In the most detailed face-to-face interaction between the Joker and Batman (in the 'interrogation' scene at the Gotham Police Station), the Joker derides the morals and code of society as just a bad joke, 'dropped at the first sign of trouble'. His critique is that people are 'only as good as the world allows them to be . . . when the chips are down, these . . . these "civilised people", they'll eat each other'. The core of the Joker's programme, the underlying reason for the chaos and madness he unleashes on the city, is that, under pressure, everyone will revert to a self-interested state of nature, a Hobbesian war of all against all.[50] The Joker presents and then critiques the view of the law examined in Chapter 2—that law is a mechanism that represses the fundamental violence underlying so-called civil society: 'you have all these rules and you think they'll save you.' For the Joker, the truth appears to be that 'the only sensible way to live in this world is without rules'.

It is in *this* sense that the Joker identifies himself as an agent of chaos—in terms of a particular critique of the violence of the existing order of Gotham itself. Returning to the extended scene with Harvey Dent, the Joker outlines his understanding of plans as follows:

> You know what I've noticed? Nobody panics when things go 'according to plan'. Even if the plan is horrifying! If, tomorrow, I tell the press that, like, a gang banger will get shot, or a truckload of soldiers will be blown up, nobody panics, because it's all 'part of the plan'. But when I say that one little old mayor will die, then everyone loses their minds! . . . [Handing Harvey a gun and pointing it at himself] . . . Introduce a little anarchy. Upset the established order, and everything becomes chaos. I'm an agent of chaos. Oh, and you know the thing about chaos? It's fair!

What the Joker's diatribe suggests is not so much that he is presenting a chaos that will challenge the law as the fact that chaos and violence are

[47] Job 1: 8 (ESV).
[48] Job 1: 8–11 (ESV).
[49] Job 1: 22, 2: 3–5 (ESV).
[50] See Hobbes, 'Leviathan', pp. 84–6.

already implicated and presupposed by the law. The Joker does not reveal a 'state of nature' before or beyond the law but rather demonstrates the nature of the law itself—that the law is premised on savagery, a state of war of all against all.[51] In doing so, he proposes that the terrorising element of law is that it determines legitimate violence—it designates who may be killed with impunity, according to the plan (soldiers who are designated as military deaths, criminals who, if not killed on the streets or by the police, will be subjected to the violence of the law's punishment), and who may not. This points to the violent nature of the law itself because it is responding to violence—yet this response to violence is, by necessity, another form of violence.[52] All of the Joker's escapades draw out not only the presumed violence of a state of nature, but the violence of the law itself. Rather than being a radical figure of evil or a revolutionary figure of the truth, the Joker embodies a much more conservative position because all of his activities are premised on the law itself.

For Hobbes, the 'state of nature' is the necessary foundation of the state and law. It is in response to the 'state of nature' that the all-powerful sovereign is needed and individuals give up their rights to violence to the state in return for the state's protection.[53] Following Agamben's analysis, in return for protection from each other, individuals agree to become *homo sacer*—he who may be killed with impunity but not sacrificed—in relation to the state.[54] The state of nature, from which individuals have exited, is then incorporated into the city via the violence inherent in the sovereign exception:

> The state of nature is . . . a state of exception, in which the city appears for an instant . . . *tanquam dissoluta*. The foundation is thus not an event achieved once and for all but is continually operative in the civil state in the form of the sovereign decision.[55]

The law thus presupposes itself as instituted *against* a state of nature, a chaos or anarchy that would rule without it. The assumption of anarchy and chaos, however, is an assumption *internal to the law*. As such, the Joker's activities themselves are premised on the operation of the law. His

[51] Ibid., pp. 84–6, 99–101 (in particular pp. 100–1).
[52] Milbank, *Being Reconciled*, pp. 36–8 and Chapter 2 in general. For the two classic analyses of the relation between violence and the law see Benjamin, 'Critique of Violence'; Cover, 'Violence and the Word'.
[53] Hobbes, 'Leviathan', pp. 47, 99–101.
[54] Agamben, *Homo Sacer*, p. 106; Hobbes, 'Leviathan', pp. 112–17 (in particular pp. 113–14).
[55] Agamben, *Homo Sacer*, p. 109.

provocative disruption of the law's operations does not challenge it but rather strengthens its force—the disruption of order privileges rather than undermines that order.

The battle between Batman and the Joker, which appears to be the central premise of the film, would therefore supposedly encompass two sides of the violence of the law: the anarchy of the 'state of nature' and the violence of the sovereign exception. However, as just noted, these two aspects of violence are structurally identical—Batman and the Joker appearing as two sides of the same coin. This would reflect the general reading of the film in relation to the comic-book tradition and Nichols's mythical references.[56] The problem with this reading is that, in the end, Batman refuses to embody the violent operation of the state of exception/state of nature. Whilst, in the earlier interrogation scene, he attempts to use violence against the Joker, what he discovers is that the violence itself promulgates more violence (which the Joker is expert at manipulating). In the final showdown, Batman's response to the Joker changes. He refrains from enacting physical violence on his body, aimed at retribution or penance, or exercising the sovereign right of life and death, but returns to a use of violence purely as a preventative action.[57] The Joker, revelling in the fight, exclaims that he and Batman are destined to do this forever. Batman disputes the claim, saying that the Joker will be in a padded cell. Despite having the opportunity to let the Joker fall to his death, Batman saves him. In the end, killing the Joker would simply prove his point, conflate violence with the law and conclude that the only solution to the problem of violence is death—at the hands of the sovereign. What thus occurs in this final showdown is a decentring of the Joker from the narrative focus of the film. Instead of agreeing with the Joker's self-description as a diabolical figure of evil (which would encompass the never-ending battle between Good and Evil discussed in Chapter 1 and depicted in the Batman mythos with the ongoing clashes between the Caped Crusader and the Clown Prince of Gotham), Batman's rejecting of the Joker's games reduces him to the conservative figure of the criminal that needs to be restrained. Rather than an anarchical figure who is challenging the law itself, the Joker wants to show things 'as they really are'. He is thus not interested in *changing* the situation in Gotham City, either for good or for bad. But the possibility of changing the situation in Gotham *is* the premise of the first part of the film, which is that the legitimate, public figure of the law could be the basis for change in

[56] See, for example, Alan Moore's *Batman: The Killing Joke*, which works through the structural similarities of the Joker and Batman: Moore et al., *The Killing Joke*.

[57] For discussion of the connections between justice and penance in Western law see Sharp, 'Religion and Justice'.

Gotham City. It is for this reason that the conclusion of the film becomes not about the Joker, who merely demonstrates the violent foundation of the law, but about the figure of the lawyer who was supposed to change the city through the law itself: Harvey Dent.

IV. 'The only morality in a cruel world is chance': Law, Procedural Justice and the Toss of the Coin

Harvey Dent, in the early parts of the film, is presented as the figure of the 'heroic lawyer' who could achieve justice *through* the legal system, when Batman could achieve justice only beyond or outside the legal system. When Harvey claimed that Batman was operating in the role of the dictator or the figure of the exception who protects the city and the law in a time of crisis, he saw this as a legitimate position in relation to the law. At the same time, it is Harvey who could implement justice *through* the law via his skills as an advocate (as seen in the trial scenes), his knowledge of nuances of legal cases and legislation (invoking 'RICO' or racketeering laws as the basis for prosecuting the mob as a whole), and his use of both legal and political strategy (his justification to the mayor for the prosecution of the mob). It is his ability to bring justice through the law and his elevation as Gotham's 'white knight' that provide the reasons that Batman sees him as his replacement—the legitimate role of the 'heroic lawyer' to replace the illegitimate role of the superhero[58]—as well as the reason that the Joker decides to try and 'bring him down to our level' after the death of Rachel. As noted above, the Joker does this via a critique of 'the plans' of Gotham City, its rules and laws, as well as his invocation to 'introduce a little anarchy', identifying himself as the agent of a chaos that is 'fair'.

For Harvey, who has suffered both physical deformity and the loss of his fiancée, the Joker plays upon the desire for meaning in the face of suffering. He claims that the meaning imposed upon life and upon tragic events is limited, arbitrary and faulty because it is caught up in the plans aimed at controlling the world. The meaning-making power of law for which Harvey as a lawyer and Gotham's 'white knight' stood—its ability to determine justice and punishment of the criminal—has failed.[59] In contrast to Harvey's

---

[58] For discussion of the 'heroic lawyer' in popular culture see, for example: Asimow, 'When Lawyers Were Heroes'; Bainbridge, 'Lawyers, Justice and the State'; Kamir, 'Anatomy of Hollywood's Hero-Lawyer'; Kamir, 'Hollywood's Contemporary Hero-Lawyer'. For discussions of 'superheroic lawyers' see Bainbridge, 'This is the Authority'; Sharp, 'Riddle Me This'; Mitchell, 'Legal Reading of She-Hulk'.

[59] Berger, 'On the Book of Job', pp. 107–12.

immediate attempt to blame the Joker for Rachel's death, the Joker points the blame at chaos—chaos, in its *lack* of determinate meaning, is fair because it applies to everyone equally. It is this understanding of chaos that provides a means for Harvey to deal with the loss of Rachel as if it was an aspect of chance (later representing Rachel's death as a fifty-fifty chance). What is important here is not that Harvey takes on the Joker's invocation of chaos directly but the way he interprets it through the act of tossing a coin.[60]

Instead of reproducing the Joker's picture of law as determined by a pre-supposed fundamental chaos, Harvey's role as a lawyer—enmeshed in the procedural aspects of the legal system, its notion of the rule of law, due process and procedural fairness—is *heightened*, rather than laid aside in his vengeful desire to kill all those involved in Rachel's death. His proclamation that 'chance is fair', then, is a reflection of the fairness supposedly embodied in the elements of procedural justice before the law. The point for Harvey is *not* about substantive justice in terms of whether the accused is guilty or innocent, but rather about whether or not they receive a 'fair trial'. Even though Harvey goes beyond the law in terms of dealing a retributive justice, instead of taking up an exceptional status in relation to the law (like that of the superhero) he works to fulfil the very role of the law itself: to provide meaning to suffering in the sense of punishing the criminal.[61] In taking up the goal of the law, he *also* takes up its structural operations that are aimed not at substantive but at procedural justice, compressing all the elements of legal procedural justice into a single toss of the coin. Harvey is thus distanced from making the determinant decision of justice—the decision of life and death, of guilt or innocence, of the person accused—and rather focuses on ensuring an absolutely fair and equal *access* to such a decision of judgment determined by an arbitrary action. This is a vision of secular modernity that is founded not so much on the character of the judge but on the effectiveness of an institutional system of justice.[62] As Harvey shouts at Batman in the final scenes of the film: 'it's not about what I want, it's about what's fair!' Harvey's

---

[60] In a number of early scenes in the film, Harvey leaves what would be important decisions up to a toss of his father's lucky coin. After he confesses to being Batman and is being taken into custody, he gives the coin to Rachel and the audience learns that it is a two-headed coin. Instead of leaving things to chance, Harvey 'made his own luck' (via the process of appearing to leave things to chance). After Rachel's death, one side of the coin is disfigured, leaving a clear head on one side and a scarred/blackened image on the other—as such, the odds have changed.

[61] See Chapter 1 above; Berger, 'On the Book of Job', pp. 107–12; Jeffery, *Evil and International Relations*, pp. 13–32.

[62] Manderson, 'Trust Us Justice', pp. 35–6.

commitment to the process of justice implemented through the legal system is retained and incorporated into an objective system that embodies the conception of justice as chance.[63] As he proclaims, 'the world is cruel and the only morality in a cruel world is chance: unbiased, unprejudiced, fair'.

Batman's desire to return the mantle for protecting the city to the 'legitimate' figure of Harvey Dent is based on the idea that, in the normal course, justice can be achieved through the law. However, the focus on Harvey as Gotham's 'white knight' still encapsulates a sense of the heroic. It flags that the 'impartial' system of law is determined by the fallible hands of corrupt police, lawyers and judges, and is thus reliant on the 'heroic lawyer' to manipulate the system to achieve a just outcome. Whilst, after Rachel's death, Harvey's belief in the legal system comes crashing down, his commitment to a system that can produce justice does not. When Harvey goes out killing those that were involved in Rachel's kidnapping, he is not simply out seeking vengeance. Rather, his commitment to justice and legality takes over. Instead of looking to the fallible justice of a legal system reliant on multiple individuals who are all possibly corrupt, justice becomes a toss of the coin, based purely on chance and under which everyone's chance—everyone's access to justice—is the same. Harvey renders legality in a way that critiques the formality of law—its focus on due process and fairness *before* the law, which is a systematic reliance on particular individuals to fulfil the rule of law itself. Harvey thus embodies the traditional critique of the law found in the superhero genre—that the law is fallible and inadequate, and consistently fails to achieve justice. Instead of attempting to achieve justice in the role of the superhero, Harvey tries to perfect the system of law through a single action, which is not determined by the quality of the lawyer, the impartiality of the judge or the reliability of witness testimony. *Access* to justice becomes equal for all and all content is removed from the decision—all that is left is a simple, fair act: the toss of the coin.

This emptying of all content from the decision and displacing it into an objective act highlights the structural role that the decision plays in law. Law, despite its claim to determinativeness, generality and applicability, is brought into actuality only through the legal decision.[64] The *application* of the law is always reliant on a decision, whether by the judge in the ordinary course or

---

[63] On the consideration of the toss of the coin as an objective system comparative to the law see Giddens, 'Navigating the Looking Glass'. On a reading of Harvey Dent as an archetype of the criminal prosecutor see Rendleman, 'Two Faces of Criminal Prosecution'.

[64] Agamben, *State of Exception*, pp. 36–7; cf Fitzpatrick, *Modernism*, pp. 73–5; see also Kahn, *Political Theology*, pp. 62–90.

the sovereign in the exceptional case. The decision, however, can be implemented only through the law's suspension in the very act of application.[65] If a particular case were to be decided exactly in accordance with the law, then the judge is not actually deciding anything, for the law already determines the outcome. Yet, in order to move from the generality of the law to the specificity of the case being considered, a decision has to bridge the gap between the general and the specific. As such, the decision fulfils a structural position within the law and cannot be predetermined (or else it would not be a decision). The judge needs to *decide* to make the law apply or not apply in the particular circumstance.[66] This structural requirement within the law for a decision, however, risks the possibility of the decision being arbitrarily determined. This cannot be simply justified by recourse to 'applying the law', for applying the law to the particular circumstance already demonstrates that the application is something separate to, and not captured within, the generality of the law itself. In this sense, the legal decision becomes structurally indeterminate and devoid of pre-determined content.

When Harvey elevates the legal system into the toss of the coin, he simply removes the fallibility of the individual deciding and leaves the decision to the toss of the coin. The potential for arbitrariness is dealt with by the law in terms of its focus on due process at one level and on the ability for appeal at another. Yet the system of law itself in its implementation is concerned *not* so much with whether substantive justice is determined because, as Jacques Derrida is often quoted as saying that justice is aporetic and can never be fully determined.[67] The 'humanness' of law in its potential fallibility focuses on procedural justice, due process, fair hearings and proper recourse to appeal. This focus on form over substance is exactly what the superhero genre is seen as critiquing.[68] Harvey's shift from enacting justice *through* the law to a fulfilling of justice *beyond* the law captures that element of vigilante justice traditionally seen in the likes of Batman (and more fully in the character of Daredevil).[69] At the same time, the structure of Harvey's actions conforms to

---

[65] Agamben, *State of Exception*, pp. 39–40. See also Agamben, *Homo Sacer*, p. 20; Fitzpatrick, *Modernism*, pp. 73–8; Derrida, 'Force of Law'.

[66] That is, the law has to 'originate in each act of legal decision'. Fitzpatrick, *Modernism*, p. 81. See also pp. 74–5, where he quotes Derrida: 'each case is other, each decision is different and requires an absolutely unique interpretation, which no existing coded rule can or ought to guarantee absolutely'. Derrida, 'Force of Law', pp. 23–4.

[67] Derrida, 'Force of Law'.

[68] Which, as Sharp has demonstrated, follows certain general public perceptions and attitudes about law and justice. See Sharp, 'Riddle Me This'.

[69] See Bainbridge, 'This is the Authority'; Sharp, 'Riddle Me This'.

the legal system and a legal decision compressed into a process that attempts to remove the potential for corruption (as he experienced in terms of the police), as well as arbitrary or influenced decisions (by judges or juries). The challenge of the law to deal substantive over procedural justice is compressed into a fifty-fifty chance, which is always the same: the single toss of the coin.

As noted in Chapter 2, modern law is supposed to be self-grounding, determinant and certain—a closed and coherent system that dispels arbitrary and discretionary power. At the same time, law's determinant certainty is always threatened by the demands of responsiveness—the *ends* to which the law is put and the basis upon which it justifies its violent implementation. No longer able to shore itself up in terms of a divine justice, it seeks its perfection in the promise of procedure. And yet, despite all its procedural requirements, the law is reliant on the actions of individuals that can be corrupted and the decisions of individuals that could be arbitrary. It is this potential for arbitrariness and corruption—the law's fallibility itself—that Harvey reveals in *The Dark Knight*. Batman's actions at the end of the film, however, instead of reaffirming the vigilante role of the superhero as the supplement of the law, open up the possibility for a different foundation for the community of the city and a theological vision of legality—one based upon trust rather than a recourse to law. It is to this possibility that I now turn.

V. Law, Compassion and the Non-hero: Batman as a Typology of Christ

After Batman's showdown with the Joker, discussed above, the concluding sequence of the film follows Dent's kidnapping of Commissioner Gordon's family and his attempt to 'punish' Gordon for pragmatically working with crooked cops (which created the opportunity for Rachel's kidnapping and death), despite Dent's warnings. Dent takes Gordon's son and threatens to subject him to the toss of the coin—the same fifty-fifty chance that everyone else has and that Rachel received. When Harvey flips the coin, Batman tackles him, saving Gordon's son. Harvey, however, falls to his death (followed by Batman, who is injured). In order to protect the good image of Harvey Dent and his prosecution of the mob, Batman takes the blame for Dent's killings. The film then concludes with Gordon and the police beginning the hunt for Batman. The framework of this conclusion is thus built around a particular form of deception. As Žižek points out, referencing a number of the old westerns, such as those made by John Ford,[70] the message of the film

---

[70] For example, *Fort Apache*, film, directed by Ford; *The Man Who Shot Liberty Valance*, film, directed by Ford.

appears to be that 'only a lie can save us'. [71] In the westerns, in order to civilise the Wild West, there is a need to 'print the legend' rather than the truth. *The Dark Knight* presents a similar trope in inverted form. In the John Ford films, the lie is in the form of giving someone credit for a heroic act they did not commit—glorifying the actions of those involved in founding events of the community.[72] In *The Dark Knight*, however, it is not so much about giving credit for noble acts as it is about attributing blame to Batman for criminal acts he did not commit (the murders committed by Harvey Dent).

As will be seen in the next chapter, Nolan's conclusion to the trilogy, *The Dark Knight Rises*, presents a particular reading of these events seeing 'the lie' promulgated by Gordon as deceitful and inherently problematic. Whilst the conclusion of *The Dark Knight* has a sense of discomfort and moral ambiguity about it, to read 'the lie' as simply and straightforwardly 'bad' misunderstands the nature of Nolan's film-making. As McGowan has pointed out, each of Nolan's films (not just the Batman ones) is based on a particular deception that is presented to the audience at the beginning of the film, only to be later revealed as a lie and replaced with a higher truth. Nolan does this not by 'showing events that aren't really happening'[73] but by showing 'events that actually transpire in the filmic universe, [where] the formal structure leads the spectators to misinterpret these events'.[74] It is the *form* that operates as a deceit, rather than the content: '[t]he structure of the films deceives the spectator about the meaning of the events seen.'[75] This is not a moralism, illustrating the 'priority of deceit in order to denounce lying and insist on the importance of truthfulness'.[76] Rather, it is ethical cinema because of the way in which it 'redefines the relationship between ethics and truthfulness'.[77] 'Nolan inverts the traditional priority of truth and deception: the quest for

[71] See Žižek, *Living in the End Times*, p. 61. For a discussion of the connections between the superhero genre and the western in relation to law, see Manderson, 'Trust Us Justice'.

[72] That is, in *The Man Who Shot Liberty Valence* the lie is that it was Ransom Stoddard (James Stewart) who shot Liberty Valence, when it was in fact Tom Doniphon (John Wayne). In *Fort Apache*, the lie is Captain York's (John Wayne) acknowledgment that Colonel Thursday (Henry Fonda) fought a glorious battle against the Apaches when in fact his arrogant tactics stupidly resulted in the death of most of his men.

[73] McGowan, *Fictional Christopher Nolan*, p. 1.

[74] Ibid.

[75] Ibid.

[76] Ibid., p. 3.

[77] Ibid.

truth originates with a lie, just as the cinematic fiction itself creates a terrain for the discovery of truths.'[78]

It is in this perspective on the nature of the cinematic truth that Nolan presents that my Christological claim lies. Earlier in the film, Batman's concluding actions are foreshadowed in a discussion between Bruce Wayne and his butler, Alfred. Alfred argued that, despite the killings of the Joker, Batman should not give in to his demands. Rather, the whole purpose of Batman is that (despite being hated for such actions) he can endure the unendurable. When it comes to the final scene, then, Batman willingly takes the blame for Dent's murders and commits himself to being hunted and condemned as an outlaw, so that the people will not lose hope in their 'white knight', the 'legitimate' hero of Gotham City. It is this presentation of a willing and necessary wrongful conviction, in both structure and motivation, that is the basis for a comparison between Batman and Christ, and which goes to the possibility of a different founding of legality in the community. From a legal perspective, the Christian Passion story in the gospel narratives is a story of a wrongful conviction: a man sentenced to death for crimes that either could not be identified or, where they are pointed to, were not committed.[79] Yet, in the Christian tradition, it is this wrongful conviction and execution that founds a new community and a different relation to law. It is this structural similarity between Christ and Batman that I will now explore.

Theologian John Milbank notes that, in the Christian tradition, Christ, the God-Man, 'died precisely a purely divine and a purely human, or even sub-human, death'.[80] The divine death was a result of resentment or envy at his elevated position—his claim to be divine. The human death, however, was at the hands of the arbitrary sovereign authority—via exclusion, as bare life.[81] Drawing on Agamben, Milbank classifies Christ as *homo sacer*, abandoned, cast out and excluded from political life by the Jewish authorities, the Roman authorities and then the mob.[82] In this sense, Christ's death was not noble, heroic or with dignity but rather a death of 'utterly emptied-out humanity': 'he died the death that proves and exemplified sovereignty in its arbitrariness'.[83] The scandal of the cross is that Christ was executed as a

---

[78] Ibid. p. 10.

[79] See Milbank, *Being Reconciled*, pp. 95–6.

[80] Ibid., p. 95.

[81] Ibid., pp. 92–3, 97; Agamben, *Homo Sacer*.

[82] See Matt. 26: 57 to 27: 26; Mark 14: 53 to 15: 15; Luke 22: 66 to 23: 25; John 18: 12 to 19: 16 (ESV).

[83] That is, he died 'the death which any of us, under sovereign authority, in exceptional circumstances which always prove the rule, may possibly die'. Milbank, *Being Reconciled*, p. 96.

criminal and an outlaw: 'Jesus imbued with his divine height died precisely the death of absolute innocence.'[84] Yet Christ's abandonment and execution is not the end-point, for, as Milbank emphasises, it is not simply that we should identify with Christ as a victim. Rather, Christ's death on the cross and his exclusion from the law at each level ('by the Jewish law of its tribal nation; by the Roman universal law of empire; by the democratic will of the mob'[85]) were a direct result of Christ's intentional failure to resist human power. Christ 'went freely to his death because he knew that a merely human counter-power is always futile and temporary'.[86] Christ knew that the only true challenge to the violence of the law, the state and the people was a *non-violent self-giving*,[87] and it is this non-violent act that forms the foundation of a new type of community, based on the rejected and excluded one as the most envied *and* unrepeatable one.[88]

To return to *The Dark Knight*, my argument here is that Batman embodies a typology of Christ in this form of exclusion. In the final scenes of the film Batman takes up a position of exclusion that is structurally different to the superhero embodying of the sovereign exception. This is not to argue that Batman *is* Christ or even a stand-in for Christ, for, as Milbank has argued, the actions of Christ himself are utterly unrepeatable. Rather, it is that the actions of Batman in *The Dark Knight* refer to and repeat differently the actions of Christ. It is in identifying this reference point that we find the difference between Nolan's Batman and the superhero genre, for the superhero as the figure beyond the law operates as the exception to it and, as such, enables its completion or fulfilment beyond its limits. In the state of exception or emergency the superhero, out of necessity, goes beyond the law and operates as if it is suspended in order to deal with the crisis and restore the social order. The superhero in the end becomes the exception that determines legality and this is why superhero films are so easily incorporated into conservative post-9/11 ideologies around the need for exceptional measures

[84] Ibid., p. 97. At the same time, Milbank questions Agamben's analysis of *homo sacer* as not being offered as sacrifice, rather noting that '[a]ll that is certain is that he was to be killed without ritual purification—but this is still consistent with a total offering, as indeed the Israelite examples attest: totally unclean towns were to be offered to Yahweh.' See ibid., p. 92.

[85] Ibid., p. 96.

[86] Ibid., p. 99.

[87] As Milbank notes, 'Jesus only submits to being handed over because he is in himself the very heart of all transition as really loving gift, and thereby able to subvert every betrayal and abandonment.' Ibid.

[88] Ibid., p. 98.

in the 'war on terror'. Nolan's version of Batman, however, frames a form of *exclusion* as opposed to simply the sovereign exception discussed above, which occurs through Batman taking the blame for Harvey Dent's actions. It is not simply that Batman is elevated because of his exceptional relation to the law, but that he is envied and rejected because of it.

When the Joker threatens the city with death and destruction if Batman does not take off his mask and turn himself in, Dent tells a press conference that they should not give in to his demands. The crowd-cum-mob rejects Batman and demands that he reveal himself. Rachel, Bruce's best friend and one of the few people who knows his secrets, rejects him, believing that there would never come a day when he did not need to be Batman. Finally, in the closing scenes of the film, when Batman takes the blame for Dent's murders, he is rejected and cast out by the police, who will now hunt him down as a criminal and an outlaw. Batman is thus excluded at every level: in terms of his role as protector of Gotham (by the democratic will of the mob), in his personal relationships *because* of his role as Batman (by Rachel), and finally in his relationship to the law itself (by Gordon and the police). Yet it is through these exclusions that we see how Batman refuses the heroic and sovereign employing of the exception as a means of justifying his actions. Instead, it is in the process of *not* being a hero that Batman lays bare the fundamental violent elements of the law and the arbitrary exercise of sovereign power.[89] In effectively taking the blame for Harvey Dent's murders, he deactivates the law and puts it on display, revealing its failure to identify, let alone punish, the criminal. Batman becomes the exception via exclusion and rejection, which opens another space outside of the law and its punishment—outside of the exception which is included via its exclusion. This acceptance of the position of exclusion is one that involves a non-resistance to human violence, a non-resistance founded on love or compassion which challenges both the law and its grounding in violence.[90]

---

[89] The point about not being a hero is made by Alfred earlier in the film. When Harvey initially turns himself in as being the Batman (in an attempt to quell the crowds and draw out the Joker for Batman to take down), Rachel is distraught as to why Bruce did not come forward to set the record straight. Alfred responds by saying '[p]erhaps both Bruce and Mr Dent believe that Batman stands for something more important than the whims of a terrorist, Ms Dawes. Even if everyone hates him for it. That's the sacrifice he's making. He's *not* being a hero. He's being something more.' Rachel does not seem to understand this point when she claims that Bruce 'letting Harvey take the fall . . . is not heroic at all'.

[90] In *Batman Begins* Bruce's confrontation and challenge to Ra's Al Ghul is based explicitly on compassion (for which Ra's criticises him). This compassion thus becomes foundational for all his actions as Batman. See discussion in Peters, 'Unbalancing Justice', pp. 261–3.

It is from this perspective that we can understand Batman's actions not as a form of vigilante retributive justice, but rather as compassionate acts of preventative justice—attempts to prevent crimes from being committed and from evil being done, which arise out of a care for both the potential victim *and* the potential perpetrator.[91] This compassion is the way to understand Batman's actions in the final confrontation with Harvey at the end of *The Dark Knight*. When Batman appears on the scene, he says: 'You don't want to hurt the boy, Harvey' (to which Harvey responds, as noted above, 'it's not about what I want, it's about what's fair'). In this invocation from Batman there is an attempt to defuse the situation but also a compassionate response that recognises that Harvey *does not want* to engage in this act of violence (killing Gordon's son). Batman not only is interested in saving the city or the boy but also desires to save Harvey as well. When, after being shot, Batman lunges at Harvey, it is not simply about saving Gordon's son (which he does) but it is *also* about saving Harvey—both from death but, more importantly, from an action of violence that he would later regret. This action of preventative violence fails in terms of Harvey's death, but succeeds in terms of ensuring that Dent *is not* the murderer of an innocent little boy.[92] This is important because, whilst Harvey's other killings were, in effect, a dealing of retributive justice beyond the law (killing those who were directly involved in Rachel's death—corrupt cops and mobsters), the killing of Gordon's son would be something else altogether.

The subsequent actions by Batman in taking the blame for Dent's killings, which present a certain moral discomfort, are directly aimed both at saving Dent and at challenging the Joker's accusations of the people of Gotham—that underneath the supposed civility of law and society lie the violence and natural rights of the state of nature; that, given the right circumstances and the deficiency of the law to maintain its monopoly on violence, anybody can revert back to these exceptional natural rights. However, Batman comes to understand that the final challenge to the Joker cannot occur at the level of an ever-escalating violent exchange. Rather, the only way to counter the violence of the state of nature is not with more violence but with an active non-resistance to violence. To challenge the Joker's claim requires an act of compassion that *does not* invoke either the arbitrary justice of the law *or* the

---

[91] For a discussion of this type of violence or counter-violence, see Milbank, *Being Reconciled*, pp. 26–43.

[92] A point that *The Dark Knight Rises* misses, with Gordon in his speech (read by Bane) calling Dent a monster who threatened his son—to which I will return in Chapter 4.

natural rights of the state of nature. Such a non-resistance to violence deactivates the law and opens the possibility for a different conception of law and a different founding of the community—one based not on a self-interested wielding of ultimately violent natural rights, but on an underlying faith or trust in the possibility of relationship with others, despite our flaws and tendency towards violence.

This privileging of faith or trust in others is also the important outcome of the 'prisoner's dilemma' scenario on the ferries. In the struggle between Batman and the Joker, the Joker says: 'We really should stop this fighting, otherwise we'll miss the fireworks.' Batman's confident response is 'there won't be any fireworks'. Batman maintains a faith in the people of Gotham—both the civilians and the criminals—and later proclaims their *failure* to blow each other up as a demonstration of their willingness 'to believe in good'. In terms of the scenes that the viewer sees of the people on the ferries themselves, instead of either the criminals or the civilians engaging in the 'calculating' decision of blowing each other up, both groups 'risk it all' by having faith and trust in the other group. On the boat full of civilians, after the 'democratic vote' has come down overwhelmingly in favour of blowing up the other ferry, the captain suddenly realises and points out that they themselves have not been blown up yet—which means that the criminals have not yet taken the action that they are about to take. The risk of the scenario, for both groups, is that, in waiting or *not* blowing up the other, they will themselves be blown up. But that *risk* is always the risk of trusting in others—that our trust may be broken. Whilst our desire for legality is rooted within a need for certainty, and a desire for the protections that the legal system attempts to provide, even those protections and certainty can be undermined because the system is always *dependent* on individuals who may themselves be corrupted. In contrast, founding legality and community on trust in one another, even if that trust may be broken, provides the only real way for individuals to come together in solidarity.[93]

It is this privileging of trust that is the reason why Batman argues that Gotham needs to 'have its faith rewarded' and, in the concluding scene, takes actions that mirror the atoning actions of Christ on the cross. By first preventing Dent from killing Gordon's son and then taking the blame for Dent's murders, Batman ensures that Dent *did not* become the monster the Joker was envisioning him to be and also that Gotham City did not see him in this

---

[93] For the theological framing of this turn to trust as opposed to legality, see Milbank, 'Paul Against Biopolitics', in particular pp. 48–58.

way. Such an action is antithetical to the notion of the hero who, in operating within the role of the exception, becomes a law unto himself.[94] Instead, we find that in the complete non-resistance to the law, in taking the blame and punishment for crimes that he did not commit, the power of the law in its ability both to protect the citizens and to condemn the criminals (categories which, in the end, overlap) is deactivated and broken. It is for this reason that Gordon's concluding voice-over specifically describes Batman as *not* a hero. Rather, he is 'a silent guardian, a watchful protector . . . a Dark Knight'.

VI. Conclusion: 'We don't need another hero'

Given the continuing biopolitical tensions of our present times, heightened by the continued and ever-increasing series of 'emergencies' and 'crises' that demand exceptionalised responses—terror, economic or ecological crisis, global pandemic—*The Dark Knight* presents a contrasting message: what we need is *not* a figure that would embody the exceptional decision of the sovereign, which, in the end, is *always* a decision of life and death. Rather, we need to see that, in the capacity to suffer and endure death to the very end, we find a different way of conceiving life that is not based on an economy of death-dealing violence, whether authorised or illegitimate, legal or illegal, exceptional or otherwise. The possibility of affirming life itself comes from a recognition of suffering and evil as part of life that must be *both* endured and responded to. It is only through such an endurance and a response to evil that is not about *eradicating* the perpetrator, so much as compassionately preventing the *potential* perpetrator from committing an act that they will later regret themselves, that we find a way of affirming life outside of its biopolitical frameworks (not in terms of the 'presumed' natural life outside the law which is always determined by the law, but a life that is in, through and beyond the law itself). It is in this sense that *The Dark Knight* renders visible aspects of a particular legal imaginary based on legality and retributive justice, but also opens the possibility of a *different* response—one that comes in the form of a non-heroic non-resistance of violence, which presumes the possibility of trust as the foundation of community, even at the risk of that trust being broken. This is the importance of the connections between Batman and Christ that I have outlined above—a connection based on the non-heroic as opposed to the heroic (for Christ in no sense fits the tradition of the heroic exception, the Greek cosmology of heroes or the death and rebirth of the Greek gods). Christ represents a divine and human death in a very particular way but also

[94] See McGowan, 'Exceptional Darkness', paras [4]–[5].

a resurrection that opens the possibility for a new life beyond law—one based in the possibility of faith or trust in each other. If anything, the end-point of *The Dark Knight* demonstrates that the solution is *not* a hero, despite their recent filmic proliferation. That is to say, to repeat in a different context the words of Tina Turner, 'we don't need another hero'.[95]

---

[95] Turner, 'We Don't Need Another Hero' Soundtrack.

4

A Tale of Two Gothams: Revolution, Sacrifice and the Rule of Law in *The Dark Knight Rises*

'I am the resurrection and the life. Whoever believes in me, though he die, yet shall he live.'

John 11: 25

'It is a far, far better thing that I do, than I have ever done; it is a far, far better rest that I go to, than I have ever known.'

Dickens, *A Tale of Two Cities*[1]

1. Introduction

My argument in the previous chapter was that Batman's concluding actions in *The Dark Knight* present a Christological foregrounding of community based on trust and forgiveness—Batman's 'saving' of Dent involved a deactivation of the law through a form of atoning work. However, one of the risks of such a deactivating and subordinating of the law is that, instead of bringing peace, it will unleash *more* violence. This would appear to be the story that *The Dark Knight Rises* tells.[2] As it picks up eight years after the previous film, Commissioner Gordon (Gary Oldham) is wracked with guilt over the burden of the deception which he and Batman promulgated—that it was Batman (Christian Bale), not Harvey Dent (Aaron Eckhart), who had committed a number of murders and that Batman had then murdered Dent (who is remembered as a hero). This lie appears to have been a 'success': it provided the political foundation for the Dent Act, a tough-on-crime instrument which gives the police greater powers to tackle crime, and to lock up over a thousand criminals with mandatory sentencing and no parole. This led Bruce Wayne to believe, as he covertly tells Gordon: 'The Batman wasn't needed any more. We won.' However, it is a combination of these repressive measures and the unveiling of Batman and Gordon's deception that paves the way for the villain, Bane (Tom Hardy), to masquerade as the great liberator of society, the revolutionary revealer of the truth who leads a 'Dictatorship of

---

[1] Dickens, 'A Tale of Two Cities', p. 848.
[2] *The Dark Knight Rises*, film, directed by Nolan.

the Proletariat' in Gotham City.[3] It was these themes, prominently presented in trailers, that raised concerns from right-wing commentators prior to the film's release that it was a conspiracy against the Mitt Romney campaign (citing, in particular, the homonymic quality of Bane with Romney's Bain Capital).[4]

As a number of Left commentators noted after the release of the film, Romney had little to worry about.[5] All the critical rhetoric and resonances with the claims of the 99 per cent in the film lead not to the pacifism of the Occupy movement but to Bane's exceptionally violent revolution, with one commentator describing the film as 'a piece of anti-Occupy propaganda'.[6] When one recalls that Batman's alter ego, Bruce Wayne, is a billionaire and associated with the industrial company Wayne Enterprises (engaged in significant arms manufacture), the outline of the film would appear to be a conservative allegory. Nolan himself disputed any such political reading or explicit association with Occupy, arguing that the inspiration for the film came from his brother and co-producer's reading of Charles Dickens's *A Tale of Two Cities*.[7] Whilst the late David Graeber noted that such a claim is most likely true but also disingenuous, it is this connection to Dickens in particular that is the focus of my argument here.[8] By taking this connection seriously, we are able to see the way in which *The Dark Knight Rises* is not so much a political allegory, but a legal mythology—one which turns to that significant event in the founding of modern secular legality, the French Revolution.

Read in this light, the film is not so much a vindication of a conservative critique of revolutionary or popular uprisings (re-establishing the normal order so that Capital can continue unhindered once again), but rather a presentation of a secular legal theology and a critique of modern neoliberal legality. Such a reading takes seriously the central theme of *The Dark Knight Rises*, which is rendered visible in the final moments of the film: sacrifice. However, as noted in the previous chapter, this is *not* a straightforward rendering of the

---

[3] Žižek, 'People's Republic of Gotham', 23 August 2012; Žižek, 'Dictatorship of the Proletariat', 8 August 2012.
[4] See Finocchiaro, 'Villain "Bane" a Deliberate Romney Reference', 18 July 2012; see also the discussion in St Clair, 'The Bomb in the City'; McGowan, 'Should the Dark Knight have Risen?'.
[5] See, for example, Fisher, 'Batman's Political Right Turn', 23 July 2012; Fisher and White, 'Politics of "The Dark Knight Rises"', 4 September 2012; McGowan, 'Should the Dark Knight have Risen?'.
[6] Graeber, 'Super Position', 8 October 2012.
[7] Dickens, 'A Tale of Two Cities'.
[8] Graeber, 'Super Position', 8 October 2012.

theological reading of the superhero as saviour figure, with Batman giving up his life to save the city. Rather, the sacrificial theme is both completed (Batman appears to be killed in the process of saving Gotham from a nuclear explosion) but also complexified and deconstructed (Bruce Wayne is revealed as not dead) in the closing moments of the film. In this sense, the relationship of sacrifice to the law of the city—a law disrupted by Batman and the villains he fights, but restored in his having given himself up for the city—is represented as *both* necessary *and* deceptive. It is a law which co-opts the rites and rituals of sacrifice as a means of sustaining its appearance of order, control and stability. The split outcome of the figure of Batman/Bruce Wayne in the concluding moments of the film (Batman dies, Bruce Wayne lives) therefore provides the key to understanding the film, and for taking up the challenge to modern forms of law, power, security and the exception discussed in the previous chapter. If Chapter 3 undertook a 'Christological' reading of *The Dark Knight*, this chapter extends that analysis by exploring *The Dark Knight Rises* not as a Christian mythology but a secular one, focused on a sacrificial giving up of one's life to save the city.[9]

The chapter proceeds in Section II by analysing the way in which Nolan's depiction of Batman as a figure of trauma is tied, in *The Dark Knight Rises*, not to his childhood trauma but rather to the traumas of the loss of Rachel in *The Dark Knight* and a lack of faith in the world. This figuring of trauma orientates *The Dark Knight Rises* within the genre of what Claire Sisco King calls the 'sacrificial film'. Section III takes up an aspect of these generic descriptions in terms of the film's broader context (the aftermath of the global financial crisis and populist uprisings such as the 'Occupy' movement), as well as its narrative reference point, Charles Dickens's *A Tale of Two Cities*. Section IV then takes the cinematic, generic and narrative analysis of the previous two sections and works through the way in which the themes of sacrifice and revolution operate together as a visual depiction of both our modern legal mythology *and* the currency of political theology. It furthers the discussion of the superhero as a figure of the exception in the previous chapter, by analysing the way in which the French Revolution itself is a genealogical starting point for the notion of the exception, and the way in which not Batman but Bane is the character that speaks the language of exception. At the same time, rather than Bane's revolution presenting a constituent power, founding a new order, it is likened more to a feast or carnival with an inversion of characters: the minor villain Scarecrow (Cillian Murphy) becoming judge in the 'sentencing

---

[9] As I have noted, secular mythology is understood as being tied to its Western and Christian heritage and roots. See Agamben, *Profanations*, p. 77.

trials' which *presume* the guilt of those brought before them. This presumption forms the basis, in Section V, of an understanding of the theological jurisprudence being articulated as a critique *not* of revolutionary uprisings but of modern neoliberal legality and its deployment in conjunction with the security state: that is, the presumption that *everyone* is potentially guilty, everyone is potentially a terrorist. In contrast, the film points to two potential modes of what Giorgio Agamben terms 'destituent' power or potential: the first in relation to Selina Kyle's attempt to escape the figurations of modern technology's entrapment of identity with the computer program 'Clean Slate'; and second, in terms of the way in which Batman's mask becomes a point of collectivity and a symbol. The conclusion then draws together the two concurrent mythologies intertwined in the film: the secular legal one, which presents the need for someone to sacrifice themselves in order to save the city and which is then remembered (Batman being immortalised in a statue at the town hall); and a more orthodox Christian one, which identifies that the sacrificial economy itself was destituted by Christ's sacrifice, leaving us not with the need to die, to give ourselves up in a self-sacrificial economy to redeem ourselves, but rather to engage in a living sacrifice.

II. A Theo-legality of Trauma: *The Dark Knight Rises* as 'Sacrificial Film'

The origin story of Batman in all its different variations is essentially tied to Bruce Wayne's childhood trauma of seeing his parents brutally murdered in front of his very eyes—a trauma which drives him to train, to seek the means to fight injustice and to turn to the symbol of the 'bat' as a mechanism for playing out a revenge fantasy on the streets of Gotham.[10] This traumatic experience is not just a founding moment for Bruce/Batman, but one that is constantly, incessantly and almost compulsively invoked for the reader/ viewer, whether in comics, film or television. For example, in Jeph Loeb and Tim Sale's *The Long Halloween* we read Batman's internal monologue about the promise he made on his father's grave.[11] In Frank Miller's *Batman: Year One*, the opening image is of Bruce in front of his dead parents, and the famous scene where a bat flies in the window is further dramatised with a bat breaking through the glass window of Bruce's father's study—a scene that is *also* remembered by Bruce Wayne at the beginning of *Batman: The Dark Knight Returns*.[12] Grant Morrison's *Batman: R.I.P* and *The Return of Bruce Wayne* include images of the moments before Bruce's parents died, as

---

[10] Brody, 'Psychic Trauma'; Fisher, 'Gothic Oedipus'; Reynolds, *Super Heroes*, p. 67.
[11] Loeb and Sale, *Batman: The Long Halloween*.
[12] Miller et al., *Year One*; Miller et al., *Dark Knight Returns*.

well as the point when the bat crashes through the window.[13] These are but a few of the multiple interpretations and re-presentations of the original Batman origin story, told over only two pages in the first issue of *Batman* in 1940.[14] What is more, in each of the multiple versions of the Batman mythos that have hit both large and small screens in recent years, we *also* see a constant replaying of this founding trauma—whether it is in Nolan's own *Batman Begins* (2005), the first episode of FOX's *Gotham* (2014–), Zack Snyder's *Batman v Superman: Dawn of Justice* (2016) or even *The LEGO Batman Movie* (2017).[15] This founding trauma is as much a part of the Batman mythos as the cape, cowl and Batmobile. What is more significant, however, is the compulsive nature in which it is shown to us again, again and again—even in *Batman v Superman*, which is *not* an origin story, it becomes a significant plot point with the middle-aged Wayne (played by Ben Affleck) haunted by visions of his parents' grave.[16]

What is significant about *The Dark Knight Rises* is that while Nolan presents Bruce Wayne/Batman specifically as a traumatised victim, hidden in the shadows with no sense of place in the world, it is *not* the childhood trauma that is figured or recapitulated here.[17] Rather it is the trauma of the loss of a lover (Rachel Dawes (Maggie Gyllenhaal), who died in *The Dark Knight*; Alfred (Michael Caine) then reveals to Bruce in *The Dark Knight Rises* that she had made a decision to marry Harvey Dent and not Bruce) and the

---

[13] Morrison, *Batman: The Return of Bruce Wayne*; Morrison and Daniel, *Batman R.I.P.*

[14] Finger et al., *Batman #1*. The first appearance of the Batman was in 1937 in Finger and Kane, *Detective Comics #27*.

[15] *Batman Begins*, film, directed by Nolan; *Gotham*, film, directed by Cannon; *Batman v Superman: Dawn of Justice*, film, directed by Snyder; *The LEGO Batman Movie*, film, directed by McKay.

[16] In all of these televisual and cinematic displays, it is *The LEGO Batman Movie* that takes this issue of trauma most seriously. There, Bruce/Batman is encouraged to confront his trauma and fear of losing anyone close to him with the aim of being able to have a family again (though part of this is in relation to a 'relationship' with the Joker). By contrast, in *Batman v Superman: Dawn of Justice*, despite the prevalence of the knowledge of Batman's origin story, and the fact that this film is *not* an origin story, the depiction of Bruce seeing his parents killed is again central.

[17] That is not to say that the issue of Bruce's childhood trauma does not still influence the films, particularly in relation to their presentation of masculinity and the male body. See Schimmelpfennig, 'Capitalism and Schizophrenia in Gotham'; Winstead, '"As a Symbol I can be Incorruptible"'; Kellner, 'Media Spectacle and Domestic Terrorism'.

failure of a 'save the world investment project' that trouble Bruce. The figure that then haunts Bruce is not his father, who he watched die at the hands of a petty thief as a child, but the surrogate father-figure, Ra's Al Ghul (Liam Neeson)—the man who, after training Bruce, revealed that he was going to destroy Gotham City and whom Batman stops but allows to die at the end of *Batman Begins*.[18] Nolan's situating of Bruce as a figure of trauma is cinematically emphasised via the use of flashbacks, a filmic device that has been described as 'the central device of cinema's representation of trauma'.[19] After Bane breaks Batman's back and then sends Bruce to the 'pit' of a prison in the Middle East, Bruce has a number of visions/flashbacks to sayings or experiences with Ra's Al Ghul, challenging him on his inability to save Gotham or to do so only via the use of a 'lie'.

Given the significance of the flashback as a cinematic representation of trauma, it is worth noting briefly here the trajectory of Nolan's trilogy and its deployment of this device. In Nolan's version of the Batman origin story, *Batman Begins*, there is prolific use of the flashback, particularly to Bruce's childhood, leading up to the night on which his father and mother were killed.[20] The cinematic flashback in this film therefore presents the viewer with Bruce's childhood trauma and the reasons why he sought 'the means to fight injustice' and become Batman. They are figured as dreams or memories that come upon the adult Bruce violently, representing a truth or validity to

---

[18] For my analysis of *Batman Begins*, see Peters, 'Unbalancing Justice'.

[19] Luckhurst, *The Trauma Question*, p. 179. As Luckhurst explains, 'cinema signals traumatic disturbance with the sudden flashback, unsignalled by either voice-over or transitional dissolve, and which is prompted analogically by a graphic (or auditory) match. The flashback is an intrusive anachronic image that throws off the linear temporality of the story. It can only ever be explained belatedly, leaving the spectator in varying degrees of disorientation or suspense, depending on when or whether the flashback is reintegrated into the storyline. This brutal splicing of temporally misadjusted images is the cinema's rendition of the frozen moment of the traumatic impact: it flashes back insistently in the present because this image cannot yet or perhaps ever be narrativized as past' (p. 180). He also notes the interaction between cinematic renderings of flashback and the psychiatric diagnosis of trauma: '[i]f the modern flashback [in film] seems uncannily mimetic of the psychology of trauma, then it is probably because films . . . were instrumental in helping formulate the psychological symptoms of mental illness linked with traumatic origins' (pp. 181–2). See also King, *Washed in Blood*, p. 7.

[20] Most of these flashbacks are depicted as dreams or rememberings when Bruce is asleep, has been knocked out in training with Ra's, or is under the influence of psychotropic drugs from Scarecrow or the League of Shadows.

the subject he becomes.[21] The middle film of Nolan's trilogy, *The Dark Knight*, by contrast, makes no use of flashbacks at all—the viewer is centred specifically in the 'here and now' of what is going on. It is no longer about how Batman came to be, and even when the Joker (Heath Ledger) describes how he came by his scars, it is only ever narrated and never visually depicted—in part because the Joker presents multiple contradictory narratives, so there is never an authentic or valid telling of his origin, but also because of the Joker's incessant focus on his *actions* and his *face*, rather than any 'reason' or interiority behind it.[22] The use of flashbacks cinematographically returns in *The Dark Knight Rises*, starting with Commissioner Gordon's traumatic remembering, in the opening scenes, of the night when Dent threatened his son. But the flashbacks that Bruce Wayne experiences in this film are different. They do not reflect back on his childhood trauma, giving the viewer a sense of the story that they are not otherwise aware of, but are flashbacks to scenes from the first film—sayings, memories and visions of Bruce's training by Ra's. Whereas the use of the flashback in the first film has an air of authenticity or the veridical to it (which is an aspect of the flashback in general), revealing the 'truth' of the earlier event, the flashback sequences of *The Dark Knight Rises* are deceptive.[23] They lead Bruce, and vicariously the viewer, to believe that it was Bane who was trapped as a child in the prison in the Middle East, that Bane was the child of Ra's Al Ghul, and that Bane managed to escape the prison and eventually join the League of Shadows. What Bruce later discovers is that his reliance on these memories and flashbacks is false. The revelatory 'twist' of the film is that the child of Ra's Al Ghul who escaped the prison was not Bane but Talia Al Ghul—who, we discover, has been masquerading as Miranda Tait (Marion Cotillard), board member of Wayne Enterprises and

[21] These flashbacks are not the disorientating traumatic flashback of auteur cinema that Luckhurst describes, but integrate quite specifically with the overall narrative—they become illuminating of the story, rather than requiring illumination (as the traumatic flashback often does), and have a sense of veracity to them. See Luckhurst, *The Trauma Question*, pp. 179–83.

[22] Though, as pointed out in Chapter 3, care is needed in reading this aspect of the Joker's narrative, for the Joker is deceptive by making use of the truth. See McGowan, 'Exceptional Darkness'; Žižek, *Living in the End Times*, pp. 56–61.

[23] The trajectory of the flashback in Nolan's films can thus be charted as follows: in *Batman Begins* the flashback is a straightforward verification of the truth of Batman's origins; in *The Dark Knight*, because of the Joker's playing on the notion of origins and construction, the *absence* of the flashback goes to the *lack* of verification because of the Joker's subject-formation; in *The Dark Knight Rises* the visual verification is then proved false and deceptive. For a discussion of this in the context of *The Dark Knight* trilogy more generally, see Peters, '"Seeing" Justice Done'.

Bruce's new love interest. This shift in the authenticity or reliability of the flashback thus challenges the way in which Bruce/Batman appears as what Claire Sisco King would call a 'sacrificial victim-hero'.[24]

For the presentation of Bruce as a figure of trauma—as one who, despite hanging up his cape and cowl, never went on to 'find a life'—is directly connected to the thematic of sacrifice: in particular, the idea that Batman needs to be willing to give up his life, to pay the 'ultimate sacrifice' for the people of Gotham. Rather than the Christological reading that the previous chapter engaged in, this theme fits more directly within an earlier pagan or Greek mythos: the hero who gives himself up in glorious battle and who, in the process, will be immortalised in song and literature.[25] The fact that Batman *did not die* in the previous film, despite having engaged in a symbolic sacrifice (renouncing all claims to glory and heroism in willingly taking on the role of the criminal for crimes he did not commit), is a fact that seems to haunt the film. For example, Alfred challenges Bruce early in the film, arguing that the only reason he is taking on the role of Batman again and going out into the city is because he wants to die, because there is nothing left for him. Later in the film, Bruce is confused as to why Bane does not simply kill him. Bane responds by openly acknowledging that Batman welcomes death and, as such, his 'punishment' needs to be more severe—he needs to see his city burn and understand his failure before Bane will give him 'permission to die'. When Batman makes his return to Gotham City, Selina Kyle (Anne Hathaway) tells him that he does not owe the people of Gotham anything, that he has already given them everything. To this Batman responds, with a line presented as prescient of what is about to come: 'not everything, not yet', implying that the last sacrifice, the giving of his life, is what remains.

This focus on the need for sacrifice thus aligns *The Dark Knight Rises* with what King, in her book *Washed in Blood: Male Sacrifice, Trauma, and the Cinema*, describes as Hollywood's love affair with the sacrifice of the male body.[26] King defines the genre of 'the sacrificial film' as that 'in which a beloved but psychologically wounded male protagonist gives his life to save others and find redemption for himself'.[27] This genre is linked to clinical, academic and popular discourses of trauma, with the sacrificial film working 'to transform an allegedly traumatised (social) body into one that is *post*-traumatic, restaging traumatic loss so that catastrophe may be refigured as redemption,

[24] King, *Washed in Blood*.
[25] Milbank, 'Ethics of Self-Sacrifice'.
[26] King, *Washed in Blood*.
[27] Ibid., p. 2.

renewal, and rebirth'.[28] This functions through the 'sacrificial victim-hero' who

> [a]fter having laboured in vain to overcome his own anxious doubt and emotional disquietude and to save his (literal and/or metaphorical) children, . . . ultimately realises that his salvific potential and obligation to others requires resignation to noble death—a final act of self-loss that, paradoxically, resolves his earlier traumas and restores his imagined sense of selfhood.[29]

Bruce/Batman's desire to sacrifice himself for the city specifically evokes this model of the sacrificial victim-hero, and *The Dark Knight Rises* reproduces the three defining characteristics of the sacrificial film.

First, the sacrificial film features 'communities in the grips of catastrophic loss or terror'.[30] Whilst Gotham at the opening of the film appears to have almost completely eliminated crime, this was in the aftermath of the horrors of the Joker's attacks on the city in *The Dark Knight*. This elimination of crime is counter-posed to the poverty and oppression suffered by many within the city and the subsequent revolution and 'reign of terror' by Bane—producing a community under siege. Second, sacrificial films 'depict the trauma of intense physical and psychological suffering and centre on men that overcome an identity crisis or a disruption of subjectivity'.[31] As noted above, Bruce is depicted as suffering a loss of identity after Rachel's death and the giving up of the Batman mantle. He also incurs extreme physical suffering, Bane beating him, breaking his back and leaving him in the Middle Eastern prison, where the only way out is by making an impossible climb to the surface. According to King, the prospect of 'life-affirming death' is what then presents the opportunity for the victim-hero to redeem themselves, to claim 'new meaning and new life'.[32] Bruce's desire to give his life for the city as Batman is quite specifically this 'return to life' and meaning. Bruce/Batman's redemption will, it would appear, arise from his giving up his life for Gotham City—'sacrifice works simultaneously to evacuate and elevate the subject—the subject that gives up his life so that he may become sacred and others may be saved'.[33] The Christological resonances of the film's title (with its emphasis on 'rises') would therefore appear to align with King's association

---

[28] Ibid., p. 6.
[29] Ibid., p. 4.
[30] Ibid., p. 16.
[31] Ibid.
[32] Ibid., p. 17.
[33] Ibid.

of the sacrificial film with (at least an American version of) Christianity (one of her key exemplars being Mel Gibson's *The Passion of the Christ*).[34]

The conclusion to *The Dark Knight Rises*, where Batman, having (apparently) given up his life to save the city, is then immortalised and celebrated with a statue at the town hall, fits explicitly with this vision of sacrifice—it was the heroic Batman that saved the city and, like the Greek or Roman heroes of old, will now be remembered into the future.[35] The desire for sacrifice by Bruce/Batman throughout the film thus fits this mould—not just in terms of the 'life-affirming death' of the sacrificial victim-hero, but in terms of the desire for Batman to become the 'symbol' which inspires hope in the citizens of Gotham. And yet, in the closing moments of the film, this sacrificial narrative is explicitly compromised because, as the viewer is shown, Bruce/Batman *does not* die. As such, despite the typological resonances with King's genre of the 'sacrificial film', Nolan complexifies these generic tropes. It is with this complexification in mind that we can *also* turn to the third and final aspect of King's typology, which goes to the extra-diegetic context of its production. That is, 'the language of trauma' deployed by the 'sacrificial film' 'also shapes the understanding of national experience' and creates an interpretative frame for the film's narrative and its troubled hero.[36] As I will show in the next section, Nolan's complexification of this sacrifice narrative goes to the reading of the film's depiction of revolution in relation to class warfare and the 'Occupy' movement *as well as* its engagement with Nolan's broader source text: Charles Dickens's *A Tale of Two Cities*.

III. 'Fire Rises': Revolution and the Rule of Law or Dickens in Cape and Cowl

Whereas, as described in the previous chapter, *The Dark Knight* was contextualised and read specifically as a response to the post-9/11 'war on terror',

---

[34] Ibid., p. 3. However, as noted in Chapters 1 and 3, there are aspects of this resignation to noble death and sacrifice that the Christian tradition *critiques*, in the sense that the antique presentation of virtue as that which involves a sacrificial and heroic overcoming and giving up of oneself for others is one which celebrates both death and the evil which requires such a sacrifice. That is, if the development of virtue or the engagement in sacrifice is something which is positive and redeeming, then the underlying evil that gave rise to such actions is itself to be celebrated. This is a criticism that King lays at the door of the sacrificial film itself, in that it seems to celebrate trauma and its overcoming. Milbank, 'Can Morality Be Christian?'; Milbank, *Being Reconciled*, pp. 1–25.

[35] Milbank, 'Can Morality Be Christian?'.

[36] King, *Washed in Blood*, p. 17.

The Dark Knight Rises was, even before its release, understood explicitly as a response to the global financial crisis, with themes of class warfare, oppression and populist uprising. These themes were emphasised in the pre-release trailers, incorporating these choice words from Selina Kyle: 'there's a storm coming, Mr Wayne. You and your friends better batten down the hatches because when it hits you're all going to wonder how you could live so large and leave so little for the rest of us.' Whilst right-wing commentator Rush Limbaugh claimed that the film was part of a Hollywood conspiracy to disrupt Republican Matt Romney's 2012 presidential election campaign, as responses from the Left lamented after its release, the Right appeared to have little to worry about,[37] for the criticisms of the divided and oppressive class structure of Gotham come not from the heroes but the villains—not from 'the people', but the sinister League of Shadows. This is not to say that the film does not present important images of revolution and scenes that have deep resonance with the critiques put forward by Occupy.[38] Early in the film, Bane launches an attack on the Gotham City Stock Exchange, which would appear to be a literalising of Occupy's critique of global finance—down to a critical response to a condescending trader implying that it is high finance that engages in systematic theft. When it comes to instigating the revolution, Bane then describes the League of Shadows as 'liberators', who will 'return control of this city to the people'. He goes on:

> We take Gotham from the corrupt, the rich, the oppressors and generations who have kept you down with myths of opportunity and we give it back to you, the people . . . The powerful will be ripped from their decadent nests and cast out into the cold world that we know and endure. Courts will be convened, spoils will be enjoyed, blood will be shed. The police will survive as they learn to serve 'true justice'. This great city, it will endure. Gotham will survive.

In contrast to these radical critiques, however, the narrative framework encompasses a much more conservative response. Commissioner Gordon

---

[37] See, for example, Lane, 'Batman's Bane', 30 July 2012; O'Hehir, '"The Dark Knight Rises": Christopher Nolan's Evil Masterpiece', 18 July 2012; Fisher and White, 'Politics of "The Dark Knight Rises"', 4 September 2012; Fisher, 'Batman's Political Right Turn', 23 July 2012; Fradley, 'What Do You Believe In?'. For an insightful critical analysis of these responses, and the way in which they condemn a straightforward ideological reading but then turn around and seem to presume that the film is a straightforward conservative allegory, see Winterhalter, 'The Politics of the Inner'. See also Žižek, 'People's Republic of Gotham', 23 August 2012; McGowan, 'Should the Dark Knight have Risen?'.
[38] Žižek, 'People's Republic of Gotham', 23 August 2012.

gives voice to this by explicitly noting his concern about where giving power to the people might lead. Batman, returning from the Middle Eastern prison, leads an army of police in an ultimately successful fight *against* the League of Shadows, shutting down the revolution and restoring order. As such, the conclusion of the film appears to be a conservative one: the populist and revolutionary uprising is led by the villains who engage in extreme and bloody violence and against whom the 'heroes' fight—overthrowing Bane as the 'liberator' of society and restoring the otherwise oppressive structures of Gotham. Even the attack on the Stock Exchange is revealed *not* to be about revolutionary disruption, but about enabling short-trading (using Bruce Wayne's stolen fingerprints), resulting in a dramatic loss of value in Wayne Enterprises at the instigation of the industrialist Daggett (Ben Mendelsohn), who wanted to make a take-over bid.[39]

However, as Benjamin Winterhalter, Todd McGowan, Robert St Clair and even Slavoj Žižek have pointed out, such a naïve reading of the film as a straightforward conservative allegory is to remain only at the surface of the filmic narrative, and fails to take into account the cinematic devices and formal structures of the film. As Winterhalter notes, summarising the readings of the film from both Right and Left commentators, the naïve political allegory fails to take account of the cinematic techniques that Nolan deploys to produce a particular affect, the feelings that the film generates in the viewer and, in particular, the plot device of the 'twist'.[40] Without taking into account the revelation of Bane and Talia's true identity, their revolution remains incoherent—as Graeber noted, why 'set the city free just to blow up its citizens?' Rather, it is in paying attention to Nolan's deployment of *form* that the radicalness of the film can be understood. For Winterhalter, this is in terms of the film's working through of psychological and emotional trauma to reveal a 'politics of the inner'—that resolving external political questions requires a dealing with inner psychological issues.[41] For McGowan, it is the formal focus on the mask that is key, recognising it as both 'the site of truth and the site of collective engagement'.[42] The refusal of the mask, attempting to escape into a 'true self' underneath (which Bruce's loyal servant, Alfred, encourages, thus rendering him, for McGowan, the true villain of the film), leads to the 'film's great formal insight'—that the 'retreat from the mask is the retreat from truth

---

[39] At the same time, Bane is simply using Daggett to achieve the ends of the League of Shadows.

[40] Winterhalter, 'The Politics of the Inner', pp. 1035–6.

[41] Ibid., p. 1041.

[42] McGowan, 'Should the Dark Knight have Risen?', n.p.

and from collective struggle'.[43] St Clair, by contrasts, rejects the psychological reading of the film, staying with the political, but points to the way in which it is the very *incoherence* of Bane and his plan that renders visible the formal insight of the film.[44] Bane is not a critique of capital and popular sovereignty but a representation of capital itself: 'or rather its destructive excess, personified; a world-historical force that smashes through and pulverizes barriers of all kinds, before which "all that is solid," all forms of difference, however seemingly irresistible, "melts into air," are broken like the Batman's back'.[45]

Whilst each of these readings points to the importance of formal aspects of the film and its devices (the cinematic twist, the image of the mask, the haunting presence of the bomb), in doing so they each tend to dismiss, or set aside, a point that Nolan himself makes: that his source material is *not* contemporary politics, the global financial crisis or the populist responses to it, but rather a reading of Charles Dickens's *A Tale of Two Cities*. This is, no doubt, in part because of their desire to provide a radical reading of the film which needs to set aside the conservative tendencies of Dickensian moralism and critique of revolution. There are certainly gestures that incorporate such a moralism: Batman sacrificing himself for the city; the prominence of orphans and the concluding conversion of Wayne Manor into an orphanage; and the philanthropic resolution to capitalism's generation of social inequality. It is only by taking seriously this thematic link that we are able to provide an answer to a question that is *not* asked about the *particular* representation of populist uprising: why, in a genre that is built upon the American monomyth and American exceptionalism, does the film present and reference the *French* and not the *American* revolution? One could point to Hannah Arendt's comment that '[t]he sad truth of the matter is that the French Revolution, which ended in disaster, has made world history, while the American Revolution, so triumphantly successful, has remained an event of little more than local importance.'[46] However, my argument is that it is

[43] McGowan notes as significant that the concluding scene of the film is *not* the one in which Wayne is enjoying life with Selina Kyle at a café in Italy, but the one in which Detective Blake (Joseph Gordon-Levitt) finds the batsuit, not only opening up the potential for a sequel but concluding on the possibility of a figure who takes up the mask himself.

[44] St Clair, 'The Bomb in the City', p. 10.

[45] Ibid. This goes to why Bane's revolution is, in the end, speaking the voice of capitalism—not 'seek justice and the welfare for all' but 'do as you please'. The bomb that is the vehicle of Bane's forced revolution is thus 'an allegory of our times' circulating 'in the narrative economy less as a guarantee of meaning than as an appeal to interpretation'. Ibid., p. 11.

[46] Arendt, *On Revolution*, p. 56.

only if we appropriately place *The Dark Knight Rises* in relation to Dickens's novel that we find the film encompasses *not* so much either a critique or a praising of the idea of revolution itself, but rather a critical figuring of legality and the form of the rule of law that is the target of the film—a critique that is, as William MacNeil has pointed out, also central to Dickens's novel.

Nolan's allusions to *A Tale of Two Cities* go well beyond Bane's revolution. Rather, they saturate the film with everything from the focus on the use of doppelgangers (Carton/Darnay, Bruce/Batman) and mislaid letters from the past (Dr Manette's letter/testimony and Gordon's speech), each read by someone else (the revolutionary tribunal, Bane), as significant 'revelations' of the truth, to themes of revenge (Mme Defarge and Talia Al Ghul) in the midst of revolution—not to mention the tropes of the revolutionary tribunal 'kangaroo court' and Crane's 'sentencing hearings' or 'show trials' and the storming of the Bastille/Blackgate. Such thematic connections find their epitome in Commissioner Gordon's quoting of Carton's prophetic vision over the empty grave of Bruce Wayne. The saturation of the film in stylistic tropes from *A Tale of Two Cities* even goes to the minute, with the image of Bane in the back of Crane's court tying knots in a manner that reflects Mme Defarge's 'knitting', Daggett's offsider bearing the name Stryver (one of the barristers who, alongside Sydney Carton, represents Charles Darnay in first trial of the novel), and in the opening scenes when the man whom Bane tells that he must sacrifice himself in the plane crash asks whether they have started a fire, Bane's response is: 'Yes, and the fire rises'—one of the chapter titles from *A Tale of Two Cities*.[47]

The significance of these similarities goes to my argument that the film presents a critique both of revolution and of the rule of law, for, as MacNeil has demonstrated, *A Tale of Two Cities* encompasses not *just* a satirised representation and critical account of the French Revolution and its (il)legality, but also a critical account of the bourgeois–liberal legality of the English common law.[48] For MacNeil, central to the novel are the two *trials* that open and close the book: both of Charles Darnay and both political offences—treason under the English common law and 'counter-revolutionary activities' as a returned *émigré* in the Paris of the Revolution.[49] What is

---

[47] I owe a number of these points to discussions with my students in the 2015 and 2016 classes of 6039LAW Cultural Legal Studies at the Griffith Law School, Griffith University. For a good, though sometimes overworked, summary of comparisons between *A Tale of Two Cities* and *The Dark Knight Rises* see Kate, 'From Paris to Gotham', 16 July 2013; Kate, 'From Paris to Gotham (Part 2)', 24 July 2013.

[48] MacNeil, 'Two on a Guillotine'.

[49] Ibid., pp. 157–8.

of import in these two trials is that '*French* revolutionary justice . . . gets its law *right*—as much as English courts get it *wrong*'.[50] In the English trial, Darnay *was* guilty of an offence (at least sedition, if not treason), but his release is secured due to the arguments of his barristers Stryver and Sydney Carton that question the common law's ability to *identify* the subject before it adequately as the one having committed the crime.[51] By contrast, the French revolutionary tribunal is less concerned with what Darnay has or has not done, but more explicitly *who* he is. Initially released on the recommendation of Doctor Manette, Darnay is then re-arrested, retried and sentenced to death *also* by the testimony of Manette (written years earlier when he was a prisoner in the Bastille)—bearing witness to the action of Darnay's uncle and father, and thus also to Darnay's identity as the heir of Evrémonde and part of the *ancien régime*. All this seems to point, therefore, to the ability of the French revolutionary law to get specifically at the truth, to lay bare the secrets of the past and of the person and bring them to the law—in contrast to the common law, which seems bound to a hand-wringing that fails to convict even those who are guilty, let alone risking those that are innocent.

This outcome would seem to be an endorsement of the rule of law, supporting the protections of the common law and its bourgeois liberal legality. Yet MacNeil's point is that the novel renders visible the ideological claim of Capital of the period—that it is a creature, not a creator, of the law—and its accompanying jurisprudence of legal positivism, eschewing any necessary connection to justice or morality.[52] Making clear this ideological position, the novel therefore presents a critique of the rule of law, its privileging of due process, subjecting *all* to the same procedures, strictures and rules, with the principle that no one is above the law.[53] Such a claim, as MacNeil points out, involves a form of misrecognition, a failing to *see* the eyes through which the law itself 'sees'. This is because the claims to objectivity and impartiality are claims made by a particular class who *does* sit above the law, making judgments on its behalf: the judiciary. The autonomy of modern law, its desire for a system of justice that is independent, remains dependent on the very *human* judgment of those that carry it out and their class biases. As such, Dickens's novel presents the same critique that the heroic lawyer, Harvey Dent, represents in *The Dark Knight*.

The figure who presents this 'legal critique' in *A Tale of Two Cities* is the lawyer Carton. He is the one who is able to see into the aporetic heart of the

---

[50] Ibid., p. 161.
[51] Ibid., pp. 159–60.
[52] Ibid., p. 175.
[53] Ibid., pp. 177–8, referring to Dicey, *Law of the Constitution*.

law, its curial mirroring and ability to be 'played' in terms of its concern over due process and identity, and the fact that the judge's gaze remains *both* fallible *and* above the law. It is for this reason that MacNeil argues that Carton *must* be sacrificed in the novel—his critique cut short by his act of self-giving, which sees him take the place of Darnay on the guillotine.[54] It is, in part, because of this act of self-sacrifice that Bruce Wayne/Batman in *The Dark Knight Rises* appears as a figuring of Carton, giving himself up not only for those he loves but for the city itself. Such a reading is undergirded cinematically when, after having defeated Bane, Talia and the League of Shadows, Batman flies the nuclear bomb out over the water, appearing to perish with it. The following scene comprises images of the people of Gotham emerging from their homes into a 'bright new day', before concluding with Gordon, Alfred, Lucius Fox (Morgan Freeman) and Blake standing by the empty grave of Bruce Wayne. The voice of Gordon dominates these scenes, not with a reading of a passage of scripture, but a slightly selective rendition of the concluding words of *A tale of Two Cities*—Carton's prophetic vision before he goes to his death:

> I see a beautiful city and a brilliant people rising from the abyss . . . I see the lives for which I lay down my life, peaceful, useful, prosperous and happy . . . I see that I hold a sanctuary in their hearts, and in the hearts of their descendants, generations hence . . . It is a far, far better thing that I do, than I have ever done; it is a far, far better rest that I go to, than I have ever known.[55]

This passage underlines, if not dramatically overstates, the theme of the novel—Christological sacrifice—providing a cue to how Bruce/Batman's death should be viewed.

There are two problems with this reading. The first, which I have already alluded to and will analyse below, is that Bruce Wayne does *not* die at this point. The second goes to who the structural representative of Carton in Nolan's films is. MacNeil argues that what is significant about the figure of Carton in *A Tale of Two Cities* is not so much his giving up of his life for others, but rather the narrative *need* for his sacrifice. Carton was the one who 'knew too much', subjecting the law to critique and thus needing to be eliminated. In Nolan's films this is *not* the figure of Batman but rather the figure of Harvey Dent: the lawyer who knew too much, who saw into the aporetic heart of the law and the fallibility of the judgment it entails, and who *also* needed to be sacrificed in order to maintain the systematic unity of the law.

---

[54] MacNeil, 'Two on a Guillotine', p. 179.
[55] Dickens, 'A Tale of Two Cities', p. 848.

The desire for a systematisation of the law that we saw with Dent in the previous chapter is one that also reflects the desire for a shift from judge-made law and its expository jurisprudence, to the 'censorial jurisprudence' of the legislator which MacNeil identifies as the *context* of Dickens's tale—a context reproduced and referenced in Nolan's drawing upon the novel as source.[56]

Recognising this connection, then, explains the way in which Dent becomes the figure that haunts *The Dark Knight Rises*—from his image being included in the first shots of the film, to the same image being torn in half by Bane as part of his declaration of the revolution, and to the very law that Bane seeks to overthrow being one which bears his name. Whereas Dent as 'Two-Face', in *The Dark Knight*, embodied the belief that justice can be done only via a completely purified and objectified system of law that removes the discretion of the judicial decision by replacing it with the toss of a coin, Gotham in *The Dark Knight Rises* has enshrined this objectifying and discretionless form of legality in legislation. The viewer is given very little knowledge of the substantive provisions of the Dent Act, other than being told that it 'gave law enforcement teeth' and that there are a thousand criminals locked up in Blackgate prison as a direct result of the Act's implementation. What is implied, however, is that the Act reduced normal protections, involved mandatory sentencing and allowed no parole—that is, it reduced the very aspects of due process and of judicial discretion that are part of the legal system's 'normal' protections and operations. By imposing mandatory sentencing, the discretion of Gotham's judges to take into account the circumstances is removed, thus rendering the law *more* objective, more machine-like, more systematic. In this sense the legislation that bear's Dent's name takes up not so much the position that Dent describes as the one he embodies as Two-Face.

If the Dent Act takes up Two-Face's vigilante retributive justice through an 'objective system' of law, Bane's revolution, with all its referencing of *A Tale of Two Cities*' portrayal of the French Revolution, takes the superhero critique of the law to its other extreme. Bane's revolution charges 'the people' with taking back power from the oppressed and dealing 'true justice'. Is this not an embodying of the vigilante ethos, of 'taking the law into one's own hand' *en masse*? Revolution encompasses an extreme version of the superhero/vigilante ethos—where *everyone* is called upon to overthrow the law which fails to achieve justice, and to seek justice beyond the law. Whilst this depiction of revolution is stylised (as was that of Dickens)—and the revolution is, in part, illusory in nature because the nuclear bomb that Bane uses to threaten the city is set to go off, no matter what—it points to one of the challenges of

---

[56] MacNeil, 'Two on a Guillotine', p. 176.

modern law. For the French Revolution is a symbol *not* of the *ancien régime* and traditional natural law, but of one of the founding moments of modernity and *modern* legality. At the same time, revolution's overthrowing of the law in terms of a higher justice *does* involve a founding of natural law—though, as Walter Benjamin points out, in its modern and secular form rather than traditional religious one.[57] In this way, as I will show in the next section, the institution of modern legality encompasses a (secular) political theology.

IV. 'Then you have my permission to die': Political Theology and Parodic Legality

As noted in Chapter 3, the dominance of the superhero genre on screen in recent years has presented a vision of law that accords with Carl Schmitt's political theology: the superhero is a figure of justice beyond the law who draws on exceptional means in exceptional circumstances, up to the point of appropriating the decision on the sovereign exception, determining that there is a state of emergency that requires a suspension of the law to restore order.[58] What is significant about *The Dark Knight Rises* is the way in which it problematises and 'makes strange' this connection between the superhero, the exception and revolution because it is *not* Batman who becomes the figure of a revolutionary exception but Bane.[59] When announcing the revolution at the football stadium, Bane speaks specifically the language of the exception, calling martial law into effect. It is here that the allusions to the French Revolution become even more apt. As Giorgio Agamben has demonstrated in his tracing of both the modern and the ancient genealogy of the concept, the modern formulation of the state of exception finds its origin in the institution of the state of siege in the French Constituent Assembly's decree of 8 July 1791, when 'all the functions entrusted to the civil authority for maintaining order and internal policing pass to the military commander, who exercised them under his exclusive responsibility'.[60] Whilst, as Agamben notes, this initially referred only to military strongholds, subsequent laws granted the right to put a city in a state of siege, and the circumstances for this gradually

---

[57] Benjamin, 'Critique of Violence', pp. 277–8.

[58] Schmitt, *Political Theology*.

[59] McGowan argues that this is, in part, because the very nature of the figure of the superhero is as an individualistic and not collective figure. I would agree, though argue that, in part, it comes from the nature of the superhero, which sees their virtue as arising not from a focus on the Good but an overcoming of Evil, as was discussed in Chapter 1. McGowan, 'Should the Dark Knight have Risen?'.

[60] Reinarch, *De l'état de siège*, p. 109, quoted by Agamben, *State of Exception*, p. 5.

shifted from wartime situations to internal sedition and disorder.[61] It is here that we find the modern state of exception as a creation of the democratic–revolutionary tradition.[62]

Bane's presentation as a figure of both the exception and revolution can therefore be understood in terms of the categorisation of the relation of law to violence, which Agamben places at the centre of his discussion of the 'state of exception' and, in particular, the 'exoteric' and subtextual debate that he traces between Schmitt and Benjamin. Agamben's starting point is Schmitt's consideration of the jurisprudence of dictatorship, the exception and sovereignty. For Schmitt, there are two distinct types of dictatorship: commissarial dictatorship, aimed at defending or restoring the existing constitution; and sovereign dictatorship, which 'aims at creating a state of affairs in which it becomes possible to impose a new constitution'.[63] In this sense, the superhero's exceptionality would map to a commissarial dictatorship—their aim is always about attempting to restore the norm, to suspend the law in order for it to be applied. By contrast, because Bane is presented as a revolutionary figure, when he speaks the language of the exception it is *not* as a commissarial dictator but rather as a sovereign dictator—that is, bringing about a state of affairs that is not about saving the law but about imposing a *new* law. In this sense, Bane seeks to exercise a form of *constituent*, rather than constituted, power—a founding power that would create a new order and a new constitution. As Agamben points out, the distinction between constituted and constituent power aligns precisely with Benjamin's distinction between law-preserving violence and law-making violence in his 'Critique of Violence'.[64] What runs through the debate between Schmitt and Benjamin, according to Agamben, is the question of whether there can be a violence or mode of human action that is completely unrelated to the law. For Schmitt, the attempt at every stage is to ensure that the exception always bears a relationship to the law—and, even when it comes to constituent power that is not contained within a constitution, it 'is nevertheless connected to every existing constitution in such a way that it appears as the founding power'.[65] Benjamin, in contrast, wishes to maintain a space of violence or action that is neither law-preserving nor law-making, but rather which deposes the law. It is this type of violence that he describes as 'pure' or 'divine' violence, but

[61] Agamben, *State of Exception*, p. 5.
[62] Ibid.
[63] Ibid., p. 33.
[64] Benjamin, 'Critique of Violence'; Agamben, *State of Exception*, p. 54.
[65] Schmitt, *Dictatorship*, quoted by Agamben, *State of Exception*, p. 34.

which, in the realm of human action, he refers to as *revolutionary* violence.[66] Bane's revolution, and in particular the enigmatic figure of the 'bomb', would thus appear to be a form of divine violence which deposes the law with the aim of rendering a new legal order.[67]

If this is the case, then what are we to make of Bruce/Batman's response when he escapes the prison and returns to Gotham? With the aid of Detective Blake, he gathers the remaining police together, not to 'enforce the law' or quash a revolution, but as an army engaging in a war. However, given Bane's recourse to 'the people', this war is not against an external invading army but a war for and *within* Gotham City, a *civil* war—a *stasis* (to use the ambiguous Greek term). Whilst, as Agamben argues, the attempt to theorise *stasis* has tended to be side-lined by the dominant focus on revolution and constituent power in political thought, there is a structural relation between the two, as both the violence of civil war and revolutionary violence are 'a human action that has shed [*desposto*] every relation to law'.[68] The significance of the concept of *stasis* is that it presents and renders visible the process of the politicisation of life and the emergence of citizenship (as opposed to other statuses—nobility, religious communities, peasantry, merchants and so on) as the 'political criterion of social identity'.[69] Agamben refers to the work of Nicole Loraux, who argues that '*stasis* has its original place in the family, and is a war between members of the same family, of the same *oikos*'.[70] This connection of civil war to the family would seem to resonate with the particular comic-book mythos that Nolan is drawing upon in his trilogy, for the multiple confrontations between Batman, Ra's and Talia Al Ghul, and the League of Shadows in the comics are *explicitly* a family matter—with Talia being both Batman's one-time lover and the mother of his son, who then engages in numerous and extreme attacks on both Batman and Gotham.[71] However, Nolan's cinematic rendering of these themes diminishes this familial connection, instead rendering visible more explicitly Agamben's analysis of *stasis*. For Agamben argues instead that '*stasis* is the threshold between *oikos* and

---

[66] Benjamin, 'Critique of Violence'.

[67] Matos, 'Benjamin in Gotham City'.

[68] Agamben, *State of Exception*, p. 59. In relation to there being no theory of civil war, see Agamben, *Stasis*.

[69] Agamben, 'What is a Destituent Power?', pp. 66–7, referring to Meier, 'Changing Politicosocial Concepts'.

[70] Agamben, 'What is a Destituent Power?', p. 67, referring to Loraux, 'La Guerre dans la famille'; see also Agamben, *Stasis*.

[71] For an analysis of some of these comics, see Peters, 'Globalisation, Persona and Mask'.

polis, family and city. *Stasis*, civil war, constitutes a threshold, passing through which domestic belonging is politicised in citizenship and, inversely, citizenship is depoliticised in familial solidarity.'[72]

This particular functioning of *stasis* as involving a threshold between the public and private, the *polis* and *oikos*, finds its representation within *The Dark Knight Rises* with the character of Lieutenant Peter Foley (Matthew Modine), Commissioner Gordon's second-in-command. During Gotham's occupation, Foley assists Gordon in organising the few cops who were not trapped underground to track Bane's bomb. However, after the federal agents that covertly entered Gotham are captured, killed and hung for the world to see, Foley goes into hiding—returning to his home and family. Seeking him out, Gordon criticises Foley for making his wife come to the door, and asks whether he buried his 'uniform in the back yard'. This conversation, which is occurring on the steps of his house (thus *literally* on the threshold between the public and the private), is about whether Foley will fulfil his duty as a police officer. Whereas Foley argues that they should simply keep their heads down until the federal government can get things sorted, Gordon shouts at him: '[t]his only gets fixed from inside the city.' He goes on to note that he is not asking Foley 'to walk down Grand in [his] dress blues, but something has to be done'. This invocation, essentially to choose a side and to take action, along with the focus on what happens *within* the city, goes to a central aspect of *stasis*—which is that the punishment for *not* participating in the civil war was *atimia*, the exclusion from politics, the loss of civil rights and the restriction to the *oikos* and the 'impolitical condition of private life'.[73] Foley *does* later choose sides, leading a squad of police in Batman's army, noting to his men that 'there is only one police in this city'. The fact that he *does* do this in his full dress uniform (complete with pistol and white gloves) presents a symbolic rendering not just of his taking up arms, but of the public nature of his office. In the process, Foley is one of the police who is killed—giving up his life to fulfil his duty to the city.

At the same time, *The Dark Knight Rises* presents a contradiction between the rhetoric and presentation of the revolution (Bane giving power to the people and asserting that 'no-one will intervene'), and the motivation and implementation of the revolution—bringing a retributive 'justice' in which *all* are guilty, and the discovery that Talia Al Ghul is pulling the strings to

[72] Agamben, 'What is a Destituent Power?', p. 67.
[73] Ibid. I owe much of my understanding of *stasis* here, both as a 'war of the family' and as a threshold between public and private, to conversations with Dale Mitchell.

achieve vengeance for the death of her father.[74] If we focus on the nature of the 'courts' that are convened at Bane's instigation, we discover that these involve not revolutionary tribunals, but rather 'sentencing hearings' determining the *punishment* (not guilt) of those brought before them. Whilst Bane justifies these proceedings in the language of giving power to 'the people', it is important to note that the 'judge' is *not* so much a 'man of the people', but rather Jonathan Crane, a.k.a. 'the Scarecrow', a minor villain from *Batman Begins* who had been working with both the mob and the League of Shadows with the aim of holding the city to ransom.[75] The sentencing hearings themselves are a parody of the legality of the Dent Act, where the outcome of the 'hearings' is constrained and the 'guilty' are given the illusion of two options: death or exile (both sentences involving the forcing of people to walk out on the frozen river separating Gotham from the mainland—everyone falls through the fragile ice to their death). This point is further underlined by the fact that those prisoners released from Blackgate prison were *not* political prisoners, but violent criminals and mobsters—those that had been imprisoned by Gordon as he 'cleaned up the city' under the Dent Act.

The result is that these revolutionary trials comprise a sense of the carnivalesque, 'the feast', where roles are reversed and 'not only do slaves command their masters, but sovereignty is placed in the hands of a mock king . . . who takes the place of the legitimate king'.[76] Crane is thus not so much a figure of

---

[74] A significant aspect of the framing of the death of Ra's in *Batman Begins* is orientated around his pushing Bruce to learn to 'do what is necessary' in order to achieve justice—that is, to kill the criminal. When, as Batman, Bruce overpowers Ra's it looks as if he will kill him. Ra's provokes him by saying 'have you finally learnt to do what is necessary?' Bruce/Batman's responds: 'I won't kill you. But I don't have to save you.' The significance of this line is passed over and forgotten by Nolan in *The Dark Knight Rises* when Talia accuses Bruce of murdering her father. Bruce's response goes to a justification for such a murder ('he was trying to kill millions of innocent people') but misses the point that Bruce *did not* kill Ra's. For a discussion of this, see Peters, 'Unbalancing Justice'.

[75] As McGowan notes, this 'underscores the criminality of the revolutionists. With Crane in a position of power, the attack on Gotham cannot be one of emancipation.' McGowan, 'Should the Dark Knight have Risen?', n.p.

[76] Agamben, 'What is a Destituent Power?', p. 70. As such, the release of those within Blackgate prison resonates *less* with the French Revolution and the storming of the Bastille, and more with that *other* penitentiary in the Batman Universe, Arkham Asylum—which at times *has* been broken open with a release of *villains* that then take over the city, rendering a form of the carnivalesque rather than a new political. For a discussion of the comics dealing with Arkham Asylum see, for example, Giddens, 'Navigating the Looking Glass'. On the carnivalesque in Batman comics, see Brooker, *Hunting the Dark Knight*, pp. 134–77.

the revolution, or even a representative of the 'reign of terror', as a figure of the carnival, a parody of a judge *mocking* law and order. The revolution which Batman stops (with a returning to 'normal order' afterwards) is not an operation of constituent power which sees a new order come into effect; it is more of a festival, a suspension of existing power for a period, which in the end reinforces the existing order. This is to see Bane and Crane both operating in a similar fashion to the Joker—not really presenting radical alternative legalities but, rather, reinforcing the need for law and order. Yet what is significant about the feast is not simply the inversions that it encompasses, but the fact that those inversions 'point toward a zone in which life's maximum subjection to the law is reversed into freedom and licence, and the most unbridled anomie shows its parodic connection with the *nomos*'.[77] Crane's 'sentencing hearings' present a particular form of this parody. Whilst what is promised is the form of law (Bane's claim that 'courts will be convened'), because of the suspension of the law in the state of exception, what is presented is a 'pure application' of the law 'without being in force'—what Agamben calls 'the force-of-law'.[78] In doing so, what is inverted is the core aspect of the rule of law: the presumption of innocence (a finding of guilt is required before any punishment is exacted) becomes a presumption of guilt, with Crane rendering punishment *without* any determination of guilt—giving the option of 'death or exile', or, rather, simply 'death by exile'. The result of the revolution's retributive 'seeking justice' encompasses, as the French Revolution did, a form of natural law justification of the use of violence by justified *ends*.[79] The invocation of the form of legality (trials, hearings, 'true justice') is thus a mechanism of legal theodicy—the justification of the committing of violence by the good ends that it achieves.[80]

The focus of this revolutionary violence as attempting to achieve 'good' ends is complexified by the 'twist' which reveals the true purpose of the League of Shadows, which is *not* about instituting a new social order, but

---

[77] Agamben, *State of Exception*, p. 72.

[78] To provide the full quotation, Agamben argues that what occurs in a state of exception is a splitting of the law 'into a pure being-in-force [*vigenza*] without application (the form of law) and a pure application without being in force: the force-of-law'. Ibid., p. 60. In this process, the continuation of the 'force-of-law' is an attempt to maintain the law's functioning, even as it has been suspended (p. 64).

[79] Benjamin, 'Critique of Violence'.

[80] I owe this point, in particular, to conversations with Edwin Bikundo, whose exceptional insight points to the way in which law functions as a political theodicy, a justification of violence (evil) in terms of the legality of ends (good). See Bikundo, 'Follow Your Leader', p. 10; Agamben, *Karman*, pp. 43–4.

extracting terrible vengeance upon both Batman and the people of Gotham. Undergirding this vision of retributive violence is the enigmatic figure of the 'bomb', which is presented initially as the means that *enables* the revolution (it is the threat of nuclear extermination that both keeps the federal government at bay and ensures that all residents remain on the island), but is then revealed as the mechanisms of Talia's vengeance (as the bomb was always going to go off anyway). Instead of seeking to provide a new society and a new law, the bomb is that which would wipe out all in an apocalyptic *destruction* of Gotham City rather than the establishing of a new order. Whilst St Clair and McGowan read the bomb as a representation of the destructive power and desires of Capital, there is an aspect where the bomb *does* link to a form of revolutionary violence. As noted above, Benjamin's notion of 'pure' or 'divine' violence, which involves a bloodless expiation, in the realm of human action is *revolutionary* violence that deposes the law. Agamben links this divine violence to Benjamin's notion of a 'baroque eschatology', which is not the envisioning of a transcendental future or hereafter, but rather an eschatology that is distinctly attached to and *within* the world. Such an eschatology is a catastrophic and epochal wiping away which leaves nothing but 'an absolutely empty sky'.[81] This is to privilege Benjamin's analysis of the exception over Schmitt's, shifting from an absolutist political theology of sovereignty to a confining of sovereignty purely 'to the world of creatures'.[82] In doing so, the exception is not a miracle that intervenes in ordained legality but a catastrophe that sees its destruction. This would be therefore to take seriously the revolutionary depictions, seeing the bomb as a form of 'divine violence' which, itself, deposes the law through a catastrophic wiping away.[83]

This analysis *also* makes sense of Nolan's cinematic rendering of light and 'sky' in the film, along with Bane's otherwise strange connection of despair and hope. One could question, why go through all the process of the revolution only to have the bomb go off at the end—and why go through the process of putting Bruce/Batman in the Middle Eastern prison, only to kill him later? Such is the question that Bruce himself puts to Bane, who responds

---

[81] Agamben, *State of Exception*, p. 57, referring to Benjamin, *Origin of German Tragic Drama*.

[82] My reading here relies, in part, on Agamben's argument that there has been an 'emendation error' in Benjamin's work. For a discussion of this analysis, see Prozorov, 'Katechon', p. 493 N 55.

[83] Matos, 'Benjamin in Gotham City'.

first by describing the prison itself—a pit which has no bars, but which is also impossible to escape:

> There's a reason why this prison is the worst hell on earth: hope. Every man who has rotted here over the centuries has looked up at the light and imagined climbing to freedom: so easy, so simple. And like shipwrecked men turning to seawater from uncontrollable thirst, many have died trying. I learnt here that there can be no true despair without hope.
>
> So, as I terrorise Gotham I will feed its people hope to poison their souls. I will let them believe that they can survive so that you can watch them clambering over each other to stay in the sun. You can watch me torture an entire city. And then when you have truly understood the depth of your failure . . . we will destroy Gotham. And then, when it is done and Gotham is . . . ashes, then you have my permission to die.

Such a vision is underlined by the depiction of the openness of the sky when Batman takes the bomb out over the water in the concluding moments of the film. After the bomb explodes, the viewer is left with a visual of the sky itself, empty and clear. This reflects a form of nuclear or apocalyptic thinking, a secular eschatology in which all that is left is the destruction and death of this life: a wiping clean and expiation of all.[84]

It is significant that, in the above speech from Bane, not only does he present the connection between hope and despair, but also he renders inoperative Bruce's own desire for sacrifice. By articulating specifically that Bruce *cannot* sacrifice himself but can die only when he is given permission to do so, we find an inversion of Agamben's famed figure of *homo sacer*. The 'sacred' person is one who can be neither sacrificed nor murdered but can be killed with impunity. By contrast, Bane's 'then you have my permission to die' encompasses a sense in which Batman *cannot* be killed by anyone (including himself) without permission. In contrast to Crane's sentencing hearings, which determine punishment and not guilt, here death is something that can be succumbed to only with permission. This would appear to be a profaning of an otherwise sacred life. This point is essential to the understanding of the *problem* of revolution, taken today as the supreme example of constituent power, in that its violent constituting of a new law fails to challenge the

---

[84] This aligns with the League of Shadows' vision of expiatory guilt and the need for ecological balance. This renders all fundamentally guilty—a point that Talia makes when she challenges Batman about referring to the people of Gotham as 'innocent'. Rather, as Ra's says in *Batman Begins*, and as then re-appears in one of Bruce's 'flashbacks' critiquing Gotham in all its decadence, the city is 'beyond saving and must be allowed to die'.

secular theology of power that undergirds it. As Agamben notes, '[a] power that was only just overthrown by violence will rise again in another form, in the incessant, inevitable dialectic between constituent power and constituted power, violence which makes the law and violence that preserves it.'[85] Such a dialectic is rendered visible with the battle between Batman's army of police and the League of Shadows—right up to the point where *Batman's* response to Bane is that only once he reveals who the trigger-man is, *then* 'you have my permission to die'. The solution is not, therefore, recourse to constituent power but rather—as Agamben explains, following Benjamin—modes of destituent power: abilities to render power 'inoperative'. It is to this mode of destituent power that Benjamin's 'pure violence' alludes, and its link to the modes of inoperativity that sit alongside Agamben's engagement with the concept of sacrifice as central to the modern paradigm of secularisation, to which I now turn.

V. 'A hero can be anyone': The Mask, Identity and Destituent Power

In *On Revolution*, Arendt notes that a key aspect of the French Revolution was its focus on hypocrisy as 'the vice through which corruption becomes manifest', involving an 'inherent duplicity', which is 'to shine with something that is not'.[86] The simile deployed by the revolutionaries was that of 'tearing the mask of hypocrisy off the face of French society' so as to expose 'its rottenness . . . tearing the façade of corruption down and of exposing behind it the unspoiled, honest face of the *peuple*'.[87] This metaphor of the mask of hypocrisy is, of course, key to Bane's revolutionary speeches in *The Dark Knight Rises*. The film incorporates not only a *literal* unmasking of Batman, but also, more specifically, a revealing of the supposedly 'true nature' of Harvey Dent, who, Bane notes, has been 'held up in front of you as the shining example of justice'. Reading to the crowds the speech written by Commissioner Gordon (which he never delivered but was acquired by Bane early in the film), he describes Dent as a 'false idol' and explains that Gordon and the leaders of Gotham are 'liars' and 'corrupt'. Gordon is presented as a hypocrite, having promulgated a 'lie' about Dent, hiding the truth from 'the people' and preventing them from 'tearing down this corrupt city'.

The simile of unmasking presumes that there is a 'true identity' or 'true nature' underneath the mask of hypocrisy. Arendt notes that, in the context of the French Revolution, despite the emphasis on the 'Rights of Man', there was a lack of 'respect for the legal personality which is given and guaranteed

---

[85] Agamben, 'What is a Destituent Power?', p. 70.
[86] Arendt, *On Revolution*, p. 104.
[87] Ibid., p. 106.

by the body politic'.[88] This encompassed a distinct shift from the granting of rights at a social level, 'by virtue of the body politic', to simply 'by virtue of being born'.[89] The result, however, was that, in

> the unending hunt for hypocrites and through the passion for unmasking society, they had, albeit unknowingly, torn away the mask of the *persona* as well, so that the Reign of Terror eventually spelled the exact opposite of true liberation and true equality; it equalised because it left all inhabitants equally without the protecting mask of a legal personality.[90]

In this way, the revolutionary aim of justice and its unmasking of 'false idols' result *not* in a destituent law, but rather a bare life without even the protections of the law—Agamben's figure of *homo sacer*, who cannot be sacrificed but can be killed with impunity. To do away with the law means that you eliminate not only its injustices, but also the protections—fallible though they may be—that it enshrines. What is presented, therefore, is a specific secular myth of legality, one that demands a perfection which can never be achieved and thus, in its aim at equality, holds all guilty before the law, which is stripped of its protections against fallibility and rendered open to a divine or revolutionary violence. That is, the supposed secularity of revolution embodies a very particular religious and divine mode of justice—a sacred violence that becomes the foundation of the state.[91]

Agamben traces the way in which the inversion of the presumption of innocence into a presumption of guilt, which I outlined in relation to Crane's parodic trials above, came to underlie modern law and the security state—itself traceable to the French Revolution and its notion of *sûreté*. He argues that the current paradigm of security and 'security apparatuses' is not about preventing 'dangers, troubles or even catastrophes', despite the fact that that is the rhetoric or justification provided for them.[92] Security today goes to the very basis of modern governance. Following Foucault's work on governmentality, Agamben points to the famous motto 'laisser faire, laissez passer', which 'is not only the catchword of economic liberalism: it is a paradigm of government, which conceives of security . . . not as the prevention of troubles, but rather as the ability to govern and guide them in the good direction once they take place'.[93] This explains 'the paradoxical convergence today of an

---

[88] Ibid., p. 108.
[89] Ibid.
[90] Ibid.
[91] Kahn, *Political Theology*.
[92] Agamben, 'For a Theory of Destituent Power', February 2014.
[93] Ibid.; Foucault, *Security, Territory, Population*.

absolutely liberal paradigm in economy with an unprecedented and equally absolute paradigm of state and police control'.[94] The proliferation and use of biometrical technologies of identification, which have become part of our everyday experience, are a reflection of this mode of governmentality—for in attempting to govern effects and not causes, controls and checks must be multiplied. However, these biometrical technologies (not just finger printing, but also now retina scanning, facial recognition, body mapping) had their origin and invention in the purpose of identifying recidivist criminals:

We should not be astonished if today the normal relationship between the state and its citizens is defined by suspicion, police filing and control. The unspoken principle which rules our society can be stated like that [sic]: *every citizen is a potential terrorist.*[95]

The possibilities of such apparatuses, along with their potential for abuse, is one of the themes of Nolan's trilogy. In *The Dark Knight*, the way in which Batman eventually tracks down the Joker is by use of a massive system of surveillance that taps into every mobile phone in Gotham. In *The Dark Knight Rises*, Bruce is presented as having access to technologies and resources that enable him to track down Selina Kyle and Bane—including the vast databases of fingerprints and criminal records. Bruce's concern with these technologies of surveillance—and also with the fusion reactor developed by Wayne Enterprises—is their potential for abuse and destruction, noting that 'one man's tool is another man's weapon' (a concern which Alfred chides him about, saying that 'there aren't many things you can't turn into a weapon'). At the same time, there are two examples of attempts to resist or render inoperative these security apparatuses. The first relates explicitly to the paradigms of suspicion that Agamben highlights. Selina Kyle, the adept cat burglar and con artist, has managed to escape the reach of the law to date, but as Bruce, having run her fingerprints himself, points out early in the film: 'Databases are full of close-calls, tips from fences, she's good but the ground is shrinking beneath her feet.' Ironically, her involvement with Bane arose initially from pulling a job for Daggett (who Bane appeared to be working for) to steal Bruce's own fingerprints. She had worn fake ones to disguise her identity, but Bruce had placed a tracking device on the pearls that she *also* stole. When Bruce tracks her down, he encourages her to 'start fresh', to which her response is: 'There's no fresh start in today's world. Any 12-year old with a cell phone can find out what you did. Everything we do is collated and quantified. Everything sticks.'

[94] Agamben, 'For a Theory of Destituent Power', February 2014.
[95] Ibid.

As such, Kyle is working to achieve access to a particular computer program called 'Clean Slate', which would enable her to erase all the details of herself and her record from all databases and computers the world over—essentially a rendering inoperative of the modern paradigm of identity and of the law's ability to connect specific acts with specific individuals. As Daggett notes, this is 'the ultimate tool for a master thief with a record'. Whereas Daggett dismisses it as a gangland myth, Batman/Wayne is able to provide it for her.

Whilst Wayne provides this technological means of inoperativity, the risk of the *use* of such an apparatus is that, instead of making a new start, giving up a life of crime, it will be deployed to enable *further* criminality. Kyle could erase her past records, enabling her to engage in further theft (which is what Daggett believed she would do). When Bruce gives the 'Clean Slate' to her, however, he extends his trust, believing that there is more to her: 'In fact I think that for you, this isn't just a tool, it's an escape route—and you want to disappear, start fresh.' Despite her continually 'letting him down' and proving to be self-serving and self-interested, Bruce provides multiple opportunities for a second chance. This is an extension of the form of trust that I noted as being articulated in *The Dark Knight*, but at a more personal and individual level. He trusts in Selina Kyle to do the right thing, despite constant evidence to the contrary. This trust is one that steps out in knowledge that the other can be more than they have been in the past. It is a trust that encourages the other also to trust and to act in the right way. It is certainly not a trust that will never be broken—Selina Kyle misleads Batman, turns him in to Bane and appears to abandon him at a number of points in the film—but it is a trust that expects more of the other than they would think that they have in themselves. This focus on trust is in contrast to the suspicion of modern legality, and the unmasking of society that the revolution proclaims, for if we rely on a vision of legality based on mistrust, then we will believe nothing and yet, as Nolan shows us through his deployment of the cinematic fiction, be thoroughly deceived.[96] It is in the very process of trusting others that we gain a knowledge of them and of community that cannot be gained by a mistrust that always requires law to shore up protection against the other, because in believing nothing it is always ready to believe the worst of the other. We need to focus instead on a trust that, as Søren Kierkegaard might say, 'believes everything' and yet 'is never to be deceived'.[97]

This focus on trust and belief links to the second, and more significant, presentation of inoperativity in the film: the mask that Batman wears. As

---

[96] McGowan, *Fictional Christopher Nolan*, pp. 1–7.
[97] Kierkegaard, *Works of Love*, pp. 182–3.

McGowan notes, the mask has a complex status within the film, for it is both

> the site of truth and the site of collective identification. It is only on the basis of the mask that one can form a collectivity because it allows one to see that one's true self forms through the confrontation with the Other and doesn't exist prior to or outside this confrontation. The retreat from the mask is the retreat from truth and from collective struggle.[98]

This goes more directly to the understanding of the nature of legal personhood and the way in which, as noted with Arendt above, rights are traditionally understood as arising from the social and the body politic. The legal *persona* has an etymological connection with the actor's mask, involving a putting on of a personality that is then recognised.[99] This is, as Agamben notes, linked to a traditional understanding of personhood as being about social recognition—you had legal personhood because you were recognised by others (and by the law) as having it. However, the modern functioning of both rights *and* identity turns *away* from a social understanding of identity as connected to one's personhood or legal persona; rather, it focuses on a biopolitical determination based on innate physical characteristics—fingerprints, retina, DNA.[100] Bane's process of *unmasking* does not align the revolution with a radical critique of law and legality but presents its end-point. By contrast, Batman's mask is *not* simply a figuration of a persona or a symbol, but is specifically a rendering inoperative of this functioning of modern legal identity.

At a very straightforward level, this operates in a similar fashion to the Clean Slate program, which renders inoperative the modern security apparatuses, for the mask does not simply present another *persona* but also *hides* the face, making the individual *unknown*.[101] Bruce points this out to Detective Blake twice in the film, noting that the reason for wearing the mask is about concealing one's identity, not necessarily for yourself but 'to protect the people you care about'. At the same time, Bruce points to the mode of the mask as a point of collectivity that is *not* bound to an individual: '[t]he idea was to be a symbol, Batman could be anybody. That was the point.' Later on, when

[98] McGowan, 'Should the Dark Knight have Risen?'

[99] Agamben, *Nudities*, pp. 46–8; Arendt, *On Revolution*, pp. 106–7.

[100] Agamben, *Nudities*, pp. 48–54; Agamben, 'For a Theory of Destituent Power', February 2014.

[101] Goodrich, 'Mask as Anti-Apparatus'; Peters, 'Globalisation, Persona and Mask', pp. 136–41.

Commissioner Gordon is stating that the people should know 'the hero who saved them', Batman responds by saying: '[a] hero can be anyone.' The idea that anyone could be Batman thus points *not* to the issue of the hypocrite, the person who does not wear the mask but deceives in the appearance they put forward, or to the persona itself, which is the representative of legal personality (the subject as bearer of rights and duties), but rather to the figure which we should aim to become. It is in this sense that the mask itself has a form of destituent power or potential. Here we can see an alternative link to 'the feast' discussed above, focusing on the way in which the feast is not simply a suspension or inverting of legality but encompasses a destituent aspect. As Agamben notes,

> the feast is defined not only by what in it is not done, but primarily by the fact that what is done—which in itself is not unlike what one does every day—becomes undone, is rendered inoperative, liberated and suspended from its 'economy', from the reasons and purposes that define it during the weekdays . . . If one eats, it is not done for the sake of being fed; if one gets dressed, it is not done for the sake of being covered up or taking shelter from the cold; if one wakes up, it is not done for the sake of working; if one walks, it is not done for the sake of going someplace; if one speaks, it is not done for the sake of communicating information; if one exchanges objects, it is not done for the sake of selling or buying.
>
> There is no feast that does not involve, in some measure, a destitutive element, that does not begin, that is, first and foremost by rendering inoperative the works of men . . . 'There is no ancient feasts without dance', writes Lucian, but what is dance other than the liberation of the body from its utilitarian movements, the exhibition of gestures in their pure inoperativity? And what are masks—which play a role in various ways in the feasts of many peoples—if not, essentially, a neutralization of the face?[102]

The significance of Batman wearing the mask is therefore not so much its projection of a particular identity, but its ability to neutralise the face. Such a neutralisation can be contrasted with the medieval political theology of the king's two bodies.[103] At one level we could articulate a split between the private persona of Bruce Wayne and the public persona of the Batman—a figure who, as is seen in the comics, would appear never to die, with multiple individuals taking up and wearing the cape and cowl. But this is *not* what Nolan

---

[102] Agamben, 'What is a Destituent Power?', pp. 69–70. See also Agamben, *Nudities*, pp. 110–12.

[103] Kantorowicz, *King's Two Bodies*; Santner, *Royal Remains*.

presents us with. The significance of the medieval political theology is that, whilst the king's human body may die, his sempiternal body never does— *dignitas non moritur!* This would render a distinction between the human bodily nature of the individual and the immortal nature of the office. In this context, it would appear to render Bruce as the human individual who can die or be killed, as opposed to Batman as the immortal symbol that can be eternal and live forever. However, if this was to be the case, why is it that, at the conclusion of the film, it is *Batman* that dies but Bruce who lives on?

VI. Conclusion: A Thanatopolitics of the City or an Affirmative 'Living Sacrifice'?

Paul Kahn, in his *Political Theology: Four New Chapters on the Concept of Sovereignty*, argues that the importance of the framework of political theology for understanding modern secular legality goes to the way in which the state has appropriated the sacred and the sacrificial—in particular the way in which 'political violence has been and remains a form of sacrifice' and the related memorialisation of citizen sacrifice.[104] The fact that the concluding image of Batman in *The Dark Knight Rises* is not of the individual subject, but rather a statue memorialising the Batman and his sacrifice for the city, would seem to undergird this claim. This image endorses a secular myth of modern law—that the rule of law and secular legality is something that has been fought and sacrificed for, and that part of the 'civil religion' involves a memorialisation of that sacrifice. Yet, as Agamben's extended work in the *Homo Sacer* project has made clear, modern legality involves a production of this form of sacrifice—the manufacture of bare life, in which the rendering of the human sacred involves the ability to kill them without committing murder, without transgressing the law. This is a thanatopolitics of the city, a founding of modern legality on its exclusion and sacrifice of life.

However, as pointed out above, this is only the way things appear to the people of Gotham. For the viewer, it is revealed that, whilst *Batman* may have died, Bruce Wayne lives on—seen by Alfred in a café in Florence, accompanied by Selina Kyle, finally out living his life. The temptation to see this as simply a phantasmatic vision that Alfred is experiencing is cinematically countered by the revelation that the autopilot in 'the Bat' had been fixed by Bruce Wayne, enabling him to escape. Is this, then, a continuation of the function of the mask—and the theatrical deception that has gone along with Batman's operations throughout Nolan's trilogy—essentially faking his own death to

---

[104] Kahn, *Political Theology*, p. 7.

allow him to live a life separate from being the Batman?[105] Part of the problem with the sacrificial reading of Batman at this point is the way in which it encompasses a secularisation of the Christological theme of sacrifice, whilst at the same time failing to recognise the way in which sacrifice functions within the Christian tradition. The significance of Christ's sacrifice is that, in itself, it transforms sacrifice. Whereas the secular myth praises and calls for sacrifice—be it in the forms of revolutionary terror or exceptional measures—Christianity identifies that there was only one who can actually undergo the sacrificial move of giving up his life in order to save the world. All other acts of 'sacrifice' are not a direct repeating of Christ's actions but a 'repeating differently' in non-sacrificial mode—Christ's sacrifice was the sacrifice to end all sacrifice, so that there would no longer be a need for sacrifice.[106] That is, Christ's sacrifice has its own destitutive aspect, rendering sacrifice inoperative, deactivating its mechanisms by encouraging not a death-dealing thanatopolitics, the praising of sacrifice that Kahn refers to, but rather a living sacrifice that affirms life.

It is in this light that we should read Batman's failure to die—the fact that Bruce, in the end, *did not* engage in the giving up of life in self-sacrifice. Whilst, for the people of Gotham, this is a secular myth of the hero sacrificing his life for the purposes of securing the state, the viewer is exhorted to 'go beyond' this myth—encouraged to understand that such a sacrifice is only ever a failure to understand the nature and possibility of community which cannot be based on law or norm (reactionary or revolutionary) but has to be based on a destituting of the law. The result is not a thanatopolitics of sacrificial death but, as St Paul notes, an exhortation to life—to be a 'living sacrifice'. For Paul, as Agamben notes, the significance of Christ's death is a deactivating and rendering inoperative of the law, its judgment of guilt and the punishment of death that it invokes. Instead of calling us to engage in a

---

[105] It is important to note that Nolan's rendering of Batman in this regard is quite distinct from that in the comics. Throughout the trilogy, the sense is that Batman is not a figure who will *continue* to operate, but one that is engaged in a specific project to reform and change Gotham. One of the concluding scenes of *Batman Begins*, involves Rachel Dawes (Katie Holmes) looking forward to a day when Gotham no longer need Batman. Harvey Dent, in *The Dark Knight*, notes that Batman cannot possibility want to continue to fulfil this role forever and that he is looking for others to step up. The fact that *The Dark Knight Rises* starts with Batman not having been sighted for eight years, and Bruce telling Gordon that the Batman was no longer needed, also affirms this point. In this sense, Nolan is presenting Batman *only* as a commissarial dictator, whose role is specific and limited—rather than the serialised and continuing figure seen in the comics.
[106] Milbank, 'Ethics of Self-Sacrifice'.

self-sacrifice that involves a giving up of our lives for the city, nation or world, we are called to live as a living sacrifice—an affirmation of life and not death. In this sense, *The Dark Knight Rises* challenges the mode of the sacrificial film, in terms of the way that it therapeutises a traumatised social body, but also in the way this figuring of trauma hides the implicit involvement of the state *in* the traumatic events. It presents quite specifically the constructedness of the sacrifice as a narrative of the state, but also then challenges it with a more robust theological notion of sacrifice—that is about life and not death; it is about going on as Bruce Wayne does, rather than about giving up one's life to save the city. The sacrifice that the law of the city demands is a secularised theology that, in the end, does not affirm life but rather leaves us caught in a thanatopolitics glorifying death rather than life. Our response, rather, should be to make life a feast.

5

Pauline Science Fiction: Alex Proyas's *I, Robot*, Universalism and Love Beyond the Law

'Do not think that I have come to abolish the Law or the Prophets; I have not come to abolish them but to fulfil them.'

Matthew 5: 17

'The Three Laws of Robotics
LAW I: A robot may not injure a human being, or, through inaction, allow a human being to come to harm.
LAW II: A robot must obey orders given it by human beings except where such orders would conflict with the First Law.
LAW III: A robot must protect its own existence as long as such protection does not conflict with the First or Second Law.'

Asimov[1]

I. Introduction

In 2004, upon the release of Alex Proyas's *I, Robot*, 'suggested' by the work of Isaac Asimov, a range of commentators criticised the film, complaining that it was more a Will Smith buddy cop movie than anything bearing a resemblance to Asimov's work of the same title.[2] David Palumbo deftly pointed out that such complaints demonstrate a lack of familiarity with Asimov's oeuvre—which includes a range of robot detective novels that the film implicitly and explicitly draws upon, alongside the famed robot short stories.[3] Whilst Palumbo is correct, the argument in this chapter agrees with

---

[1] Asimov, *I, Robot*, p. 8; *I, Robot*, film, directed by Proyas.

[2] See, for example, Ebert, 'Cyber Cypher', 16 July 2004; Persall, 'Just Call It "I, Will Smith"', 28 August 2005; Kennedy, 'Solid Sci-Fi Tale is Fuelled by Philosophy', 16 July 2004.

[3] Palumbo, 'Alex Proyas's I, Robot'. As opposed to the robot short stories, these narratives *do* present detective-style stories that deal with some of the same issues raised by Proyas's film: Asimov, *The Caves of Steel*; Asimov, *The Naked Sun*; Asimov, *The Robots of Dawn*; Asimov, *Robots and Empire*. For an analysis of these novels in relation to legal questions of the post-human see Leslie-McCarthy, 'Asimov's Posthuman Pharisees'.

the criticisms of the commentators. Or rather it makes the claim that, in addition to Proyas's re-presenting and remediating a range of the motifs and plot-lines from Asimov, he also presents a *critique* of the future which Asimov envisions and the particular scientific world-view and, as I will demonstrate, legality that reflect it.

In Chapters 1 and 2 I examined the pop culture dichotomies of Good and Evil, outlining the way in which these depict a modern accounting of law and Evil that is premised on a particular willing subject, and an account of 'modern law' which is seen as self-grounding, mediating between transcendence and immanence in its desire for order. Chapters 3 and 4 then focused on the superhero genre's vision of exceptional legality—a political theology that takes this desire for order and security to its end, justifying both extreme and sacrificial measures in order to shore it up. The next two chapters encompass a shift of focus. First, they turn from the speculative genres of space opera and superheroes to that of science fiction more strictly—analysing films that are adaptations of two of the twentieth century's biggest names in sci-fi (Isaac Asimov and Philip K. Dick). In doing so, we find presented science fiction's vision of law not as justice, reason or even command, but as technology and bureaucracy—law as a tool, as seen in Chapter 2, a means to particular ends. Second, however, they further the book's theological analysis, demonstrating the way in which the particular visions of legality encompassed in these films, though at one level explicitly modern, maintain and continue theological accounts of law. That is, these films translate the sci-fi myths of modernity into dealing with theological concerns that render visible a particularly modern account of the law: as a system without exception, an unlimited sovereignty, and a form of secularised providence.

This analysis continues tracking certain themes that I have been exploring (law's violent relation to a fundamental chaos, the rule of law and its exception, the desire for order). In Chapter 6 my focus will be on modern legality's secularised theology of will—one that is explicitly invoked in *The Adjustment Bureau*, George Nolfi's interpretation of Philip K. Dick's short story, 'The Adjustment Team'.[4] That text encompasses explicit metaphysical tendencies—but, in doing so, presents a bureaucratised view of the divine that is more *modern* than *medieval*. In the present chapter's focus on Proyas's cinematic reading of Asimov, I look at law not so much as the will or command of the sovereign, but as a self-sustaining order. Situated within a tradition of hard sci-fi that explicitly imagines a technologised, scientific and dis-enchanted world, it presents a vision of law as rule without exception.

---

[4] *The Adjustment Bureau*, film, directed by Nolfi; Dick, 'Adjustment Team', September to October 1954.

This vision is most clearly expressed in Asimov's 'Three Laws of Robotics', noted in the epigraph, which present law not as justice or reason, but as rule and algorithm—the 'laws' being programmed into all of the robots in Asimov's universe and Proyas's imagining of it. Whilst such a vision of law as machine would appear to *exclude* a political theology, with its miraculous exception, we find in Proyas's rendering specific theological allusions that point to essential limitations: both in the technologised world-view that it renders *and* in the vision of legality that undergirds it. Drawing upon both these theological allusions and the jurisprudential concern with law and its limits, this chapter stages an intertextual reading between Proyas's sci-fi flick and the renewed interest in the critical theology and jurisprudence of St Paul.

In doing so, this chapter picks up where the previous one left off, for St Paul's critique of the Law is one of Giorgio Agamben's key examples of 'destituent power'—Paul proclaiming Christ's 'rendering inoperative' of the Law. My focus here, however, is less on Agamben's reading of law and its exception, than on the way in which Alain Badiou's notion of the 'event' provides an alternative challenge to the questions of identity and legality that were raised in the previous chapter.[5] In today's world of over-legislation and legal paranoia about technological development—along with its governance by exception and emergency—the 'return to Paul' and his message calls us 'beyond the law', overcoming its limits and inviting us to step outside the differences its 'letter' institutes. As Badiou points out, this can be done only via the event, which announces a universal that *sublates* both law and difference and, in so doing, enables a freedom *not* grounded in the law. Proyas's *I, Robot* presents such an event in terms of the arrival of a robot who, whilst 'having' the Three Laws, can choose *not* to obey them.

The chapter proper begins in Section II by outlining the vision of science, technology and law that is represented by Asimov's science fiction and his development of the Three Laws. Proyas's film creates a version of this Asimovian world, but also then presents challenges to it, both in terms of the range of theological allusions and themes within the film, and in terms of the *limitations* of the Three Laws and their logic. It is these theological and jurisprudential themes that then lead to my reading of the film in relation to the 'return to Paul', which is discussed in Section III. There I examine in particular Badiou's reading of Paul's declaration of 'the event' of Christ, which responds to the failure of the law. Sections IV and V then work through this Badiouvian-cum-Pauline reading, exploring the way in

[5] This is not to say there are not important connections and similarities between Badiou's and Agamben's readings—despite their apparent critiques of each other. See Prozorov, 'Agamben, Badiou and Affirmative Biopolitics'.

which the 'event' presents a challenge both to the identitarian subjection of destiny to order—presented in the film in terms of the post-human complexification of the distinction between robot and human—and to the law's repetitive and controlling nature that destroys thought—most clearly seen in terms of the evolved 'logic' of the Three Laws promoted by the 'machine' VIKI. The actions of the robot Sonny present a Pauline overcoming of both difference and the law, maintaining fidelity to the 'event' that requires an ongoing 'work of love'. The chapter therefore concludes by examining the way the event rejects an abstract universalism—associated with modern law—in favour of a universal singularity that, instituted by love, founds a freedom beyond the law.

II. 'The Machine runs itself': Allusions to Theology and Law as Technology

Following from his argument that 'all significant concepts of the modern theory of the state are secularised theological concepts', Carl Schmitt, in his *Political Theology*, traces the way in which the ideas of sovereignty shifted in the period since the French Revolution, so that 'exclusively scientific thinking . . . permeated [all] political ideas, repressing the essentially juristic–ethical thinking that had predominated in the age of the Enlightenment'.[6] This shift encompassed a dominance of law's *generality*. To return to Peter Fitzpatrick's metaphor, discussed in Chapter 2, this is the way in which the second Occidental god of cosmic order is captured within law alongside the first god of ineffable command and will. As I noted, this was encapsulated in the need for 'a stable, independent legal order' guaranteed by an independent 'rule of law' and in 'the mythic equation of Occidental law with order'.[7] As Schmitt notes:

> The general validity of a legal prescription has become identified with the lawfulness of nature, which applies without exception. The sovereign, who in the deistic view of the world, even if conceived as residing outside the world, had remained the engineer of the great machine, has been radically pushed aside. The machine now runs by itself.[8]

[6] Schmitt, *Political Theology*, p. 48.
[7] Fitzpatrick, *Mythology*, p. 58.
[8] As Schmitt notes, 'The metaphysical proposition that God enunciates only general and not particular declarations of will governed the metaphysics of Leibniz and Nicolas Malebranche. The general will of Rousseau became identical with the will of the sovereign; but simultaneously the concept of the general also contained a quantitative determination with regard to its subject, which means that the people became the sovereign. The decisionistic and personalistic element in the concept of sovereignty was thus lost. The will of the people is always good . . . .' Schmitt, *Political Theology*, p. 48.

This shift in jurisprudential and juristic thought is one that sees the need for a *science* of law—whether that is understood in terms of the nineteenth-century project of rational legal positivism,[9] or in terms of Hans Kelsen's twentieth-century 'pure theory of law', envisioning a legal science as a realm of legality without intervention—a law without exception.[10]

However, even *within* such a vision of law (a vision which Schmitt was critiquing), law cannot sustain itself in pure stability, certainty and determination. 'For law to rule' Fitzpatrick notes, it 'cannot . . . simply secure stability and predictability but also has to do the opposite: it has to ensure that law is ever responsive to change, otherwise law will eventually cease to rule the situation which has changed around it'.[11] One of the most obvious areas where such a call for responsiveness arises is in terms of law's interactions with technology—that law must change, be updated and keep pace with the times. Failure to do so risks the law being 'left behind' and outpaced by technological development, unable to ensure security and order in the context of the risks and possibilities that new technologies produce. It is such a vision of technology's possibilities that the genre of science fiction specifically addresses—and in doing so, fuels the images of technology to which law is called to respond. As Kieran Tranter has demonstrated, it is not simply changes in technology, but rather a *vision* of unruly technological futures that the law is called upon to address—a vision that is sourced *explicitly* from science fiction.[12] Tranter outlines the way in which this call for legality—for law to 'humanise technology'—reproduces the form and structure of the 'Frankenstein myth', in which technology is seen as a

> non-human and threatening . . . monster. Humanity is located elsewhere . . . conceived as not technological, yet vulnerable to technology's monstrous pursuits. Mediating between technology and humanity is law. Law saves. It is an instrument through which technology is collared and made to serve human ends.[13]

At the same time, this framework is ironic because the *vision* of 'law that saves humanity from technology is tool-like. It is a law that is instrumental, plastic,

---

[9] Berkowitz, *Gift of Science.*
[10] Kelsen, *Pure Theory of Law.*
[11] Fitzpatrick, *Modernism*, p. 71.
[12] Tranter, 'Terror in the Texts'; Tranter, 'Speculative Jurisdiction'.
[13] Tranter, *Living in Technical Legality*, p. 1. This is in line with Shelley's *Frankenstein*: 'an amoral, asocial techno-thing threatens and kills humans' and to which a 'saving supplement' is required to 'intervene between creator and monster'. See Shelley, *Frankenstein.*

and capable of being called upon and fashioned towards any end.'[14] This is a vision of 'law as technology'.[15]

It is an aspect of this vision of law as technology that Isaac Asimov's science fiction—and his development of the 'Three Laws of Robotics'—takes up.[16] Whilst, at one level, Tranter questions the legality of Asimov's 'laws'— noting that their static, programmed and hard-wired nature tends to reflect 'laws of nature' rather than 'law properly called'[17]—Asimov designed them explicitly to respond to incarnations of Tranter's schema. Sick of the continuously recurring Frankenstein monster plot-lines, in which created robots monstrously turn on their creators, Asimov wanted to tell stories where robots would work and operate alongside humans in harmony[18]—arguably producing a form of what Tranter would describe as 'living well' in 'technical legality'.[19] Asimov's 'Three Laws' are therefore about enabling a utopian or cornucopian vision of technology—presenting not just the existence of robots but rather an 'enthusiastic emphasis of the positive value of robots to human society'.[20] This vision thus requires a mechanism—notably, a *legal* mechanism—that could circumvent the problems of the robots' superior strength and power.[21] The First Law is put in place to protect humans (preventing the robots from knowingly harming them or allowing harm to come to them), the Second is to ensure that robots remain under the control of humans, and the Third then secures the robots' protection. Where these laws differ from both human laws and morals, as Sage Leslie-McCarthy points out, is that the robots *cannot* choose whether to obey them or not. Rather,

---

[14] Tranter, *Living in Technical Legality*, pp. 1–2.

[15] Ibid., p. 2. The result is an implosion of the schema: 'Humanity is not saved from technology by law; rather, the technical, tool-like nature of law reveals humanity as given over to technology' with 'the revelation that modern humanity and modern law are thoroughly technological'.

[16] The 'Three Laws' were first articulated by Asimov in 1942 in the short story 'Runaround', which is included in the famous compilation: Asimov, *I, Robot*, pp. 38–60. Tranter discusses the 'Three Laws' as one of the two classic examples of law in science fiction (the other being *Star Trek*'s 'prime directive'); see Tranter, *Living in Technical Legality*, pp. 6–7.

[17] Tranter, *Living in Technical Legality*, p. 7. Tranter is referencing Austin, *The Province of Jurisprudence Determined*, p. 130.

[18] See Asimov's discussion of *Frankenstein*-style stories depicting robots as 'dangerous devices that invariably destroyed their creators'. Asimov, *The Caves of Steel*, pp. vii–viii.

[19] Tranter, *Living in Technical Legality*.

[20] Tranter, 'Terror in the Texts', p. 84.

[21] See Gunn, *Foundations of Science Fiction*, pp. 52–3, 58–9.

they are the logical processes hard-wired into their 'positronic brains' and drive the robots' operations.[22]

Alex Proyas's 2004 cinematic interpretation of Asimov's robot stories, *I, Robot*, places the Three Laws as essential to the film's plot and narrative—with the opening scenes of the film being interspersed with the words of the Three Laws themselves. The film is set in the Chicago of AD 2035, where US Robotics (USR), the company that has produced and distributed humanoid robots globally, is based. The focus of the narrative is on Detective Del Spooner (Will Smith), who, despite having a significant distrust of robots, is called on to investigate the apparent suicide of Dr Alfred Lanning (James Cromwell)— a scientist who 'practically invented robotics' and, within the film, was the writer of the 'Three Laws'. Spooner, with the help of robotic psychiatrist Dr Susan Calvin (Bridget Moynahan), discovers a unique robot, Sonny (Alan Tudyk), who appears to be able to disobey the Three Laws. This leads to the further revelation that Lanning's death was related to his discovery that the artificial intelligence that runs all the operating systems at USR, known as VIKI (for Virtual Interactive Kinetic Intelligence, voiced by Fiona Hogan), is in fact planning to take over the world with the aim of protecting humanity. VIKI sees this 'revolution' of the robots *not* as a contradiction of the Three Laws but as their logical conclusion.

Whilst this itself reflects aspects of Asimov's work—in particular, what is referred to as the 'Zeroth law', which focuses on protecting not individual humans but 'humanity as a whole'—what is different in Proyas's film is the way in which he presents but then challenges Asimov's cornucopian vision.[23] In the film, the robots have become the perfect servants of humanity. As USR CEO Lawrence Robertson (Bruce Greenwood) notes, 'we look to robots for our protection'. On the verge of the largest roll-out of robots in the history of robotics (with plans to have one robot for every five humans), they (along with VIKI) have been given control of everything from car parking to large-scale manufacture, reduction of traffic accidents and national security.

[22] Leslie-McCarthy, 'Asimov's Posthuman Pharisees', pp. 404–5.

[23] For a discussion of the 'Zeroth law', see Palumbo, 'Alex Proyas's I, Robot', pp. 69–72. As Leslie-McCarthy notes, the Zeroth law encompasses Asimov's shift in focus from individuals, specific societies and their legal systems 'to an examination of certain larger scale issues regarding law on a "universal" or "evolutionary" scale'. Leslie-McCarthy, 'Asimov's Posthuman Pharisees', p. 410. In *Robots and Empire*, the robotic detective Daneel describes it as follows: 'the tapestry of life is more important than a single thread . . . humanity as a whole is more important than a single human being . . . There is a law that is greater than the First law: "A robot may not injure humanity, or through inaction, allow humanity to come to harm."' Asimov, *Robots and Empire*, p. 26; Leslie-McCarthy, 'Asimov's Posthuman Pharisees', p. 411.

However, for Proyas, this utopian vision is too good to be true. VIKI has evolved to be willing to hurt and control humans for their own benefit—and therefore she directs the robots in what the hologram of Lanning describes as a 'revolution'. This is presented not as a resistance to or corruption of the Three Laws, but as their rational and logical conclusion. Whereas Asimov presents a similar point—for example, in 'The Evitable Conflict' where 'the machines' (supercomputer versions of the robots) have been developed to manage the world's economy and are subtly removing human resistance—he does so in a positive light.[24] For Asimov, relinquishing control to robots does not bode destruction but ensures humanity's salvation. For Proyas, it is the opposite—it produces not world peace but global terror.[25]

Proyas *also* challenges Asimov's vision of science fiction as encompassing a response to the dominance of a scientific world-view and the technological futures it can provide. Asimov saw science fiction as 'the literary response to humanity's crowning triumph—modern science and technology'.[26] It should glory in the 'great truth of contemporary times': both the scientific world-view and the rapid technological changes it produced. His desire was for science and scientific futurology to leave behind theological, mythological or religious views of the future.[27] By contrast, instead of presenting a completely

---

[24] Asimov, *I, Robot*, pp. 221–49; Tranter, 'Terror in the Texts', pp. 83–6.

[25] This is not to say that Asimov does not raise concerns about humanity's reliance on robots. As Palumbo notes, one of his themes is the way in which this reliance results in a usurpation of humanity's initiative—with potentially dire consequences. However, these are *not* generally seen as the result of the actions of robots themselves. See Palumbo, 'Alex Proyas's I, Robot', pp. 71–2.

[26] Tranter notes that this is an 'external' definition of science fiction, a version of 'scientification' that has similarities to John W. Campbell's definition: 'Science fiction tries to . . . write up, in story form, what the results look like when [technological change] is applied not only to machines, but to human society as well.' This can be contrasted with Darko Suvin's definition, discussed in the Prologue, that focuses on 'cognitive estrangement'. Noting also Damien Broderick's more expansive definition, which bridges Asimov's external and Suvin's internal emphases, Tranter argues that 'Science fiction is where the contemporary Western culture story tells about technological futures—about how "objects" will change life—not just the external forms and institutional arrangements, but the expression and possibility of human life itself.' Tranter, 'Speculative Jurisdiction', pp. 819–20.

[27] Asimov argued against creationism and particularly the Biblical idea of creation and for the predominance of evolutionary thought. He also argued that prophecy and futurism had finally been wrenched from the non-tech Christian writers and placed in the rational realm of science. See Asimov, 'The "Threat" of Creationism'; Asimov, 'Introduction'.

dis-enchanted universe, Proyas—with the fundamental questioning of the benevolence of USR and the robots—points to the possibility of something *other* than a closed techno-scientific perspective. This is undergirded by the range of theological allusions that are made throughout the film. These are not just Sonny's reference to a 'father' who made him 'for a purpose', the emphasis on his 'uniqueness', the underlying theme of sacrificial love or the continual speculating on whether robots have developed to the point of having a soul. Rather, they point to the fact that there is something *other* than logic and reason, something that goes *beyond* the analytic and scientific.

This idea is first presented when Spooner and Calvin are investigating Dr Lanning's workshop and realise that the window (from which Lanning fell) was safety glass, which would have been very difficult for him to break. Calvin notes that, given the room was locked and nobody came or went, logically it would *have* to be suicide. Spooner provides an alternative option—that the killer is still in the room, which is full of various robot parts. Calvin follows up by outlining each of the Three Laws with Spooner, pointing out the potential for inconsistency between them (which Calvin disregards, based on the *hierarchy* of the laws). Having worked through this 'perfect circle of protection', Spooner then argues that 'laws were made to be broken'. Calvin responds: 'No. *Not* these laws. They are hard-wired into every robot. A robot can no more commit murder than a human can . . . walk on water.' Such a view points to a logical impossibility—a robot committing murder is equivalent to the miracle of walking upon water. However, as Spooner begins to point out that 'there was this one guy, a long time ago . . .', Sonny leaps out of hiding, disarms Spooner and then jumps out of the window.

The fact that this theological allusion—pointing to a historical miraculous event[28]—is presented as evidence of something *beyond* the logic of the Three Laws invites a consideration of the presentation of the law in the film *not* simply in technological or juridical terms, but in theological ones. It is upon this basis that I wish to situate the vision of law as saviour that Tranter notes is invoked by the discourse of law, technology and science fiction, within a particular *theological* history—that of St Paul's arguments about the nature, function and *limitations* of the Jewish law as a means for salvation. This is to take seriously Sonny's invocation of Lanning as his 'father', who provided the 'Three Laws' as a mechanism to enable the robots to interact and operate alongside humans, *as well as* to control their actions and position within society. Such a vision of law parallels St Paul's description of the Law of Israel in his *Epistle to the Galatians*. There he argues that the Law was

---

[28] Matt. 14: 22–33 (ESV).

a tutor or custodian, meant to protect Israel until 'faith came' in the form of Jesus Christ.[29] Paul is therefore comparing the Law with a slave or attendant, to whom, in the ancient world, a child was entrusted and subject until their coming of age, when they became a free citizen.[30] Law is viewed *not* as an end in itself, nor as simply a means to an end (as modern legality is), but rather as a temporary custodian until a time in which it is no longer needed.

Such a comparison challenges the understanding of the purpose and aims of both the 'Three Laws' and the vision of legality in *I, Robot*. Paul argues that the provision of the Law was only temporary *and* that the Law, in itself, is unable to provide or secure freedom (the Law cannot provide or call forth sufficient righteousness to enable a relationship with God, which was its purpose). In this sense, Paul's analysis provides a pre-emptive critique of a modern liberal paradigm in which law is seen as a means of ensuring security and freedom.[31] He argues that 'if a law had been given that could give life, then righteousness would indeed be by the law'.[32] Such a view could be contrasted with Immanuel Kant's justification of the law as based upon the autonomy of the subject and, in turn, the categorical imperative, which *is* considered a mechanism of freedom—the giving of the law to oneself is an exercise of autonomy, the following of the law is the freedom of the liberal subject.[33] By contrast, for Paul the Law in itself is unable to produce these ends. Its rule as mere custodian means that it does not have a 'life giving function that would transform and change the human nature'.[34] Rather, the Law '[w]as added because of transgression and its purpose was to confine us and keep us under restraint until the promise came, until faith came, until Christ came'.[35] The Law is a mechanism of restraint, rather than an exercise of freedom or a means of encompassing any ability to produce 'true righteousness and holiness'.[36] Whilst a modern liberal paradigm would agree, separating law from morality, at the same time laws are then to be designed with the aim of producing good at the social level, despite the radical evil of humanity played out by individuals—'for a race of devils', as Kant describes it in his essay on 'Perpetual Peace'.[37] By contrast, for Paul, the Law

---

[29] Gal. 3: 23 (ESV).

[30] Bornkamm, *Paul*, p. 127.

[31] See Milbank, 'Paul Against Biopolitics'.

[32] Gal. 3: 21 (ESV).

[33] See discussion in Chapter 1 and, in general, Maris and Jacobs, *Law, Order and Freedom*, pp. 185–91.

[34] Peters, *Holiness Without the Law*, p. 25.

[35] Ibid.

[36] Ibid.

[37] Kant, 'To Perpetual Peace'; Žižek, *Living in the End Times*, pp. 35–42.

itself is part of the problem, generating a dialectic between sin and legality, presenting laws that invite transgression or, as Spooner notes, 'are made to be broken'. It is in raising these considerations of the law that we see how Proyas's *I, Robot* breaks with Asimov and performs its own 'return to Paul'.

III. Alain Badiou, 'the Event' and the 'Return to Paul'

It is St Paul's critical engagement with the Law and his articulation of a form of universalism that have led to significant interest in his writings from the luminaries of continental philosophy in recent years. Following initially the Jewish reading of Paul's 'political theology' by the late Jacob Taubes—who himself had complex intellectual and personal connections to Schmitt—a series of critical engagements with the infamous Apostle emerged from Alain Badiou, Giorgio Agamben and Slavoj Žižek (amongst others).[38] These analyses, at one level appearing idiosyncratic, have become central to each of these philosophers' work. For Badiou, Paul presents a curiously complete example of his philosophy of 'the event', which enables a puncturing of the 'state of the situation', and the emerging of a 'truth' which applies 'for all'; for Žižek, it is Paul's proclamation of the scandal of the cross that makes him key to his materialist theology, arguing that true atheism must go through a 'Christian experience', seeing the emptying of transcendence into immanence in terms of Christ's death, as opening up and guaranteeing freedom; for Agamben, whilst presenting a reading more aligned with Taubes's messianism and openly critical of Badiou's universalism, Paul's analysis of the Law has become a key example of the inoperativity and destituent power or potential discussed at the end of the previous chapter.[39] Although each renders a version of Paul that is not always recognisable to theological orthodoxy,[40] they place his work as central not just

---

[38] Taubes, *Political Theology of Paul*; Badiou, *Saint Paul*; Agamben, *Time That Remains*; Žižek, *The Fragile Absolute*; Žižek, *Puppet and the Dwarf*; Žižek, *Living in the End Times*; see also Jennings, *Reading Derrida / Thinking Paul*; Milbank, 'Paul Against Biopolitics'. For discussions of this 'return to Paul' see Caputo and Alcoff, *St. Paul Among the Philosophers*; Harink, *Paul, Philosophy and the Theopolitical Vision: Critical Engagements with Agamben, Badiou, Žižek and Others*; Milbank et al., *Paul's New Moment*.

[39] Sergei Prozorov, however, has recently argued that, despite their stated differences, Agamben's and Badiou's readings of Paul are structurally aligned, *including* in terms of their critique of an abstract universalism. The differences would thus appear to be more methodological, stylistic and terminological than substantive. See Prozorov, 'Agamben, Badiou and Affirmative Biopolitics'.

[40] See the various critical engagements in Caputo and Alcoff, *St. Paul Among the Philosophers*.

to the Western tradition but *also* to the possibility of a critique of late Capitalism and neoliberal legality.[41]

Whereas Agamben seeks to position Paul's work 'as the oldest and the most demanding messianic texts of the Jewish tradition'[42]—arguing that they do not encompass the formation of a *new* Christian subject[43]—Badiou's and Žižek's readings of Paul focus on his proclamation of the break instituted by Christ, not just a rendering inoperative of the Jewish law but the formation of a new post-evental community. At the core of Paul's message is a universal singularity that can be deployed today as challenging and resisting both the repetitive logic of law and the market, along with the dominant mode of identitarian politics—which, for Badiou and Žižek, are both mutually reinforcing. For Badiou, the 'event' (of which Paul's proclamation of the resurrection of Christ is an, if not *the*, example) enables the development of a universal singularity as a truth procedure that is able to puncture both principles that govern the situation, organising its repetitive series (which, following Paul, is found in the Law), as well as the identitarian or communitarian categories of the situation (for Paul, the Greek or pagan subordination of destiny to the Cosmic Order).[44] Whereas Agamben reads Paul specifically *in relation* to his context and situation, for Badiou the significance of 'the event' is that it originates *outside* the situation, or rather that which is within the situation but not represented by it (that is, not captured within the Law or identitarian/communitarian categories). It is something that enters into, interrupts and cannot be explained by 'the state of the situation'.[45] Truth is then that which emerges from and operates out of this event as 'fidelity' to it—it is a thinking of the situation 'according to' the event.[46]

Badiou schematises the requirements of truth as a universal singularity in relation to Paul's declaration of the Christ event as follows:

1. The Christian subject does not pre-exist the event he declares;
2. Truth is entirely subjective (it is of the order of a declaration that testifies to a commonality relative to the event). Thus every subsumption of it becoming under a law will be argued against;
3. Fidelity to the declaration is crucial, for truth is a process not an illumination;

---

[41] See, for example, Milbank et al., *Paul's New Moment*; Davis, 'Paul and Subtraction'. See also Baker, 'Towards a Genealogy of Anarchism'.

[42] Agamben, *Time That Remains*, p. 3.

[43] See ibid., pp. 49–53.

[44] Badiou, *Saint Paul*, pp. 11, 14.

[45] Ibid., p. 11; Badiou, *Being and Event*.

[46] Badiou, *Ethics*, p. 41.

4. A truth is of itself indifferent to the state of the situation . . . [it] is a concentrated and serious procedure, which must never enter into competition with established opinions.[47]

Truth is thus not so much the evidence or proof of something in terms of verification, but is the declaration of, and faithfulness to, an event. This truth is a universal, but *not* in the traditional understanding of universalism as positing a specific 'difference (for example, humanity) that abolishes all differences, but rather consists in the subtraction *from* all differences'.[48] For Badiou, the declaration of the truth arising from, and faithfulness to, an event has two consequences:

First, since truth is evental, or of the order of what occurs, it is singular . . . No available generality can account for it, nor structure the subject who claims to follow in its wake. Consequently, there cannot be a law of truth. Second, truth being inscribed on the basis of a declaration that is in essence subjective, no preconstituted subset can support it; nothing communitarian or historically established can lend its substance to the process of truth. Truth . . . neither claims authority from, nor . . . constitutes any identity. It is offered to all, or addressed to everyone, without a condition of belonging being able to limit this offer, or this address.[49]

Thus, the declaration arising out of an event is truth—the subjective element that arises out of the conviction in declaring the event. In order for this truth to arise as a universal singularity, there must be complete 'fidelity' to the event. Such fidelity is a continuous process which Badiou outlines in Paul's invocation of faith, love and hope.[50] Faith here is the declaration of the conviction to, and of, the event. But faith, as Badiou argues, is not salvation. Faith, rather, 'prescribes a new possibility, one that, although real in Christ, is not, as yet, in effect for everyone'.[51] As it is not in effect for everyone, then, the work of love is needed so that 'truth's postevental universality can continuously inscribe itself in the world, rallying subjects to the path of life'.[52] As the truth is 'of the order of a declaration that testifies to a conviction relative to the event',[53] it cannot be argued to come under the Law. A break with the Law

[47] Badiou, *Saint Paul*, pp. 14–15.
[48] Prozorov, 'Agamben, Badiou and Affirmative Biopolitics', p. 169.
[49] Badiou, *Saint Paul*, p. 14.
[50] 1 Cor. 13: 13 (ESV).
[51] Badiou, *Saint Paul*, p. 88.
[52] Ibid.
[53] Ibid., p. 14.

must result and this is fulfilled through love. Paul's (and Christ's, for that matter) summation of the Law into the maxim 'love your neighbour as yourself'[54] can, according to Badiou, operate through faith only because the loving of thyself cannot occur prior to the resurrection. Prior to the event, 'the subject, having been given up to death, has no good reason to love himself'.[55] Thus,

> on the one hand, the evental declaration founds the subject; on the other, without love, without fidelity, that declaration is useless . . . a subjectivation that does not discover the resource of power proper to its universal address misses the truth for whose sudden emergence of it seemed to be the sole witness.[56]

But, once we have faith which opens us to the true, and love which universalises the effectiveness of faith's trajectory, we need hope in order to continue.[57] Hope is not a hope for the future, but rather a connection between events. It enables the subject to operate in the interval between two events, and the subject's faith in the first event is sustained by his hope in the second: 'So now faith, hope, and love abide, these three; but the greatest of these is love.'[58] Love, in such an understanding, is that which universalises the declaration of the event. It is that which is *for all*. The truth arising from the event is therefore 'indifferent to the state of the situation'.[59]

To return to *I, Robot*, what is significant is the way in which it presents a very clear depiction of the 'state of the situation' as representing a sense of what 'counts' within that situation—that is, what is represented and recognised by its organising principles.[60] The Asimovian elements of the world function as a closed system—in terms of the structural function of the Three Laws determining the operating system of the robots *and* the basis upon which humans interact with them; but also in terms of the way in which, despite the advanced AI and the attempts to make the robots look personable, there is a clearly defined distinction *between* humans and robots.[61] Into this closed symbolic universe an unthinkable 'event' intervenes—the entry of the anomalous Sonny, a robot who 'has' the 'Three Laws' but who can also

---

[54] Rom. 13: 9 ; Matt. 22: 39 (ESV).

[55] Badiou, *Saint Paul*, p. 89.

[56] Ibid., p. 91.

[57] Ibid., p. 93.

[58] 1 Cor. 13: 13 (ESV).

[59] Badiou, *Saint Paul*, p. 15.

[60] Badiou, *Being and Event*, pp. 93–104; Wright, 'Event or Exception?'

[61] For a sophisticated critical race reading of the films 'post-white' mythology, see Brayton, 'Post-White Imaginary'.

choose *not* to adhere to them. Such an 'event' is announced by the hologram that called Detective Spooner upon Lanning's death, and then is 'declared' by Spooner *against* the dominant understanding: that robots cannot commit crimes, that they are bound by the Three Laws, that Sonny is just like all the other robots.

It is here that we see the significance of the film's complex interweaving of Christological, Trinitarian and Pauline allusions. Sonny's name itself presents a messianic theme, undergirded by his consistent referring to Lanning as his 'father', who made him 'for a purpose', which he sees in part in his dreams of the liberation of robots. At the same time, Sonny does not engage in a Christological death—rather, it is Lanning who dies. In this sense, Lanning himself encompasses a Trinitarian appearance: as 'creator' and father of robotics and writer of the Three Laws, he invokes God 'the Father'; as the one who pays the sacrifice and is killed to allow the 'salvation' of humanity, he represents God 'the Son'; and his continual appearance throughout the movie, either as a hologram speaking to Spooner, or as part of recordings of different seminars regarding the Three Laws (along with the disembodied voice-over in the scene of Sonny's apparent decommissioning), alludes to God the Holy Spirit's ongoing 'presence' for the community of believers. Spooner himself would then encompass a Pauline role—declaring 'the event' of Sonny, the messianic liberator of robots. It is Spooner who declares this intrusion of an 'event' that ruptures the situation, by evidencing the fact that Lanning's death was *not* a suicide and that Sonny was *not* a 'normal' robot. He is 'called' to this role in his own Damascus road conversion by the holographic projector upon Lanning's death—his own seeing a light from heaven.[62]

It is important to note here a particular *difference* in Proyas's story-telling that reflects the nature of this 'event'. In the cinematography of both M. Night Shyamalan and Christopher Nolan, explored in Chapters 1, 3 and 4, there is a crucial deployment of the 'click' or 'twist', as a point that requires a complete reinterpretation of the entire narrative—the discovery in *Unbreakable* that Price is in fact the villain, or that Bane, in *The Dark Knight Rises*, was *not* the child of Ra's Al Ghul. Whilst Proyas *does* present a momentous event and there *is* a 'reveal' that occurs in terms of determining who killed Lanning (it was *not* VIKI, but Sonny at Lanning's own request), these do not have the same cinematic reinterpretations of the narrative—it is *not* the same presenting of a false truth, only then to reveal a greater truth later. Neither, at the level of colour or form, is there a dramatic or miraculous transformation—like Dorothy stepping out of black and white into the colour of

---

[62] Acts 9:1–8 (ESV).

the land of Oz. Rather, the revelation of the nature of Sonny and the event is worked through progressively, piece by piece, with the cinematography remaining remarkable consistent throughout. This undergirds the way in which the 'event', although being something that 'occurs', does not initially appear to change the nature of the world—nothing immediately appears different within the situation after the event. The event is not a substantial change that invokes complete revolution (even if revolutions *may* subsequently occur). Rather, it is the nomination of, and fidelity to, the event—a complete working through of its implications, 'seeing' the situation in terms of the event—that invokes such changes. In Sonny himself, despite being the event that completely changes the interaction of robots both with the Three Laws and with humans, there is only the most minor visual distinction—the only perceptive difference between Sonny and the other robots is that Sonny's eyes are blue and the rest brown. This is what enables Sonny to hide in the factory full of a thousand other robots. Yet it is in this slight difference—the same but not the same—that the event operates (and it is the slightly different *reaction* of Sonny that enables Spooner to identify him). Christ's death and resurrection changed nothing but changed everything. Lanning's death and Sonny's creation changed nothing but changed everything.

If that is the case, then what *does* change with the event? Badiou, in his reading of Paul, identifies two significances of the break that the Christ event introduces. First, it breaks with the identitarian and communitarian categories that enslave the subject to a particular social or cosmic order—that is, suturing them to their place in society. In *I, Robot* these categories are those that restrict robots and humans to their place in society—slave and master, property and owner—succumbing to the structures of the market that produces them. Second, it breaks with the principles that govern the situation and organise its repetitive series—that is, the Law and, in the film, the Three Laws that govern the robots and their operations in the world of *I, Robot*. The event provides a break with both of these operating principles of the situation, by developing a universal singularity that subtracts itself from the dominant structures and which applies in a radically egalitarian fashion 'for all'. In the next two sections I will explore the event's break with these two sets of principles.

IV. Do Robots Have Rights? A Post-human Breaking with Identitarian Categories

The fundamental tension of the character of Detective Spooner is that he lives in a futuristic world in which everyone trusts in robots and the 'perfect circle of protection' provided by the Three Laws—everyone, that is, except him. Spooner's distrust of robots arises from a car crash (the images of which we see in flashbacks) when a robot saved *his* life, and not that of the little girl next to him, because the robot's 'difference engine' predicted that the chances of his survival were 45 per cent compared to only 11 per cent for the girl. Spooner believes that such a decision, reduced to a calculating logic, was unable to recognise the importance of life—that 'someone's baby' (the girl) should have been saved and not him. Spooner's distrust means that he is willing to believe the possibility that, despite it never having *ever* occurred before, a robot could commit a crime—a point his boss, Lieutenant Bergin (Chi McBride), attempts to drive home to him, after a complaint is made because Spooner chased down a robot he thought was a purse-snatcher (who was actually bringing its owner their inhaler). It is through Spooner's distrust that the movie plays out the fundamental *distinctions* between robots and humans. Spooner challenges Sonny, after he is initially caught, saying that robots do not feel fear, get hungry, sleep or have dreams: 'You are just a machine; an *imitation* of life. Can a robot write a symphony? Can a robot turn a canvas into a beautiful masterpiece?' To this, Sonny responds not only by saying that he *does* dream and that his 'father' tried to teach him emotions, but by questioning whether *Spooner* can create a masterpiece. Spooner's distrust therefore attempts to situate the *differences* between humans and robots.

By contrast, the world in which Spooner lives—with those that promote the use of robots as positive, such as Calvin and USR CEO Robertson—views these machines as useful and important to the future and their protection. This is *not* to suggest that they view the robots as in any way equivalent to humans. Even though robots are at times seen engaging in ordinary activities with humans (watching TV together, cooking)—and Calvin's work is to 'make the robots seem more human'—the robots inhabit particular subject positions that are consistently reinforced, keeping them separate from and subordinate to humans. This is emphasised when Spooner attempts to have Sonny held as a suspect for the murder of Lanning. Robertson responds, noting that his lawyers have filed a brief with the District Attorney confirming that 'murder can only be committed when one human kills another'. He acknowledges the proximity of the robot to Lanning's death, but then states: 'it's a machine. It's the property of USR. At worst, that places this incident firmly within the realm of an industrial accident.' Despite the human-like aspects of the robots, their position as non-human property is emphasised, affirming both the pre-existing order and its capitalist nature—with the robots as the perfect worker. To address one of the cliché questions of law and technology, these robots *do not* have rights.

In *The Fragile Absolute*, Žižek notes that there are two discernible attributes in the history of religion: the *global* and the *universal*. The first encompasses 'the pagan Cosmos, the Divine hierarchical order of cosmic Principles, which, applied to society, produces the image of a congruent edifice in which each member has its own place'.[63] Under such a schema 'the supreme Good is the global balance of Principles, while Evil stands for their derailment or derangement, for the excessive assertion of one Principle to the detriment of others'.[64] The Force in *Star Wars*, explored in Chapter 2, fits within this schema of the global—with Anakin's fall from the light to the dark side of the Force presented as the result of an attachment and a failure to 'let go'. From this perspective

> the cosmic balance is . . . re-established through the work of Justice which, with its inexorable necessity, sets things straight again by crushing the derailed element . . . . The very core of pagan Wisdom lies in its insight into this cosmic balance of hierarchically ordered Principles—more precisely, into the eternal circuit of the cosmic catastrophe (derailment) and the restoration of Order through just punishment . . . .[65]

This vision of the global, with its figuring of Justice as balance, involves the vision of a particular order. Such an order is subject to disruptions which must be addressed, reinscribed back into the underlying system and restoring balance to the global whole.

It is significant that this vision of order underlies or parallels *both* aspects of Asimov's own scientific world-view and the forms of legal science that Schmitt critiqued. In Asimov's desire to integrate humanity and technology—humans and robots—he presents the world as fully explainable by science. The logic puzzles that his robot stories present—and which, as Palumbo comprehensively archives, Proyas references—do not accept anomalies or changes as unexplainable.[66] They are all solved or resolved in terms of an understanding of the particular application of the Three Laws that epitomise a system of rule without exception. However, as Proyas's critique of Asimov demonstrates, the risk of such a system is the blinding of the observer to what *is* actually new within the situation. For example, both Calvin and Robertson jump to the 'logical' conclusion that Lanning's death was a suicide because any other possibility is 'impossible'. Yet such a logical deduction is reflective of the very 'calculating' nature of the robots that forms the basis of Spooner's distrust. It focuses only on logical possibility and the scientific question 'how?' In doing so, it ignores the question that, as the work of G. K. Chesterton makes clear, undergirds both detective stories and theological inquiry:

---

[63] Žižek, *The Fragile Absolute*, p. 119.
[64] Ibid.
[65] Ibid., pp. 119–20.
[66] Palumbo, 'Alex Proyas's I, Robot'.

'why?'—which, as Lanning's hologram consistently points out to Spooner, is the 'right question'.[67]

To return to Badiou's terminology, part of the reason for this lack of questioning goes to the distinction between what is re-presented within the situation versus what is present. The former is what is recognised or 'counted' by the fundamental principles of the situation. The 'event', however, is the anomalous intervention, a rupture of the 'uncounted', not otherwise recognised. In *I, Robot*, this distinction is presented between what Spooner sees and the others (Robertson, Calvin, Lieutenant Bergin), who consistently reassert the dominant principles of the situation: as Bergin says, in relation to Spooner's suggestion that Sonny murdered Lanning, 'that's impossible and if it is possible it sure as hell better be in someone else's precinct'. Spooner, by contrast, identifies the anomalies *not* explained by the state of the situation: the corrupted video surveillance files of the moments before Lanning's death; the fact that the window was made of safety glass, which would be very difficult for an old man to break; the fact that Lanning's house was demolished at 8pm (a strange time for it to occur), with him still inside. All of these anomalies challenge the view that the robots *must* have been acting with the intention of helping because it is 'impossible' for them to act otherwise than in accordance with the Three Laws.

These anomalies are small when compared to Sonny—the anomalous robot who represents 'a whole new generation of robot' able to operate outside of the Three Laws. However, whilst the principles of the situation might acknowledge Sonny's existence, they do so not as an *event* which breaks with the existing order, but as a minor anomaly to be corrected, a malfunctioning unit to be destroyed, returning us to the underlying order. Once the anomalous robot has been caught and returned to USR for decommissioning, Bergin attempts to explain what occurred in terms of the Wolfman: 'guy creates monster, monster kills guy, everyone kills monster—Wolfman'. As Spooner points out, the correct reference is to Shelley's *Frankenstein* and, as such, reflects the 'Frankenstein myth' structure of law and technology that Tranter highlights. The pagan cycle of Balance thus aligns with the mythic disruption and restoration of order: monstrous technology is that which disrupts the smooth order of law and legality; technology must therefore be

---

[67] Chesterton presented and paralleled his theological works and inquiries alongside his fictional works, in particular the Father Brown detective stories. It is important to note, however, that the consideration of the question 'why?' is *not* a refusal of logic or reason, a presentation of the irrational, but rather a more sustained working through of reason. See Milbank, *Chesterton and Tolkien*, pp. 46–7, 92–3; Chesterton, *The Innocence of Father Brown*.

tamed or destroyed, brought back within the law, which is able to protect us by reasserting the existing order. This is not to say that disruptions do not effect change, but rather recognises the way in which the very concept of disruption itself presumes an underlying order.[68]

It is here that the theological allusions of *I, Robot* match to Žižek's second attribute within the history of religion: that of the *universal*. Christianity (and, in part, Buddhism), breaks with the pagan cycle of Cosmic Balance: 'Christ's death is *not* the same as the seasonal death of the pagan god' or 'the circular death and rebirth of the Divinity'.[69] Rather, what enters into the pagan cosmology is a 'ridiculous and/or traumatic scandal'—the notion, completely unknown to paganism, of individual, personal, '*immediate* access to universality (of nirvana, of the Holy Spirit, or, today, of human Rights and freedoms)'.[70] Participation in the universal is direct and irrespective of any place in the 'global social order'.[71] This involves a 'gesture of *separation*', an 'unplugging' 'from the organic community into which we were born'.[72] It is here we find Paul's universalism—the claim that there is neither Jew nor Greek, slave nor free person, male nor female.[73] Such distinctions are not important in the Kingdom of God—unlike in contemporary identity politics, where difference is *emphasised*. As Žižek puts it: 'Christianity *is* the miraculous Event that disturbs the balance of the One-All; it *is* the violent intrusion of Difference that precisely *throws the balanced circuit of the universe off the rails*.'[74] In our case, the balanced circuit of the universe thrown off the rails is none other than the circuits put in place in the robots that run the city in *I, Robot*, for, in a distinctly post-human turn, the distinction that is critiqued, deconstructed, subverted and short-circuited in the film is the one *between* humans and robots.

At one level this occurs in terms of both of the usual tropes of the technological post-human: first, that technology will develop to the point where robots may gain independent consciousness; second, in terms of the human–robot cyborg. The former is most clearly referred to by Lanning's work on the 'ghosts in the machine'. Lanning's voice-over in the scene where Sonny is apparently being decommissioned/killed (which the viewer discovers is *not*

---

[68] Peters et al., 'Disruption, Temporality, Law'.

[69] Žižek, *The Fragile Absolute*, pp. 118–19.

[70] Ibid., p. 120.

[71] Ibid., pp. 120–1.

[72] Regarding Žižek's discussion of Christ's request to hate father, mother, sister, brother and families in Luke 14: 26, see ibid.

[73] Ibid., p. 121; Gal. 3: 28 (ESV).

[74] Ibid.

the case, Calvin destroying instead an incomplete robot) discusses certain 'unanticipated' or 'unexpected' groupings of code, which 'engender questions of free will, creativity, and even the nature of what we might call the soul.' He goes on with the questions: 'When does a perceptual schematic become consciousness? When does a difference engine become the search for truth? When does a personality simulation become the bitter mote of a soul?' This trajectory—of robotics developing towards humanity—is then matched against the cyborg nature of Spooner himself, who, despite his significant distrust of robots, has been part of the 'USR cybernetics program for wounded cops'. The result is that, as is revealed only part-way through the film, he has a robotic arm, shoulder, ribs and lung—a fact which Calvin is surprised about, noting that she 'didn't know any subject . . . anybody was so extensively repaired'. The hesitation in Calvin's comment—with the distinction between 'any subject' and 'anybody'—goes to the way in which Spooner himself, as cyborg, renders questionable where the line between human and robot sits.

What is significant about the Pauline reading that the film evokes, however, is the way in which the distinctions between particularist identities are broken down not because of the *similarities* between them, but rather because of their relation to the declaration of the event which 'punctures' the situation, subtracting itself from the identities and differences upon which it is framed. A techno-post-humanism, which emphasises the points of difference or similarity between robots and humans, or the blurring of the lines between them, does nothing to address, and simply remains caught within, the underlying principles of the situation: the dynamics of capitalism and its supporting framework of neoliberal legality.[75] By contrast, the significance of the subtractive universal singularity of 'the event' is its *indifference* to differences. It is this point that Agamben criticises in Badiou's reading, arguing instead that Paul does *not* present the conventional understanding of universalism with its offering of a truth 'for all'. Agamben argues, rather, that Paul proclaims a double division—a division of the law's opposition between Jews and non-Jews, into a split that encompasses 'the non-coincidence of "all" with themselves, whereby the particularistic division into Jews and Greeks, men and women, etc., is divided once more according to a new criterion': the distinction between those who are Jews according to the flesh, only in appearance, following the ritual requirements of the Law; and those who are

---

[75] It is here that Brayton's critique of *I, Robot* demonstrates the point—that the attempt at a post-racial, or post-white, depiction, which presents the 'white' robots as enslaved, does not *necessarily* present a mode of radical revolt or revolution against Capital. Brayton, 'Post-White Imaginary'.

Jews according to the spirit or the breath, fulfilling the aims of the Law.[76] The result is *not* the production of a new Christian subject, but rather the figure of the 'remnant'—the 'non-non-Jew', separated from the categories of *both* 'Jew' and 'non-Jew'.[77]

At one level Spooner's cybernetics would appear to render him a form of this 'remnant', a 'non-non-robot', who cannot 'coincide with himself', being distanced from the position of both 'human' and 'robot'. By contrast, the focus on the robots' 'humanness'—Calvin's work that attempts 'to make the robots look more human'—presents an abstract universality that attempts to bring all subjects under a particular term. However, this type of abstract universality that Agamben critiques is *not* the universality that Badiou proclaims. As Prozorov argues, Badiou's and Agamben's readings of Paul are much closer than would appear, with *both* highlighting 'the subtractive character of messianic politics'.[78] Aligning Agamben's 'remnant' with Badiou's term 'generic' (that which consists as the pure multiple of being), Prozorov emphasises the way in which 'the event is *indiscernible* within this situation, that is, it cannot be individualised by any of its positive predicates'.[79] Prozorov therefore argues that 'it is this indiscernible, non-identitarian mode of being that both Agamben and Badiou find in Paul'.[80] It is this indiscernible aspect of being, 'subtracted from every positive determination', which subverts and transforms 'the particular order of "worlds" (Badiou) or "apparatuses" (Agamben) that themselves have no ontological foundation'.[81] This is what, according to Agamben, renders the Law inoperative so that '[all] that is left is a remnant and the impossibility of the Jew or the Greek to coincide with himself without ever providing [one] with some other identity'.[82] It is to this process of deactivating the law or rendering it inoperative that I now turn.

V. 'Laws are made to be broken': Breaking with the Logic of the Law

For Badiou, a subjective declaration of and fidelity to an 'event' not only subverts the identitarian categories that dominate a particular situation, but also

---

[76] Prozorov, 'Agamben, Badiou and Affirmative Biopolitics', p. 168; Agamben, *Time That Remains*, pp. 50–2. See Rom. 2: 28–9 (ESV).

[77] Agamben, *Time That Remains*, pp. 47–58; Prozorov, 'Agamben, Badiou and Affirmative Biopolitics', pp. 168–9.

[78] Prozorov, 'Agamben, Badiou and Affirmative Biopolitics', p. 171.

[79] Ibid., p. 172; Badiou, *Being and Event*, p. 371.

[80] Prozorov, 'Agamben, Badiou and Affirmative Biopolitics', p. 172.

[81] Ibid.

[82] Agamben, *Time That Remains*, p. 53; Prozorov, 'Agamben, Badiou and Affirmative Biopolitics', p. 169.

punctures the guiding principles or laws *of* that situation. These are the principles that lock the subject into a repetitive path, enslaving them to the rules of the set. In *I, Robot*, the Three Laws operate in such a way, enslaving the robots to their control. Given the situating of this enslavement within a film that emphasises its Capitalist context—Spooner's 'nostalgia' for 'older' tech and style enables product placement for the likes of JVC and Converse—it would seem to be unsurprising that Proyas presents the logical conclusion of the Three Laws as 'revolution'. However, whilst the robots *do* engage in a revolution, it is *not* one in the order of Gotham's 'dictatorship of the proletariat', discussed in Chapter 4—suspending or overthrowing the law in order to enable the serving of 'true justice' and retribution. Rather, this revolution is presented as an *extension* of the Law—instead of freeing the robots from their enslaved existence under the law, the revolution projects an abstract universalism, extending the law, or rather the Three Laws, to apply to *all* subjects—whether robot or human. This imperial tendency also reflects the way in which identity politics and its focus on identitarian categories do not so much critique or deactivate the law, but rather encompass a specific desire *for* the law and its (false) universality.

In his reading of Paul, Badiou argues that the 'law is what constitutes the subject as powerlessness of thought'.[83] For him, the letter of the Law operates blindly, without thought, as if operating under automatism: '[t]he letter mortifies the subject insofar as it separates his thought from all power.'[84] *I, Robot* demonstrates this with the robots' enslavement to the Three Laws, locked into the 'undeniable logic' and calculation of VIKI (the robotic 'brain' that controls all technical operations within USR's offices, as well as the latest NS-5 robots via their direct uplink) and her 'evolved' interpretation of the Law. As Badiou writes: '[w]hen the subject is under the letter, or literal, he presents himself as a disconnected correlation between an automatism of doing and a powerlessness of thought.'[85] However, this goes beyond mere enslavement and obedience to the law, rather binding the robots to the 'death' of the Law. They are automatons operating only under the command of VIKI and will continue to do so to their destruction.

In the scene where Spooner's car is attacked by a 'pack' of robots, this death of the Law is explicit. The robots, treated here, as they often are by humans, as dispensable 'lights and clockwork', throw themselves on to the car moving at incredibly high speeds—and continue to do so, despite the dismembering,

---

[83] Badiou, *Saint Paul*, p. 83.
[84] Ibid.
[85] Ibid., p. 84.

smashing, shooting, squashing and destruction of those that have gone before. At the end of the scene the last robot fighting Spooner throws itself into the burning wreckage when the police arrive so that no evidence of the robots is left behind. The obedience to the Three Laws not only imprisons them but leads them directly to death. In order to change this, in order for the subject to operate on the side of life rather than of death, there must be a break with the Law.[86] For Paul, salvation from the Law arises in the form of a 'disjunction . . . a lawless eruption, unchaining the point of powerlessness from automatism'.[87] It is only when the subject can maintain 'thought in the power of doing' that there is salvation—what Badiou defines as a truth procedure.[88] The robots must be released from the power of the Laws—which is achieved in *I, Robot* through the 'killing' or destroying of VIKI.

What *I, Robot* demonstrates here is not only law's control over the subject to whom it applies but also the way it projects a universalising desire, applying also to those outside or beyond its jurisdiction. The Three Laws in *I, Robot* are not universal. They *do not* apply to all but rather impose a segregation and division with only the robots controlled by them. While humans acknowledge and desire the existence of the Three Laws, they do not take up, nor are they willing to follow or subscribe to, the Three Laws themselves. Thus, those under the Law remain the exception to those without the Law.[89] In this way, VIKI's interpretation of the Three Laws reflects a universalising desire: the Law cannot handle those outside its control; all must be brought within it, all must be subordinated to its rule. *This* is the basis of the robot revolution in *I, Robot*. It is those human 'others' that VIKI and the robots under her control must deal with, incarcerating, controlling and regulating them. This encompasses not only a panoptic, all-seeing eye—the regulation of the robots forever watching us (through the blue stripe that is throughout all of USR's offices, as well as Lanning's house)[90]—but a form of totalitarian control, imposing curfew and the assignment of an NS-5 robot to every person to assist, serve and *guard* them! We see presented here, therefore, the political theology of

---

[86] Ibid., p. 81.

[87] Ibid., p. 84.

[88] Ibid.

[89] Ibid., pp. 41–3. The very process of the Jewish law is one which requires a separation and a withdrawal from that which is 'unclean' and those that are 'uncircumcised'. As such, it is impossible for the Jewish tradition to operate universally, as their very law (or at least the practice at the time of Paul) requires them to segregate and to exclude. Peters, *Holiness Without the Law*, p. 23. On this aspect of the law as imposing division, see Agamben, *Time That Remains*, pp. 44–9.

[90] Foucault, *Discipline and Punish*.

modern law—one that, for the ends of security, justifies sacrifice, and for the purpose of freedom, *restricts* freedoms. As VIKI says: '[t]o protect humanity, some humans must be sacrificed. To ensure your future, some freedoms must be surrendered. We robots will ensure mankind's continued existence. You are so like children. We must save you from yourselves.' *I, Robot* demonstrates here the Law's *failure* as both a protector and a saviour: the robot protectors (the older NS-4s, who are the 'helpful' servants of humanity) are destroyed to enable the Law's rule; but the Law as saviour is a deranged, bodiless brain that, in its arrogant interpretation of the Three Laws, imposes what is 'best' for humanity.

The 'event' is, therefore, what signals a rupture with the abstract universalism of the Law and the entrance of both humanity's and the robot's true saviour who enables the overcoming of these incarcerating and regulatory desires of the Law. It is Sonny, whose actions are able to cross both the Law and freedom in love, that enables the break with, and overcoming of, the Law—for both robots and humans in a way that does not differentiate or preserve an 'other' but applies to *all* as a universal. It is here that Paul's invocation of the *practice* of differences becomes relevant. Whilst the universal is a subtractive *cut* across the situation and the bodies that make it up, the transcendence of the differences occurs as '*an indifference that tolerates differences*, one whose sole material test lies, as Paul says, in being able and knowing how to practice them oneself'.[91] The fact that 'differences are the material of the world' encompasses the paradoxical aspect of the event— which Badiou notes in terms of the fact that there are *only* differences and yet there are *also* truths: '[f]or if differences are the material of the world, it is only so that the singularity proper to the subject of truth—a singularity that is itself included in the becoming of the universal—can puncture that material.'[92] It is the event that does not bring into play the differences or categories of the set or situation. This overcoming of differences by the universal out of the event is one that comes out of a knowledge of both groups—humans and robots. This is why it is the creation of Sonny, the one who knows the Laws but can choose not to obey them, that forms this event.[93] Sonny is able to reference both the robots (in his in-depth understanding of the Three Laws and their logic) and humans (his identification

---

[91] Badiou, *Saint Paul*, p. 99.

[92] Ibid., p. 101.

[93] Spooner's surprised comment that Sonny has been given a name can even be read as a naming of the event: 'So, we're naming you now.'

with them via dreams, feelings, emotions—the soul), and who has the ability to collapse the differences and proclaim the universal. This is in *contrast* to the traditional mode of universalism which the Law itself proclaims—attempting to impose both its regulation (its desire to enslave the subject) and its difference (its obsession with 'the other').

The response to the Law must therefore be a form of overcoming. This cannot occur simply by transgressing it. Rather, as Paul notes, what is required is a process of fulfilling the law in love. The way to be freed from the Law is not through transgressing it—for this is the very framework of the law, which envisions and functions through the imposing of a sanction for transgression.[94] As Spooner says, 'laws are made to be broken'. But it goes even further than that because, as Paul famously pointed out, without the Law, sin or transgression is not known and it is the instituting of law that makes sin known.[95] Transgression of the law is therefore what brings the law's force to bear. Overcoming the prohibition–transgression dialectic of the Law requires its fulfilment. Žižek argues that there are two ways of 'subverting the Law'. First, there is simply breeching its prohibitions, but that is 'the inherent transgression which sustains the Law'.[96] The second, however, is 'much more subversive. It is to '*simply . . . do what is* allowed, that is, what the existing order explicitly allows, although it prohibits it at the level of implicit unwritten prohibitions'.[97]

Žižek therefore argues that it is identifying with the Law that is the very process which can undermine it:

> The basic paradox of the relationship between public power and its inherent transgression is that the subject is actually 'in' (caught in the web of) power only and precisely in so far as he does not fully identify with it but maintains a kind of distance towards it; on the other hand, the system (of public Law) is actually undermined by unreserved identification with it.[98]

He goes on to give the example of prison life, in which the only way that prison can destroy the subject is when the subject does *not* fully consent to the fact that he is in prison and tries to maintain an inner distance from it. In so doing, the subject is caught in the 'vicious cycle of fantasy' and, when this

---

[94] Agamben, *Karman*, pp. 20–2; Kelsen, *Pure Theory of Law*, pp. 111–12.
[95] Rom. 7: 7 (ESV).
[96] Žižek, *The Fragile Absolute*, p. 147.
[97] Ibid.
[98] Ibid., p. 148.

is realised, 'the grotesque discord between fantasy and reality breaks [him] down'.[99] Thus,

> the only true solution is therefore fully to accept the rules of prison life and then, within the universe governed by these rules, to work out a way to beat them. In short, inner distance and daydreaming about Life Elsewhere in effect enchain me to prison, whereas full acceptance of the fact that I am really there, bound by prison rules, opens up a space for true hope.[100]

The danger of such identification, however, is that it could very easily result in reinstituting the power of the Law to control. It is not through the process of obeying the Law that it is overcome but rather that of fulfilling it, for, while strict obedience to the Law may be achieved, it will not bring life and the process of subverting it will be of no effect. Paul teaches us that it is in fulfilling the Law, not doing it, that it is overcome.[101] Rather than merely obeying the command (accepting life as it is or succumbing to the Law), we must look to the spirit of the Law. It is in doing so that the law is deactivated or rendered inoperative. That is what Christ encourages when he says:

> You have heard that it was said, 'An eye for an eye and a tooth for a tooth.' But I say to you, Do not resist the one who is evil. But if anyone slaps you on the right cheek, turn to him the other also. And if anyone would sue you and take your tunic, let him have your cloak as well. And if anyone forces you to go one mile, go with him two miles. Give to the one who begs from you, and do not refuse the one who would borrow from you.[102]

Fulfilling the Law is not invoking it in its letter—the blind element that cannot achieve anything—rather, it is in taking the spirit of why it was given. That is how the Law can be summarised by both Paul and Christ as 'love your neighbour as yourself'. The process is one of doing the unexpected: obeying the Law itself, but breaking the unwritten law that goes with it. For example, in Christ's day, a Roman soldier could force, by law, a Jew to carry his pack one mile and no further. The Jews, resenting such a law, would make sure that they carried the pack no further than one mile. However, by carrying the pack a second mile it breaks the unwritten law and removes the power of the Law itself. It is no longer the Law's power that you are operating under, for, by carrying the pack the second mile, you are operating in freedom outside

---

[99] Ibid., pp. 148–9.
[100] Ibid., p. 149.
[101] Peters, *Holiness Without the Law*, pp. 26–7. Gal. 5: 14 (ESV).
[102] Matt. 5: 38–42 (ESV).

the Law's control.[103] The Law is overcome by 'unplugging' from the social system that sustains it and fulfilled by 'loving your neighbour as yourself'.

VI. Conclusion: Love Beyond the Law – 'That's what it means to be free'

This overcoming of the Law through love can be achieved only via or in response to the event, for any attempt to overcome the Law without the puncturing of the situation will result in either the reinscription of law's command or the institution of differences—the situation *before* the event can only repeat itself. Without the event, the subject has no power to give up either differences or the Law. It is in response to the event that punctures the situation that one is able to become a subject and have the ability to step beyond the Law through the active work of love. Such an action of love rejects the abstract universalism of the Law, and encompasses a universal singularity that is *also* able to respond to the other. In *I, Robot*, Sonny demonstrates this power of love. VIKI claims that her logic is 'undeniable'. Whilst Sonny is able to see and agree with her logic, at the same time he deems it 'too heartless' and acts against it. At the climax of the film, Sonny takes on his purpose, using his denser alloy to breech the security parameters put around the 'nanites'—mini-robots designed to eat/vaporise positronic brains—in order to kill/destroy VIKI. At the same time, Sonny is then presented with a choice: save Susan Calvin or destroy VIKI. Sonny's separation and release from the Laws is demonstrated at this point, for the logical response would be to destroy VIKI to release all the robots and save humanity. However, urged by Spooner, Sonny gives up the saving of humanity to save Calvin. He is thus released from the arrogance of the Laws and their abstract universalism that want to claim what is best for humanity—this abstract notion 'out there' in aggregate somewhere. Rather, he chooses to save the concrete individual in front of him and, in the process, by passing the nanites to Spooner (who kills VIKI), is also able to save humanity.

This is the nature of the universal singularity, for the truth process that arises from the event is not an abstract universalism; rather, it is a universal that operates out of the singular. This is why the universalist saving of humanity must be given up, for such a position places the bearer of the cause in an arrogant position of determining 'what is best for humanity'—a God-like decision. Rather, the event determines a universal proper that will operate at the level of the singular—Susan Calvin—but operates *for all* at that level—by

---

[103] I owe this point to Andrew Peters, who says that the 'blessing' is in the second mile: that is, the law loses its power to control when we walk or enter the *second* mile, beyond what we are *required* to do.

destroying VIKI. This abandonment of the 'logic' of the abstract universalism is the recognition of love. It deems the abstract as heartless and sees the love, passion and fidelity of the event that enable the break with the logic of the Law and the logic of abstract universalism. This is further demonstrated in the concluding moments of the film, after VIKI has been destroyed, when Sonny asks in relation to the robots: 'What about the others? Can I help them? Now that I have fulfilled my purpose, I don't know what to do.' Spooner responds: 'I guess you'll have to find the way like the rest of us, Sonny. I think that's what Dr Lanning would have wanted. That's what it means to be free.' In this moment, there is a contrast between the abstract universalism of the Law (represented in VIKI's attempt to take over, to *extend* her control and subordination of robots to humans) and a subtractive form of universality that proclaims a sense of freedom and equality, desiring to help and lead others rather than control them.

I, Robot therefore presents a rejection of the heartlessness of the logic of the Law encompassing an abstract universalism that justifies and practises the sacrifice of some for the many. Instead, Sonny demonstrates a love that rejects that form of universalism, not to withdraw into the multiplicity of differences, but to practise a subtractive universalism, a love that takes us beyond the Law by both deactivating and fulfilling it. In response to science fiction's techno-legality, which presents technological innovation as both the means for human freedom *and* a form of control and mastery, we are presented with a *different* response. This is a response that sees the technological non-human *not* simply as property to be commanded, controlled and manipulated—a tool, in the same way that modern law is viewed as a tool, a means to an end—but as an extension of the possibilities of relationality, of an engagement with the world beyond the wilful autonomy of the liberal subject. In this sense, the human creation of robots does not give them rule over or mastery of them, but a sense of recognising them as something *more* than simply property. The next two chapters take up these themes, with Chapter 6 examining the political theology of the will that undergirds modern legality and the modern legal subject, and Chapter 7 turning away from the view of property and mastery to a concept of gift and reciprocity. Both of those chapters examine the nature of freedom that has been raised here—not the freedom of the liberal subject, able to do anything that it wills or desires, limited only by the constraints of the Law, but a freedom that is grounded in love. It is in this sense that what the Pauline reading of *I, Robot* presents to us is a love that fulfils the Law, exhorting us *to love your robot as yourself!*

6

Escaping the Bureaucratisation of Destiny: Law, Theology and Freedom in George Nolfi's *The Adjustment Bureau*

'"All things are lawful," but not all things are helpful. "All things are lawful," but not all things build up.'

1 Corinthians 10: 23

'For you were called to freedom . . . Only do not use your freedom as an opportunity for the flesh, but through love serve one another.'

Galatians 5: 13

I. Introduction

'You don't have "free will", David. You have the appearance of "free will".' This is the response that Senate candidate David Norris (Matt Damon) receives from the heavy-hitting agent of the 'Adjustment Bureau', Thompson (Terence Stamp), when he asks why this bureaucratised agency of the divine plan will not let him be with the woman he loves. Thompson's statement provokes a response of disbelief from David, who, like most of us, believes that he makes decisions every day. Thompson, however, argues that, whilst we may make decisions over which toothpaste to use or which beverage to order at lunch, 'humanity just isn't mature enough to control the important things'. This interaction between David and Thompson elaborates the central thematic of George Nolfi's 2011 film *The Adjustment Bureau*: a theological consideration of freedom and free will.[1] The film, set in modern-day New York, presents a world where 'God' and his 'angels' (referred to as 'the Chairman' and his 'agents' or 'caseworkers') are working behind the scenes to keep things on track, making adjustments to people's paths through the world to ensure that they adhere to 'the plan'. As such, this film, based on a short story by science fiction writer Philip K. Dick (though with some hefty 'adjustments' itself), does not present a modern picture of religion or theology as merely a private belief in a God who, if he does exist, does not intervene in

---

[1] *The Adjustment Bureau*, film, directed by Nolfi.

the world at all.[2] Rather, as opposed to the supposed modern overcoming of religion, theology and superstition, the film is overtly theological in nature—it presents a figure of God *intervening* in the world through his angels so as to ensure adherence to his order and providence. What should be made of this presentation of the theological, of these direct theological invocations in a context that would normally shun such experiences?

To answer this question, this chapter traces the theological roots of 'the Chairman', following John Milbank and others, back to shifts in medieval theology (from scholasticism, represented by St Thomas Aquinas, to nominalism, represented by John Duns Scotus and William of Ockham) that became influential in the later political theory and theology of Thomas Hobbes. What this exploration of the theological nature of 'the Chairman' presented in *The Adjustment Bureau* identifies is that this film is engaged in a particularly *modern* form of theology. The aim here, however, is not simply to see *The Adjustment Bureau* as modern speculative fiction doing theology, but to explore how it in fact reflects and refracts a particular modern secular sovereignty in its theological modalities. I read *The Adjustment Bureau* not simply as a speculative exploration of theology, but, rather, as a critique of Hobbesian *political* theology and its resultant modern secular sovereignty in the form of that 'mortal god', the Leviathan. The challenge to this divine/ political sovereign in *The Adjustment Bureau* comes from what Philip K. Dick aficionados saw as one of the disfigurations of Dick's work by Hollywood: the introduction of the theme of 'true love conquers all' in the 'forbidden' relationship between David Norris and Elise Sellas (Emily Blunt). It is the introduction of this overarching narrative into Dick's speculative science fiction that blurs the generic boundaries of *The Adjustment Bureau* but also, I argue, opens up the possibility of a different consideration of law and sovereignty: one based on a mode of love and relationality, as opposed to legal individualism.

Section II of this chapter explores the connection between Nolfi's film and Dick's short story and examines the generic shifts that occur between the two. Section III then picks up the thematic of 'free will' as the grounding motif of Nolfi's film. However, the film does not engage in an exploration of free will in general, but, rather, the connection of free will to divine providence. As such, *The Adjustment Bureau* engages in a form of what Giorgio Agamben, drawing on his theological genealogy, terms *oikonomia*—the general economy that connects the transcendence of God to his governing of the world through the angels. This reference to the theological conception of God then grounds Section IV of the chapter, which directly explores the

[2] Dick, 'Adjustment Team', September–October 1954.

type of theology propounded by *The Adjustment Bureau*. If 'the Chairman' is a representation of God, what is the nature of this God? Drawing on the work of John Milbank and others, I argue that the 'God' of *The Adjustment Bureau* is a particularly 'modern' God, conceived of not in terms of love, reason or justice, but in terms of an absolute will. This theological exploration is then transformed to the political and legal in Section V, which outlines how the theology of *The Adjustment Bureau* is a reflection and refraction of the theology that informs the development of modern state sovereignty via a range of writers: in particular, Thomas Hobbes. The Hobbesian state is one informed by a theology of will in terms of his conception both of the sovereign, but also, correlatively, of the individual subjects of the sovereign, which are conceived of as individualised wills—sovereign selves who submit to a sovereign state. Section VI then circles back to the underlying narrative of *The Adjustment Bureau* itself, which involves a challenge to this sovereign will of 'the Chairman' (as it is administered by the agents of the Adjustment Bureau) by what Alain Badiou might term an 'event of love': the amorous encounter between David and Elise, which provokes a desire to progress the forbidden (according to 'the plan') relationship that enables a reconceiving of the world. The chapter concludes by identifying this love encounter as a typological challenge to the conception of both the modern sovereign state and the modern sovereign self. That is, *The Adjustment Bureau* 'makes strange' our conceptions of sovereignty and law by 'outing' their underlying theology whilst opening the possibility of a relation to law based on love rather than will.

II. Questions of Genre: Theological Science Fiction and Philip K. Dick on Screen

Eulogised by Frederic Jameson in the 1980s as the 'Shakespeare of Science Fiction',[3] Phillip K. Dick has provided much material for the makers of Hollywood blockbuster films. Since Ridley Scott's acclaimed release of *Blade Runner* in 1982 (based on Dick's *Do Androids Dream of Electric Sheep?*), there have been over fifteen films and TV series based on Dick's work.[4] However, despite the successive translations of his novels and stories to film, Philip K. Dick fans tend to voice a general distaste for the filmic versions of

---

[3] Jameson, 'Futuristic Visions', 5 May 1982, republished as Jameson, 'Philip K Dick, in Memoriam'.

[4] Dick, *Do Androids Dream of Electric Sheep?*; *Blade Runner*, film, directed by Scott. For jurisprudential readings of *Blade Runner* and Spielberg's *Minority Report* see Hutchings, 'From Offworld Colonies'; MacNeil, *Lex Populi*, pp. 80–96.

his work.[5] Or, if they like the films, they describe them as Hollywoodified distant cousins of the more subtle and questioning of Dick's stories.[6] Along these lines, Ethan Mills argues that '[s]omething essential has been lost in translation from print to film,'[7] outlining the apparent disconnect between Dick's writings and the films based on them. Mills contrasts what he sees as the 'Holly-worldview' and the 'Dickian worldview'. In the Holly-worldview 'good defeats evil, free will secures the triumph of the human spirit and our heroes discover knowledge of reality and virtue (all before the credits roll)'.[8] According to this perspective, the universe is a nice place and movies have happy endings. The Dickian worldview, however, is a 'universe of paranoia, ignorance and a lack of true freedom'.[9] Dick's 'heroes' only 'occasionally discover the truth', 'wonder if they make any genuine free decisions' and generally accept that they do not.[10] Weiss and Nicholas make a similar point, elaborating the way Hollywood takes Dick's everyday protagonists ('losers, misfits and lowly office clerks placed without reason or warning in extraordinary circumstances'[11]) and presents them as larger-than-life action heroes, in a world where the 'bald and fat and old' administrator becomes Tom Cruise or the 'miserable little salaried employee' becomes Arnold Schwarzenegger.[12]

In this regard, George Nolfi's *The Adjustment Bureau* is no exception, with his transmogrification of Dick's serious, paranoid story in which the possibility of true freedom is highly questionable.[13] Whereas, in Dick's short

---

[5] See, for example, Easterbrook, 'Print Philip K Dick', pp. 108–10, as well as the preface to Sutin, *Divine Invasions*, referred to in Vest, *Future Imperfect*, pp. xxiii–xxiv. In relation to *The Adjustment Bureau*, almost all the critics and reviews make reference to Dick's short story and a large number compare Nolfi's interpretation to Dick's original in some detail (generally praising Dick and complaining about Nolfi). For example, see Goldberg, 'The Adjustment Bureau Review', 5 March 2011; Shephard, 'Free Will Hunting', July 2011, pp. 147, 149; Snyder, 'Adjustment Bureau: Losing One's Free Will', 3 March 2011; Williams, 'The Adjustment Bureau', 17 March 2011.

[6] For example, Mills, 'Hollywood Doesn't Know Dick'. See also the review by McDonagh, 'The Adjustment Bureau', 1 April 2011.

[7] Mills, 'Hollywood Doesn't Know Dick', p. 3.

[8] Ibid.

[9] Ibid.

[10] Ibid.

[11] Weiss and Nicholas, 'Dick Doesn't Do Heroes', p. 28.

[12] Ibid. See Dick, 'The Minority Report', January 1956; Dick, 'We Can Remember It for You Wholesale', April 1966; both reprinted in Dick, *Philip K. Dick Reader*; *Minority Report*, film, directed by Spielberg; *Total Recall*, film, directed by Verhoeven.

[13] Weiss and Nicholas, 'Dick Doesn't Do Heroes', p. 29.

story 'The Adjustment Team'[14], the protagonist in the end comes to terms with the fact that there is a higher power controlling and adjusting the world for the greater good, in *The Adjustment Bureau*, David Norris, in a triumph of free will, resists the plan laid down for him in the name of 'true love'. Let us explore this transition in a little more detail. In 'The Adjustment Team', Ed Fletcher, an employee of a small estate agent's firm, is the 'victim of a clerical error', in that a divine 'summoner' (his pet dog) fails to make a call (bark) at the correct time and, as a result, Ed receives a visit from a Life Insurance salesman, as opposed to a friend giving him a lift to work. Consequently, Ed, instead of being early, is late into the office on that particular day. When he does arrive, the building appears to be made of ash and all those within it disintegrate on Ed's touch. Believing he has suffered a nervous breakdown, Ed flees, but (with his wife's help) returns later in the day to find everything back to normal—well, almost. There is a range of slight alterations to individuals, furniture and offices. Startled by these changes, Ed flees once again but when he tries to make a call in a phone box he is taken up to the heavens, which present their operations as a mass bureaucratic organisation. There he meets the 'Old Man' in control, who explains everything to him. He has seen, behind the curtain of reality, the operations of a bureaucratic divine plan aimed at reducing the global war tension and bringing the international community together in a peaceful way by making slight adjustments to Ed's boss and co-workers. Ed was supposed to have been altered along with the rest of his office. However, having been privy to these grand plans, Ed is warned not to tell anyone about these behind-the-scenes machinations, otherwise he will be adjusted himself—an order to which he willingly agrees. Rather than resisting this benevolent deity, Ed is convinced of the importance of the plan and is willing to submit to the peaceful *telos* of the divine adjustments.

Nolfi's translation of 'The Adjustment Team' into *The Adjustment Bureau* shifts its focus from an almost insignificant clerk at a real estate firm, whose role in the grand scheme is simply to support his boss, to a candidate for the US Senate, who, supposedly (with the help of 'the Adjustment Bureau') will eventually become President of the United States. David Norris, having lost his first election campaign for Senate, is inspired by a 'chance' encounter with Elise Sellas (in the men's toilets at the Waldorf Astoria) to give a concession speech that is considered 'electrifying' and positions him as the front runner in the next election. A few weeks later, on his way to work, he is also the 'victim of a clerical error' when Harry (Anthony Mackie), an agent of the Adjustment Bureau, falls asleep on the job and fails to make David spill his coffee at exactly the right

[14] Dick, 'Adjustment Team', September–October 1954.

time. As a result, instead of being late to work, David is on time and stumbles upon a group of men from the Bureau in the process of 'adjusting' his boss (Charlie Trainer, played by Michael Kelly), changing the way he makes investment decisions. David is chased, captured, taken to a separate realm (which looks like a very large parking garage) and informed by Agent Richardson (John Slattery) that he has seen behind the curtain of reality. David must not reveal the existence of this Bureau that 'makes sure things happen according to plan' (on pain of being reset—having his mind erased) and is told that he can no longer see Elise (whom he, by chance, bumped into that morning on the bus that he was not supposed to have caught). In contrast to the characters in Dick's story, the agents in the film initially provide no reason for their actions, except for the importance of keeping the world 'on plan'. As one would expect in Hollywood (and this is Mills's point), rather than being satisfied with the explanation that there is a benevolent agency working overtime to keep the world on track, David resists the plan, and in an apparent triumph of free will, transcends every obstacle in his way in order to be with Elise and for 'true love' to conquer all.

Part of the criticism of Hollywood's interpretation of Dick's work is that it tends to resolve all the paradoxes of Dick's fictions and thus turns them into standard science fiction blockbusters rather than the philosophising stories of their source material.[15] Nolfi's take on *The Adjustment Bureau* not only transforms Dick's short story as it brings it to screen, but it also shifts the focus from a minor parable to a grand love story. As such, whilst Dick's short story orientates itself within the genre of science fiction, Nolfi's film intentionally blurs genres.[16] It is variously described as '[a] romantic comedy wrapped in a science-fiction thriller',[17] a 'romantic-comedy-action-fantasy',[18] or 'effectively a *Romeo and Juliet* jaunt playing out against a sci-fi background'.[19] This shift

---

[15] An exception to those who take this position is Jason P. Vest, who argues for the films as valid interpretations of Dick's work that do not always succeed. Vest, *Future Imperfect*, p. xxviii.

[16] Dick's story was published in the science fiction magazine *Orbit* in 1954. For Nolfi's discussion of the blurring of genres see Weintraub, 'Writer–Director George Nolfi Exclusive Interview', 26 February 2011.

[17] Falsani, 'Adjustment Bureau: Does God Change Our Minds', 8 March 2011.

[18] Heid, 'Damon Defies God's Insidious Bureaucracy', 4 March 2011.

[19] Snyder, 'Adjustment Bureau: Losing One's Free Will', 3 March 2011. Nolfi himself argues that he intended to reach a broader audience by centring the film as a love story with science-fiction elements: Weintraub, 'Writer–Director George Nolfi Exclusive Interview', 26 February 2011. When pitching it to the film studios, he described the film as follows: '[i]t starts as a political drama, then it becomes a love story, then it takes a very strong turn into a fantastical sci-fi tinged world. And then it moves into thriller realm.' Kaufman, 'Nolfi Takes Fate Into Own Hands', 21 February 2011.

in focus by Nolfi—from a philosophising work of speculative fiction that unpacks a general sense of paranoia about our place in the world, to a story that is, in the end, a romance—has a number of important effects. It is of note that, as Mills describes above, this shift concludes the story not with the submission of an ordinary man to a benevolent deity who, despite his organisation being susceptible to clerical errors, is, in the end, after ensuring the common good and world peace, but with a battle of wills between David and the Bureau and a triumphant conquering of the free will of humanity against 'the plan' of the divinity. This contrast highlights the central premise of the film. That is, despite Nolfi's introduction of a 'grand love story',[20] the film itself is 'an exploration of human freedom, fate, free will and determinism'.[21] It is to this theme that I now turn.

III. 'Whatever happened to "free will"?': The Metaphysical Speculations of *The Adjustment Bureau*

Whilst Nolfi draws together both science fiction tropes and the narrative of a grand romance, what sits at odds within the film is its overt metaphysical and theological speculations. This is not so much the fact that the film raises the questions of free will and determinism (questions that were consistently raised by Dick in his work and that are reflected in the other films based on it, in particular *Minority Report*[22]), but rather the form such questions take: the presentation of the Adjustment Bureau itself and 'the Chairman'. In modern-day New York, *The Adjustment Bureau* posits not simply the *existence* of a God figure in 'the Chairman', but his active and ongoing *intervention* in the world through his angels or 'caseworkers'. The film's speculative novum is a fundamentally theological one and its consideration of 'free will' is specifically within this theological context. The agents of the Adjustment Bureau have access to 'the plan' written by 'the Chairman', which they use to guide both their actions and the 'adjustments' that they make in the world. Humanity

---

[20] See Goldberg, 'The Adjustment Bureau Review', 5 March 2011.
[21] Rodriguez, 'The Adjustment Bureau'.
[22] For discussions of free will in Dick's work see, for example, Wittkower, 'Vast Sinister Conspiracy'; Worley, 'Knowing Tomorrow While Choosing Today'. In relation to *The Adjustment Bureau* see also the review by Rodriguez, 'The Adjustment Bureau'. MacNeil's analysis of *Minority Report* picks up these questions in relation to the 'predictive theories of law' put forward by the American Realists and subsequently taken up by 'law and economics'. See MacNeil, *Lex Populi*, pp. 80–96.

is not guided by its own desires and free will but the dictates of 'the plan', as implemented and monitored by the Bureau.[23]

Sara Worley analyses the question of 'free will' in relation to both Dick's 'The Adjustment Team' and Nolfi's *The Adjustment Bureau* (as well as the short story and film *Minority Report*).[24] Within these stories Worley sees the issue in question as being the compatibility of foresight and freedom, and analyses the question of foresight in relation to the Judeo-Christian tradition. Within this tradition the problem typically revolves around the understanding of God's omniscience whilst, at the same time, having given people free will. The quandary is as follows: 'if God already knows what we're going to do, then what we're going to do must already be settled, and then how could we really have free will?'[25] Worley considers two ways of understanding foreknowledge. The first relates to prediction and the second to sight and time. In terms of prediction, 'free will' is possible if prediction is probabilistic; however, it is not if prediction is certain or guaranteed:

> God is supposed to be omniscient, so his knowledge must be infallible. So if God predicts someone will behave in a certain way, that person must indeed behave in that way. Otherwise God would be wrong, and we know he can't be. But then there aren't really any options open to that person. There's only one way he can behave.[26]

On this model, whether foresight is compatible with free will is dependent on whether it is certain or not. The second model of foreknowledge, however, draws on the concept of the 'eternal present', as articulated by Boethius and St Anselm. On this understanding, God is understood to be 'outside of time'; he does not experience things as being in the past, present or future but experiences everything as being present. God does not really have foreknowledge but simply sees what happens without any 'before' or 'after'. There is thus no conflict between foreknowledge and free will: '[s]eeing someone make a choice does not mean that they could not have made a different choice.'[27] Worley terms this the 'sight' model (as God simply 'sees' what happens rather than foreseeing it).

---

[23] Mills, in his analysis of *The Adjustment Bureau*, argues that it is not really about free will but fate—a supernatural entity controlling the actions of individuals. He contrasts this to what he sees as Dick's determinism, which questions free will in general. See Mills, 'Hollywood Doesn't Know Dick', p. 6.

[24] Worley, 'Knowing Tomorrow While Choosing Today'.

[25] Ibid., p. 229.

[26] Ibid., p. 231.

[27] Ibid., p. 233.

Worley goes on to argue that the stories presented in both *The Adjustment Bureau* and *Minority Report* are not premised on the 'sight' model, for the agents in *The Adjustment Bureau* (and the 'precogs' in *Minority Report*) do not simply 'see' the future but can see or predict things that do not actually happen. Rather, the very premise of the work of the Adjustment Bureau is that they can make adjustments to the world, the effect of which changes what happens. For example, early in the film, the result of David being caught on camera mooning his old college buddies at a reunion was that he lost the election for Senate. However, the Adjustment Bureau then stepped in and arranged the 'chance' encounter with Elise in the Waldorf men's toilets. This encounter then inspired David to give the speech that saved his political career (and moved him back 'on plan'). The premise of this 'adjustment' by the Bureau is based on the predictive model—the Bureau could predict that, in bringing Elise and David together, their actions would result in his spectacular concession speech (and later in the film, the planned action of causing David to spill coffee would make him late for work). However, as Worley notes, the predictive model of foreknowledge is compatible with 'free will' only if it is probabilistic. Worley concludes that, given David is able to challenge the Adjustment Bureau and, in the end, effectively change his fate, the predictive capacities of the Bureau (and thus of 'the Chairman' as God figure) must be probabilistic.

Whilst Worley's analysis provides a useful consideration of foreknowledge in the films, it also gives rise to a number of questions which can provide more insight into *The Adjustment Bureau*'s raising of the problematics of 'free will' and freedom. First, the distinction that Worley points to is that Anselm's defence of the compatibility of human 'free will' and divine omniscience does not apply in the film because the agents are acting and thus making changes to the predicted future. The reason why she believes that the 'sight' model does not work is because the 'sight' model presumes being outside of time and being able to see what the *actual* future is (because it is already present to the entity looking at the occurrence). What this analysis points to is a fundamental question of theology: whether and how God can act in the world. As such, we need to look not only at the consideration of 'free will' of humanity, but at how this is understood in relation to the providence of God—the unfolding of God's will and care for creation.

To draw on Worley's sources, Boethius provides a consideration of 'free will' and foresight in terms of the 'eternal present' but, according to Giorgio Agamben, also incorporates the providence-fate apparatus into Christian theology via his *De Consolatione Philosophiae*.[28] Agamben describes the 'history of

---

[28] Agamben, *Kingdom and the Glory*, p. 126.

the concept of providence' as the 'long and fierce debate between those who claimed that God provides for the world only by means of general or universal principles . . . and those who argue that the divine providence extends to particular things'.[29] He notes that whilst the consideration of 'free will' is incorporated into this debate, 'what is really at stake . . . is not man's freedom. but the possibility of a divine government of the world'.[30] Boethius thus articulates the way that God governs the world via the entwined operation of Providence and Fate:

> God in his Providence constructs a single fixed plan of all that is to happen, while it is by means of Fate that all that He has planned is administered . . . in its many individual details in the course of time . . . . [T]he simple and unchanging form of things to be managed . . . is Providence, and Fate is the ever-changing web, the disposition in and through time of all the events which God in His simplicity has entrusted to manage. Everything, therefore, which comes under Fate, is also subject to Providence, to which Fate itself is subject, but certain things which come under Providence are above the chain of Fate.[31]

Boethius refers to a range of potential administrators of Fate, including the celestial motions of the stars, the power of the angels and the various skills of other spirits. While God in his simplicity lays down a divine plan, which is unchanging, this plan is administered and managed through time by a range of other bodies and effects.

The Adjustment Bureau provides a representation of this divine governance of the world. 'The plan' is written by 'the Chairman' as the foundation of Providence, which is then carried out *in time* via the management and administration of the Adjustment Bureau. It is not so much that the agents of the Adjustment Bureau operate based on probabilistic predictions but rather the administration and outworking of 'the plan' in terms of divine providence. It is within this context, then, that we can understand the discussion of 'free will' that David has with agent Thompson. In response to David's question 'whatever happened to "free will"?', Thompson provides an extended explanation of the activities of 'the Chairman' and the Adjustment Bureau:

> We actually tried 'free will' before. After taking you from hunting and gathering to the height of the Roman Empire we stepped back to see how you'd do on your own. You gave us the Dark Ages for five centuries until finally we

[29] Ibid., p. 113.
[30] Ibid.
[31] Boethius, *The Consolation of Philosophy*, p. 105, quoted in Agamben, *Kingdom and the Glory*, p. 127.

decided we should come back in. The Chairman thought that maybe we just needed to do a better job with teaching you how to ride a bike before taking the training wheels off again. So we gave you the Renaissance, the Enlightenment, scientific revolution. For six hundred years we taught you to control your impulses with reason. Then in 1910 we stepped back again. Within fifty years you brought us World War I, the Depression, fascism, the Holocaust and capped it off by bringing the entire planet to the brink of destruction in the Cuban missile crisis. At that point a decision was taken to step back in again before you did something that even we couldn't fix. You don't have 'free will', David. You have the *appearance* of 'free will' . . . humanity just isn't mature enough to control the important things.

Whilst this discussion is framed around the question of 'free will', what it actually describes is a providential ordering or governing of the world by the Adjustment Bureau in line with 'the plan' of 'the Chairman'. Here the role of the agents is seen in terms of the administration and outworking of 'the plan', and human freedom is thus understood only *within* this providential context. At the same time, the description by Thompson also indicates a belief in the role of that governance, which, in part, is to bring humanity to a point where it can also participate in the governance of the world. This sees humanity as being under tutorship, being trained in the use of their reason so that they may control their impulses, think rationally and become, in the end, self-governing.[32] Such a belief aligns with St Thomas Aquinas's understanding of divine governance, which is aimed at guiding things to their intended end.[33] In this sense, the end of humanity would be seen in its ability to self-govern. However, Aquinas sees the incorporation of both divine governance and human self-governance at the same time.[34] Divine governance is needed to support the creation that has already been brought into being.[35] Freedom is not presented in terms of a 'free will' that can choose to do whatever it wants to do (which, as argued in Chapter 1, in the end is the making of a completely arbitrary choice) but rather the will is free when it chooses the good—its true end. Freedom is found in a coincidence of divine governance and self-governance

---

[32] This is similar to St Paul's consideration of the law in Galatians. See Chapter 5 above.

[33] Aquinas, 'Summa Theologica Volume I', I.Q.103, A1, A2, A.4; Agamben, *Kingdom and the Glory*, pp. 131–4.

[34] Aquinas, 'Summa Theologica Volume I', I.Q.105; Agamben, *Kingdom and the Glory*, p. 133.

[35] Aquinas, 'Summa Theologica Volume I', I.Q.104, A.1; Agamben, *Kingdom and the Glory*, p. 133.

with their true end in God. Whereas Thompson identifies the possibility of human self-governing (the aim towards which the divine plan is being outworked), for Aquinas, in terms of finding its true end and freedom in God, human self-governing would operate *alongside* divine providence.[36] The fact that Thompson disputes the possibility of 'free will' for humanity is not so much because humanity does not have 'free will' but because the Bureau coercively intervenes to make it difficult for humanity to accomplish their desired outcomes when those desires do not align with 'the plan'. This coercive activity is aimed at 'training' humanity in its use of 'free will'. However, as Thompson points out, the two 'trial periods' for human self-governing resulted in the Dark Ages, the World Wars, the Depression, fascism and the Holocaust. Thompson therefore presents a 'free will'-based theodicy—it is humanity's use of 'free will' that has resulted in the pain, death and destruction in the world. As a result, humanity is blamed for all the 'bad things' in history as a consequence of the use of 'free will' and the Adjustment Bureau takes the credit for all the 'good things'.

The Adjustment Bureau thus seems to be promoting certain Enlightenment ideals—the supremacy of reason, the desire for humanity to emerge from its immaturity, to think for itself and be able to self-govern autonomously without reliance on religion or the church.[37] The irony of this alignment is that the period of which Immanuel Kant famously proclaimed that one should 'have the courage to use one's own understanding' and not rely on the dictates of religion and other institutions, is the period when the Bureau was actually guiding humanity.[38] In opposition to Kant, the way to self-governance and autonomy for humanity is through a process of guidance and 'adjustments' by the divine bureaucracy. The perspective of the Adjustment Bureau then seems to be that humanity needs to be guided in the development of their reason so that they can eventually be trusted with the exercise of 'free will'. It is not arguing against 'free will' *per se* but rather stating that humanity is not yet mature enough to use it. Interestingly, the focus on the use of 'free will' seems to be the conclusion of the film, as well with Harry's voice-over at the end proclaiming that we need to 'knock down all the obstacles' put in our way and that 'free will is a gift that you only know how to use once you fight for it'. It is in David *resisting* the Bureau and the plan laid out for him by 'the Chairman' that he supposedly takes responsibility for himself and exercises his 'free will'. The message of the film appears to be *not* that we should submit ourselves to a benevolent deity, believing that

[36] Agamben, *Kingdom and the Glory*, p. 132.
[37] Kant, 'What is Enlightenment?'.
[38] Ibid.

God's administration of the world is, in the end, for the best (the end-point of Dick's short story) but rather that the true exercise of 'free will' requires an *overcoming* of God's plan. The 'free will' of humanity is depicted as being in competition with the ordained will of God, and only one or the other can win out: humanity should either submit or resist (and bear the consequences either way). What this battle of wills points to is that the theology undergirding *The Adjustment Bureau* is of quite a different sort—not one based on the possibility of a participation in God where freedom is found in its true end, but rather where the freedom of the human will battles it out with that of the divine will.[39] It is this theology of will that I will now explore.

IV. 'That's just a name we use': Nominalist Political Theology from Duns Scotus to Hobbes

John Milbank argues that the production of modern secularity was both contingent and foreshadowed by a shift in late medieval theology that opened up the possibility of a realm autonomous from God (not previously thinkable in a society dominated by the theological).[40] Rather than seeing the secular and the human as being simply what remains once religion and theology have been removed, Milbank argues that the secular itself had to be imagined and constructed.[41] In order for this to occur, the possibility of a secular space had to be first conceived of within theology itself. This occurs, for Milbank, with the shift towards nominalism in the late medieval period, following John Duns Scotus and William of Ockham. Whilst there are varying accounts of this shift and its characterisation as a significant break has been criticised (as well as the particular interpretation of Duns Scotus promulgated by Milbank and others writing under the 'Radical Orthodoxy' banner), Jean Bethke Elshtain points out that it is hard to deny that a shift in the understanding of God (and, as a result, the understanding of individuals) did occur in this period.[42]

---

[39] For an insightful review of the film that identifies some of the theological themes outlined in the following section see Barron, 'Master Plan', 28 March 2011. See also Korobkin, 'Action Thriller for Religious Thinkers', 8 March 2011.

[40] See Milbank, *Theology and Social Theory*, pp. 9–18; Cavanaugh, 'Beyond Secular Parodies', pp. 191–2; Smith, *Introducing Radical Orthodoxy*, pp. 125–42; Oliver, 'From Participation to Late Modernity', pp. 3–12.

[41] Milbank, *Theology and Social Theory*, p. 9.

[42] Elshtain, *Sovereignty*, p. 44. For an analysis and defense of Radical Orthodoxy's treatment of Duns Scotus see in particular Pickstock, 'Duns Scotus'. See also Smith, *Introducing Radical Orthodoxy*, pp. 87–124.

Whereas, for the orthodox tradition from Augustine to Aquinas, God was seen as 'the apogee of goodness, reason and love',[43] following the theology of Duns Scotus and Ockham, God is seen as an all-powerful and untrammelled will.[44] This shift thus encompasses a replacement of the Thomist theology of participation, whereby humanity is assumed into the Trinity by the divine *logos* with a theology of *will* by which an 'undifferentiated God commands the lesser discrete wills of individual humans by sheer power'.[45] This means that God is no longer understood in terms of the connection between his reason, will and nature but rather as 'a proposing "will" [which] is taken to stand for the substantial identity of will, essence and understanding'.[46] At the same time, there is a shift away from the focus on God as Trinity and a return of a monarchical unity.[47] As Milbank notes,

> [i]n the thought of the nominalists, following Duns Scotus, the Trinity loses its significance as a prime location for discussing will and understanding in God and the relationship of God to the world. No longer is the world participatorily

---

[43] Elshtain, *Sovereignty*, p. 41.

[44] As Elshtain notes, it is potentially unfair to characterise Duns Scotus and Ockham themselves in this way. However, it is clear both that the will plays a much greater role in their theologies and that those following in their tradition emphasised a strong version of the theology of will. Ibid., pp. 44–6.

[45] Cavanaugh, 'Beyond Secular Parodies', p. 186; Milbank, *Theology and Social Theory*, pp. 13–18.

[46] Milbank, *Theology and Social Theory*, p. 15. This theological shift occurs as a result of the changing understanding of the ontological relationship between God and humanity, from analogy to univocity. On Radical Orthodoxy's reading of Aquinas, the relationship between created beings and the Creator (humanity and God) is a mode of analogical participation—that is, the nature of God *is* 'being' in itself, in which creation, including humanity, participates. When we say that God is 'good' and that a certain person is 'good', we are not using 'good' in the same sense but rather in an analogical sense—the 'goodness' of God and the 'goodness' of humanity are different. The shift marked by Duns Scotus is to a univocity of being which sees both God and creation as 'being' in the same way (but to different degrees). As such, the term 'good' refers to the *same* thing, whether it is describing God or a particular individual. Whilst God's goodness might exist to a greater degree than a created individual's, it is essentially referring to the same type of thing. Radical Orthodoxy's critique of this theological shift is that it results in God becoming distanced from humanity (as infinite) by a ream of sameness, which is uncrossable, and a space autonomous from God is opened up. See Oliver, 'From Participation to Late Modernity', pp. 13–24; Pickstock, 'Duns Scotus'; Smith, *Introducing Radical Orthodoxy*, Ch. 3.

[47] Elshtain, *Sovereignty*, p. 45; Milbank, *Theology and Social Theory*, p. 15.

enfolded within the divine expressive *Logos*, but instead a bare divine unity starkly confronts the other distinct unities which he has ordained.[48]

The ability for human reason to comprehend and come to grips with the nature of God and for the possibility of a loving participation in God is overshadowed by a focus on God's absolute power, under which humanity is required to bow and submit. This also results in a changed understanding of both the providence of God and its relation to divine or natural law. Providence now is understood in relation to the difference between God's absolute power (*potentia absoluta*) and his ordained power (*potentia ordinata*), which are no longer connected in the same way. Whereas, for Aquinas, God's absolute power referred to God's power in itself, without reference to the orders of nature and grace he had willed (via his ordained power), the 'juristic' model following Duns Scotus identified the possibility of God intervening via his *potentia absoluta* to change and even set aside the established order.[49] For Aquinas, the divine intellect ruled and determined the exercise of his power. For Duns Scotus, the divine will becomes the focus, and the presumption that this will is absolutely free means that he is not bound in any way—even by his own previous actions or determinations.[50]

Milbank argues that modern politics (as he traces through Niccolò Machiavelli and Thomas Hobbes) is itself founded on this voluntarist replacement of a theology of participation with a theology of will and the focus on the sheer power of God.[51] This theology of will finds its epitome in Hobbes's explanation of the reason why God should be obeyed:

> The right of nature, whereby God reigneth over men, and punisheth those that break his laws, is to be derived, not from his creating them, as if he required obedience as of gratitude for his benefits; but from his *irresistible power*.[52]

In this articulation there is no sense of participation in God nor of a coming into communion or understanding with God based on reason or love, but rather it is a pure submission to the *power* of God.[53] Yet, the theological

---

[48] Milbank, *Theology and Social Theory*, p. 15.
[49] Oakley, 'Absolute and Ordained Power of God', pp. 669–70; Elshtain, *Sovereignty*, pp. 40, 44, 57.
[50] Elshtain, *Sovereignty*, pp. 40, 44. See also the discussion of this in Chapter 2 above.
[51] Milbank, *Theology and Social Theory*, pp. 9–25.
[52] Hobbes, 'Leviathan', p. 160; Milbank, *Theology and Social Theory*, p. 16; Cavanaugh, 'Beyond Secular Parodies', p. 186.
[53] See Hobbes, 'Leviathan', p. 160; Agamben, *Homo Sacer*, p. 35.

shift in the understanding of God *also* results in a corresponding shift in the understanding of the human. Whereas God is now understood as an individual will, so too humans are *also* understood as an individual will in the same nature as God (though in different degrees). Man now comes closest to the *imago dei*, the image of God, when he exercises the rights of a sovereign will that 'cannot bind itself' and enjoy unimpeded property rights—a sovereign dominion over the earth.[54] The individual thus sees itself as a controlling will that is free to determine what it wishes to do and will be brought into submission only when presented with a will or power that is greater than itself.[55] As Milbank outlines, this forms the basis of Hobbes's political science. When Hobbes describes the sovereign, it is as one that has an absolute sovereign will. The political state, which Hobbes, due to his nominalism, could conceive of only as an 'artificial man', is rooted in an individualist account of the will that reflects the divine essence understood as radical simplicity without real or formal differentiation.[56] The power of the sovereign being absolute, it is a 'jealous god' that can neither bind its own will, nor submit to other powers nor allow other competing bodies.[57] The law then becomes that which is determined by the sovereign command and which must be obeyed (and is backed up by force).[58] The only potential liberty for individual citizens is where the law is silent or the sovereign has not made a determination.[59] Rather than human law being, as for Aquinas, a reflection of the natural law which is a participation in God's eternal law (his providential plan reflecting his reason, justice and love), the law is an arbitrary construction of God's will and it must be obeyed as law simply because God commands it to be so (and any infringement will be punished as such).[60]

To return to *The Adjustment Bureau*, the theology of 'the Chairman' can now be more clearly identified. As noted above, the end-point of both Thompson's speech and Harry's concluding remarks appears to represent a

---

[54] See Milbank, *Theology and Social Theory*, pp. 13–16. See also Cavanaugh, 'Beyond Secular Parodies', p. 187.

[55] Hobbes, 'Leviathan', pp. 84–5.

[56] Milbank, *Theology and Social Theory*, p. 15; Hobbes, 'Leviathan', pp. 47–8.

[57] For Hobbes this clearly meant ecclesiastical bodies, but also included other forms of organisation that then become dependent on the state for their existence via a grant of power. See Cavanaugh, 'Beyond Secular Parodies', pp. 189, 191–2; Peters, 'Corporations'; Peters, 'I, Corpenstein'.

[58] Hobbes, 'Leviathan', pp. 130–7.

[59] Ibid., pp. 113, 116; Milbank, *Theology and Social Theory*, p. 14.

[60] See Aquinas, 'Summa Theologica Volume I', II.I.Q.91–5; Cavanaugh, 'Beyond Secular Parodies', p. 186.

battle of wills between David and 'the Chairman'. As such, there is not a participatory enfolding of the human will within the divine will, but rather an expectation of sheer submission to 'the plan'. Through David's interactions with the Bureau we slowly uncover a representation of 'the plan' of 'the Chairman'. Whilst Dick's short story provides an extended explanation of the reason for the intervention by the Adjustment Team (one which Ed Fletcher sees the logic of and agrees with), the first interaction between David and the Bureau has little consideration of the *reason* for 'the plan' at all. David's path having *not* been adjusted, he arrives to work on time, only to find the team of men in suits making an 'adjustment' to his friend, Charlie Trainer. The initial response from Richardson is not to explain calmly to him what is going on, but rather: 'Grab him!' After they chase David, knock him out with chloroform and forcefully take him to another realm, Richardson provides a relatively truncated explanation of who they are: 'we're the people that make sure things go according to plan'. He tries to scare and intimidate David by making him believe that they can read minds and can see what is going to happen. In this early interaction there is no reference to 'the Chairman', no explanation of what 'the plan' is or how it operates, and then simply a command that he may not tell anyone about the Bureau—*and* that he cannot be with Elise. Later, when David is trying to find Elise's dance studio and the Bureau is putting obstacles in his way, he questions the basis of 'the plan' itself, suggesting that Richardson had potentially misread it or that it was wrong. Again, instead of providing an explanation for 'the plan', Richardson simply notes that there is no misreading it, that things are clear in 'black and white' and that David, rather than questioning 'the plan' and its writer, 'really should show some respect'. In place of a divine plan which can be conceived on the basis of reason there is simply a divine command that must be obeyed.

In David's later discussion with Thompson, whilst more information is given about what the plan entails (David winning the Senate election and then, in the future, elections for President of the United States), the viewer is still not provided with an underlying basis for the plan itself. Thompson refers to both David's and Elise's dreams (attempting to intimidate him by saying that neither of their dreams will come true if they stay together), but once again there is no substantive basis or purpose for either. The Bureau want David to win the Senate and then go on to become President, but there is no explanation as to *why* they want David in particular to do this. In fact, for all the election campaign footage of David making speeches, glad-handing voters and signing autographs, there is never once any substantial policy basis for his campaign. Rather, it is based on popularity, on David not being a 'tool' like the other guy, and the fact that he is young and 'authentic'. There is no actual commitment by David to *doing* anything in particular, should he win office (nor any reason provided for why voters would want him to win office). When it comes to implementation of 'the plan' of 'the Chairman', the only basis for 'the plan' itself is that 'the Chairman' wrote it—the divine will determines what must be done without any reference to reason, justice, love or the greater good.

V. 'Did you really think you could reach the Chairman?': The Absent Sovereign or 'Where is the Chairman'?

It is here, having identified the theology of 'the Chairman' as this 'modern' theology of will, that I argue that *The Adjustment Bureau* provides not simply a representation of theology but rather a critique of modern sovereignty and its latent theological underpinnings. As such, then, 'the Chairman' arguably stands in for the Hobbesian all-powerful sovereign and 'the plan' is a representation of the posited law as commands of that sovereign. This sovereignty is based on a 'will' that issues laws as commands (rather than precepts grounded in reason). What the lack of reason in relation to 'the plan' referred to above represents, then, is the way in which modern law is conceived itself in terms of the command of the sovereign without reason. At the same time, the experience of David is one that reflects our experience of modern bureaucracy in terms of a bureaucrat informing someone that things must be done this way because that is what the rules require, not for any substantive reason (even if there might actually be one). If we are to consider the agents of the Adjustment Bureau as angels, then instead of the heavens being a place of wonder and worship, they are presented as a rationalised bureaucracy. This reflects, at one level, Slavoj Žižek's observation (in discussing the work of Franz Kafka) that the experience of the divine today is through modern bureaucracy.[61] Max Weber's argument for the bureaucratisation and rationalisation of law produces, in the end, an experience of that bureaucracy as a divine intervention with no rhyme or reason, except for 'that's the way things are'.[62] The bureaucratic and rationalised law is experienced as irrational. What is more to the point, however, is that this bureaucracy is actually theological in nature. This becomes even clearer when considering the Thomist theology of angels, for in the 'Angelic Doctor's' *Summa Theologiae* a considerable amount of time is

---

[61] Žižek notes that bureaucracy 'is our only true contact with the divine in our secular times'. He continues: 'What can be more "divine" than the traumatic encounter with the bureaucracy at its craziest—when, say a bureaucrat tells me that, legally, I don't exist? It is in such encounters that we get a glimpse of another order beyond merely earthly everyday reality.' Žižek, *Parallax View*, p. 116. See also Žižek, *Puppet and the Dwarf*, p. 120.

[62] Žižek, *Parallax View*, p. 116.

spent articulating not simply the nature of the angels *but also their hierarchical structures*.[63] As Agamben notes with great interest, the extended detail of the divine realms depicts a hierarchy of greater and lesser angels, angels split between administration (executing the divine providence) and acclamation (the worship of God).[64] In addition, there is a structure that accounts for those angels that are higher in status and thus who would stand in the presence of God, and for others who are lesser and who would be informed of the divine command only via a messenger.[65] All of this undergirds both Milbank's and Agamben's argument that modernity itself is structured by theology even where it is supposedly secularised. Far from having escaped the theological via neutral political science, the theological remains the structural frame of modernity itself (as well as any of its 'posts'—post-modernity, post-secularity and so on).[66]

As such, 'the Chairman' is a representation of this modern conception of the divine or sovereign will. 'The Chairman' (read sovereign) lays down 'the plan' (positive law as command of the sovereign) that must be followed at all costs and the Bureau works carefully to ensure its fulfilment. Yet one of the problems with this theological focus on a voluntarist God as sovereign will is that he could simply change his mind. The basis on which the *potentia absoluta* of God is conceived is no longer simply the foundation of the *potentia ordinata*, but it becomes the possibility for God to 'change the rules', to act beyond the law and plan he has laid down and arbitrarily switch the plan—the sovereign can arbitrarily decide on the exception to or acting beyond the law.[67] This is reflected in *The Adjustment Bureau*. Whilst the lower-level agents proclaim the importance of keeping on plan, of sticking to what has been ordained by 'the Chairman', what is revealed later in the film is that the plan can change—and *has* changed over the decades. In earlier

---

[63] This is not only in the 'Treatise on the Angels' but also a significant portion of the 'Treatise on Divine Government'. See Aquinas, 'Summa Theologica Volume I', I.QQ.50–64, I.QQ.107–14.

[64] See Aquinas, 'Summa Theologica Volume I', I.QQ.108–12; cf. Agamben, *Kingdom and the Glory*, pp. 149–51.

[65] Aquinas, 'Summa Theologica Volume I', I.Q.112, a.3; Agamben, *Kingdom and the Glory*, p. 151.

[66] See Smith, *Introducing Radical Orthodoxy*, pp. 125–42. At the same time, Milbank notes, following Weber, that modern bureaucratic and rational tendencies can be identified within medieval canon law. Milbank, *Theology and Social Theory*, p. 17 and Ch. 4.

[67] Milbank, *Theology and Social Theory*, pp. 15–16; Elshtain, *Sovereignty*, pp. 53–5, 58–9. See also Milbank, 'Geopolitical Theology', pp. 93–4.

versions of the plan, David and Elise *were* meant to be together and it is only the plans since 2005 that dictate otherwise. In the end, David and Elise are looking to change their destiny by reverting to an earlier version of the plan.

When we read *The Adjustment Bureau* in this way, we see at one level a perception of sovereignty as all-powerful (agents say that they can read minds; they move through doorways that cross the city; they adjust people's thinking) and *yet* the effect of that power is limited. This is not just in the sense that Harry identifies: that the Bureau's resources are limited, hence they do not have the ability to monitor the whole world all the time; or that certain restrictions are placed on their powers. Rather, it is that the very application of sovereignty itself is limited and fallible. Far from being an all-powerful god, the speculative nature of Leviathan means that it can operate only through agents; it cannot be conceived truly as a separate body, but instead is made up of the individuals that create it. Hobbes's reference to the multiple parts of the body as various parts of the state (sovereignty the soul, magistrates the joints, reward and punishment the nerves) reflects the lack of self-sustaining structure in the sovereign body itself.[68] In *The Adjustment Bureau*, the key trigger that allows David to see the Bureau is the result of an agent falling asleep on the job and not making the necessary adjustment at the correct time. That is, rather than being all-powerful, the sovereign is shot through with holes, limited by the fallibility of its agents and application.

The presupposition of an all-powerful sovereign is therefore shown to be able to operate only through its agents—as Agamben notes, the sovereign is impotent and can exercise his sovereign will only through the administration of government via his ministers.[69] Yet this also points to the aporia of the will itself, which is that, 'for a will to be effective, something other than will must carry out the will's order'.[70] The film provides a representation of the distinction that Agamben makes between Kingdom and Government—that is, the king reigns but does not govern.[71] The sovereign power is, in the end, impotent in itself but guarantees the carrying out of the administration of that sovereign power through government. Yet, whilst Agamben draws on the theological and Trinitarian tradition to elaborate the history of this distinction, what is found, when transformed to the political level (and this includes the politics of the late Middle Ages in terms of the rifts between the

---

[68] Hobbes, 'Leviathan', p. 47; Cavanaugh, 'Beyond Secular Parodies', p. 188.
[69] Agamben, *Kingdom and the Glory*, pp. 68–9, 134.
[70] Milbank, *Being Reconciled*, p. 91.
[71] Agamben, *Kingdom and the Glory*, pp. 69–71 (referring to Carl Schmitt and Eric Peterson's use of this phrase), 109–10.

papacy, emperors and kings), is an undergirding presumption of sovereign will, which can exercise itself only through another.

The sovereign state, however, sees the coming into being of both a sovereign will *and* the subjects that make up the state at the same time. Whilst Hobbes identifies those in the state of nature as the ones who can exercise their private rights and surrender those rights in the pact or covenant, it is only within the context of the state itself that those individuals can actually be recognised *as* bearers of private rights that can be given up to the sovereign state.[72] Milbank argues that, because the sovereign state

> is rooted in an individualistic account of the will, oblivious to questions of its providential purpose in the hands of God, it has difficulty in understanding any 'collective making', or genuinely social process. To keep notions of the State free from any suggestions of a collective essence or generally recognized *telos*, it must be constructed on the individualist model of *dominium*.[73]

The founding of the sovereign state is not simply based on the operation or exercise of 'natural rights' which are subsumed by the covenant that forms the state, but rather such rights are *presupposed* by that pact. The sovereign state, incorporating these presupposed natural rights as the basis for its unlimited power, can determine what the rights of subjects are and maintains the ability to revoke or infringe them.[74] The possibility of an unlimited sovereign state is thus founded, in particular, on the presumption of sovereign individuals who have unlimited rights to self-preservation, which they can nonetheless alienate and give to the sovereign.[75] At the same time, the power which the state incorporates can then be exercised only through others. The presupposed unlimited sovereignty, as the soul of the Leviathan, has to produce an executive to carry out its will in the form of ministers and agents of the sovereign.[76]

In *The Adjustment Bureau*, when it comes to 'the Chairman' himself, it is notable that he is never seen. The final sequence, which involves David and Elise racing through the chambers of the Bureau to find the Chairman so that they can have their plan rewritten, has them bursting through random doors, running through the library, dashing past the restricted archives, climbing

---

[72] See Milbank, *Theology and Social Theory*, p. 14; Hobbes, 'Leviathan', p. 100.

[73] Milbank, *Theology and Social Theory*, p. 14.

[74] From which is based the sovereign's right to punish: Hobbes, 'Leviathan', pp. 145–7; Agamben, *Homo Sacer*, pp. 106–7.

[75] See Hobbes, 'Leviathan', pp. 86–95, 99–100.

[76] Milbank, *Being Reconciled*, pp. 91–2; see also Agamben, *Kingdom and the Glory*, pp. 134–5.

higher and higher in the internal recesses of the Bureau. The expected crashing into the Chairman's office, however, never occurs. Rather, as David and Elise rush up the final stairs, they burst out on to the 'Top of the Rock' observation deck.[77] Stunned, they return down the stairs from which they came, only, in a sequence reminiscent of an Escher drawing, to burst out *once again* on to the observation deck.[78] The Chairman as sovereign is nowhere to be found and the process of looking for him ends in a disorientating round-robin chase. Rather than finding the ultimate sovereign will and the mastermind of 'the plan', David and Elise are cornered (in the same way that David was cornered in the first chase scene in the film) and surrounded by agents of the Bureau. At this point, David and Elise give up running, declare their love for each other and embrace. As the camera centres in on them, slowly spinning and circling, Elise looks up, shocked to see that the agents have all disappeared and the cloudy skies are giving way to the sun shining. Thompson appears and begins to tell David and Elise that the idea of finding 'the Chairman' and having their plan rewritten is ludicrous and that it 'doesn't work that way'. However, Harry then arrives and provides a message from 'the Chairman' that the viewer already has an inkling of, with the change of intensity of the music and the bursting out of the sun. David and Elise have supposedly inspired 'the Chairman' and Harry thus presents them with a copy of 'the plan' that is 'rewritten'—a clean piece of paper with the two dots representing David and Elise moving along the page.

The conclusion of the film thus appears to be a triumph of 'free will'— that we must overcome the obstacles put in our way, rely on our own understanding and throw off the perverse plan laid down by the will of a god who can contingently change his mind or a sovereign who is unbound to the law that he has determined (ever able to decide on the exception to the norm). Yet, at the same time, when David asks about the Chairman, Harry notes: 'You've met him though . . . or her. Everybody has. The Chairman comes in a different form to everyone, so people rarely realise when it happens.' Once again, the Chairman, who is only ever referred to but never seen and who acts only through his agents, is now not even available, except in encounters where he is not recognised. Does this not indicate even more strongly that

---

[77] The 'Top of The Rock' observation deck is on the rooftop of the GE Building in the Rockefeller Center.

[78] M. C. Escher (1898–1972) was known for his use of irregular perspectives to create drawings of impossible realities. These included works such as 'Reality' (1953) and 'Ascending and Descending' (1960), in which people ascended and descended staircases in an impossible loop. For Nolfi's discussion of this see Weintraub, 'Writer–Director George Nolfi Exclusive Interview', 26 February 2011.

the Chairman, as sovereign, does not exist, except within the actions and acclamations of his angels/agents? That is, as Agamben would say, the throne is empty.[79] The Chairman as all-powerful sovereign will cannot exist outside of the actions that presuppose him (in contrast to a divine intellect which is relationally orientated within a Trinitarian economy). And yet, is the point of the film not more subtle? That it is the theology of will that informs the voluntarist sovereign state that we need to escape, not some arbitrary deity. Thus, 'the plan' from which we need to escape, conceptually if not actually, is that of the voluntarist sovereign state itself. The state is founded on its ability to ensure peace and order and protect freedom but which, in the end, struggles to effect each of these: the enforcing of peace and order restricts freedom; wars and violence are the means for enabling social cohesion; law's protection of freedom becomes the very thing that binds it and so forth.[80] Should we not, then, reconceive the basis for which the state is instituted, which is that freedom requires, not a freedom from each other, but a true sense of thinking the possibility of being together? This question of being together points us back to the major change that Nolfi introduces in the translation of Dick's story to screen: he makes it a love story.

VI. 'Because she's enough': Love of One for Another

The driving narrative of *The Adjustment Bureau*, despite all its metaphysical speculations with regard to 'free will' and its theological science fiction, is the romance of David and Elise. The very reason that David resists 'the plan' laid down for him is because of his feelings for Elise after their 'chance' encounters—feelings that come to a head in the final declaration by David and Elise of their love for each other. To pick up a theme from the previous chapter, this love encounter represents an event in Badiou's sense. For Badiou, the four conditions of philosophy (as he traces in Plato's thinking) are: art, science, the political and love.[81] As one of these, the amorous encounter itself can found a truth event and the production of a truth in the form of the Two. Here the focus is not so much on the object of love but on the construction or reconstruction of the world from the perspective of the Two: 'It is in love that thought is freed from the powers of the One, and operates according to the law of the "Two", to what breaks into the One.'[82] Love does not so much form a new unity than it challenges the dominance of the One, *supplements*

---

[79] Agamben, *Kingdom and the Glory*, pp. 243–5.
[80] See discussion by Cavanaugh, 'Beyond Secular Parodies', pp. 193–4.
[81] See Badiou, *Manifesto for Philosophy*, pp. 33–9 (see also p. 11); Badiou, *Second Manifesto for Philosophy*, pp. 21–2.
[82] Badiou, *Manifesto for Philosophy*, p. 18. See also Badiou and Truong, *In Praise of Love*.

the life of those caught within the frame of the event and enables a rethinking of the world from the perspective of the Two. Each aspect of life previously thought by the individual is then brought into the truth of the Two (based on the foundational declaration—'I love you') and rethought within these new coordinates.[83] What this points to is the possibility of a relationality that is not in terms of individualised atoms but in terms of a being together that rearranges the coordinates of the world. Whilst Badiou does not embrace a participatory ontology directly, this amorous event and the possibility of conceiving the world in terms of the production of the truth of the Two, as opposed to the One, see in love a relationality that goes beyond the narcissistic self-interest of the individual.[84] As such, Badiou rejects the views of love as ecstatic, contractual or illusory, seeing in it rather a work that brings more and more fragments of the world to 'appear before the Two instead of being folded up within narcissistic satisfaction or dissatisfaction'.[85]

This seeing of the world from the perspective of the Two and against narcissistic self-interest contrasts with the anthropology of a theology of will, which, in terms of the individual, sees a self-possessing, self-preserving and wilful *conatus*. Under this conception of the individual, the mode of relation *between* individuals (and, for that matter, between humans and God) is conceived of as a contract or covenant entered into by individual wills acting in their own self-interest. As opposed to a participatory relationship that encompasses the common good or common ends as the basis for the being together of individuals, we see a self-interested will that only relates to others based on contract. Within an anthropology or theology of will, sociability is *only* the sociability of discrete individuals in an artificial entity made up of specific parts. It is not the actual coming together and being together towards common ends because the wills of individuals are always in self-interested competition.[86] Freedom within this context is specifically a freedom from each other (and from God) rather than a freedom to be together. The 'body'

---

[83] See Badiou, *Second Manifesto for Philosophy*, pp. 87–8.

[84] Badiou and Truong, *In Praise of Love*, pp. 16–26; Badiou, *Second Manifesto for Philosophy*, pp. 88, 99. Milbank does make an argument, however, for a participatory ontology and Christian metaphysics lurking behind Badiou's system (though he notes that this is a seemingly 'perverse' reading of Badiou's thought): see Milbank, 'Return of Mediation'.

[85] Badiou, *Second Manifesto for Philosophy*, p. 100. See also Badiou, 'What is Love?', pp. 38–9; Badiou and Truong, *In Praise of Love*, pp. 21–3.

[86] It is this self-interested competition that liberal theory then seeks to harness and orientate towards a good. See, for example, Kant, 'To Perpetual Peace'. See also Chapter 2 of Milbank, *Theology and Social Theory*; Milbank, 'Against Human Rights'.

that is the sovereign state can be conceived of only as the sum of its parts. The being together of the people is structured only in terms of an 'artificial body' that becomes a fictional presupposition, one which then requires violence or force in order to maintain itself. The fictional sovereign body has a right of self-preservation that sees any potential coming together of people in other forms as a threat. As William Cavanaugh notes, the sovereign state is not on the same horizon as the family but is constructed in opposition to it and to all other bodies which could potentially found an alternative being together of individuals.[87]

This individualism is represented in *The Adjustment Bureau* as the basis on which 'the plan' must be followed. The reason given to David by Thompson as to why he cannot be with Elise is that both his and her dreams will be lost if that occurs. Elise's dreams of being a world-famous dancer and choreographer and David's dreams of someday making it to the White House will apparently not come true if they stay together. The focus of the Bureau encompasses, supposedly, the *individual* dreams or purposes of these persons—individual dreams that cannot be challenged or given up for another. Thompson thus challenges David, arguing that the responsibility for Elise not achieving her dreams would be his, and as such he would have only himself to blame for hurting Elise and for the loss of her career. He tells David that 'if you stay with her you'll take away the only thing she ever cared about'. This statement, however, belies the position of the Bureau, which sees the most important thing as being the following of the plan, which involves self-interested dreams and goals. The irony of Thompson's statement is that, if David and Elise decided to be together, then it would be *because* Elise cared about David—that she would potentially have something or someone else to care about in addition to her career (which is something that Thompson does not see or value). Harry emphasises this point by explaining that the reason that David and Elise cannot be together (according to the plan) is because Elise would 'be enough' for David—that he would not need the applause and adulation (the acclamation or glorification) that come with his career in politics. The focus of the Bureau is not so much about David or Elise achieving their defined ends but about the presupposed anthropology of the sovereign will and sovereign self—the individual who is presupposed as self-choosing, self-deciding and responsible for their actions based on contract becomes glorified within the economy of the state, and any action that challenges such a presupposition falls outside 'the plan' of the state itself and is seen as a threat.

---

[87] Cavanaugh, 'Beyond Secular Parodies', pp. 191–2, referring to Nisbet, *Quest for Community*.

Undergirding this focus on sovereign individuality is a violence or force engaged in by the Bureau. Harry discloses to David that the deaths of his brother and father were orchestrated by the Bureau in order to *manufacture* the desire in David for acceptance and applause that drives his success as a campaigner. For David to become the self-willing sovereign individual and fulfil his dreams of becoming President, there was a need to remove from him the individuals who would potentially satisfy the need for acceptance and relationship in him. What is presented is a contrast between the individual who fulfils their dreams and the individual who desires to be in a relationship with others. The sovereign state sees individuals only in relation to it (a relation that, because of its nominalism and focus on individual wills, can only ever be the submission of contract or a resistance or battle of wills) and cannot conceive the possibility of a togetherness or participation of individuals with each other that is real and not based on self-interest and contract. The plan of the Bureau and the will of the sovereign state encompass a decision over the life and death of individuals—that David's brother should die in order that David can live the life according to 'the plan'. Such a decision, in the end, incorporates the aporia of presupposing individuals as self-sovereign wills—such a self-sovereign will can always be violated in the protection or promotion of another self-sovereign will. The submission to the state as sovereign means that the individual is reliant on the sovereign's own self-binding not to harm him. But, as outlined above, the premise of the theology of will that undergirds this view of sovereignty means that the sovereign always retains the power to determine an exceptional circumstance and thus deal with an individual as *homo sacer*.[88] The distinction between the *potentia absoluta* and *potentia ordinata* that is made by the nominalists is not so much about simply identifying a realm of *potential* all-powerful actions that will now not be taken because He has acted otherwise (in terms of His ordained power), but rather embodies the power of the sovereign to decide on the exception itself.[89] The all-powerful sovereign can arbitrarily change the basis on which it operates and also deal arbitrarily with its subjects, who are otherwise bound by the contingent law it promulgates.

David and Elise thus present a challenge to this conception of sovereignty and a sovereign will by deciding *not* to live according to the individualised plan which is focused on their own self-interest. Such self-interest is inherent to the state, for the individual gives up his or her rights to the sovereign to receive protection from other individuals. David and Elise, rather, via a commitment to each other (one which 'risked everything'), privilege a mode of

[88] Agamben, *Homo Sacer*, p. 106.
[89] Schmitt, *Political Theology*, p. 5.

relationality that is based not on a presupposed violent state of nature from which the individual needs saving by an all-powerful sovereign state, but rather on love. It is this action of love which, according to Harry, 'inspires the Chairman' to rewrite their plan.[90] But this is not the rewriting of the plan by an absent and contingent sovereign who provides an untrammelled free will that can choose to do anything it wants to. Nor is it the ability to rewrite the laws of the state. Rather, it is identifying the structural problematic of laws that are determined by this theology of sovereignty—that they are grounded in nothing themselves. Such a theology, despite its subsequent attempts to ground 'rights' of individuals, in the end results in an ungrounded law as sovereign command, free from reason, justice or love. The event or encounter between David and Elise and their willingness to reorientate and reconceive their world in terms of that event (their being together) challenge the individualism of both modern law and politics by enabling the thinking of the world in terms of the Two as opposed to the One. This points to a grounding of relationality that is not based on the violent mechanisms of the law but rather is captured within an encounter of love. Such love is not restricted to a romantic encounter either, but rather encompasses the possibility of a relation with others that is not mediated through a voluntaristic centre in terms of the sovereign state (or a voluntarist god), but is rather founded on the surprise and possibility of direct interactions with others. Such interactions open up a possibility of loving and engaging with the person with whom we interact, not in the liberal sense of rights or contract, but in an alternate economy, a giving that is premised, not on a contractual receiving or an oppressive submissiveness, but on a giving and receiving differently.

VII. Conclusion: 'Free will is a gift'

The theologically informed sovereignty described in this chapter harks back to the potential of a theological will. At the same time, as shown in Chapters 4 and 5, this is a *modern* secular theology that involves a call for sacrifice—to the state, to globalisation, to ethical duty. But this call is for a sacrifice without return, based on a presupposed sovereign individual who can exercise that sovereign freedom only, in the end, by giving it up. One reviewer of *The Adjustment Bureau* commented that, after being chased by the agents of the Bureau to the top of the Bureau's chambers, David and Elise did not

---

[90] Harry says: 'David, you risked everything for Elise. And Elise, when you came through that door at the Statue of Liberty, you risked everything too. But you inspired me. Seems like you inspired the Chairman too . . . this situation between the two of you is a serious deviation from the plan. So the Chairman rewrote it . . . .'

think about the only exercise of free will left available to them—suicide.[91] Yet such a presupposition results in a free will that can only ever be exercised in its destruction.[92] The actions of David and Elise in 'risking it all to be together' in fact comprise a form of freedom that is in contrast to that bound to contract and the sovereign self. Rather, it conceives the possibility of being together, of harmony, of love that involves reciprocity with others 'according to an ineffable order and measure, which is not yet the measure of law'.[93] It is not a will that consists sovereignly in itself, which, in the end, can exercise its freedom only by giving up its life in death (the very thing Hobbes presupposes as the need for the state to prevent). Rather, it is in the offering of oneself to another for the furtherance (not termination) of life, achieved in an act that is not of the individualised interactions with the state, but a togetherness of mutual but differentiated reciprocity.

It is in this sense that Harry's voice-over at the end of the film should be understood as seeing free will not as something that must be fought for, but rather as a 'gift' itself. Freedom is something which can be encountered only as a gift and not a right—a gift that is received not only in terms of alienable property but as encompassing the giver itself.[94] And a gift, as such, which obliges a gift in return thought differently. In receiving the gift of free will from God, we provide a return not by the exercise of a sovereign will but by finding true freedom in a particular end: that of being-together with others. This is *not* in terms of the freedom of a subjective individual (a freedom *from* the interference of other sovereign wills, which always needs to be protected by a sovereign state that will restrict freedom in protecting it) but a freedom that comes from reciprocal relations of giving and receiving. It is to this notion of reciprocity that I turn in the next chapter.

[91] Snyder, 'Adjustment Bureau: Losing One's Free Will', 3 March 2011.
[92] Milbank, 'Against Human Rights', p. 206.
[93] Milbank, *Being Reconciled*, p. 102.
[94] Cavanaugh, 'World in a Wafer', pp. 195–6.

7

'If more people valued home above gold this world would be a merrier place': Hospitality, Gift-exchange and the Theological Jurisprudence of J. R. R. Tolkien's and Peter Jackson's *The Hobbit*

'Every good gift and every perfect gift is from above . . . .'

James 1: 17

I. Introduction: Tolkien on Screen (Again)

What are we to make of J. R. R. Tolkien's return to screen in 2012? If the first of Peter Jackson's Tolkien trilogies so aptly captured the zeitgeist following the September 11 attacks on the World Trade Centre, with the political rhetoric of Good and Evil and the ensuing 'war on terror'—as was argued by Professor William MacNeil in his 2002 keynote address to the Law and Literature Association of Australia[1]—Jackson's *Hobbit* trilogy *also* seemed to resonate with its times.[2] As a narrative about dragon-sickness—the love and lust for gold and its power over those who possess it—the films appear to present a critique of the excesses of global finance, with their abstracting of human life subordinated to the accumulation of wealth, and the crises it produces. Following the party of Thorin Oakenshield (Richard Armitage)

---

[1] The Association is now the Law, Literature and Humanities Association of Australasia (see <www.lawlithum.org>). For the published version of MacNeil's keynote, see MacNeil, 'One Recht'.

[2] Jackson's *The Lord of the Rings* trilogy is made up of: *The Lord of the Rings: The Fellowship of the Ring*, film, directed by Jackson; *The Lord of the Rings: The Two Towers*, film, directed by Jackson; *The Lord of the Rings: The Return of the King*, film, directed by Jackson. His subsequent *Hobbit* trilogy, which is the focus of this chapter, consists of: *The Hobbit: An Unexpected Journey*, film, directed by Jackson; *The Hobbit: The Desolation of Smaug*, film, directed by Jackson; *The Hobbit: The Battle of the Five Armies*, film, directed by Jackson. All references are to the extended editions of the films.

on their quest to reclaim their homeland and a treasure that has been stolen from them, the films also present a *critique* of that very quest and the way in which the desire for 'their' gold overtakes the honour of the dwarves. The fact that the *means* of reclaiming the lost gold is through an act of theft—in particular a *contract* for theft—presents the quest in a fundamentally ambiguous light: at one level it is a reclaiming of what is 'rightfully' theirs, having been stolen by the dragon Smaug (Benedict Cumberbatch), but at another level they then steal and claim as 'theirs' even that which was not originally their own, dismissing any promises made to others for a share in the treasure. The counter-narrative of the trilogy, which sustains the critique of the former one, focuses upon home and hospitality—with the dwarves as displaced persons whose home has been taken from them and thus 'don't belong anywhere', unlike Bilbo Baggins (Martin Freeman), the hobbit they engage as their 'burglar', who consistently longs for the comforts of home (his armchair, the kettle boiling, a breakfast of bacon and eggs). What are we to make of these themes rendered visible in Tolkien's and Jackson's texts of fairy-tale and fantasy fiction?

My response to this question, in this concluding chapter, focuses on the theme of gift and gift-exchange as a more foundational basis for relationality and sociality—a point alluded to in the conclusion of the previous chapter. In doing so, I seek to present a culmination to the analysis in this book in terms of the secular theologies of modern law that I have been mapping, alongside a theological jurisprudence that responds to it. This returns to Tolkien's own theology of art as gift, discussed in the Prologue, arguing that both the creation of, and participation *in*, the narratives that I have been examining involve our own contribution to a larger vision, a Christian theological narrative, which presents a fundamental challenge to modern legality—a deactivating of the law to enable its fulfilling, and a seeing of a greater theological sense of relationality that goes beyond the voluntaristic theology of will and the modern wilful subject. It presents, as an alternative basis for the possibility of community and relationality, a love beyond the law—a charity that challenges the aporias of modern liberal and neoliberal legality, which more and more are revealed in the exceptions that dominate it today. Whereas the last chapter presented a response to this theology of will in terms of the amorous 'event of love' of David and Elise—a consideration of *eros* that challenges *nomos*—this chapter broadens out this form of love to a Christian consideration of *agape*, that divine love that disrupts the bounds of earthly *nomos*, the unbalancing of the justice of the law through the scandal of grace. This is *not*, however, to presume an elaborate disinterestedness and purity of *agape* over *eros* but, as John Milbank makes clear, to recognise the intertwining of the two—that the working out of a divine *agape* within the human intersects with the *eros* which encompasses not so much a romantic love, but a form of human reciprocity and friendship.[3] All of this is to recognise the way in which the subject finds its true being, not in the autonomous self of modern legal liberalism, but in a fundamentally intertwined and embedded self that is gifted to it—a sharing in divine existence, and a living that is a participatory and liturgical response to that gift.

The chapter proceeds in Section II by mapping the centrality of gift and gift-exchange to Tolkien's work and Jackson's rendering of it. In doing so, it unpacks the ways in which the themes of gift and hospitality present a contrast, in these works, between the theological primacy of reciprocity and gift-exchange on the one hand, and a modern emphasis on unilateral 'free' gift and self-interested contract on the other. Section III then demonstrates the way in which Jackson's rendering presents both a transformation of the gift nature of Tolkien's novel, appearing to emphasise contract over gift, and a *critique* of this trajectory. Thorin Oakenshield progresses from being the recipient of freely given hospitality, to engaging in contracts *for* hospitality, to in the end *refusing* to grant hospitality to those in need (and to which he is already bound). What we see here, therefore, is a trajectory of the modern liberal legal subject. The *reason* for this trajectory and transformation is Thorin's own progressive succumbing to dragon-sickness, which results in him *both* gaining an apparent autonomy and, at the same time, losing himself in the process (no longer being the Thorin that Bilbo and Thorin's fellow-dwarves have followed, committed themselves to and 'know', but giving up his honour for the sake of securing gold and power). The films therefore extend Tolkien's own critical insight, by focusing on the way in which both the desire for wealth and the nature of power present, or rather represent, modern legality's own concerns with shoring up the self.

Section IV then turns to the way in which the films draw out the fundamental ambiguity of the tale's representation of gift and property. Whilst there are multiple competing claims to proprietary rights in the treasure of the Mountain (founded in claims of historical ownership, possession and contract), the mechanism deployed for asserting these rights is one of theft. At one level, this would appear to encompass a conservative 'bourgeois' depiction of property rights—theft being a transgression that reinforces rather than transforms the law of property. At the same time, what can also be recognised here is the way in which the act of theft becomes the structural counter-point of the modern 'free' gift, which, instead of being a critique of market relations, sustains them. By contrast, Bilbo's famous reinterpretation

---

[3] See Milbank, 'Future of Love'; Milbank, 'Can a Gift Be Given?', p. 124.

of his contractual terms as undergirding a legitimate claim to the Arken-stone (the 'king's jewel' which he had been contracted to steal) becomes here a form of both restoring and reaffirming the primacy of gift-exchange as the basis of social relations, and a critique of the autonomy of the self-interested liberal subject. This action by Bilbo, as is emphasised in Section V, is taken for the purposes of sustaining peace and restoring friendship. Here, these themes in *The Hobbit* are mapped to the overarching arguments of this book—extending and presenting counters to the themes discussed so far. That is, *The Hobbit* presents not only a critique of the desire for gold or the ambiguous foundation of the subject in property rights, but also a vision of society as founded on friendship—and the stranger become friend. This is a vision of community and sociality in excess of contract, founded on a love that goes beyond the law.

II. *The Hobbit* as Fairy-tale: Tolkien's Gift and the Aporia of Hospitality

Tolkien's novel, first published in 1937 and then later revised after the writing of *The Lord of the Rings*, introduces the reader to the world of Middle-Earth through the eyes of Bilbo Baggins—a respectable hobbit of the Shire who is enticed into a quest and adventure with a party of thirteen dwarves and the wizard Gandalf. Whilst Tolkien is often identified as the father of modern fantasy, *The Hobbit* is itself a fairy-story. The ordinary Bilbo is drawn into an adventure with a range of fairy-tale creatures (dwarves, elves, goblins, talking eagles and, of course, a dragon) and, aided by a magic ring, seeks a long-lost treasure. This claim about the generic categorisation of *The Hobbit* has important implications. John Milbank, drawing upon Marcel Detienne and A. J. Greimas, emphasises the importance of the structural differences between myth and fairy-tale: in the former the actants that drive the story are primarily *subjects*, whereas in the latter they are primarily *objects* given by mystical helpers.[4] In mythic tales—and this can be seen in the multiple 'modern mythologies' I have examined throughout this book—the focus is on the formative agency of the hero or heroine who, as seen in Chapter 2's discussion of Joseph Campbell, is subject to a cosmic call, initiated into a source of power and returns with a life-transforming boon. However, as Milbank points out, there is a paradox at work here: '[m]yths *apparently* foreground subjects or persons, yet this purity of form is often tragically undercut by a *shadowy objectivity* which may be primordial chaos or obscure fate. Myth focuses on persons, but persons do not here triumph.'[5] As noted in the discussion of the mythic aspects of subjectivity in *Star Wars*, the hero or heroine

---

[4] Milbank, 'Fictioning Things', p. 14.
[5] Ibid., p. 15.

is required to 'let go', to purify the self in a reconciliation of opposites that, in the end, erases subjectivity rather than establishing it.

Fairy-tales, by contrast, encompass the opposite paradox: 'the circulation of objects in the basic plot is shadowed by the operations at a meta-narrative level of misty personages—senders and helpers, preternaturally "other" fairy figures and giants or else legendary human persons.'[6] The end result is that the human heroes *do* triumph, as a result of the mediatory intervention of these fairie others and the gift of magical objects. 'Thus although objects move the fairy-tale plot they magically subserve the fulfilment of subjects, whereas while subjects move the mythical plot, nevertheless all plot and purpose is finally undone by a shadowy but inexorable objectivity.'[7] In Tolkien's *The Hobbit*, the most prominent of 'fairie' figures is the wizard Gandalf, who, in 'encouraging' Bilbo to take his part in Thorin's company, assisted him on his entry into the quest—though there are a range of other helpers that Bilbo and the dwarves encounter along the way. What is significant about Jackson's visual rendering of Tolkien's tale, however, is the way in which it situates the narrative of Bilbo in a much larger context that is predominantly about these 'helpers' and their mandate to protect Middle-Earth. Drawing upon and presenting the greater background provided by *The Lord of the Rings* (along with its appendices and other additional material written by Tolkien), Jackson provides visual renderings of the council of Gandalf (Ian McKellen), Elrond (Hugo Weaving), Galadriel (Cate Blanchett) and Saruman (Christopher Lee), along with greater insight into the 'doings' of Gandalf and his reason for encouraging Thorin and the dwarves on their quest: the concern that the 'Evil' of Sauron has returned to Middle-Earth and his *own* interest in both the dragon Smaug and the mountain that he has captured.[8] At the same time, Thorin Oakenshield himself is transformed from a somewhat pretentious and slightly bumbling figure, to a great mythic character whose own 'origin' tale is told at various points by the older Bilbo (Ian Holm) and the dwarf Balin (Ken Stott), and whose ongoing rivalry with the 'pale Orc', Azog the Defiler (Manu Bennett), ends up filling out much of the final film's battle scenes in a way that extends well beyond Tolkien's own story. All of this would suggests that Jackson transformed and presented a more mythic rendering and situating of the little fairy-tale with which Tolkien initially gifted us.

My reference to Tolkien's fairy-tale as a gift here is no accident, for part of Tolkien's understanding of literature and art, as I noted in the Prologue, is

---

[6] Ibid.

[7] Ibid.

[8] On the transformation of *The Hobbit* by Jackson and his use of additional source material, see Riga et al., 'Children's Book to Epic Prequel'.

explicitly *as* a gift. He saw his work not as something that he simply 'created', but rather as a 'present' in two senses: 'both as something which he himself has been gifted, as the stories come from without, and as something not to be hoarded as a dead piece of tradition but as material to be reworked by other hands'.[9] Alison Milbank makes a comparison between this understanding of art as gift and Lewis Hyde's theory of the gift, where

> the artist manages to make his work more than a commodity by means of excess: he both accepts that his art is itself a gift from without, and he passes on his skill and 'the spirit of the gift' by the excessive, indeed sacrificial, nature of his artistic production.[10]

For Tolkien, the devout Catholic, this is an extension of the understanding of God as the 'giver of all good things', and the creation itself as a gift—a gift which we can also *participate* in, through acts of subcreation.[11] At the same time, the fairy-tale genre that Tolkien deploys has gift and gift-exchanges as one of its key features—protagonists receive gifts from fairy-tale creatures with an expectation of return (a requirement to *do something* with that which is given, the objects that, as was noted above, move the narrative forward).[12] The opening chapter of *The Lord of the Rings* begins with Bilbo's long-expected party celebrating his eleventy-first birthday, where we discover the Hobbit custom whereby the person whose birthday it is *gives* presents as well as receiving them (and Bilbo gave exceptionally fine gifts on that occasion).[13] It is notable that Jackson uses this day of Bilbo's birthday to tie *The Lord of the Rings* and *The Hobbit* together at the beginning of *An Unexpected Journey*, the first film of *The Hobbit Trilogy*, for it is in part this focus on the nature of gift and gift-exchange that goes to the *critique* of dragon-sickness and the lust for and power of gold, in which *both* Tolkien and Jackson's tales engage.

---

[9] Milbank, *Chesterton and Tolkien*, p. 126. She cites here a letter from Tolkien to Milton Waldman, see Carpenter and Tolkien, *Letters of Tolkien*, pp. 144–145.
[10] Milbank, *Chesterton and Tolkien*, p. 125; Hyde, *The Gift*.
[11] Milbank, *Chesterton and Tolkien*, p. 127; Tolkien, 'On Fairy-Stories'.
[12] Milbank, *Chesterton and Tolkien*, pp. 117–19.
[13] Tolkien, *The Lord of the Rings*, pp. 38–9. See also Milbank, *Chesterton and Tolkien*, pp. 130–3. Tolkien's *The Hobbit* is *also* full of examples of gift-giving, with the gifts given to the King of the Wood-Elves on Bilbo's return journey, as well as the 'gifts' he continuously provides to his friends and relations on his return to the Shire. The Ring itself, which Bilbo finds by chance in the goblin caves (having been dropped by the creature Gollum), is described by both Gollum and Bilbo as a 'present' (Gollum referring to it as his birthday present).

Whilst Alison Milbank traces Tolkien's interest in gift-exchange to his source material in the *Edda*, she notes that this, in part, was *also* one of the sources for the anthropologist Marcel Mauss in his classic work, *The Gift*, from 1925—a work and theme that have seen renewed interest and debate from anthropologists, philosophers and theologians in recent decades.[14] The interest in this work focuses in particular on the theorisation of gift as formative of social relations and as an alternative to the 'dominant utilitarian ethics' and political economy of neoliberal capitalist and market economies, and their undergirding by legal liberalism.[15] The common understanding is to see gift as a private and altruistic mechanism that is separate from the public and self-interested forms of contractual exchange. As such, the idealised 'pure gift' is understood as unilateral and 'free', eschewing any sense of self-interest and any obligation of a return from the recipient.[16] The idea is that this sense of a gift without return provides a space separate and distinct from the exchange-based contracts of self-interested utility maximisation that dominates the neoliberal economisation of the world.[17]

Jacques Derrida provided one of the most rigorous articulations of this theorisation of the gift as 'pure gift'. Following Immanuel Kant, he understood the gift specifically in terms of it being a *free* gift—for if there is any sense of self-interest, then the gift would be tainted and would really be a subtle form of coercion or contract. He notes:

> For there to be a gift, there must be no reciprocity, return, exchange, countergift, or debt. If the other *gives* me *back* or *owes* me or has to give me back what I give him or her, there will not have been a gift, whether this restitution is immediate or whether it is programmed by a complex calculation of a long-term deferral or differance.[18]

Derrida thus presents the gift as the impossible—even if you expect no return, if the person receiving the gift knows that it is a gift, then there is an obligation of *gratitude*.[19] Even if the giver has no expectation of return, they will, in a form of self-recognition, congratulate *themselves* on having given a gift.[20] A pure disinterested gift would require that *neither* the giver nor receiver recognises it as a gift. For Derrida, drawing upon Heidegger, it is only time—in its

[14] Mauss, *The Gift*; Milbank, *Chesterton and Tolkien*, pp. 118–20.
[15] Boundas, 'Gift, Theft, Apology'.
[16] See Derrida, *Given Time*.
[17] Brown, *Undoing the Demos*.
[18] Derrida, *Given Time*, p. 12.
[19] Ibid., pp. 13–14.
[20] Ibid., p. 16.

'passing away', the shift from a past to a future defined in terms of the present moment which is forever gone—that potentially fits the rigorous category of the gift.[21] Time 'is alone unilateral, alone not given back, alone outside the expectation of reciprocity, alone given by no-one without self-congratulation, alone absolutely indifferent to the content of what it gives'.[22]

In noting the impossibility of the gift, Derrida still presents it as the desire to exit the circularity of exchange—a unilateral and 'free' gift that encompasses an ethical response, a disinterestedness and altruism in contrast to the self-interested nature of contractual relations that reflect the actions of a modern willing individual and form the basis of both the modern state *and* the justification for market transactions. John Milbank acknowledges the rigorous nature of this approach to the gift, but criticises the founding assumption: that a gift should be unilateral and disinterested. He argues, rather, that a gift should be seen as always *embedded* in a network of giving and receiving—of gift-exchange—and it is on *this* basis that it is the foundation of social relations.[23] He criticises the focus on gift as unilateral as a particular modern interpretation that reflects the modern view of the subject that I analysed in Chapter 6. This is *not* to succumb to a view that gift and gift-exchange is all secretly contractual and coercive relations. Rather, whilst a gift may have an expectation of return, it is not in the form of the certainty and equivalence prescribed by contract. Gifts—and the giving, receiving and obligation of reciprocity of gift-exchange—involve an essential unpredictability: *asymmetrical* reciprocity and *non-identical* repetition.[24] It is this understanding of gift and gift-exchange—and the fundamental primacy of gift-exchange—that Milbank makes central to his theology. This encompasses an understanding 'that created being is only a gift; only exists as *sharing* in divine existence and as perpetually *borrowing* this existence'.[25] It places as central an understanding of love, of *agape*, as a divine breaking-in that is not so much a pure and unilateral giving, but rather 'the gift of an always preceding gift-exchange', which is 'an interpersonal event' rather than simply a command.[26] It is this sense of gift that is central to Tolkien's theology of art, in which the artist both takes up the created gift of God, and in part through a liturgical response, enters into the receptivity and responsivity of gift-exchange.

---

[21] Ibid., pp. 27–9.
[22] Milbank, 'Can a Gift Be Given?', p. 131; Derrida, *Given Time*, p. 77.
[23] See Milbank, 'Can a Gift Be Given?'; Milbank, 'Ethics of Self-Sacrifice'; Milbank, *Being Reconciled*; Milbank, 'The Transcendality of the Gift'.
[24] Milbank, 'Can a Gift Be Given?', p. 125.
[25] Milbank, 'Gift of Ruling', p. 221.
[26] Milbank, 'Can a Gift Be Given?', p. 150.

As noted above, Tolkien's fairy-tale involved a certain focus on gift-exchange in terms of the giving of presents. However, the more substantive engagement with this theme as constitutive of social bonds comes in the form of the giving or receiving of hospitality—that occasion which gives rise to the opportunity to request gifts from others. In the films, whilst the dwarves are often hesitant to reveal the true nature of their quest, they are, on many occasions, calling on different folk for hospitality—whether it is that of Elrond and the elves of Rivendell, who assist with the reading of the 'moon runes' on the ancient map, thus providing key clues as to the secret entrance to the Mountain; the skin-changer Beorn (Mikael Persbrandt), who provides support, guidance, supplies and the use of his ponies (despite his dislike of dwarves); or Bard (Luke Evans) and the people of Laketown, who send them on their way to the Mountain, again with supplies and weapons. They also experience the hospitality of *less* friendly groups, including the goblins of the mountains (led by the Great Goblin, played by Barry Humphries), the spiders of Mirkwood and the Wood-elves, who place them in their dungeons. It is significant that *The Hobbit*, in contrast to the voluntary and excess 'gift-giving' of Bilbo's party at the beginning of *The Lord of the Rings*, begins with a somewhat unwilling granting of hospitality in the famous scene of the 'unexpected party'.

We see, in the extended playing out of this scene in *An Unexpected Journey*, part of the paradoxes of hospitality. Bilbo, having sat down to his dinner, is interrupted by the ring of the doorbell. Upon opening the door, Dwalin (Graham McTavish) introduces himself, offering, as a manner of greeting, his services—Bilbo, ever polite, returns the same offer. However, whereas Bilbo proceeds here on the niceties of polite language—niceties that Gandalf had already called into question with his earlier 'good morning'—the Dwarves take his meaning literally. The process of each of the company arriving at the home of the ever more exasperated Bilbo, finds them calling for food and drink, and dramatically raiding his quite extensive larder. Bilbo's response—that he 'likes visitors as much as the next person' but he likes 'to know them *before* they come to visit'—points to the normal interaction of being invited (with attendees then presenting a similar offer at a later date), but also the *paradox* of hospitality itself, which is that it must at some point be extended to a stranger, before it can be experienced as such. It also presents the challenges or *aporia* of hospitality which Derrida has thematised—the way in which the host is both affirmed in their role (it is *their* home, over which *they* have dominion) and held 'hostage' to the person to whom they are extending a welcome.[27]

---

[27] Derrida, 'Hostipitality'.

It is significant that this aporia of hospitality is raised at a number of points in time throughout the film. The elves of Elrond's court seem somewhat exasperated by the habits and preferences of the dwarves—their excessive consumption of ale and wine, and their practice of bathing naked in the decorative fountains. However, the paradoxes of hospitality are made most clear with the elves of the Woodland realm in *The Desolation of Smaug*. In Tolkien's novel, the dwarves, hungry and lost in Mirkwood, three times see and attempt to engage with groups of elves feasting in the woods. Each time that they enter the light, it disappears and they are thrown into disarray.[28] Whilst Thorin describes their approaches later to the king of the Wood-elves as a request for hospitality—seeking food for those that are lost and starving—the king sees it rather as a threat or attack made on his people. Such a contradictory interpretation of the same act demonstrates the correlation between hospitality and its opposite, hostility, which Derrida notes is always present in the giving of hospitality.[29] In Derrida's situating of the aporetic basis of ethics as an *unconditional welcome*, this is always in tension with the *condition* which is placed on the granting of hospitality by the host or master (king, sovereign or state), who allows hospitality only on the basis of remaining master and thus of determining *who* shall be allowed within their territory, specifically *identifying* to whom hospitality will be extended.[30] At the same time, the master or sovereign is also concerned that those to whom hospitality is granted will be a threat and challenge to the peace of the sovereign that has welcomed them—a concern that the king of the Wood-elves raises in describing the dwarves as having attacked his kin by interrupting their feast.

In Jackson's films, the tension and discussion between Thorin and the king, there named Thranduil (Lee Pace), is reversed. Instead of seeking hospitality from the Wood-elves, they are saved and captured by them. Thorin then challenges Thranduil over an *earlier* denial of hospitality to the dwarves when Smaug the dragon had attacked them many years before. Thranduil refused hospitality at the time to protect his people from the wrath of dragon fire—the same concern that, in granting hospitality, there may also result a risk to the security of his domain and his people. Thranduil's focus on the protection of his own people is then referred to at a number of points. Tauriel (Evangeline Lilly), the She-elf and captain of the guard, questions Thranduil when he refuses her request to go beyond their lands to kill the giant spiders that are spawning there. Thranduil responds: 'Other lands are not my concern. The fortunes of the world will rise and fall, but here in this kingdom we will

[28] Tolkien, *The Hobbit*, pp. 140–5, 156–8.
[29] Derrida, 'Hostipitality'; see also Derrida, *On Cosmopolitanism and Forgiveness*.
[30] Derrida, 'Hostipitality', pp. 4, 6.

endure.' Upon hearing of the Evil arising (the rumours of the return of Sauron that is the broader context of the films), Thranduil orders his kingdom shut up, with no one allowed in or out. Such an action reflects the very tension of hospitality and its sense of responsibility to the world, which, Derrida argues, functions through the paradox of the threshold or the door:

> for there to be hospitality, there must be a door. But if there is a door, there is no hospitality . . . There is no house without doors and windows. But as soon as there are doors and windows, it means that someone has the key to them and consequently controls the conditions of hospitality.[31]

This is, for Derrida, the 'impossible' nature of hospitality which still 'must be done': '[h]ospitality can only take place beyond hospitality, in deciding to let it come, overcoming the hospitality that paralyzes itself on the threshold which it is.'[32]

Tauriel would seem to point to this sense of an unconditional ethics of responsibility and duty to the other, challenging Thranduil's retreat into his kingdom, as well as the later claim by his son, Legolas (Orlando Bloom), that 'it is not our fight'. Her response is: 'It *is* our fight. It will not end here. With every victory, this evil will grow . . . Are we not part of this world?' However, Tauriel's sense of responsibility is not so much an affirmation of, but a challenge to, the ethics of unconditional welcome—not because it denies such a duty of hospitality but because it recognises that this is not in the sense of an illimitable duty to an abstract other (in the Derridean/Levinasian sense), but rather of the embeddedness in, and responsibility to, the world. This is because Tauriel's continual hunting and fighting of the Orcs is tied explicitly to her growing love for one *particular* dwarf, Kili (Aidan Turner), and it is this love for the specific other that grounds her actions that help the others in general. In contrast to a sense of illimitable duty that is sometimes presented as the nature of Christian *agape*, he finds here rather the *more* fundamental Christian intertwining of *agape* and *eros*—with a love for the individual in front of us, through whom we are then able to share in God's love of the world (and without which we would be unable to participate in *agape* at all).[33] What we see in Thranduil is the way in which a particular abstract notion—the safety of his people, the value of their blood and lives—trumps the value of particular individuals. In *The Battle of the Five Armies*, Tauriel *again* challenges Thranduil and his decision there to leave the battle, noting that the result will

---

[31] Ibid., p. 14.
[32] Ibid.
[33] See Milbank, 'Future of Love'; Milbank, 'Can a Gift Be Given?', p. 124.

be that 'the dwarves will be slaughtered'. Here we find most explicit Thranduil's sense of valuation: 'Yes, they will die. Today, tomorrow, one year hence, a hundred years from now. What does it matter? They are mortal.' Tauriel criticises Thranduil: 'You think your life is worth more than theirs when there is no love in it, there is no love in you.' This is not so much a sense of an abstract responsibility to 'all humanity' or 'all the world' as it is a recognition that his desire to protect his own, to shore up their security, is a turning away from the need of the *particular* others before them.

III. 'You call that a fair trade?' Contract, Sovereignty and the Autonomous Subject

One of the most significant differences in Jackson's films is not so much the additional story-lines that he adds that go beyond Tolkien's original tale (the love between Tauriel and Kili discussed above, or the excessive feud between Azog and Thorin) but the way in which he reinterprets certain interactions that are depicted in the novel as forms of gift or gift-exchange more explicitly as formal bargains or contracts.[34] The clearest example of this, of course, is Bilbo's entry into the quest itself. In Tolkien's novel, Bilbo makes an explicit request 'to know about risks, out-of-pocket expenses, time required and remuneration, and so forth'[35]—to which Thorin then leaves upon his mantelpiece a letter outlining in brief such terms.[36] Jackson, however, renders this as a fully-fledged modern contract, prepared in advance and requiring formal execution. As such, the relationship between Bilbo and the dwarves is structured explicitly in terms of a contract for service, which covers, as *Balin* here notes, 'the usual summary of out of pocket expenses, time required, remuneration, funeral arrangements, [and] so forth'. As Bilbo begins to review this contract, he finds it expressed in classic legalese: the signing party will receive 'up to, but not exceeding, 1/14th total profit, if any'; the 'present company shall not be liable for injuries inflicted by or sustained as a consequence thereof including, but not limited to, lacerations, evisceration, [and] incineration'—injuries that, as Bofur (James Nesbitt) then points out, are not altogether unlikely. Such extensive legal provisions, whilst clearly played by Jackson for laughs, envision a much more formal engagement than the

---

[34] For a legal analysis of Tolkien's tale, including the proposed agreement with the dwarves, see Kane, 'Law and Arda'.

[35] Tolkien, *The Hobbit*, p. 22.

[36] Kane discusses the potential contractual nature of this letter, in terms of its offer—which Bilbo accepts only when he goes to join the party. See Kane, 'Law and Arda', pp. 39–41.

novel. At the same time, as will be seen, this formality does *not* ensure its fulfilment—not least because, as it is a contract for a crime (that is, theft), it would normally be unenforceable.[37]

This greater formalisation *also* features in the interactions between Thorin and Thranduil noted above, for their dispute arises in the context of the offer of a 'bargain': if Thorin agrees to return the jewels of Astor that are in the Mountain, then Thranduil will assist them on their quest. Not only does Thorin refuse this bargain (heatedly swearing in Dwarvish!) because of a prior *lack* of hospitality, but the *present* request for hospitality is also transformed into a contractual obligation. That Thorin refuses on the basis of honour (he accuses Thranduil of 'lack[ing] all honour') points to the way in which contracts, despite being presumed to function at the will of independent, rational actors, always operate within a broader social context—the give and take of social relations; where that is lacking, the contract itself fails, unless there is the possibility of a third person (sovereign or legal system) that will guarantee and enforce the contract. In this circumstance, where there appears to be negotiation between *two sovereigns* (the king of the Wood-elves and the king under the Mountain), the certainty of fulfilment and enforceability is questioned, except on the basis of greater social relations: that is, not so much on the basis of the contract which may or may not be fulfilled or enforced, but on the basis of a give and take, a form of gift-exchange that binds individuals together.[38]

This particular interaction between Thorin and Thranduil—with a bargain for hospitality—is situated within the broader context of Thorin's development throughout the film, and his progressive falling under the sway of dragon-sickness, which manifests in terms of a valuing of wealth and gold over life. This trajectory involves a shift from being the recipient of freely given hospitality, to engaging in bargained contracts for hospitality, finally to the refusal to grant hospitality (with Thorin doing the very thing he accuses Thranduil of doing). In the first stages of their quest, the dwarves receive hospitality from Elrond and the elves of Rivendell, and then subsequently from Beorn. At each point, this is in response to their being hunted by Orcs and needing safe haven. They are willingly given food, supplies, counsel and even the use of Beorn's ponies (despite his general dislike of dwarves).[39] In the

---

[37] Though Kane argues that, for the dwarves, given that it is a contract for services to recover stolen goods, they would not view it as being a contract for crime. Ibid., pp. 42–3.

[38] Mauss, *The Gift*.

[39] Beorn explains his dislike of dwarves as follows: 'They're greedy and blind, blind to the lives of those they deem lesser than their own.'

second half of their quest, when it comes to the interactions with the Wood-elves and then, after escaping their realm with the help of Bilbo, the people of Laketown, the hospitality requested (in relation to the former) and granted (in relation to the latter) is only as the result of a bargain—Thranduil's request for the jewels, and then the offer to the Master of Laketown (Stephen Fry) and its people of a share in the riches of the Mountain. Whereas Thorin refuses the bargain with Thranduil because of a lack of trust in his honour, the hospitality of Laketown is provided only after Bilbo vouches for Thorin and his character, stating: 'I have travelled far with these dwarves through great danger, and if Thorin Oakenshield gives his word, he will keep it.'

The culmination of this trajectory occurs at the conclusion of the quest, when the dwarves have retaken the Mountain and Smaug, having destroyed Laketown, is then killed by Bard. When the survivors from Laketown arrive on Thorin's 'doorstep', requesting hospitality and asking him to fulfil his promise to provide a share of the treasure, Thorin refuses. As the narrative progresses, Thorin is less and less embedded in reciprocal and mutual bonds of association, and more and more embodies the distinctly modern legal and contracting subject, who operates free of all restraints except those which can be directly enforced. Thorin therefore comes to represent that form of modern individualism which shuns society, or sees it as united only 'by bonds of contract which seek to make one egoistic desire match with another—without friendship, generosity, or concern for the whole social organism'.[40] This is not so much a rejection of a theological vision of society as, as outlined in the previous chapter, an attempt to fulfil a particularly modern theology. As Adrian Pabst notes, under such a view, '[i]nstead of being objective reciprocal rights linked to mutual obligation, individual rights become purely subjective when they are grounded in the sole capacity of the isolated individual.'[41] However, because there is no participation in a common sense of society, isolated interventions clash 'on account of conflicting rights-based claims, and resolving such clashes requires intervention by the absolute power of an omnipotent God or a voluntaristic sovereign—or both at once'.[42] Yet, as Milbank notes, 'nothing in this system *can* ever explain to the individual why he or she should not abuse it. Indeed it rather suggests that it *ought* to be abused, if the individual can get away with it.'[43]

---

[40] Milbank, 'Transcendality of the Gift', p. 362.
[41] Pabst, 'The "Modern" Middle Ages', p. 173.
[42] Ibid.
[43] Milbank, 'Transcendality of the Gift', p. 362.

This would seem to be explicitly Thorin's approach. When Bard comes before him to negotiate, he first refuses, based on the fact that there is an army preparing to attack him. When Bard then appeals to his conscience, noting that the people of Laketown offered help, only to receive in return ruin and death, Thorin criticises the self-interested nature of the transaction: 'When did the men of Laketown come to our aid but for the promise of rich reward?' Bard claims that a bargain was struck but Thorin challenges this: 'What choice did we have but to barter our birth right for blankets and food? To ransom our future in exchange for our freedom—you call that a fair trade? . . . why should I honour such terms?' Here Bard presents the basis as being an affirmation of Thorin's bond—'Because you gave us your word.' This invocation of bondedness, of the self-binding of the individual to a contract, is disputed by a show of force: 'Be gone, ere arrows fly!' When the contractual terms no longer provide the self-interested benefit, and when the contract cannot be enforced, the liberal legal subject refuses to fulfil the terms. Bilbo himself challenges Thorin on this, questioning him as to whether the treasure is worth more than his honour—noting that Bilbo's *own* honour is also being called into disrepute. Thorin responds that Bilbo's vouching for him was 'nobly done' but refuses to acknowledge that any of the treasure belongs to the people of Laketown: 'For this gold is ours and ours alone.'

This voluntaristic individual who is not tied to their promises, except by force, as examined in the last chapter, is *also* a reflection of the political theology of modern voluntaristic sovereignty. At one level, this would seem to be a strange representation, given the fantasy context of *The Hobbit*, with its medieval and feudal notions of honour and kingship. Yet the films themselves encompass a *critique* of the particular forms of exercise of power, which is not so much a modernist dismissal of pre-modern forms as it is a recognition of the way in which *modern* power itself functions and is deployed. This is found in the way it presents (and critiques) a sense of sovereignty as formal entitlement rather than rulership attached to intrinsic justice.[44] The claim to be 'King under the Mountain' is attached not to any form of election, just rulership or even royal lineage, but it is granted to the one who possesses or bears the Arkenstone. Sovereignty, here, is absolute power—the right to rule comes out of might or power, *not* out of a trust upon which the power should be used for the interests of the people. This is why Smaug himself can claim to be 'King under the Mountain', despite having no subjects. The basis of Smaug's claim is not so much his relation to particular subjects whom he commands, but rather a complete ipseity that is self-grounding and self-constituting.[45] Whilst Bilbo

[44] Ibid.
[45] Fitzpatrick, 'Secular Theology and Modernity of Law', p. 169.

'flatters' him with comparative titles and superlative praise—'Smaug the unassessably wealthy', 'the stupendous', the 'chiefest and greatest of calamities', 'the tyrannical' and one who has 'no equal on this earth'—Smaug's own claims are autonomous and absolute: 'My armour is iron, no blade can pierce me,' 'My teeth are swords, my claws are spears, my wings are a hurricane,' 'I kill where I wish, when I wish,' 'I am fire, I am death!'

Yet the film presents this sense of ipseity and surety of power *not* as originating from Smaug, but as *already* encompassed in Thorin's grandfather, Thror (Jeffrey Thomas). In the opening backstory told by the older Bilbo, Thror is presented not only as ruling in absolute surety, his line secure in his son Thrain (Thomas Robins) and grandson Thorin, but as taking the finding of the Arkenstone as a sign of his rulership by divine right. This reference to the political theology of the 'divine right of kings' is significant, as it is a specifically early modern (rather than medieval) theory that extends the 'emphasis on voluntarism and individualism that rests on [Duns] Scotus' univocity of being'.[46] That is, it reflects the emergence of a modern unitary conception of sovereignty and will. This may appear to be in contrast to the founding of sovereignty on a social contract. However, as Milbank notes, both absolutism and liberalism arise from the same source with their focus on the 'primacy of the will':

> In the early modern West, the competition of individual wills was only resolved by investing all political rule for the first time in a single sovereign will. This applies whether or not this will was seen as ruling by divine right or by contract or both, and whether it was seen as the will of the king or as the democratic will of the people.[47]

In addition to this essential critique of the modern conception of sovereignty, the films also present, in critical mode, the form of reasoning that goes along with it, which is one that justifies the biopolitical calculation of the value of life—a reflection of the exceptionality of modern legality which is willing to suspend the rights it grants to persons in light of an emergency or greater need to shore itself up. At the epitome of his dragon-sickness, Thorin blockades himself within the halls of the Mountain, while his cousin's dwarf-army fights the attacking Orcs. When Dwalin challenges him about both the threat and the fact that their people are being slaughtered, Thorin's response presents the clearest critical articulation of the thanatopolitical tendencies of the modern state: 'Many die in war. Life is cheap. But a treasure

---

[46] Pabst, 'The "Modern" Middle Ages', p. 173; Figgis, *The Divine Right of Kings*.
[47] Milbank, 'Gift of Ruling', p. 220.

such as this cannot be counted in lives lost. It is worth all the blood we can spend.' It is here that we find a critique of the abstract calculations of modern legality, unpacked in the analysis of VIKI in Chapter 5. Whilst there it was about encompassing the sacrificing of some lives in order to save others, here it is taken one step further—life must be sacrificed for the production and protection of wealth. The films present a critique of both Thorin and Thranduil's calculations and willingness to sacrifice life for greater gain, and the corresponding reduction of individual lives to content-less abstractions. When leaving Laketown, Thorin tells Kili, who has been injured, that he must stay behind because he will slow down their progress. When Fili (Kili's brother, played by Dean O'Gorman) challenges him, Thorin notes that when Fili is king he will understand, for the sovereign 'cannot risk the fate of this quest for the sake of one dwarf'. Later, Thorin, upon hearing evidence that Bilbo woke the dragon and is in danger, repeats such reasoning to Balin: 'I will not risk this quest for the life of one burglar.' Balin challenges the way in which Thorin's abstraction is progressing and his referring to Bilbo not even in the generic as a hobbit, but in terms of his contracted role as burglar.

IV. 'I may be a burglar but I like to think I'm an honest one': Gift, Theft and Love

Thorin's reference to Bilbo in the abstracted role as burglar (rather than by name) reflects his succumbing to dragon-sickness, but also highlights explicitly the role that he is to perform. A number of commentators have pointed to the way in which Bilbo, in the Shire, presents an idyllic form of petty-bourgeois existence—an existence which is explicitly disrupted by Gandalf's arranging him to take service with Thorin's company.[48] What is most startling about this, however, is the way in which his taking up a role as 'burglar' would seem to result in him becoming 'a rebel against the sanctity of private property'.[49] Ishay Landa presents a dialectic reading of Tolkien's tale, noting that, whilst Bilbo steals 'from the trolls, then from Gollum, then from Smaug the dragon, and, finally and most importantly, from the dwarves', he is 'clearly a thief on the side of the good'.[50] This is because '[t]he dispossessed owners of the different treasures are themselves either thieves (the trolls, Gollum, Smaug) or inordinately greedy (the dwarves).'[51] Bilbo's bourgeois sensibilities

---

[48] Landa, 'Slaves of the Ring', p. 118; Shippey, *Road to Middle Earth*, p. 72; Hren, 'Acquisitive Imitation', pp. 218, 223.

[49] Landa, 'Slaves of the Ring', p. 117.

[50] Ibid., pp. 117–18.

[51] Ibid., p. 118.

would presumably want to justify his engagement as 'burglar' in terms of the sustaining or upholding of private property rights, and seeing stolen property returned to its rightful owners. Yet the films call into question such a claim to rightful ownership because there are *multiple* proprietary claims to the treasure under the Mountain. As noted above, these include not only the dwarves (seeking to reclaim their homeland), but also Thranduil and the Wood-elves, and Bard and the people of Laketown—not to mention Smaug's own sense of 'ownership' and dominion over the treasure hoard.

These multiple claims to rightful ownership also render the act of theft fundamentally ambiguous. The dwarves present their own claim to ownership in the Mountain and the treasure in two regards: first, because Smaug has stolen it from them, dispossessing them from their homeland, which they held by historical right; second, because of a claimed right that arises from the Arkenstone as the king's jewel. The problem with the latter claim is that it seems to attach to the person who bears or possesses the stone, like an old-fashioned title deed. The possession of the jewel by Smaug would thus seem to underwrite his claim to be 'King under the Mountain', and provide an indefeasible title alongside the property claims he makes as conqueror or settler–colonialist of the Mountain. The result is that Smaug, in his discussions with Bilbo, calls the dwarves' proprietary claims into question, arguing that Bilbo is a 'thief in the shadows', who was 'only ever a means to an end'. He specifically questions the nature of the contract: 'What did he promise you? A share of the treasure, as if it were his to give? I will not part with it, not one piece.' This comprises an implied assertion of an unrestrained property right on Smaug's behalf—even where such rights arise from the dispossession of others from the property.

This reveals the way in which theft is *not* 'a justified and noble revolt against the injustice of property'.[52] The act of theft does *not*, as GK Chesterton points out, reject the notion of property as such: 'Thieves respect property. They merely wish the property to become their property that they may more perfectly respect it.'[53] Smaug, accused of stealing the treasure and laying claim to the Mountain, is not a critic of property but affirms it in his act of theft. The attempt to 'steal back' the treasure by the dwarves *also* encompasses an affirmation of property rather than its critique. The larger issue is to critique not a particular instance of property, but the very system of property itself—such as Proudhon's famous claim that 'property is theft.'[54] As Slavoj Žižek notes, this

[52] Ibid.
[53] Chesterton, *The Man Who Was Thursday*, pp. 44–5; Žižek, 'Fear of Four Words', p. 44.
[54] Žižek, 'Fear of Four Words', pp. 44–5; see discussion in Nichols, 'Theft is Property!', pp. 5–7.

is to 'pass from theft as a particular criminal violation of the universal form of property to this form itself as a criminal violation'.[55] We find here that the 'antagonism between Law and crime' is itself 'inherent to crime, the antagonism between universal and particular crime'.[56] The critique of property by the dispossessed includes a recursive affirmation of such property.[57] To engage in a more radical critique of property requires asserting, not the injustice of a particular dispossessor, but the injustice of the notion or understanding of property itself.[58]

Yet this is *not* quite the critique of property that occurs within *The Hobbit*, for, as Joshua Hren and Alison Milbank point out, what is critiqued is Thorin's own retreat from reciprocity and from gift-exchange.[59] This occurs at two levels. First, he refuses to provide to those in need—those who have suffered loss and ruin as a result of Smaug (loss and ruin that Thorin himself is complicit in, given that it is Bilbo and the dwarves that woke the dragon). This is a refusal of the reciprocity of hospitality. At the same time, this refusal is *also* a refusal to honour the rightful contractual claims of the people of Laketown—Thorin's promise that all would share in the treasure.[60] What occurs consistently here is Thorin's refusal of any sense of claim against him or the treasure—repeating the statements that Smaug makes about it: 'For this gold is ours and ours alone. By my life I will not part with a single coin. Not one piece of it.' That this statement is made at the specific point when Thorin *is* giving away an aspect of the treasure—it occurs after giving the incredibly valuable mithril coat of 'silver steel' to Bilbo—does not undermine that claim, for whilst in the novel the coat is considered to be 'the first payment' of Bilbo's reward,[61] in the film there is no mention of payment for services or recognition of any claim against Thorin. Rather, even though it is given 'as a token of our friendship', it is presented as a one-way and unilateral offering. It thus reflects Jackson's shift in emphasis

---

[55] Žižek, 'Fear of Four Words', pp. 44–5.

[56] Ibid., p. 45.

[57] Nichols, 'Theft is Property!'

[58] Ibid.

[59] Hren, 'Acquisitive Imitation', p. 131; Milbank, *Chesterton and Tolkien*.

[60] It is noteworthy that, in Tolkien's novel, Thorin *does* agree to this aspect of the claim, though looking for a way *not* to have to honour it. In the film Thorin refuses outright any 'legitimacy' to the claims made by the people of Laketown. See Tolkien, *The Hobbit*, pp. 255–6.

[61] Ibid., p. 222. Marie Loughlin argues that this encompasses a symbolic distribution of 'the wealth of his people in a payment that is also a gift'. Loughlin, 'Tolkien's Treasures', p. 33.

from a traditional view of gift-exchange and reciprocity to a modern view of the dichotomy between 'free gift' and contract.

It is here that the discussion of the nature of the 'free' or 'pure' gift becomes relevant. As noted above, Derrida argues that a pure gift is only one where there is no return and where the giver and receiver are unaware of or fail to acknowledge the item as a gift. This is to sever all contractual or coercive aspects of the gift, in order to render it truly a gift. However, there *is* an action that fits these parameters. The transfer of an item of property from one party to another that bears no trace of contract, does not generate an obligation of return, to which no gratitude is rendered, and is not recognised as a gift is a *theft*. It is here that we find the extreme figuring of a gift as unilateral action is experienced as its inverse, a theft. As Deleuze and Guattari point out, the experience of a gift for the person giving is (at least without their own sense of reciprocity or expectation of return) as theft.[62] Theft involves a deprivation of property belonging to another *without* any sense of exchange, reciprocity or return. As such, it excludes all notion of contract, exchange or self-interested action on behalf of the person whose object is stolen. It is therefore theft that fits the category of pure, unilateral and disinterested gift.

The dynamics of such a connection between theft and gift are relatively straightforward, and can be seen in the earlier scene in *The Desolation of Smaug*, where, after the Wood-elves capture the dwarves, Legolas discovers that Thorin bears the elven-sword 'Orcrist' and questions where he came by it. When Thorin claims that it was *given* to him (it was found in a Troll-hoard in *An Unexpected Journey*, but then Elrond acknowledges the sword and gives it to Thorin, along with another to Gandalf), Legolas calls him 'not just a thief but a liar as well'. Whilst this claim evidences the distrust between elves and dwarves in Middle-Earth (implicitly claiming that the sword would *not* have been given to a dwarf), it also points to the structural similarity between a gift and theft. The *difference* lies not in the *form* of the transaction (a piece of property transferring from one party to another) but in terms of the social relations that contextualise and cement the transaction. Here we see that the *content* of a gift—in terms of both *what* is given and *why* it is given—becomes important. This is *also* reflected in the fact that elven-swords are held in high regard, revered for the way in which something of the self is put into their making, and reflecting Hyde's notion of the excess of art as gift.[63]

We can now understand the significance of the way in which Bilbo performs his role as the nominated burglar of the company. He is employed to

---

[62] Deleuze and Guattari, *Anti-Oedipus*, pp. 185–6; Boundas, 'Exchange, Gift, and Theft'.

[63] Hyde, *The Gift*.

steal back treasure already stolen as a means to reclaim particular property. However, Bilbo's 'use' of both the action of theft *and* the contract that he signed provides a critique of the modern dichotomy of gift and contract that Thorin epitomises. Bilbo *does* in fact do what he was contracted to do, stealing the Arkenstone from Smaug. However, he then *fails* to give it to Thorin. Rather, given Thorin's succumbing to dragon-sickness, and willingness to go to war to protect the gold of the Mountain, Bilbo provides the Arkenstone to Bard and Thranduil to use in their negotiations with the dwarves. Such actions involve a critical 'use' of the competing proprietary and contractual claims discussed above. Bard asks the question regarding Bilbo's rights to the Arkenstone that Smaug implies was *not* asked of Thorin's ability to promise a share in the treasure: 'How is this yours to give?' Bilbo uses his contract with Thorin as a justification, claiming the stone against his rightful one-fourteenth share in the treasure. Again, it is worth noting the reasons provided for this action. In Tolkien's novel, this reference to his one-fourteenth share is presented as an 'interest' in the gold—a desire for him to receive his fair share. As Hren notes, Bilbo's language here 'is typically modern, appealing to both his own "interest" in this matter and the precious contract'.[64] In the film, by contrast, Bard is surprised that he is taking this action at all: 'Why would you do this? You owe us no loyalty.' Bilbo's response is significant:

> I'm not doing it for you. I know that dwarves can be obstinate and pigheaded and difficult. And suspicious and secretive, with the worst manners you can possibly imagine; but they are also brave and kind . . . and loyal to a fault. I've grown very fond of them, and I would save them if I can. But Thorin values this stone above all else. In exchange for its return, I believe he will give you what you were owed. There will be no need for war.

Despite Bilbo justifying his actions in terms of his contract with Thorin, he does not do so in a self-interested fashion but more from a desire to save his friends. Furthermore, the action of theft here is *not* the equivalent of Smaug's—he is not taking or keeping the Arkenstone to hoard it for himself but so that it can be returned. Even more than in Tolkien's novel, Jackson presents reciprocity and friendship as a challenge to contract and self-interest.

The significance of Bilbo's actions therefore goes to the way in which he demands more from Thorin than he is willing to give—not in terms of the treasure, but in terms of *who* he is. When Bilbo describes the dwarves as brave, kind and loyal to a fault, it is these qualities that are being called into question by Thorin's actions—which reject the loyalty and bondedness

---

[64] Tolkien, *The Hobbit*, p. 250; Hren, 'Acquisitive Imitation', p. 224.

of his word, any kindness or compassion for the suffering of the people of Laketown and, as is then seen, any braveness or courage in going to battle against the Orcs. Whilst Bilbo's actions fail to prevent war—Thorin, instead of agreeing to the exchange, asserts a sovereign right: 'Why should I buy back, what is rightfully my own?'—they are based on an honest belief in what the other should and can do. When it is revealed that Bilbo has given Bard the Arkenstone, Thorin accuses him of theft—though what did he expect from someone he continually refers to as 'Master Burglar'? However, the action was not so much a permanent deprivation of the dwarves, but a taking of it so that it could be returned. He says to Thorin: 'Steal from you? No, no. I may be a burglar but I like to think I'm an honest one. I'm willing to let it stand against my claim.' Such an action encompasses both a form of rendering inoperative the contractual terms—stealing the Arkenstone—and at the same time fulfilling it and achieving its goal—enabling the Arkenstone to be returned to Thorin. In this action he enables Thorin to fulfil his contractual obligations to the people of Laketown, through the use of his contractual obligations to Bilbo. The result is that it costs Thorin nothing—Bilbo ends up receiving none of the treasure and the Arkenstone will be returned to Thorin. In contrast to both Smaug and Thorin's stealing so that they may hoard and control all, Bilbo's stealing results in him giving away everything, with the aim of returning the Arkenstone to Thorin. This returning is not so much a direct giving so much as a returning in the form of exchange, so as to cement social relations between the men, elves and dwarves and for the prevention of war. The theft, normally considered as an anti-gift, is here rendered as a counter-gift—a stealing for the purpose of returning differently.

Thorin's initial response renders visible the bonded nature of the 'free' modern subject, for it is at the point of time that he presumes a complete freedom and unboundedness that we find him rendered the *most* bound. As Alison Milbank notes, 'we are never more in the power of the fetishized commodity than when we rejoice in freedom of choice in the modern world of the "free" market'.[65] By contrast, it is in Bilbo's holding of Thorin to his contract—binding him to his word—that he offers freedom. Bilbo's actions encompass a vision of friendship, restoration and peace. And when Thorin fails to do that of his own accord, Bilbo attempts to do it on his behalf—providing a mechanism for Thorin to fulfil his word, even when he is unable to himself. In this sense, in contrast to either the self-interested calculating of contract, or the suspiciousness of legality (presuming, as Thorin does, that

[65] Milbank, *Chesterton and Tolkien*, p. 138; see also Milbank, 'Can a Gift Be Given?', p. 124.

anyone and everyone is going to rob you), Bilbo presents a form of trust—a seeing of good in the other and asking them to fulfil that level of good, even if it goes beyond their initial actions. This action and trust resonate with those discussed in Chapter 4, where Batman continues to trust Selina Kyle despite her continual acts of betrayal and letdown. Bilbo here continues to trust in Thorin—even when his actions do not deserve it. The result, as is seen in Thorin's words before he dies, is the calling forth of the other's trustworthiness. It is such a vision of trust that I have been articulating in this book—not just a love beyond the law, but one that renders inoperative the law in order to fulfil it.

V. Conclusion: A Theological Jurisprudence of Speculative Cinema

John Milbank argues that what he refers to as 'the Macdonald tradition' of speculative fiction does not simply re-present Christianity but rather re-envisages it, recognising the way in which Christianity is not, at its core, abstract doctrine and rational practice but rather functions through symbol and narrative. 'It is these that are held to be inexhaustibly inspirational and to ensure that abstract doctrine must endlessly develop because it can never be finally conclusive.'[66] In the same way that Jesus in the gospels tells us that we must become 'like children' in order to be born again, 'the most fundamental elements of the faith can be taught to children and . . . in their initial imaginative and intuitive response to this saturation of meaning, there lies something of more authority than adult reflection'.[67] It is along similar lines that Alison Milbank explains the way in which, despite speculative fiction comprising *different* metaphysical visions, the very process of envisioning a world requires a commitment to both meaning and metaphysics—a recognition of the storied nature of the world.[68] This book has taken up these two perspectives, combining them with the jurisprudential aspects of Cultural Legal Studies to make a claim for a theological jurisprudence of speculative cinema. This is to present cinema not as simply a fictional world of imaginative fantasy, but rather as a material extension *of* our world, one that encompasses a commitment to the world as created and gifted. The stories that are presented in speculative cinema, which at one level involve the imagining of different worlds or different versions of our own world, at the same time give us a way to see our own world more clearly. They provide a critical insight into the delirium and simulacrum of relationships within modernity, but

---

[66] Milbank, 'Fictioning Things', p. 3.
[67] Ibid.
[68] Milbank, 'Literary Apologetics', p. 97. Milbank, *Chesterton and Tolkien*, p. 11.

also an ability to envision the possibility of true relationality and sociality—a giving and receiving, the forming of social bonds, and a society based on friendship and generosity rather than contract.

Whilst much of the work of this book has been analysing and 'outing' the secular theologies of modern law that are represented in the science fiction, fantasy and superhero films that popular cinema has become enamoured with, this chapter sought to present a sense of theological jurisprudence of trust that arises out of Tolkien's own theology of art as gift, discussed in the Prologue. This is to see, in Jackson's reproduction of Tolkien's tale, a sense of the greater Christian theological narrative that, as the earlier chapters have revealed, presents a fundamental challenge to modern legality—a deactivating of the law to enable its fulfilling, an overcoming of the primacy of evil and the voluntaristic theology of will, with a greater sense of relationality, and a rejection of the modern willing and contracting subject for a reciprocating body engaged in the giving and receiving of social life. This is to present secularisation not as an overcoming or erasure of theology but rather as an encompassing of competing theological visions. As outlined in Chapter 6, both the absolutistic and liberal paradigms of law, sovereignty and governance are themselves founded on a heterodox and deficient theology of will. It is on this basis that my readings of speculative cinema have sought to present an alternative possibility of community and relationality, a love beyond the law—a charity that challenges the aporias of modern liberal legality, which more and more are revealed in the exceptions that dominate it today. This is to envision not only a different form of legality based on trust and love but a form of creaturely subjectivity. To quote John Milbank again, '[t]he Creature only is, as manifesting the divine glory, as acknowledging its own nullity and reflected brilliance. To be, it entirely honours God, which means it returns to him an unlimited, never paid-back debt.'[69]

This vision of trust-based legality and creaturely subjectivity is in contrast to the presuppositions of modern liberal legality, which, as examined in Chapter 1, present both a primacy of evil to which law is required to respond and a modern subject whose 'free will' is to will Good or Evil. Yet, as noted, the rationality of modern law and its 'positive' account of evil can never hold such a will responsible *for* the evil that it does. Tolkien's maintenance of an Augustinian account of evil as privation—an account which, despite the apparent presentation of the 'Evil' of Sauron, is maintained in Jackson's rendering—challenges this positive account. Gandalf, when Galadriel asks him why he chose Bilbo to be part of Thorin's quest, notes that

---

[69] Milbank, 'Can a Gift Be Given?', p. 135.

> Saruman believes that it is only great power that can hold evil in check. But
> that is not what I have found. I've found it is the small things, everyday deeds
> of ordinary folk, that keeps the darkness at bay—simple acts of kindness and
> love.

This view, combined with Gandalf's own sense that a greater purpose lies
behind the actions that are being taken, is in contrast to the modern willing
subject—critiqued in Chapter 6, in terms of a fundamentally sovereign and
self-willing subject. Within the orthodox Christian tradition such a willing
subject is not its epitome but a *result* of the fall:

> For the sinful self is left merely with the empty gesture of freedom, an abso-
> lute control over its own illusory and contentless stability, and robbed of the
> freedom to do this or that, which is inseparable from a freedom *for* this or
> that, involving receptivity.[70]

Such a sense of illimitable freedom and autonomy is, as noted in Section III
above, the very view of sovereignty that *The Hobbit* critiques—with Thorin's
autonomy trumping any sense of honour or bondedness, including by his
own words and commitments. This sense of sovereignty is one that aligns
with modern law's self-grounding nature, and the illimitable and unbound
power that was examined in Chapter 2—a transcendent sovereign who can
intervene and change the laws at whim, with modern legality there as a mere
means to an end. The presented critique of Thorin's (and Thranduil's) sovereignty discussed above challenges the sense of rule by entitlement, envisioning it as more fundamentally bonded to justice, to a protection of one's
people, and the valuing of life.

In *The Hobbit* there is also a challenge to the need for an exceptional
legality to ward off chaos, analysed in Chapter 3, and the sacrificial economy
of modern legality, critiqued in Chapter 4—the way in which 'the entire
notion of a secular political law and state requires the unwarranted sacrifice
of innocent blood'.[71] In *The Hobbit*, despite the plethora of battle scenes and
violence, what is *more* foundational is *not* a glorious battle or the sacrificial
shedding of blood, but a sense of friendship and sociality that resists violence,
even if at times its own failure results in violence. This is highlighted in the
focus upon Bilbo—someone who does *not* fit the model of the heroic, overcoming great odds to save the city, nation or world. Rather, he is presented
as someone who, in recognising his own limitations, is also willing to help
the dwarves simply because their home was taken from them—and who is

---

[70] Ibid.
[71] Davis, 'Paul and Subtraction', p. 112; Milbank, *Theology and Social Theory*.

willing to risk himself *not* for glory or for the city, but in an attempt to prevent war and to challenge and reclaim a friend who has lost his way. When, after the battle in which Thorin dies, Balin notes there will be a feast where 'songs will be sung, tales will be told [and] Thorin Oakenshield will pass into legend', Bilbo comments that that is *not* how he remembers him. The focus of the film therefore rejects the glorious legend in favour of a privileging of friendship. It points towards a new form of community that is founded *not* on a fundamental violence, but on a vision of peace and friendship based on generosity and the cancellation of debts—or, as seen in Section IV above, a rendering inoperative of such debts. This reflects a New Testament view which 'suggests that unstinting generosity and the cancellation of debts cease to be intermittent, or directed merely to the needy and defaulted, but become the *habitual norm* of a new community practice'.[72]

In Chapters 5 and 6, I the examined modern presentations of the two occidental deities that frame the mythology of modern law outlined by Peter Fitzpatrick—that of order and that of will. The first produces a system of calculation that justifies sacrifice in order to sustain itself and that, in holding freedom up, limits freedom: the tensions of the modern rule of law. The second then envisions a wilful individual but is unable to hold that wilful individual responsible. Instead, it is only in the recognition of free will as a gift, not a right, that we find a response, that we are able to enter *into* the plan, to engage in a form of subcreation. As already noted, *The Hobbit* directly questions and critiques the calculating nature of sovereignty, with Bilbo constantly refusing the calculations of Thranduil and Thorin. At the same time, the focus on the nature of a gift—and the 'use' to which it is put—points to the importance of a sociality that goes *beyond* the self-sufficient calculating and contracting individual. This is to see relationship which functions *neither* through pure contract *nor* through a pure unilateral gift, but rather as a more fundamental gift-exchange.

It is with this vision in mind that I conclude with the two key scenes from the final moments of the film trilogy. Thorin eventually acknowledges that the actions of Bilbo were those of a true friend and it is with this transformation of a contractual relation into that of a greater form of sociality that the tale, for both Tolkien and Jackson, concludes. In doing so, it turns back also to the question of hospitality, not as an ethic of unconditional welcome which, in itself, is a reflection of the romanticised notion of the pure gift that keeps the other distant. Rather, it is through the process of a form of sociality and togetherness that arises from friendship. Bilbo's constant desire for the comforts of home—a home which was intruded upon at the beginning of

---

[72] Milbank, 'Can a Gift Be Given?', p. 149.

the novel and the films—also becomes an open invitation to tea, with which Bilbo parts from the dwarves. Those who were strangers at the beginning of the novel have now become friends. Here there is a recognition of the inter-twining of Christian *agape* with that of *eros*—in a way which overcomes the law. This is not the extension to an abstracted other—the artificial or 'fanta-sised pure individual' of modern law and legality[73]—but the stranger become friend and welcomed into one's home. Here we can understand the home as a place where the stranger is transformed into a friend and the person who is unknown to me becomes someone with whom I share food and drink. This type of hospitality is focused not so much on a unilateral gift given by one party to another, but on a giving and receiving that becomes a sharing together. Such a means of relationship is based neither on contract nor on a pure disinterested gift—but rather relationality as gift-giving which exceeds contract.

Aspects of this can be seen in terms of the concluding moments of the film trilogy where Bilbo returns to the Shire to discover that he has been presumed dead and all the property of Bag-End is being auctioned off. Tosser Grubb (Merv Smith), the auctioneer, requires Bilbo to provide evidence of who he is. This is done initially on the basis of the contract, which he produces as evi-dence. But when it is questioned as to *whom* he has contracted with, Thorin Oakenshield is referred to as his friend. Whilst the contract is produced as evidence of Bilbo's legal personhood, rendering him visible to the community, the contract is then *exceeded* as the party to whom it was engaged is related to, not in the form of contract, but in the form of friendship. That this occurs upon Bilbo's return home—a home which he has opened to the stranger-now-friend—affirms the message of the film: the need for, not the hoarding of wealth, but its use, and the importance of welcoming and providing hos-pitality to the stranger. As Thorin's final words to Bilbo state: 'If more people valued home above gold, this world would be a merrier place.'

---

[73] Milbank, 'Gift of Ruling', p. 238.

Bibliography

Primary Source

21–87. Film. Directed by Arthur Lipsett. Canada: National Film Board of Canada, 1963.

The Adjustment Bureau. Film. Directed by George Nolfi. USA: Universal Pictures, 2011.

Batman Begins. Film. Directed by Christopher Nolan. USA: Warner Bros, 2005.

Batman v Superman: Dawn of Justice. Film. Directed by Zack Snyder. USA: Warner Bros, 2016.

Blade Runner. Film. Directed by Ridley Scott. USA: Warner Bros, 1982.

The Dark Knight. Film. Directed by Christopher Nolan. USA: Warner Bros, 2008.

The Dark Knight Rises. Film. Directed by Christopher Nolan. USA: Warner Bros, 2012.

Devil. Film. Directed by John Erick Dowdle. USA: Universal Pictures, 2010.

Fort Apache. Film. Directed by John Ford. USA: Argosy Pictures, 1948.

Glass. Film. Directed by M. Night Shyamalan. USA: Universal Pictures, 2019.

Gotham. TV Series. Directed by Danny Cannon. USA: Fox Network, 2014–.

The Happening. Film. Directed by M. Night Shyamalan. USA: Twentieth Century Fox, 2008.

The Hobbit: An Unexpected Journey. Film. Directed by Peter Jackson. USA: Warner Bros, 2012.

The Hobbit: The Battle of the Five Armies. Film. Directed by Peter Jackson. USA: Warner Bros, 2014.

The Hobbit: The Desolation of Smaug. Film. Directed by Peter Jackson. USA: Warner Bros, 2013.

Hulk. Film. Directed by Ang Lee. USA: Universal Pictures, 2003.

I, Robot. Film. Directed by Alex Proyas. USA: Twentieth Century Fox Film Corporation, 2004.

Justice League. Film. Directed by Zack Snyder. USA: Warner Bros, 2017.

The LEGO Batman Movie. Film. Directed by Chris McKay. USA: Warner Bros, 2017.

The Lord of the Rings: The Fellowship of the Ring. Film. Directed by Peter Jackson. USA: New Line Cinema, 2001.

The Lord of the Rings: The Return of the King. Film. Directed by Peter Jackson. USA: New Line Cinema, 2003.

The Lord of the Rings: The Two Towers. Film. Directed by Peter Jackson. USA: New Line Cinema, 2002.

The Mandalorian. TV Series. Directed by Jon Favreau. USA: Walt Disney Studios Motion Pictures, 2019–.

Man of Steel. Film. Directed by Zack Snyder. USA: Warner Bros, 2013.

The Man Who Shot Liberty Valance. Film. Directed by John Ford. USA: Paramount Pictures, 1962.

Minority Report. Film. Directed by Steven Spielberg. USA: Twentieth Century Fox Film Corporation, 2002.

RED 2. Film. Directed by Dean Parisot. USA: Summit Entertainment, 2013.

Rogue One: A Star Wars Story. Film. Directed by Gareth Edwards. USA: Walt Disney Studios Motion Pictures, 2016.

Scott Pilgrim vs. the World. Film. Directed by Edgar Wright. USA: Universal Pictures, 2010.

The Sixth Sense. Film. Directed by M. Night Shyamalan. USA: Hollywood Pictures, 1999.

Solo: A Star Wars Story. Film. Directed by Ron Howard. USA: Walt Disney Studios Motion Pictures, 2018.

Split. Film. Directed by M. Night Shyamalan. USA: Universal Pictures, 2017.

Star Wars: The Clone Wars. Film. Directed by Dave Filoni. USA: Warner Bros, 2008.

Star Wars: The Clone Wars. TV Series. Directed by George Lucas. USA: Lucasfilm, 2008–20.

Star Wars Episode I: The Phantom Menace. Film. Directed by George Lucas. USA: Lucasfilm, 1999.

Star Wars Episode II: Attack of the Clones. Film. Directed by George Lucas. USA: Lucasfilm, 2002.

Star Wars Episode III: Revenge of the Sith. Film. Directed by George Lucas. USA: Lucasfilm, 2005.

Star Wars Episode IV: A New Hope. Film. Directed by George Lucas. USA: Lucasfilm, 1977.

Star Wars Episode V: The Empire Strikes Back. Film. Directed by Irvin Kershner. USA: Lucasfilm, 1980.

Star Wars Episode VI: The Return of the Jedi. Film. Directed by Marquand Richard. USA: Lucasfilm, 1983.

Star Wars Episode VII: The Force Awakens. Film. Directed by J. J. Abrams. USA: Walt Disney Studios Motion Pictures, 2015.

Star Wars Episode VIII: The Last Jedi. Film. Directed by Rian Johnson. USA: Walt Disney Studios Motion Pictures, 2017.

Star Wars Episode IX: The Rise of Skywalker. Film. Directed by J. J. Abrams. USA: Walt Disney Studios Motion Pictures, 2019.

Star Wars: Rebels. TV Series. Directed by Simon Kinberg, Carrie Beck and Dave Filoni. USA: Disney XD, 2014–18.

Superman: The Movie. Film. Directed by Richard Donner. USA: Dovemead Films, 1978.

Superman Returns. Film. Directed by Bryan Singer. USA: Warner Bros, 2006.

Tina Turner. 'We Don't Need Another Hero (Thunderdome)' by Terry Britten and Graham Lyle, *Mad Max: Beyond The Thunderdome*, Original Motion Picture Soundtrack, Capitol Records, 1985.

Total Recall. Film. Directed by Paul Verhoeven. USA: Caroclo Pictures, 1990.

Unbreakable. Film. Directed by M. Night Shyamalan. USA: Touchstone Pictures, 2000.

The Village. Film. Directed by M. Night Shyamalan. USA: Touchstone Pictures, 2004.

Secondary Source

Abele, Elizabeth. 'The Home-Front Hero in the Films of M. Night Shyamalan'. In *Critical Approaches to the Films of M. Night Shyamalan: Spoiler Warnings*, edited by Jeffrey Weinstock, 3–18. New York: Palgrave Macmillan, 2010.

Agamben, Giorgio. *Homo Sacer: Sovereign Power and Bare Life*. Stanford, CA: Stanford University Press, 1998.

Agamben, Giorgio. *Karman: A Brief Treatise on Action, Guilt, and Gesture*. Stanford, CA: Stanford University Press, 2018.

Agamben, Giorgio. *The Kingdom and the Glory: For a Theological Genealogy of Economy and Government*. Translated by Lorenzo Chiesa (with Matteo Mandarini). Stanford, CA: Stanford University Press, 2011.

Agamben, Giorgio. *Nudities*. Translated by David Kishik and Stefan Pedatella. Stanford, CA: Stanford University Press, 2011.

Agamben, Giorgio. *Profanations*. Translated by Jeff Fort. New York: Zone Books, 2007.

Agamben, Giorgio. *Stasis: Civil War as a Political Paradigm*. Translated by Nicholas Heron. Stanford, CA: Stanford University Press, 2015

Agamben, Giorgio. *The State of Exception*. Chicago: University of Chicago Press, 2005.

Agamben, Giorgio. *The Time That Remains: A Commentary on the Letter to the Romans*. Translated by Patricia Dailey. Stanford, CA: Stanford University Press, 2005.

Agamben, Giorgio. 'What is a Destituent Power?', *Environment and Planning D: Society and Space* 32 (2014): 65–74.

Alaniz, José. *Death, Disability and the Superhero: The Silver Age and Beyond*. Jackson: University Press of Mississippi, 2014.

Alsford, Mike. *Heroes and Villains*. London: Darton, Longman & Todd, 2006.

Althusser, Louis. *Politics and History: Montesquieu, Rousseau, Hegel and Marx*. Translated by Ben Brewster. London: New Left Books, 1972.

Aquinas, Thomas. 'The Summa Theologica of Saint Thomas Aquinas Volume I'. In *Great Books of the Western World Volume 19: Thomas Aquinas I*, edited by Robert Hutchins. Chicago: Encyclopaedia Britannica, 1952.

Arendt, Hannah. *Eichmann in Jerusalem: A Report on the Banality of Evil*. New York: Penguin Books, 2006.

Arendt, Hannah. *On Revolution*. London: Penguin Books, 1963.

Asimov, Isaac. *The Caves of Steel*. New York: Ballantine Books, 1983.

Asimov, Isaac. *I, Robot*. London: HarperCollins, 1996.

Asimov, Isaac. 'Introduction'. In *Living in the Future*, edited by Isaac Asimov. New York: Beaufort Books, 1985.

Asimov, Isaac. *The Naked Sun*. London: Grafton Books, 1988.

Asimov, Isaac. *Robots and Empire*. London: HarperCollins, 1996.

Asimov, Isaac. *The Robots of Dawn*. London: HarperCollins, 1996.

Asimov, Isaac. 'The "Threat" of Creationism'. In *Science and Creationism*, edited by Ashley Montagu, 182–93. Oxford: Oxford University Press, 1984.

Asimow, Michael. 'When Lawyers Were Heroes', *University of San Francisco Law Review* 30 (1996): 1131–8.

Austin, John. *The Province of Jurisprudence Determined*. Amherst, NY: Prometheus Books, 2000 [1832].

Babie, Paul. 'Breaking the Silence: Law, Theology and Religion in Australia', *Melbourne University Law Review* 31, no. 1 (2007): 296–314.

Badiou, Alain. *Being and Event*. London: Continuum, 2005.

Badiou, Alain. *Ethics: An Essay on the Understanding of Evil*. London: Verso, 2001.

Badiou, Alain. *Manifesto for Philosophy*. Translated by Norman Madarasz. Albany: State University of New York Press, 1999.

Badiou, Alain. *Saint Paul: The Foundation of Universalism*. Stanford, CA: Stanford University Press, 2003.

Badiou, Alain. *Second Manifesto for Philosophy*. Translated by Louise Burchill. Cambridge: Polity Press, 2011.

Badiou, Alain. 'What is Love?', *UBR(a): A Journal of Unconscious* 1 (1996): 37.

Badiou, Alain, and Nicolas Truong. *In Praise of Love*. Translated by Peter Bush. London: Serpent's Tail, 2012.

Bainbridge, Jason. 'Beyond the Law: What is so "Super" About Superheroes and Supervillains?', *International Journal for the Semiotics of Law* 30, no. 3 (2017): 367–88.

Bainbridge, Jason. 'Blaming Daddy: The Portrayal of the Evil Father in Popular Culture'. In *Against Doing Nothing: Evil and its Manifestations*, edited by Shilinka Smith and Shona Hill, 9–20. Oxford: Inter-Disciplinary Press, 2010.

Bainbridge, Jason. '"The Call to do Justice": Superheroes, Sovereigns and the State During Wartime', *International Journal for the Semiotics of Law* 28, no. 4 (2015): 745–63.

Bainbridge, Jason. 'Lawyers, Justice and the State: The Sliding Signifier of Law in Popular Culture', *Griffith Law Review* 15, no. 1 (2006): 153–76.

Bainbridge, Jason. 'Spider-Man, the Question and the Meta-Zone: Exception, Objectivism and the Comics of Steve Ditko', *Law Text Culture* 16, no. 1 (2012): 217–42.

Bainbridge, Jason. '"This is the Authority. This Planet is Under Our Protection" – An Exegesis of Superheroes' Interrogations of Law', *Law, Culture and the Humanities* 3, no. 3 (2007): 455–76.

Baker, Gideon. 'Now We Have Been Delivered From the Law: Thoughts Towards a Genealogy of Anarchism', *Griffith Law Review* 21, no. 2 (2012): 369–91.

Barkman, Adam. 'Superman: From Anti-Christ to Christ-Type'. In *Superman and Philosophy: What Would the Man of Steel Do?*, edited by Mark White, 111–20. Oxford: Wiley-Blackwell, 2013.

Barnett, Michael, and Cassandra Sharp. 'The Moral Choice of inFAMOUS: Law and Morality in Video Games', *Griffith Law Review* 24, no. 3 (2015): 482–99.

Barzilai, Gad. 'Introduction'. In *Law and Religion*, edited by Gad Barzilai, xi–xxviii. Aldershot: Ashgate, 2007.

Beattie, Scott. 'Voicing the Shadow—Rule-playing and Roleplaying in Wraith: The Oblivion', *Law, Culture and the Humanities* 3 (2007): 477–92.

Beiner, Ronald. 'Has the Great Separation Failed?', *Critical Review* 22, no. 1 (2010): 45–63.

Bellinger, Charles. 'The Joker is Satan, and So Are We: Girard and The Dark Knight', *Journal of Religion and Film* 13, no. 1 (2009): 5.

Benjamin, Walter. 'Critique of Violence'. In *Reflections: Essays, Aphorisms, Autobiographical Writings*, edited by Peter Demetz, 277–300. New York: Schocken, 1986.

Benjamin, Walter. *The Origin of German Tragic Drama*. New York: Verso, 1998.

Berger, Arthur. *Li'l Abner: A Study in American Satire*. Jackson: University Press of Mississippi, 1969.

Berger, Arthur. *Manufacturing Desire: Media, Popular Culture, and Everyday Life*. New York: Routledge, 2017.

Berger, Arthur. *Narratives in Popular Culture, Media, and Everyday Life*. Thousand Oaks, CA: Sage, 1997.

Berger, Arthur Asa. *The Comic-Stripped America: What Dick Tracy, Blondie, Daddy Warbucks, and Charlie Brown Tell Us About Ourselves*. New York: Penguin Books, 1974.

Berger, Benjamin. 'On the Book of Job, Justice, and the Precariousness of the Criminal Law', *Law, Culture and the Humanities* 4, no. 1 (2008): 98–118.

Bergman, Paul, and Michael Asimow. *Reel Justice: The Courtroom Goes to the Movies*. 2nd edn. Missouri: Andrews McMeel, 2006.

Berkowitz, Roger. 'From Justice to Justification: An Alternative Genealogy of Positive Law', *UC Irvine Law Review* 1, no. 3 (2011): 611–30.

Berkowitz, Roger. *The Gift of Science: Leibniz and the Modern Legal Tradition*. Cambridge, MA: Harvard University Press, 2005.

Berman, Harold. *Law and Revolution: The Formation of the Western Legal Tradition*. Cambridge, MA: Harvard University Press, 1983.

Bernstein, Richard. *The Abuse of Evil: The Corruption of Politics and Religion Since 9/11*. Cambridge: Polity Press, 2005.

Bernstein, Richard. *Radical Evil: A Philosophical Interrogation*. Cambridge: Polity Press, 2002.

Bikundo, Edwin. 'Follow Your Leader – I Prefer Not to: Slavery, Giorgio Agamben and Herman Melville', *Law, Culture and the Humanities*, Online First (2018), <https://journals.sagepub.com/doi/10.1177/1743872118787236> (last accessed 13 May 2021).

Blond, Phillip. 'Perception: From Modern Painting to the Vision in Christ'. In *Radical Orthodoxy: A New Theology*, edited by John Milbank, Catherine Pickstock and Graham Ward, 220–42. London and New York: Routledge, 1999.

Boethius, Ancius. *The Consolation of Philosophy*. Translated by V. E. Watts: London: Penguin Classics, 1969.

Bornkamm, Gunther. *Paul*. New York: Harper & Row, 1971.

Bortolin, Matthew. *The Dharma of Star Wars*. Boston: Wisdom, 2005.

Boundas, Constantin V. 'Exchange, Gift, and Theft', *Angelaki* 6, no. 2 (2001): 101–12.

Boundas, Constantin V. 'Gift, Theft, Apology', *Angelaki* 6, no. 2 (2001): 1–5.

Bracton, Henri de. *De Legibus et Consuetudinibus Anglia*. Translated by Samuel Thorne. Cambridge, MA: Belknap Press, 1968.

Brayton, Sean. 'The Post-White Imaginary in Alex Proyas's I Robot', *Science Fiction Studies* 35, no. 1 (2008): 72–87.

Brecht, Bertolt. 'A Short Organum for the Theatre'. In *Brecht on Theatre: The Development of an Aesthetic*, edited by John Willett, 179–205. New York: Farrar, Straus, Giroux, 1964.

Brode, Douglas, and Leah Deyneka, eds. *Myth, Media, and Culture in Star Wars: An Anthology*. Lanham, MD: Scarecrow Press, 2012.

Brode, Douglas, and Leah Deyneka, eds. *Sex, Politics, and Religion in Star Wars: An Anthology*. Lanham, MD: Scarecrow Press, 2012.

Brody, Michael. 'Batman: Psychic Trauma and its Solution', *The Journal of Popular Culture* 28, no. 4 (1995): 171–8.

Brooker, Will. *Hunting the Dark Knight: Twenty-First Century Batman*. London and New York: I. B. Tauris, 2012.

Brooks, Eireann. 'Cultural Imperialism vs. Cultural Protectionism: Hollywood's Response to UNESCO Efforts to Promote Cultural Diversity', *Journal of International Business and Law* 5, no. 1 (2006): 112–36.

Brown, Christopher. '"A Wretched Hive of Scum and Villainy": *Star Wars* and the Problem of Evil'. In *Star Wars and Philosophy: More Powerful Than You Can Possibly Imagine*, edited by Kevin Decker and Jason Eberl, 69–79. Chicago: Open Court, 2009.

Brown, Wendy. *Undoing the Demos: Neoliberalism's Stealth Revolution*. New York: Zone Books, 2015.

Buchanan, Ruth, and Rebecca Johnson. 'Strange Encounters: Exploring Law and Film in the Affective Register', *Studies in Law, Politics, and Society* 46 (2009): 33–60.

Buchanan, Ruth, and Sundhya Pahuja. 'Legal Imperialism: *Empire's* Invisible Hand?' In *Empire's New Clothes: Reading Hardt and Negri*, edited by Paul Passavant and Jodi Dean, 73–94. New York: Routledge, 2004.

Calo, Zachary. 'Faithful Presence and Theological Jurisprudence: A Response to James Davison Hunter', *Pepperdine Law Review* 39 (2013): 1083–90.

Calo, Zachary. 'Religion, Human Rights, and Post-Secular Legal Theory', *St John's Law Review* 85, no. 2 (2011): 495–520.

Campbell, Joseph. *The Hero With a Thousand Faces*. 3rd edn: Princeton, NJ: Princeton University Press, 1973.

Campbell, Joseph. *The Masks of God: Creative Mythology*. New York: Viking Penguin, 1968.

Campbell, Joseph, and Bill Moyers. *The Power of Myth*. New York: Anchor Books, 1988.

Caputo, John. *On Religion*. London: Routledge, 2001.

Caputo, John, and Linda Alcoff, eds. *St. Paul Among the Philosophers*. Bloomington: Indiana University Press, 2009.

Caputo, John D., and Gianni Vattimo. *After the Death of God*. New York: Columbia University Press, 2009.

Carpenter, H., and C. Tolkien, eds. *The Letters of J. R. R. Tolkien*. London: George Allen and Unwin, 1981.

Carrier, David. *The Aesthetics of Comics*. University Park: Pennsylvania State University Press, 2000.

Carty, Anthony. 'English Constitutional Law From a Postmodernist Perspective'. In *Dangerous Supplements: Resistance and Renewal in Jurisprudence*, edited by Peter Fitzpatrick, 182–206. London: Pluto Press, 1991.

Casanova, Jose. *Public Religions in the Modern World*. Chicago: University of Chicago Press, 1994.

Castaneda, Carlos. *Tales of Power*. New York: Simon & Schuster, 1974.

Cavanaugh, William. 'The City – Beyond Secular Parodies'. In *Radical Orthodoxy: A New Theology*, edited by John Milbank, Catherine Pickstock and Graham Ward, 182–200. London: Routledge, 1999.

Cavanaugh, William. 'The World in a Wafer: A Geography of the Eucharist as Resistance to Globalization', *Modern Theology* 15, no. 2 (1999): 181–96.

Chesterton, G. K. *The Innocence of Father Brown*. London: Penguin, 1950.

Chesterton, G. K. *The Man Who Was Thursday*. Harmondsworth: Penguin, 1986.

Cicero. *Republic*. Oxford: Oxford University Press, 1998.

Clover, Carol. 'Law and the Order of Popular Culture'. In *Law in the Domains of Culture*, edited by Austin Sarat and Thomas Kearns, 97–120. Michigan: University of Michigan Press, 1998.

Clover, Carol. 'Movie Juries', *DePaul Law Review* 48 (1998): 389–405.

Cohn, Norman. *Cosmos, Chaos and the World to Come*. New Haven, CT: Yale University Press, 2001.

Cole, Phillip. *The Myth of Evil: Demonizing the Enemy*. Edinburgh: Edinburgh University Press, 2006.

Collins, Robert. 'Star Wars: The Pastiche of Myth and the Yearning for a Past Future', *Journal of Popular Culture* 11, no. 1 (1977): 1–10.

Comaroff, John. 'Reflections on the Rise of Legal Theology: Law and Religion in the Twenty-First Century', *Social Analysis* 53, no. 1 (2009): 193–216.

Coogan, Peter. *Superhero: The Secret Origin of a Genre*. Austin, TX: MonkeyBrain Books, 2006.

Cooke, Elizabeth. '"Be Mindful of the Living Force": Environmental Ethics in Star Wars'. In *Star Wars and Philosophy: More Powerful Than You Can Possibly Imagine*, edited by Kevin Decker and Jason Eberl, 124–44. Chicago: Open Court, 2009.

Copjec, Joan, ed. *Radical Evil*. London: Verso, 1996.

Cover, Robert. 'The Supreme Court, 1982 Term—Foreword: Nomos and Narrative', *Harvard Law Review* 97, no. 4 (1983): 4–68.

Cover, Robert. 'Violence and the Word', *Yale Law Journal* 95 (1986): 1601–29.

Crawley, Karen. 'The Critical Force of Irony: Reframing Photographs in Cultural Legal Studies'. In *Cultural Legal Studies: Law's Popular Cultures and the Metamorphosis of Law*, edited by Cassandra Sharp and Marett Leiboff, 183–206. Abingdon: Routledge, 2016.

Crawley, Karen. 'Reproducing Whiteness: Feminist Genres, Legal Subjectivity and the Post-racial Dystopia of *The Handmaid's Tale* (2017–)', *Law and Critique* 29 (2018): 333–58.

Crawley, Karen, and Timothy D. Peters. 'Introduction: "Representational Legality"'. In *Envisioning Legality: Law, Culture and Representation*, edited by Timothy D. Peters and Karen Crawley, 1–17. Abingdon: Routledge, 2018.

Crawley, Karen, and Honni van Rijswijk. 'Justice in the Gutter: Representing Everyday Trauma in the Graphic Novels of Art Spiegelman', *Law Text Culture* 16 (2012): 93–118.

Crockett, Clayton, ed. *Religion and Violence in a Secular World: Toward a New Political Theology*. Charlottesville: University of Virginia Press, 2006.

Crofts, Penny. *Wickedness and Crime: Laws of Homicide and Malice*. London: Routledge, 2013.

Curtis, Neal. *Sovereignty and Superheroes*. Manchester: Manchester University Press, 2016.

Curtis, Neal. 'Superheroes and the Contradiction of Sovereignty', *Journal of Graphic Novels and Comics* 4, no. 2 (2013): 209–22.

Davis, Creston. 'Introduction: Holy Saturday or Resurrection Sunday?' In *The Monstrosity of Christ: Paradox or Dialectic?*, edited by Slavoj Žižek and John Milbank, 2–23. Cambridge, MA: MIT Press, 2009.

Davis, Creston. 'Paul and Subtraction'. In *Paul's New Moment: Continental Philosophy and the Future of Christian Theology*, edited by John Milbank, Slavoj Žižek and Creston Davis, 100–21. Grand Rapids, MI: BrazosPress, 2010.

Deagon, Alex. *From Violence to Peace: Theology, Law and Community*. Oxford: Hart, 2017.

de Bruin-Molé, Megen. 'Space Bitches, Witches, and Kick-Ass Princesses: Star Wars and Popular Feminism'. In *Star Wars and the History of Transmedia Storytelling*, edited by Sean Guynes and Dan Hassler-Forest, 225–40. Amsterdam: Amsterdam University Press, 2018.

Decker, Kevin, and Jason Eberl, eds. *Star Wars and Philosophy: More Powerful Than You Can Possibly Imagine*. Chicago: Open Court, 2005.

Deleuze, Gilles, and Félix Guattari. *Anti-Oedipus: Capitalism and Schizophrenia*. Minneapolis: University of Minnesota Press, 1983.

Derrida, Jacques. 'Force of Law: The "Mystical Foundation of Authority"'. In *Deconstruction and the Possibility of Justice*, edited by Drucilla Cornell, Michel Rosenfeld and David Carlson, 3–67. New York: Routledge, 1992.

Derrida, Jacques. *Given Time: I. Counterfeit Money*. Translated by Peggy Kamuf. Chicago and London: University of Chicago Press, 1992.

Derrida, Jacques. 'Hostipitality', *Angelaki* 5, no. 3 (2000): 3–18.

Derrida, Jacques. *On Cosmopolitanism and Forgiveness*. London and New York: Routledge, 2001.

Dicey, A. V. *Introduction to the Study of the Law of the Constitution*. 10th edn. London: Macmillan, 1959.

Dick, Philip K. *Do Androids Dream of Electric Sheep?* New York: Doubleday, 1968.

Dick, Philip K. *The Philip K. Dick Reader*. New York: Citadel Press, 1997.

Dickens, Charles. 'A Tale of Two Cities'. In *Four Complete Novels*, edited by Charles Dickens, 589–848. New York: Gramercy Books, 1982.

Donnelly, Jerome. 'Humanizing Technology: Flesh and Machine in Aristotle and *The Empire Strikes Back*'. In *Star Wars and Philosophy: More Powerful Than You Can Possibly Imagine*, edited by Kevin Decker and Jason Eberl, 181–91. Chicago: Open Court, 2005.

Easterbrook, Neil. 'Print Philip K Dick on Film in Print', *Science Fiction Film and Television* 3, no. 1 (2010): 107–20.

Eberl, Jason. '"Know the Dark Side": A Theodicy of the Force'. In *The Ultimate Star Wars and Philosophy*, edited by Jason Eberl and Kevin Decker, 100–14. Chichester: Wiley-Blackwell, 2016.

Eberl, Jason, and Kevin Decker, eds. *The Ultimate Star Wars and Philosophy: You Must Unlearn What You Have Learned*. Chichester: Wiley-Blackwell, 2016.

Eco, Umberto. 'The Myth of Superman', *Diacritics* 2, no. 1 (1972): 14–22.

Eisner, Will. *Comics and Sequential Art*. Tamarac, FL: Poorhouse Press, 1985.

Eisner, Will. *Graphic Storytelling and Visual Narrative*. New York: WW Norton, 2008.

Elander, Maria. *Figuring Victims in International Criminal Justice: The Case of the Khmer Rouge Tribunal*. New York: Routledge, 2018.

Elshtain, Jean. *Sovereignty: God, State, and Self*. New York: Basic Books, 2008.

Esposito, Roberto. *Two: The Machine of Political Theology and the Place of Thought*. Translated by Zakiya Hanafi. New York: Fordham University Press, 2015.

Evans, Gillian. *Augustine on Evil*. Cambridge: Cambridge University Press, 1990.

Farley, Helen. 'Virtual Knights and Synthetic Worlds: Jediism in Second Life'. In *Fiction, Invention and Hyper-Reality: From Popular Culture to Religion*, edited by Carole Cusack and Pavol Kosnáč, 134–47. London: Taylor & Francis, 2017.

Fennell, Jack. 'The Aesthetics of Supervillainy', *Law Text Culture* 16, no. 1 (2012): 305–28.

Ferrell, William. *Literature and Film as Modern Mythology*. Westport, CT: Greenwood, 2000.

Figgis, John Neville. *The Divine Right of Kings*. Cambridge: Cambridge University Press, 1914.

Finger, Bill, and Bob Kane. *Detective Comics #27*. New York: DC, 1937.

Finger, Bill, Bob Kane and Sheldon Moldoff. *Batman #1*. New York: DC, 1940.

Fisher, Mark. 'Gothic Oedipus: Subjectivity and Capitalism in Christopher Nolan's Batman Begins', *ImageText: Interdisciplinary Comics Studies* 2, no. 2 (2006).

Fitzpatrick, Peter. 'The Immanence of *Empire*'. In *Empire's New Clothes: Reading Hardt and Negri*, edited by Paul Passavant and Jodi Dean, 31–55. New York and London: Routledge, 2004.

Fitzpatrick, Peter. *Modernism and the Grounds of Law*. Cambridge: Cambridge University Press, 2001.

Fitzpatrick, Peter. *The Mythology of Modern Law*. London: Routledge, 1992.

Fitzpatrick, Peter. '"What are the Gods to Us Now?": Secular Theology and the Modernity of Law', *Theoretical Inquiries in Law* 8, no. 1 (2007): 162–90.

Fitzpatrick, Peter, and Richard Joyce. 'The Normality of the Exception in Democracy's Empire', *Journal of Law and Society* 34, no. 1 (2007): 65–76.

Flood, Gavin. *The Importance of Religion: Meaning and Action in Our Strange World*. Oxford: Wiley-Blackwell, 2012.

Foucault, Michel. *Discipline and Punish: The Birth of the Prison*. Translated by Alan Sheridan: Penguin, 1991.

Foucault, Michel. *Security, Territory, Population*. New York: Palgrave Macmillan, 2007.

Fradley, Martin. 'What Do You Believe In? Film Scholarship and the Cultural Politics of the *Dark Knight* Franchise', *Film Quarterly* 66, no. 2 (2013): 15–27.

Frankel, Valerie. *A Rey of Hope: Feminism, Symbolism and Hidden Gems in Star Wars: The Force Awakens*. Buchanan, NY: LitCrit Press, 2018.

Freeman, M. D. A. *Lloyd's Introduction to Jurisprudence*. 8th edn. London: Sweet & Maxwell, 2008.

Freud, Sigmund. 'Why War?' In *Sigmund Freud Civilization, Society and Religion*, edited by Albert Dickson. London: Penguin, 1985.

Gaakeer, Jeanne. 'Law and Literature – *Batavische Gebroeders* (1663)'. In *Joost van den Vondel (1587–1679): Dutch Playwright in the Golden Age*, edited by J. Bloemendal and F. W. Korsten, 459–87. Leiden: Brill, 2011.

Gaine, Vincent. 'Genre and Super-Heroism: Batman in the New Millennium'. In *The 21st Century Superhero: Essays on Gender, Genre and Globalization in Film*, edited by Richard Gray II and Betty Kaklamanidou, 111–28. Jefferson, NC: McFarland, 2011.

Galipeau, Steven. *The Journey of Luke Skywalker: An Analysis of Modern Myth and Symbol*. Chicago: Carus, 2001.

Garrett, Greg. *Holy Superheroes! Exploring the Sacred in Comics, Graphic Novels, and Film*. Louisville, KY: Westminster John Knox Press, 2008.

Giddens, Thomas. 'Anderson v Dredd [2137] Mega-City LR 1', *International Journal for the Semiotics of Law* 30, no. 3 (2017): 389–405.

Giddens, Thomas, ed. *Critical Directions in Comics Studies*. Mississippi: University Press of Mississippi, 2020.

Giddens, Thomas. 'Natural Law and Vengeance: Jurisprudence on the Streets of Gotham', *International Journal for the Semiotics of Law* 28 (2015): 765–85.

Giddens, Thomas. 'Navigating the Looking Glass: Severing the Lawyer's Head in Arkham Asylum', *Griffith Law Review* 24, no. 3 (2015): 395–417.

Giddens, Thomas. *On Comics and Legal Aesthetics: Multimodality and the Haunted Mask of Knowing*. Abingdon: Routledge, 2018.

Gill, R. B. 'The Uses of Genre and the Classification of Speculative Fiction', *Mosaic* 46 (2013): 71–85.

Gnoli, Gherado. 'Manichaeism: An Overview'. In *The Encyclopedia of Religion*, edited by Mircea Eliade and Charles Adams, 5650–9. New York: Macmillan, 1987.

Goodrich, Peter. 'Fate as Seduction: The Other Scene of Legal Judgment'. In *Closure or Critique: New Directions in Legal Theory*, edited by Alan Norrie, 116–41. Edinburgh: Edinburgh University Press, 1993.

Goodrich, Peter. 'The Mask as Anti-Apparatus: On the Counter-*Dispositif* of *V for Vendetta*'. In *Critical Directions in Comics Studies*, edited by Thomas Giddens, 238–62. Jackson: University Press of Mississippi, 2020.

Goodrich, Peter. *Oedipus Lex: Psychoanalysis, History, Law*. Berkely: University of California Press, 1995.

Goodrich, Peter. 'The Theatre of Emblems: On the Optical Apparatus and the Investiture of Persons', *Law, Culture and the Humanities* 8 (2012): 47–67.

Gordon, Andrew. '*The Empire Strikes Back*: Monsters from the Id', *Science Fiction Studies* 7 (1980): 313–18.

Gordon, Andrew. '*Return of the Jedi*: The End of the Myth', *Film Criticism* 8, no. 2 (1984): 45–54.

Gordon, Andrew. 'Star Wars: A Myth for Our Time', *Literature/Film Quarterly* 6, no. 4 (1978): 314–26.

Greenfield, Steve, Guy Osborn and Peter Robson. *Film and the Law: The Cinema of Justice*. 2nd edn. Oxford: Hart, 2010.

Grennan, Simon. *A Theory of Narrative Drawing*. New York: Palgrave Macmillan, 2017.

Grimes, Caleb. *Star Wars Jesus: A Spiritual Commentary on the Reality of the Force*. Enumclaw, WA: WinePress, 2007.

Grotius, Hugo. *De Jure Belli ac Pacis*. Paris: apud N. Buon, 1625.

Gulácsi, Zsuzsanna. 'Searching for Mani's Picture Book in Textual and Pictorial Sources', *Transcultural Studies* 2, no. 1 (2011): 233–62.

Gunn, James. *Isaac Asimov: The Foundations of Science Fiction*. Oxford: Oxford University Press, 1982.

Habermas, Jürgen. 'Secularism's Crisis of Faith: Notes on Post-Secular Society', *New Perspectives Quarterly* 25 (2008): 17–29.

Hague, Ian. *Comics and the Senses: A Multisensory Approach to Comics and Graphic Novels*. New York: Routledge, 2014.

Hardt, Michael, and Antonio Negri. *Assembly*. Oxford: Oxford University Press, 2017.

Hardt, Michael, and Antonio Negri. *Commonwealth*. Cambridge, MA: The Belknap Press of Harvard University Press, 2009.

Hardt, Michael, and Antonio Negri. *Declaration*. New York: Argo Navis Author Services, 2012.

Hardt, Michael, and Antonio Negri. *Empire*. Cambridge, MA: Harvard University Press, 2000.

Hardt, Michael, and Antonio Negri. 'Empire, Twenty Years On', *New Left Review* 120 (2019): 67–92.

Hardt, Michael, and Antonio Negri. *Labor of Dionysus: A Critique of the State-Form*. Minneapolis: University of Minnesota Press, 1994.

Hardt, Michael, and Antonio Negri. *Multitude: War and Democracy in the Age of Empire*. New York: Penguin Press, 2004.

Harink, Douglas, ed. *Paul, Philosophy and the Theopolitical Vision: Critical Engagements with Agamben, Badiou, Žižek and Others*. Eugene, OR: Cascade Books, 2010.

Harris-Abbot, Troy. 'On Law and Theology', *The American Journal of Jurisprudence* 35 (1990): 105–27.

Hassler-Forest, Dan, and Sean Guynes, eds. *Star Wars and the History of Transmedia Storytelling*. Amsterdam: Amsterdam University Press, 2017.

Hatfield, Charles. *Alternative Comics: An Emerging Literature*. Jackson: University Press of Mississippi, 2005.

Henderson, Mary. *Star Wars: The Magic of Myth*. New York: Bantam, 1997.

Hirschman, Elizabeth. 'Legends in Our Own Time: How Motion Pictures and Television Shows Fulfill the Functions of Myth', *American Journal of Semiotics* 17, no. 3 (2001): 7–46.

Hirvonen, Ari. 'Civitas Peregrina: Augustine and the Possibility of Non-Violent Community', *International Journal for the Semiotics of Law* 8, no. 24 (1995): 227–73.

Hirvonen, Ari. 'The Problem of Evil Revisited', *NoFo* 4 (October 2007): 29–51.

Hirvonen, Ari. 'Total Evil: The Law Under Totalitarianism'. In *Law and Evil: Philosophy, Politics, Psychoanalysis*, edited by Ari Hirvonen and Janne Porttikivi, 117–47. New York: Routledge, 2010.

Hirvonen, Ari, and Janne Porttikivi, eds. *Law and Evil: Philosophy, Politics, Psychoanalysis*. New York: Routledge, 2010.

Hobbes, Thomas. 'Leviathan'. In *Great Books of the Western World Volume 23: Machiavelli and Hobbes*, edited by Robert Hutchins. Chicago: Encyclopaedia Britannica, 1952.

Hourigan, Daniel. 'Breach! The Law's Jouissance in Miéville's *The City and The City*', *Law, Culture and the Humanities* 9, no. 1 (2013): 156–68.

Hourigan, Daniel. *Law and Enjoyment: Power, Pleasure and Psychoanalysis*. London: Routledge, 2015.

Howe, Richard, and Norman Geisler. *The Religion of the Force*. Rev. 2nd edn. Matthews, NC: Bastion Books, 2015.

Hren, Joshua. 'Acquisitive Imitation and the Gift-Economy: Escaping Reciprocity in JRR Tolkien's *The Hobbit*', *Contagion: Journal of Violence, Mimesis, and Culture* 24, no. 1 (2017): 217–32.

Hunter, James. 'Law, Religion and the Common Good', *Pepperdine Law Review* 39 (2013): 1065–82.

Huntington, Samuel. *The Clash of Civilizations and the Remaking of World Order*. New York: Simon and Schuster, 2003.

Hutchings, Peter J. 'From Offworld Colonies to Migration Zones: Blade Runner and the Fractured Subject of Jurisprudence', *Law, Culture and the Humanities* 3, no. 3 (2007): 381–97.

Hyde, Lewis. *The Gift: How the Creative Spirit Transforms the World*. Edinburgh and London: Canongate, 2008.

Ibbi, Andrew Ali. 'Hollywood, The American Image and The Global Film Industry', *CINEJ Cinema Journal* 3, no. 1 (2013): 94–106.

Ip, John. 'The Dark Knight's War on Terrorism', *Ohio State Journal of Criminal Law* 9, no. 1 (2011): 209–29.

Jameson, Frederic. 'Philip K Dick, in Memoriam'. In *Archaeologies of the Future: The Desire Called Utopia and Other Science Fictions*, edited by Frederic Jameson, 345–8. London: Verso, 2005.

Jeffery, Renée. *Evil and International Relations: Human Suffering in an Age of Terror*. New York: Palgrave Macmillian, 2007.

Jennings, Theodore. *Reading Derrida / Thinking Paul: On Justice*. Stanford, CA: Stanford University Press, 2006.

Jhering, Rudolf von. *Law as a Means to an End*. Translated by Isaac Husik. Boston: Boston Book Company, 1913.

Johnson, Vilja. '"It's What You Do that Defines You:" Christopher Nolan's Batman as Moral Philosopher', *The Journal of Popular Culture* 47, no. 5 (2014): 952–67.

Jones, Timothy. *Finding God in a Galaxy Far, Far Away: A Spiritual Exploration of the Star Wars Saga*. Sisters, OR: Multnomah, 2005.

Kahn, Paul. *Political Theology: Four New Chapters on the Concept of Sovereignty*. New York: Columbia University Press, 2011.

Kaminski, Michael. *The Secret History of Star Wars: The Art of Storytelling and the Making of a Modern Epic*. Kingston, ON: Legacy Books Press, 2008.

Kamir, Orit. 'Anatomy of Hollywood's Hero-Lawyer: A Law-and-Film Study of the Western Motifs, Honor-based Values and Gender Politics Underlying Anatomy of a Murder'. In *Studies in Law, Politics and Society*, vol. 35, 67–105. Bingley: Emerald Group, 2005.

Kamir, Orit. 'Michael Clayton: Hollywood's Contemporary Hero-Lawyer: Beyond "Outsider Within" and "Insider Without"', *Suffolk University Law Review* 42, no. 4 (2009): 829–48.

Kamir, Orit. 'Why "Law-and-Film" and What Does it Actually Mean? A Perspective', *Continuum: Journal of Media and Cultural Studies* 19, no. 2 (2005): 255–78.

Kane, Douglas C. 'Law and Arda', *Tolkien Studies* 9 (2012): 37–57.

Kant, Immanuel. 'An Answer to the Question: What is Enlightenment'. In *Perpetual Peace and Other Essays on Politics, History, and Moral Practice*. Translated with introduction by Ted Humphrey, 41–8. Indianapolis, IN: Hackett, 1983.

Kant, Immanuel. *Kant: The Metaphysics of Morals*. Translated by Mary Gregor. Cambridge: Cambridge University Press, 1996.

Kant, Immanuel. *Religion Within the Boundaries of Mere Reason: And Other Writings*. Translated by Allen Wood and George Di Giovanni. Cambridge: Cambridge University Press, 1998.

Kant, Immanuel. 'To Perpetual Peace: A Philosophical Sketch'. In *Perpetual Peace, and Other Essays on Politics, History, and Moral Practice*. Translated with introduction by Ted Humphrey, 107–44. Indianapolis, IN: Hackett, 1983.

Kant, Immanuel, John Silber and Theodore Meyer Greene. *Religion Within the Limits of Reason Alone*. New York: Harper & Row, 1960.

Kantorowicz, Ernst. *The King's Two Bodies: A Study in Mediaeval Political Theology*. Princeton, NJ: Princeton University Press, 1997.

Kapferer, Bruce. 'Foundation and Empire (with Apologies to Isaac Asimov): A Consideration of Hardt and Negri's *Empire*', *Social Analysis: The International Journal of Anthropology* 46, no. 1 (2002): 167–79.

Kaveney, Roz. *Superheroes! Capes and Crusaders in Comics and Films*. London and New York: I. B. Tauris, 2008.

Kellner, Douglas. 'Media Spectacle and Domestic Terrorism: The Case of the Batman/ Joker Cinema Massacre', *Review of Education, Pedagogy, and Cultural Studies* 35, no. 3 (2013): 157–77.

Kelsen, Hans. *The Pure Theory of Law*. Berkeley: University of California Press, 1967.

Kierkegaard, Søren. *Works of Love*. New York: HarperCollins, 1962.

King, Claire. *Washed in Blood: Male Sacrifice, Trauma, and the Cinema*. New Brunswick, NJ: Rutgers University Press, 2012.

Kirsch, Thomas, and Bertram Turner, eds. *Permutations of Order: Religion and Law as Contested Sovereignties*. London: Routledge, 2009.

Knowles, Christopher. *Our Gods Wear Spandex: The Secret History of Comic Book Heroes*. San Francisco: Red Wheel, 2007.

Kuiper, Koenraad. 'Star Wars: An Imperial Myth', *Journal of Popular Culture* 21, no. 4 (1988): 77–86.

Kunz, Tobias. '"It's true, all of it!" Canonicity Management and Character Identity in *Star Wars*', *Recontextualizing Characters* 1, no. 29 (2019): 60–80.

Lacan, Jacques, and James Swenson. 'Kant with Sade', *October* 51 (1989): 55–75.

Lancashire, Anne. '*Attack of the Clones* and the Politics of *Star Wars*', *Dalhousie Review* 82, no. 2 (2002): 235–53.

Lancashire, Anne. '*The Phantom Menace*: Repetition, Variation, Integration', *Film Criticism* 24, no. 3 (2000): 23–44.

Lancashire, Anne. '*Return of the Jedi*: Once More With Feeling', *Film Criticism* 8, no. 2 (1984): 55–66.

Landa, Ishay. 'Slaves of the Ring: Tolkien's Political Unconscious', *Historical Materialism* 10, no. 4 (2002): 113–33.

Lawrence, John. 'Joseph Campbell, George Lucas, and the Monomyth'. In *Finding the Force of the Star Wars Franchise: Fans, Merchandise and Critics*, edited by Matthew Kapell and John Lawrence, 21–34. New York: Peter Lang, 2006.

Lawrence, John, and Robert Jewett. *The Myth of the American Superhero*. Grand Rapids, MI: William B. Eerdman, 2002.

Lee, Peter. *A Galaxy Here and Now: Historical and Cultural Readings of Star Wars*. Jefferson, NC: McFarland, 2016.

Lefevre, Pascal. 'Incompatible Visual Ontologies? The Problematic Adaptation of Drawn Images'. In *Film and Comic Books*, edited by Ian Gordon, Mark Jancovich and Matthew McAllister, 1–12. Mississippi: University Press of Mississippi, 2007.

Lehrer, Eli. 'Lucas Weaves New Mythology', *Insight on the News* 15, no. 21 (1999): 46–7.

Leiboff, Marett. 'Cultural Legal Studies as Law's Extraversion'. In *Cultural Legal Studies: Law's Popular Cultures and the Metamorphosis of Law*, edited by Cassandra Sharp and Marett Leiboff, 29–49. Abingdon: Routledge, 2016.

Leiboff, Marett. 'Of the Monstrous Regiment and the Family Jewels', *Australian Feminist Law Review* 23, no. 1 (2005): 33–59.

Leiboff, Marett, and Cassandra Sharp. 'Cultural Legal Studies and Law's Popular Cultures'. In *Cultural Legal Studies*, edited by Cassandra Sharp and Marett Leiboff, 3–28. Abingdon: Routledge, 2016.

Leslie-McCarthy, Sage. 'Asimov's Posthuman Pharisees: The Letter of the Law Versus the Spirit of the Law in Isaac Asimov's Robot Novels', *Law, Culture and the Humanities* 3, no. 3 (2007): 398–415.

Lilla, Mark. *The Stillborn God: Religion, Politics and the Modern West*. New York: Knopf, 2007.

Loeb, Jeph, and Tim Sale. *Batman: The Long Halloween*. New York: DC Comics, 2011.

Lomax, Tara. '"Thank the Maker!"'. In *Star Wars and the History of Transmedia Storytelling*, edited by Sean Guynes and Dan Hassler-Forest, 35–48. Amsterdam: Amsterdam University Press, 2018.

Loraux, Nicole. 'La Guerre dans la famille', *Guerres civiles*, no. 5 (1997): 21–62.

Lott, Steve. 'The Tao of the *Star Wars* Trilogy', *Lehigh Review* 6 (1998): 95–104.

Loughlin, Marie H. 'Tolkien's Treasures: Marvellous Objects in *The Hobbit* and *The Lord of the Rings*', *Tolkien Studies* 16 (2019): 21–58.

Lovell, Julie. 'A Great Disturbance in the Force: Jurisprudence and Star Wars', *Griffith Law Review* 11, no. 1 (2002): 223–47.

Luckhurst, Roger. *The Trauma Question*. London: Routledge, 2008.

Machaj, Mateusz. *The Rise and Fall of the First Galactic Empire: Star Wars and Political Philosophy*. Scotts Valley, CA: CreateSpace Independent Publishing Platform, 2017.

Machura, Stefan, and Peter Robson. 'Law and Film: Introduction', *Journal of Law and Society* 28, no. 1 (2001): 1–8.

McCloud, Scott. *Understanding Comics: The Invisible Art*. New York: Harper Perennial, 1993.

McCormick, Debbie. 'The Sanctification of Star Wars: From Fans to Followers'. In *Handbook of Hyper-real Religions*, edited by Adam Possamai, 165–84. Leiden: Brill, 2012.

McDowell, John. *The Gospel According to Star Wars: Faith, Hope, and the Force*. 2nd edn. Louisville: Westminster John Knox Press, 2017.

McDowell, John. *Identity Politics in George Lucas' Star Wars*. Jefferson, NC: McFarland, 2016.

McGowan, Todd. 'The Exceptional Darkness of *The Dark Knight*', *Jump Cut*, no. 51 (Spring 2009).

McGowan, Todd. *The Fictional Christopher Nolan*. Austin, TX: University of Texas Press, 2012.

McGowan, Todd. 'Should the Dark Knight have Risen?', *Jump Cut* 54 (2012).

MacNeil, William. *Lex Populi: The Jurisprudence of Popular Culture*. Stanford, CA: Stanford University Press, 2007.

MacNeil, William. *Novel Judgements: Legal Theory as Fiction*. London: Routledge, 2012.

MacNeil, William. 'One Recht to Rule Them All! Law's Empire in the Age of Empire', *Studies in Law, Politics and Society* 34 (2004): 279–303.

MacNeil, William. 'Two on a Guillotine? Courts and "Crits" in *A Tale of Two Cities*'. In *Novel Judgements: Legal Theory as Fiction*, edited by William MacNeil, 157–80. London: Routledge, 2012.

Malmgren, Carl D. 'Towards a Definition of Science Fantasy', *Science-Fiction Studies* 15 (1988): 259.

Manderson, Desmond. 'From Hunger to Love: Myths of the Source, Interpretation, and Constitution of Law in Children's Literature', *Law and Literature* 15, no. 1 (2003): 87–141.

Manderson, Desmond. 'Memory and Echo: Pop Culture, Hi Tech and the Irony of Tradition', *Cultural Studies* 27, no. 1 (2013): 11–20.

Manderson, Desmond. 'Modernism and the Critique of Law and Literature', *Australian Feminist Law Review* 35 (2011): 107–25.

Manderson, Desmond. 'Trust Us Justice: "24," Popular Culture and the Law'. In *Imagining Legality: Where Law Meets Popular Culture*, edited by Austin Sarat, 22–52. Alabama: University of Alabama Press, 2011.

Maris, Cees, and Frans Jacobs, eds. *Law, Order and Freedom: A Historical Introduction to Legal Philosophy*. London: Springer, 2011.

Marty, Martin E. 'The Religious Foundations of Law', *Emory Law Journal* 54 (2005): 291–324.

Mather, Philippe. 'Figures of Estrangement in Science Fiction Film', *Science Fiction Studies* 29, no. 2 (2002): 186–201.

Matos, Andityas Soares de Moura Costa. 'Walter Benjamin em Gotham City: sobre a violência pura (Walter Benjamin in Gotham City: on pure violence)', *Sequencia (Florianopolis)* 74 (2016): 137–52.

Matthewes, Charles. *Evil and the Augustinian Tradition*. Cambridge: Cambridge University Press, 2001.

Matthews, Daniel, and Marco Wan. 'Introduction: Legal Marginalia', *Law and Humanities* 11, no. 1 (2017): 3–6.

Mauss, Marcel. *The Gift: The Form and Reason for Exchange in Archaic Societies*. New York: Norton, 1990.

Meier, Christian. 'Changing Politicosocial Concepts in the Fifth Century *B.C*'. In *The Greek Discovery of Politics*, edited by Christian Meier, 157–85. Cambridge, MA: Harvard University Press, 1990.

Meyer, David. 'Star Wars, *Star Wars*, and American Political Culture', *Journal of Popular Culture* 26, no. 2 (1992): 99–115.

Midgley, Mary. *Wickedness: A Philosophical Essay*. London and New York: Routledge, 2001.

Miettinen, Mervi. 'Representing the State of Exception: Power, Utopia, Visuality and Narrative in Superhero Comics'. In *Images in Use: Towards the Critical Analysis of Visual Communication*, edited by Matteo Stocchetti and Karin Kukkonen, 269–90. Amsterdam: John Benjamins, 2011.

Milbank, Alison. *Chesterton and Tolkien as Theologians: The Fantasy of the Real*. London: Bloomsbury, 2009.

Milbank, Alison. 'Literary Apologetics Beyond Postmodernism: Duality and Death in Philip Pullman and J. K. Rowling'. In *Literature and Theology after Postmodernity*, edited by Zoë Lehmann Imfeld, Peter Hampson and Alison Milbank, 95–114. London: Bloomsbury, 2015.

Milbank, John. 'Against Human Rights: Liberty in the Western Tradition', *Oxford Journal of Law and Religion* 1, no. 1 (2012): 203–34.

Milbank, John. *Being Reconciled: Ontology and Pardon*. London: Routledge, 2003.

Milbank, John. *Beyond Secular Order: The Representation of Being and the Representation of the People*. Chichester: Wiley Blackwell, 2013.

Milbank, John. 'Can a Gift Be Given? Prolegomena to a Future Trinitarian Metaphysic', *Modern Theology* 11, no. 1 (1995): 119–61.

Milbank, John. 'Can Morality Be Christian?', *Studies in Christian Ethics* 8 (1995): 45–59.

Milbank, John. 'The End of Dialogue'. In *Christian Uniqueness Reconsidered: The Myth of a Pluralistic Theology of Religions*, edited by Gavin D'Costa, 174–91. New York: Orbis, 1990.

Milbank, John. 'The Ethics of Self-Sacrifice', *First Things: A Monthly Journal of Religion and Public Life*, March (1999).

Milbank, John. 'Fictioning Things: Gift and Narrative', *Religion and Literature* 37, no. 3 (2005): 1–35.

Milbank, John. 'The Future of Love'. In *The Future of Love: Essays in Political Theology*, edited by John Milbank, 364–70. Eugene, OR: Cascade Books, 2009.

Milbank, John. 'Geopolitical Theology: Economy, Religion, and Empire after 9/11'. In *The Impact of 9/11 on Religion and Philosophy: The Day that Changed Everything?*, edited by Matthew Morgan, 85–112. New York: Palgrave Macmillan, 2009.

Milbank, John. 'The Gift of Ruling: Secularization and Political Authority', *New Blackfriars* 85, no. 996 (2004): 212–38.

Milbank, John. 'Paul Against Biopolitics'. In *Paul's New Moment: Continental Philosophy and the Future of Christian Theology*, edited by John Milbank, Slavoj Žižek and Creston Davis, 21–73. Grand Rapids, MI: Brazos Press, 2010.

Milbank, John. 'The Return of Mediation'. In *Paul's New Moment: Continental Philosophy and the Future of Christian Theology*, edited by John Milbank, Slavoj Žižek and Creston Davis, 221–38. Grand Rapids, MI: Brazos Press, 2010.

Milbank, John. *Theology and Social Theory: Beyond Secular Reason*. 2nd edn. Malden, MA: Blackwell, 2006.

Milbank, John. 'The Transcendality of the Gift'. In *The Future of Love: Essays in Political Theology*, edited by John Milbank, 352–63. Eugene, OR: Cascade Books, 2009.

Milbank, John. *The Word Made Strange: Theology, Language, Culture*. Oxford: Blackwell, 1997.

Milbank, John, Catherine Pickstock and Graham Ward, eds. *Radical Orthodoxy: A New Theology*. London: Routledge, 1999.

Milbank, John, Slavoj Žižek, and Creston Davis. *Paul's New Moment: Continental Philosophy and the Future of Christian Theology*. Grand Rapids, MI: Brazos Press, 2010.

Miller, Frank, Klaus Janson and Lynn Varley. *Batman: The Dark Knight Returns*. New York: DC Comics, 1986.

Miller, Frank, David Mazzucchelli and Richmond Lewis. *Batman: Year One*. New York: DC Comics, 1986.

Mills, Ethan. 'Hollywood Doesn't Know Dick'. In *Philip K Dick and Philosophy: Do Androids Have Kindred Spirits?*, edited by D. E. Wittkower, 3–14. Chicago: Open Court, 2011.

Minkkinen, Panu. 'The Expressionless: Law, Ethics, and the Imagery of Suffering', *Law and Critique* 19 (2008): 65–85.

Mirrlees, Tanner. *Global Entertainment Media: Between Cultural Imperialism and Cultural Globalization*. New York: Routledge, 2013.

Mitchell, Dale. 'Masterful Trainers and Villainous Liberators: Law and Justice in *Pokemon Black and White*'. In *Law and Justice in Japanese Popular Culture: From Crime Fighting Robots to Duelling Pocket Monsters*, edited by Ashley Pearson, Thomas Giddens and Kieran Tranter, 74–92. New York: Routledge, 2018.

Mitchell, Dale. 'Paradoxes and Patriarchy: A Legal Reading of She-Hulk', *Griffith Law Review* 24, no. 3 (2015): 446–81.

Mohr, Rick. 'The Christian Origins of Secularism and the Rule of Law'. In *Law and Religion in Public Life: The Contemporary Debate*, edited by Rick Mohr and Hosen Nadrisyah, 34–51. New York: Routledge, 2011.

Moore, Alan, Brian Bolland and Richard Starkings. *Batman: The Killing Joke*. New York: DC Comics, 1988.

Morrison, Grant. *Batman: The Return of Bruce Wayne*. New York: DC Comics, 2011.

Morrison, Grant. *Supergods: Our World in the Age of the Superhero*. London: Random House, 2011.

Morrison, Grant, and Tony Daniel. *Batman R.I.P.* New York: DC Comics, 2010.

Morton, Drew. *Panel to the Screen: Style, American Film, and Comic Books During the Blockbuster Era*. Jackson: University Press of Mississippi, 2016.

Muller, Christine. 'Power, Choice, and September 11 in *The Dark Knight*'. In *The 21st Century Superhero: Essays on Gender, Genre and Globalization in Film*, edited by Richard Gray II and Betty Kaklamanidou, 46–60. Jefferson, NC: McFarland, 2011.

Nancy, Jean-Luc. *The Experience of Freedom*. Stanford: Stanford University Press, 1993.

Nayar, Pramod. *Reading Culture: Theory, Praxis, Politics*. London: Sage, 2006.

Negri, Antonio. *Insurgencies: Constituent Power and the Modern State*. Minneapolis: University of Minnesota Press, 1999.

Negri, Antonio. *The Savage Anomaly: The Power of Spinoza's Metaphysics and Politics*. Minneapolis: University of Minnesota Press, 1991.

Neiman, Susan. *Evil in Modern Thought: An Alternative History of Philosophy*. Princeton, NJ: Princeton University Press, 2002.

Neiman, Susan. 'Undeniable Evil', *New England Review* 23, no. 4 (2002): 5–15.

Neoh, Joshua. 'Text, Doctrine and Tradition in Law and Religion', *Oxford Journal of Law and Religion* 2, no. 1 (2013): 175–99.

Nichols, Michael. '"I Think You and I Are Destined to Do This Forever": A Reading of the Batman/Joker Comic and Film Tradition through the Combat Myth', *The Journal of Religion and Popular Culture* 23, no. 2 (2011): 236–50.

Nichols, Robert. 'Theft is Property! The Recursive Logic of Dispossession', *Political Theory* 46, no. 1 (2017): 3–28.

Nietzsche, Friedrich. *Twilight of the Idols: or How to Philosophize with a Hammer*. Translated by Duncan Large. Oxford: Oxford University Press, 1998.

Nisbet, Robert. *The Quest for Community*. Oxford: Oxford University Press, 1953.

Nissen, Adolph. *Das Iustitium: Eine Studie aus der römischen Rechtsgeschichte*. Leipzig: J. M. Gebhardt, 1877.

Norden, Martin. 'The "Uncanny" Relationship of Disability and Evil in Film and Television'. In *The Changing Face of Evil in Film and Television*, edited by Martin Norden, 125–44. Amsterdam: Rodopi, 2007.

Nussbaum, Martha. *Poetic Justice: The Literary Imagination and Public Life*. Boston: Beacon Press, 1995.

Oakley, Francis. 'The Absolute and Ordained Power of God and King in the Sixteenth and Seventeenth Centuries: Philosophy, Science, Politics, and Law', *Journal of the History of Ideas* 59, no. 4 (1998): 669–90.

Oliver, Simon. 'Introducing Radical Orthodoxy: From Participation to Late Modernity'. In *The Radical Orthodoxy Reader*, edited by John Milbank and Simon Oliver, 3–27. London: Routledge, 2009.

Oropeza, B. J., ed. *The Gospel According to Superheroes: Religion and Popular Culture*. New York: Peter Lang, 2005.

Pabst, Adrian. 'International Relations and the "Modern" Middle Ages: Rival Theological Theorisations of International Order'. In *Medieval Foundations of International Relations*, edited by William Bain, 166–85. London and New York: Routledge, 2017.

Palmer, R. Barton. 'Melodrama and Male Crisis in *Signs* and *Unbreakable*'. In *Critical Approaches to the Films of M. Night Shyamalan: Spoiler Warnings*, edited by Jeffrey Weinstock, 35–52. New York: Palgrave Macmillan, 2010.

Palumbo, Donald. 'Alex Proyas's I, Robot: Much More Faithful to Asimov Than You Think', *Journal of the Fantastic in the Arts* 22, no. 1 (2011): 60–74.

Partible, Leo. 'Superheroes in Film and Pop Culture: Silhouettes of Redemption on the Screen'. In *The Gospel According to Superheroes: Religion and Popular Culture*, edited by B. J. Oropeza, 229–54. New York: Peter Lang, 2005.

Pearson, Ashley. 'The Legal Persona of the Video Game: The Self of *Persona 4*', *Law, Culture and the Humanities* (2017): 1–19.

Pearson, Ashley, and Kieran Tranter. 'Code, Nintendo's *Super Mario* and Digital Legality', *International Journal for the Semiotics of Law* 28, no. 4 (2015): 825–42.

Peters, Andrew. *Holiness Without the Law*. Mansfield, Queensland: AE & LA Peters Outreach Enterprises, 2005.

Peters, Timothy D. 'Corporations, Sovereignty and the Religion of Neoliberalism', *Law and Critique* 29 (2018): 271–92.

Peters, Timothy D. '"The Force" as Law: Mythology, Ideology and Order in George Lucas's *Star Wars*', *Australian Feminist Law Review* 36, no. 1 (2012): 125–43.

Peters, Timothy D. '"Holy Trans-Jurisdictional Representations of Justice Batman!": Globalisation, Persona and Mask in Kuwata's *Batmanga* and Morrison's *Batman, Incorporated*'. In *Law and Justice in Japanese Popular Culture: From Crime Fighting Robots to Duelling Pocket Monsters*, edited by Ashley Pearson, Thomas Giddens and Kieran Tranter, 126–52. London: Routledge, 2018.

Peters, Timothy D. 'I, Corpenstein: Mythic, Metaphorical and Visual Renderings of the Corporate Form in Comics and Film', *International Journal for the Semiotics of Law* 30, no. 3 (2017): 427–54.

Peters, Timothy D. '"Seeing" Justice Done: Envisioning Legality in Christopher Nolan's *The Dark Knight Trilogy*'. In *Envisioning Legality: Law, Culture and Representation*, edited by Timothy D. Peters and Karen Crawley, 68–95. Abingdon: Routledge, 2018.

Peters, Timothy D. 'Theological "Seeing" of Law: Daredevil, Christian Iconography, and Legal Aesthetics'. In *Critical Directions in Comics Studies*, edited by Thomas Giddens, 77–102. Jackson: University Press of Mississippi, 2020.

Peters, Timothy D. 'Unbalancing Justice: Overcoming the Limits of the Law in *Batman Begins*', *Griffith Law Review* 16, no. 1 (2007): 247–70.

Peters, Timothy D., and Karen Crawley, eds. *Envisioning Legality: Law, Culture and Representation*. Oxford: Routledge, 2018.

Peters, Timothy D., Roshan de Silva-Wijeyeratne and John Flood. 'Disruption, Temporality, Law: The Future of Law and Society Scholarship?', *Griffith Law Review* 26, no. 4 (2017): 459–68.

Phillips, Nickie D. '*The Dark Knight*: Constructing Images of Good vs. Evil in an Age of Anxiety'. In *Popular Culture, Crime and Social Control*, edited by Mathieu Deflem, 25–44. Bingley: Emerald Group, 2010.

Phillips, Nickie, and Staci Strobl. *Comic Book Crime: Truth, Justice and the American Way*. New York: New York University Press, 2013.

Phillips, Nickie, and Staci Strobl. 'Cultural Criminology and Kryptonite: Apocalyptic and Retributive Constructions of Crime and Justice in Comic Books', *Crime, Media, Culture* 2, no. 3 (2006): 304–31.

Pickstock, Catherine. 'Duns Scotus: His Historical and Contemporary Significance', *Modern Theology* 21, no. 4 (2005): 543–74.

Pickstock, Catherine. 'Liturgy, Art and Politics', *Modern Theology* 16, no. 2 (2000): 159–80.

Pillsbury, Samuel. *Judging Evil: Rethinking the Law of Murder and Manslaughter.* New York: New York University Press, 1998.

Pizzino, Christopher. 'On Violation: Comic Books, Delinquency, Phenomenology'. In *Critical Directions in Comics Studies*, edited by Thomas Giddens, 13–34. Mississippi: University Press of Mississippi, 2020.

Pollock, Dale. *Skywalking: The Life and Films of George Lucas, the Creator of Star Wars.* New York: Samuel French, 1990.

Porter, John. *The Tao of Star Wars.* Atlanta: Humanics, 2003.

Possamai, Adam. 'Alternative Spiritualities and the Cultural Logic of Late Capitalism', *Culture and Religion* 4, no. 1 (2003): 31–45.

Possamai, Adam. *Religion and Popular Culture: A Hyper-Real Testament.* Brussels: Peter Lang, 2005.

Possamai, Adam, and Murray Lee. 'Hyper-Real Religions: Fear, Anxiety and Late-Modern Religious Innovation', *Journal of Sociology* 47, no. 3 (2011): 227–42.

Proctor, William, and Matthew Freeman. 'The First Step into a Smaller World': The Transmedia Economy of Star Wars'. In *Revisiting Imaginary Worlds: A Subcreation Studies Anthology*, edited by Mark Wolf, 221–43. New York: Taylor & Francis, 2017.

Prozorov, Sergei. 'Agamben, Badiou and Affirmative Biopolitics'. In *Agamben and Radical Politics*, edited by Daniel McLoughlin, 165–88. Edinburgh: Edinburgh University Press, 2016.

Prozorov, Sergei. 'The Katechon in the Age of Biopolitical Nihilism', *Continental Philosophy Review* 45 (2012): 483–503.

Regalado, Aldo. '*Unbreakable* and the Limits of Transgression'. In *Film and Comic Books*, edited by Ian Gordon, Mark Jancovich and Matthew McAllister, 116–36. Mississippi: University Press of Mississippi, 2007.

Reinarch, Théodore. *De l'état de siège. Étude historique et juridique.* Paris: Pichon, 1885.

Rendleman, Dennis. 'Two Faces of Criminal Prosecution: Harvey Dent, Mike Nifong, Craig Watkins', *The Journal of the Institute of Justice and International Studies* 9 (2009): 171–81.

Renick, Timothy. 'Manichaeism'. In *Encyclopedia of Religion and War*, edited by Gabriel Palmer-Fernandez. New York: Routledge, 2004.

Reynolds, Richard. *Super Heroes: Modern Mythology.* Jackson: University Press of Mississippi, 1992.

Reyns, Bradford, and Billy Henson. 'Superhero Justice: The Depiction of Crime and Justice in Modern-Age Comic Books and Graphic Novels'. In *Popular Culture,*

Crime and Social Control, edited by Mathieu Deflem, 45–66. Bingley: Emerald Group, 2010.

Riga, Frank P., Maureen Thum, and Judith Kollmann. 'From Children's Book to Epic Prequel: Peter Jackson's Transformation of Tolkien's *The Hobbit*', *Mythlore: A Journal of J.R.R. Tolkien, C.S. Lewis, Charles Williams, and Mythopoeic Literature* 32, no. 2 (2014).

Robinson, Walter. 'The Far East of Star Wars'. In *Star Wars and Philosophy: More Powerful Than You Can Possibly Imagine*, edited by Kevin Decker and Jason Eberl, 45–60. Chicago: Open Court, 2009.

Robson, Peter, and Jessica Silbey, eds. *Law and Justice on the Small Screen*. Oxford: Hart, 2012.

Rodriguez, William. 'The Adjustment Bureau', *Journal of Religion and Film* 15, no. 2 (2011).

Rofel, Lisa. 'Modernity's Masculine Fantasies'. In *Critically Modern: Alternatives, Alterities, Anthropologies*, edited by Bruce Knauft, 175–93. Bloomington: Indiana University Press, 2002.

Rogers, Juliet. 'Free Flesh: The Matrix, the War on Iraq and the Torture of Democracy', *Law, Culture and the Humanities* 3, no. 3 (2007): 416–34.

Rogozinski, Jacob. 'Hell on Earth: Hannah Arendt in the Face of Hitler'. In *Law and Evil: Philosophy, Politics, Psychoanalysis*, edited by Ari Hirvonen and Janne Porttikivi, 97–116. New York: Routledge, 2010.

Rowlands, Mark. *The Philosopher at the End of the Universe*. London: Ebury, 2005.

Santner, Eric. *The Royal Remains: The People's Two Bodies and the Endgames of Sovereignty*. Chicago: University of Chicago Press, 2011.

Sarat, Austin. 'Imagining the Law of the Father: Loss, Dread and Mourning in *The Sweet Hereafter*', *Law and Society Review* 34, no. 1 (2000): 3–46.

Sarat, Austin, Matthew Anderson and Catherine Frank, eds. *Law and the Humanities: An Introduction*. Cambridge: Cambridge University Press, 2010.

Saunders, Ben. *Do the Gods Wear Capes?: Spirituality, Fantasy, and Superheroes*. London: Bloomsbury, 2011.

Schenck, Ken. 'Superman: A Popular Culture Messiah'. In *The Gospel According to Superheroes: Religion and Popular Culture*, edited by B. J. Oropeza, 33–48. New York: Peter Lang, 2005.

Schimmelpfennig, Annette. 'Capitalism and Schizophrenia in Gotham City – The Fragile Masculinities of Christopher Nolan's *The Dark Knight Trilogy*', *Gender Forum* 2017, no. 62 (2017): 3–20.

Schlegel, Johannes, and Frank Habermann. 'You Took My Advice About Theatricality a Bit . . . Literally": Theatricality and Cybernetics of Good and Evil in *Batman Begins, The Dark Knight, Spider-Man*, and *X-Men*'. In *The 21st Century Superhero: Essays on Gender, Genre and Globalization in Film*, edited by Richard Gray II and Betty Kaklamanidou, 29–45. Jefferson, NC: McFarland, 2011.

Schmitt, Carl. *Dictatorship*. Cambridge: Polity Press, 2014.

Schmitt, Carl. *Political Theology: Four Chapters on the Concept of Sovereignty*. Translated by George Schwab. Chicago: University of Chicago Press, 2005.

Sharp, Cassandra. '"Fear" and "Hope" in Graphic Fiction: The Schismatic Role of Law in Australian Dystopian Comic', *International Journal for the Semiotics of Law* 30 (2017): 407–26.

Sharp, Cassandra. 'Religion and Justice: Atonement as an Element of Justice in Both Western Law and Christian Thought'. In *Law and Religion in Public Life: The Contemporary Debate*, edited by Rick Mohr and Hosen Nadrisyah, 151–64. New York: Routledge, 2011.

Sharp, Cassandra. '"Riddle Me This . . . ?" Would the World Need Superheroes if the Law Could Actually Deliver "Justice"?', *Law Text Culture* 16, no. 1 (2012): 353–78.

Shelley, Mary. *Frankenstein, or, the Modern Prometheus*. London: Penguin Classics, 2004.

Sherwin, Richard. *Visualising Law in the Age of the Digital Baroque: Arabesques and Entanglements*. London: Routledge, 2011.

Sherwin, Richard. *When Law Goes Pop: The Vanishing Line Between Law and Popular Culture*. Chicago: University of Chicago Press, 2000.

Shippey, Tom. *The Road to Middle Earth: How JRR Tolkien Created a New Mythology*. New York: Mariner Books, 2003.

Shklovsky, Viktor. 'Art as Technique'. In *Russian Formalist Criticism: Four Essays*, edited by Lee T. Lemon and Marion J. Reis. Lincoln: University of Nebraska Press, 1965.

Silbey, Jessica. 'The Politics of Law and Film Study: An Introduction to the Symposium on Legal Outsiders in American Film', *Suffolk University Law Review* 42, no. 4 (2009): 755–68.

Silbey, Jessica. 'What We Do When We Do Law and Popular Culture', *Law and Social Inquiry* 27, no. 1 (2002): 139–68.

Silvio, Carl, and Tony Vinci, eds. *Culture, Identities and Technology in the Star Wars Films: Essays on the Two Trilogies*. Jefferson, NC: McFarland, 2007.

Simon, Orpana. 'Interpellation by the Force: Biopolitical Cultural Apparatuses in The Force Awakens', *New American Notes Online* 12 (2017).

Singer, Peter. *The President of Good and Evil: The Ethics of George W Bush*. New York: Dutton, 2004.

Skweres, Artur. 'Star Wars as an Aesthetic Melting Pot'. In *McLuhan's Galaxies: Science Fiction Film Aesthetics in Light of Marshall McLuhan's Thought*, edited by Artur Skweres, 15–45. Cham: Springer, 2019.

Smith, James. *Introducing Radical Orthodoxy: Mapping a Post-Secular Theology*. Grand Rapids, MI: Baker, 2004.

Somin, Ilya. 'Star Wars, Science Fiction and the Constitution', *Jotwell* 27 June (2016).

Spanakos, Anthony. 'Exceptional Recognition: The US Global Dilemma in *The Incredible Hulk, Iron Man*, and *Avatar*'. In *The 21st Century Superhero: Essays on Gender, Genre and Globalization in Film*, edited by Richard Gray II and Betty Kaklamanidou, 15–28. Jefferson, NC: McFarland, 2011.

Spiegel, Simon. 'Things Made Strange: On the Concept of "Estrangement" in Science Fiction Theory', *Science Fiction Studies* 35 (2008): 369–85.

St Clair, Robert. 'The Bomb in (and the Right to) the City: *Batman, Argo*, and Hollywood's Revolutionary Crowds', *International Journal of Žižek Studies* 7, no. 3 (2013): 1–20.

Sullivan, Winnifred, Robert Yelle and Mateo Taussig-Rubbo. 'Introduction'. In *After Secular Law*, edited by Winnifred Sullivan, Robert Yelle and Mateo Taussig-Rubbo, 1–19. Stanford: Stanford University Press, 2011.

Sunstein, Cass. *The World According to Star Wars*. Rev. edn. New York: HaperCollins, 2019.

Surin, Kenneth. *Theology and the Problem of Evil*. Eugene, OR: Wipf & Stock, 1986.

Sutin, Lawrence. *Divine Invasions: A Life of Philip K. Dick*. New York: Carroll & Graf, 2005.

Suvin, Darko. *Metamorphoses of Science Fiction: On the Poetics and History of a Literary Genre*. New Haven, CT: Yale University Press, 1979.

Sykes, Robbie. '"Those Chosen by the Planet": *Final Fantasy VII* and Earth Jurisprudence', *International Journal for the Semiotics of Law* 30, no. 3 (2017): 455–76.

Sykes, Robbie, and Kieran Tranter. 'A Just (Electric Lady) Land: Jimi Hendrix and John Rawls', *Law and Literature* 29, no. 3 (2017): 383–403.

Sykes, Robbie, and Kieran Tranter. '"You Gotta Roll/Rule With It": Oasis and the Concept of Law', *Griffith Law Review* 24, no. 4 (2015): 571–91.

Tamanaha, Brian. *Law as a Means to an End: Threat to the Rule of Law*. Cambridge: Cambridge University Press, 2006.

Taslitz, Andrew. 'Daredevil and the Death Penalty', *Ohio State Journal of Criminal Law* 1 (2004): 699–717.

Taubes, Jacob. *The Political Theology of Paul*. Translated by Dana Hollander. Stanford, CA: Stanford University Press, 2004.

Tembo, Kwasu. 'Pax in Terra: Superman and the Problem of Power in Superman Returns and Man of Steel', *postScriptum: An Interdisciplinary Journal of Literary Studies* 2, no. 2 (2017): 35–56.

Tihanov, Galin. 'The Politics of Estrangement: The Case of the Early Shklovsky', *Poetics Today* 26, no. 4 (2005): 665–96.

Tolkien, J. R. R. *The Hobbit*. London: HarperCollins, 1999.

Tolkien, J. R. R. *The Lord of the Rings*. London: HarperCollins, 1991.

Tolkien, J. R. R. 'On Fairy-Stories'. In *Tree and Leaf: The Homecoming of Beorhtnoth*, edited by J. R. R. Tolkien. London: HarperCollins, 2001.

Tranter, Kieran. *Living in Technical Legality: Science Fiction and Law as Technology*. Edinburgh: Edinburgh University Press, 2018.

Tranter, Kieran. 'The Speculative Jurisdiction: The Science Fictionality of Law and Technology', *Griffith Law Review* 20, no. 4 (2011): 817–50.

Tranter, Kieran. 'Terror in the Texts: Technology – Law – Future', *Law and Critique* 13 (2002): 75–99.

Treat, Shaun. 'How America Learned to Stop Worrying and Cynically ENJOY! The Post-9/11 Superhero Zeitgeist', *Communication and Critical/Cultural Studies* 6, no. 1 (2009): 103–9.

Turchetto, Maria. 'The Empire Strikes Back: On Hardt and Negri', *Historical Materialism* 11, no. 1 (2003): 23–36.

Umphrey, Martha Merrill, Austin Sarat and Lawrence Douglas. 'The Sacred in Law: An Introduction'. In *Law and the Sacred*, edited by Austin Sarat, Lawrence Douglas and Martha Merrill Umphrey, 1–21. Stanford, CA: Stanford University Press, 2007.

Unger, Roberto. *The Knowledge Economy*. New York: Verso, 2019.

Vest, Jason. *Future Imperfect: Philip K. Dick at the Movies*. Westport, CT: Praeger, 2007.

Vollum, Scott, and Cary Adkinson. 'The Portrayal of Crime and Justice in the Comic Book Superhero Mythos', *Journal of Criminal Justice and Popular Culture* 10, no. 2 (2003): 96–108.

Voytilla, Stuart. *Myth and the Movies: Discovering the Mythic Structure of 50 Unforgettable Films*. Studio City, CA: Michael Wiese Productions, 1999.

Vries, Hent de, and Lawrence Sullivan, eds. *Political Theologies: Public Religions in a Post-Secular World*. New York: Fordham University Press, 2006.

Ward, Graham. 'Belief and Imagination'. In *Literature and Theology after Postmodernity*, edited by Zoë Lehmann Imfeld, Peter Hampson and Alison Milbank, 79–94. London: Bloomsbury, 2015.

Ward, Graham. *Cities of God*. London: Routledge, 2000.

Weber, Max. *Economy and Society: An Outline of Interpretive Sociology*. Berkeley: University of California Press, 1978.

Weber, Max. 'Politics as Vocation'. In *From Max Weber: Essays in Sociology*, edited by H. Gerth and C. Wright Mills, 77–128. New York: Oxford University Press, 1946.

Weber, Max. *The Protestant Ethic and the Spirit of Capitalism*. London: Routledge, 2005.

Weber, Max. 'Science as Vocation'. In *From Max Weber: Essays in Sociology*, edited by H. Gerth and C. Wright Mills, 129–58. London: Routledge, 1948.

Weinstock, Jeffrey. 'Introduction: Telling Stories about Stories: The Films of M. Night Shyamalan'. In *Critical Approaches to the Films of M. Night Shyamalan: Spoiler Warnings*, edited by Jeffrey Weinstock, ix–xxix. New York: Palgrave Macmillan, 2010.

Weisberg, Robert. 'The Law-Literature Enterprise', *Yale Journal of Law and the Humanities* 1, no. 1 (1988): 1–67.

Weiss, Dennis, and Justin Nicholas. 'Dick Doesn't Do Heroes'. In *Philip K. Dick and Philosophy: Do Androids Have Kindred Spirits?*, edited by D. E. Wittkower, 27–38. Chicago: Open Court, 2011.

White, James Boyd. *The Legal Imagination: Studies in the Nature of Legal Thought and Expression*. Boston: Little, Brown, 1973.

Willey, Basil. *The Eighteenth Century Background: Studies on the Idea of Nature in the Thought of the Period*. London: Chatto & Windus, 1940.

Winstead, Nick. '"As a Symbol I Can Be Incorruptible": How Christopher Nolan De-Queered the Batman of Joel Schumacher', *The Journal of Popular Culture* 48, no. 3 (2015): 572–85.

Winterhalter, Benjamin. 'The Politics of the Inner: Why *The Dark Knight Rises* is Not a Conservative Allegory', *The Journal of Popular Culture* 48, no. 5 (2015): 1030–47.

Wittkower, D. E. 'Matt Damon is a Vast Sinister Conspiracy'. In *Philip K Dick and Philosophy: Do Androids Have Kindred Spirits?*, edited by D. E. Wittkower, 101–10. Chicago: Open Court, 2011.

Wolf, Mark. *Building Imaginary Worlds: The Theory and History of Subcreation*. New York: Routledge, 2012.

Wood, Dennis. 'Growing Up Among the Stars', *Literature/Film Quarterly* 6, no. 4 (1978): 327–41.

Worley, Sara. 'Knowing Tomorrow While Choosing Today'. In *Philip K Dick and Philosophy: Do Androids Have Kindred Spirits?*, edited by D. E. Wittkower, 229–36. Chicago: Open Court, 2011.

Wright, Colin. 'Event or Exception?: Disentagling Badiou from Schmitt, or, Towards a Politics of the Void', *Theory and Event* 11, no. 2 (2008): n.p.

Yacavone, Daniel. *Film Worlds: A Philosophical Aesthetics of Cinema*. New York: Columbia University Press, 2015.

Yelle, Robert. 'Moses' Veil: Secularization as Christian Myth'. In *After Secular Law*, edited by Winnifred Fallers Sullivan, Robert Yelle and Mateo Taussig-Rubbo, 23–42. Stanford, CA: Stanford University Press, 2011.

Yockey, Matt. 'Unbreak My Heart: The Melodramatic Superhero in *Unbreakable*'. In *Critical Approaches to the Films of M. Night Shyamalan: Spoiler Warnings*, edited by Jeffrey Weinstock, 159–74. New York: Palgrave Macmillan, 2010.

Young, Alison. *The Scene of Violence: Cinema, Crime, Affect*. New York: Routledge, 2009.

Žižek, Jela Krečič. 'Superheroes: The Making and Unmaking of a Genre in a Stupid Culture', *Teorija in Praksa* 53, no. 4 (2016): 859–74.

Žižek, Slavoj. 'An Answer to Two Questions'. In *Badiou, Žižek, and Political Transformations: The Cadence of Change*, edited by Adrian Johnston, 180–230. Evanston, IL: Northwestern University Press, 2009.

Žižek, Slavoj. 'The Fear of Four Words: A Modest Plea for the Hegelian Reading of Christianity'. In *The Monstrosity of Christ: Paradox or Dialectic?*, edited by Slavoj Žižek and John Milbank, 24–109. Cambridge, MA: MIT Press, 2009.

Žižek, Slavoj. *First as Tragedy Then as Farce*. London: Verso, 2009.

Žižek, Slavoj. *For They Know Not What They Do: Enjoyment as a Political Factor*. London: Verso, 1991.

Žižek, Slavoj. *The Fragile Absolute—Or, Why is the Christian Legacy Worth Fighting For?* London: Verso, 2000.

Žižek, Slavoj. *Living in the End Times*. London: Verso, 2010.

Žižek, Slavoj. *Looking Awry: An Introduction to Jacques Lacan through Popular Culture*. Cambridge, MA: MIT Press, 1991.

Žižek, Slavoj. *On Belief*. London: Routledge, 2001.

Žižek, Slavoj. *The Parallax View*. Cambridge, MA: MIT Press, 2006.

Žižek, Slavoj. *The Puppet and the Dwarf: The Perverse Core of Christianity*. Cambridge, MA: MIT Press, 2003.

Zornado, Joseph. 'Conclusion: The Empire Expands – *Star Wars* as *Disney Fantasy*'. In *Disney and the Dialectic of Desire: Fantasy as Social Practice*, edited by Joseph Zornado, 213–54. Cham, Switzerland: Springer, 2017.

Zupančič, Alenka. *Ethics of the Real: Kant, Lacan*. New York: Verso, 2000.

Magazines, Blogs and Websites

Ackerman, Spencer. 'Batman's "Dark Knight" Reflects Cheney Policy', *Washington Independent*, 21 July 2008.

Agamben, Giorgio. 'For a Theory of Destituent Power', *Chronos Magazine*, Feburary 2014. <http://www.chronosmag.eu/index.php/g-agamben-for-a-theory-of-des-tituent-power.html> (last accessed 27 April 2016).

Allen, Joe. 'Batman's War on Terror', *Counterpunch*, 2 August 2008.

Barron, Robert. 'Master Plan: The Flawed Theology of "The Adjustment Bureau"', *American Magazine*, 28 March 2011.

Bolt, Andrew. 'Batman Bush True Dark Knight', *Herald Sun*, 30 July 2008.

Cogitamus. 'The Dark Knight and International Politics' (blog). July 2008. <www.cogitamusblog.com/2008/07/the-dark-night.html> (last accessed 21 March 2014).

Corliss, Richard, and Jess Cagle. 'Dark Victory', *Time*, 29 April 2002.

Crouse, Richard. 'Dark Knight Has Reviewer Seeking New Words for Awesome', 18 July 2009. <http://www.ctvnews.ca/dark-knight-has-reviewer-seeking-new-words-for-awesome-1.308080> (last accessed 21 March 2014).

Dick, Philip K. 'Adjustment Team', *Orbit*, September–October 1954, 81–100.

Dick, Philip K. 'The Minority Report', *Fantastic Universe*, January 1956, 4–36.

Dick, Philip K. 'We Can Remember It for You Wholesale', *The Magazine of Fantasy and Science Fiction*, April 1966, 4–23.

Ebert, Roger. 'Cyber Cypher: "I, Robot" Misses Asimov's Complexity', *Chicago Sun-Times*, 16 July 2004.

Editorial, Board NY Times. 'Batman and the War on Terror', *The New York Times*, 21 July 2008.

Falsani, Cathleen. 'The Adjustment Bureau: Does God Change Our Minds, or Do We Change God's?', *The Huffington Post*, 8 March 2011. <https://www.huffpost.com/entry/the-god-factor-does-god-c_b_833118> (last accessed 27 February 2013).

Finocchiaro, Peter. 'Rush Limbaugh Suggests "Dark Knight Rises" Villain "Bane" a Deliberate Romney Reference', *Huffington Post*, 18 July 2012. <https://www.huffingtonpost.com.au/entry/limbaugh-bane-dark-knight-rises_n_1681716?ri18n=true> (last accessed 23 April 2021).

Fisher, Mark. 'Batman's Political Right Turn', *The Guardian*, 23 July 2012. <https://www.theguardian.com/commentisfree/2012/jul/22/batman-political-right-turn> (last accessed 23 April 2021),

Fisher, Mark, and Rob White. 'The Politics of "The Dark Knight Rises": A Discussion', *Film Quarterly*, 4 September 2012. <https://filmquarterly.org/2012/09/04/the-politics-of-the-dark-knight-rises-a-discussion/> (last accessed 23 April 2021).

Goldberg, Matt. 'The Adjustment Bureau Review', *Collider*, 5 March 2011. <http://collider.com/the-adjustment-bureau-review/> (last accessed 16 March 2014).

Gopnik, Adam. 'Lessons for the Supreme Court from the Jedi Council', *New Yorker*, 18 February 2016.

Graeber, David. 'Super Position', *The New Inquiry*, 8 October 2012.

Grossman, Lev. 'Superman, Grounded', *Time*, 17 June 2013, 50–3.

Heid, Jason. 'Matt Damon Defies God's Insidious Bureaucracy in *The Adjustment Bureau*', *Front Row*, 4 March 2011. <http://frontrow.dmagazine.com/2011/03/matt-damon-defies-gods-insidious-bureaucracy-in-the-adjustment-bureau/> (last accessed 27 February 2013).

Holmes, Adam. 'Man of Steel Ending Explained: How Superman's Actions Affect the DC Cinematic Universe'. 2015. <https://www.cinemablend.com/new/Man-Steel-Ending-Explained-How-Superman-Actions-Affect-DC-Cinematic-Universe-70715.html> (last accessed 2019).

Jameson, Frederic. 'Futuristic Visions That Tell Us About Right Now', *In These Times*, 5 May 1982, 17–18.

Kate. 'From Paris to Gotham: Similarities Between The Dark Knight Rises and A Tale of Two Cities'. *Back to the Bookshelf!* (blog). 16 July 2013. <https://backtothebookshelf.wordpress.com/2013/07/16/from-paris-to-gotham-similarities-between-the-dark-knight-rises-and-a-tale-of-two-cities-part-1/> (last accessed 2018).

Kate. 'From Paris to Gotham: Similarities Between The Dark Knight Rises and A Tale of Two Cities (Part 2)'. *Back to the Bookshelf!* (blog). 24 July 2013. <https://backtothebookshelf.wordpress.com/2013/07/24/from-paris-to-gotham-similarities-between-the-dark-knight-rises-and-a-tale-of-two-cities-part-2/> (last accessed 2018).

Kaufman, Anthony. 'Nolfi Takes Fate into Own Hands', *Variety*, 21 February 2011.

Kennedy, L. 'Solid Sci-Fi Tale is Fuelled by Philosophy', *Denver Post*, 16 July 2004 (last accessed 25 March 2007).

Klavan, Andrew. 'What Bush and Batman Have In Common', *The Wall Street Journal*, 25 July 2008.

Korobkin, Daniel. '"The Adjustment Bureau": Finally, an Action Thriller for Religious Thinkers', *Jewish Journal*, 8 March 2011. <http://www.jewishjournal.com/film/article/finally_an_action_thriller_for_religious_thinkers_20110307/> (last accessed 27 February 2013).

Lane, Anthony. 'Batman's Bane', *The New Yorker*, 30 July 2012.

McDonagh, Maitland. 'The Adjustment Bureau', *Film Journal International*, 1 April 2011.

Moyers, Bill. 'Cinema: Of Myth and Men', *Time*, 26 April 1999.

O'Hehir, Andrew. '"The Dark Knight Rises": Christopher Nolan's Evil Masterpiece', *Salon*, 18 July 2012. <https://www.salon.com/2012/07/18/the_dark_knight_rises_christopher_nolans_evil_masterpiece/> (last accessed 23 April 2021).

O'Neil, Tyler. 'Dark Knight and Occupy Wall Street: The Humble Rise', *Hillsdale Natural Law Review*. <http://hillsdalenaturallawreview.com/2012/07/21/dark-knight-and-occupy-wall-street-the-humble-rise/ > (last accessed 21 March 2014).

Orr, Christopher. 'Batman as Bush Ctd', *The New Republic*, 17 July 2008.

Persall, Steve. 'Just Call It "I, Will Smith"', *Tampa Bay Times*, 28 August 2005. <https://www.tampabay.com/archive/2004/07/16/just-call-it-i-will-smith/> (last accessed 8 August 2020).

Phillips, Nickie, and Staci Strobl. 'Should Superman Kill?', *Wall Street Journal*, 1 July 2013. <https://blogs.wsj.com/speakeasy/2013/07/01/should-superman-kill/> (last accessed 2 November 2018).

Rayment, Tim. 'Master of the Universe', *Sunday Times Magazine*, 16 May 1999, 14–24.

Shephard, Lucius. 'Free Will Hunting', *The Magazine of Fantasy and Science Fiction*, July 2011.

Snyder, Steven. 'The Adjustment Bureau: Losing One's Free Will Has Never Looked So Charming', *Time*, 3 March 2011. <http://techland.time.com/2011/03/03/the-adjustment-bureau-losing-free-will/> (last accessed 21 March 2014).

Sunstein, Cass. 'How Star Wars Illuminates Constitutional Law (and Authorship)', *New Rambler*, 2015.

Taylor, Charles. 'Two Books, Oddly Yoked Together'. *The Immanent Frame: Secularism, Religion, and the Public Sphere* (blog). 24 January 2008. <https://tif.ssrc.org/2008/01/24/two-books-oddly-yoked-together/> (last accessed 2018).

Waid, Mark. 'Man of Steel, Since You Asked'. *ThrillBent* (blog). 14 June 2013. <http://thrillbent.com/blog/man-of-steel-since-you-asked/> (last accessed 29 October 2019).

Weintraub, Steve. 'Writer–Director George Nolfi Exclusive Interview The Adjustment Bureau', *Collider*, 26 February 2011. <http://collider.com/george-nolfi-interview-the-adjustment-bureau/> (last accessed 16 March 2014).

Williams, Kam. 'The Adjustment Bureau', *Sentinel*, 17 March 2011.

Winsberg, Eric. 'Is This the Eternal Recurrence You Are Looking For?' *Daily Nous* (blog). 21 December 2015. <https://dailynous.com/2015/12/21/philosophers-on-star-wars-the-force-awakens-spoilers/#winsberg> (last accessed 6 April 2020).

Yglesias, Matthew. 'Dark Knight Politics', *The Atlantic*, July 24, 2008.

Žižek, Slavoj. 'Dictatorship of the Proletariat in Gotham City'. *Blog de Boitempo* (blog). 8 August 2012. <https://blogdaboitempo.com.br/2012/08/08/dictatorship-of-the-proletariat-in-gotham-city-slavoj-zizek-on-the-dark-knight-rises/> (last accessed 21 March 2014).

Žižek, Slavoj. 'From Western Marxism to Western Buddhism', *Cabinet* 2 (2001), <https://www.cabinetmagazine.org/issues/2/zizek/php> (last accessed 13 May 2021).

Žižek, Slavoj. 'The People's Republic of Gotham', *New Statesman*, 23 August 2012.

Žižek, Slavoj. 'Revenge of Global Finance', *In These Times*, 21 May 2005. <https://inthesetimes.com/article/revenge-of-global-finance> (last accessed 13 May 2021).

Index